SATURDAY AM

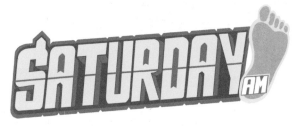

PRESENTS...

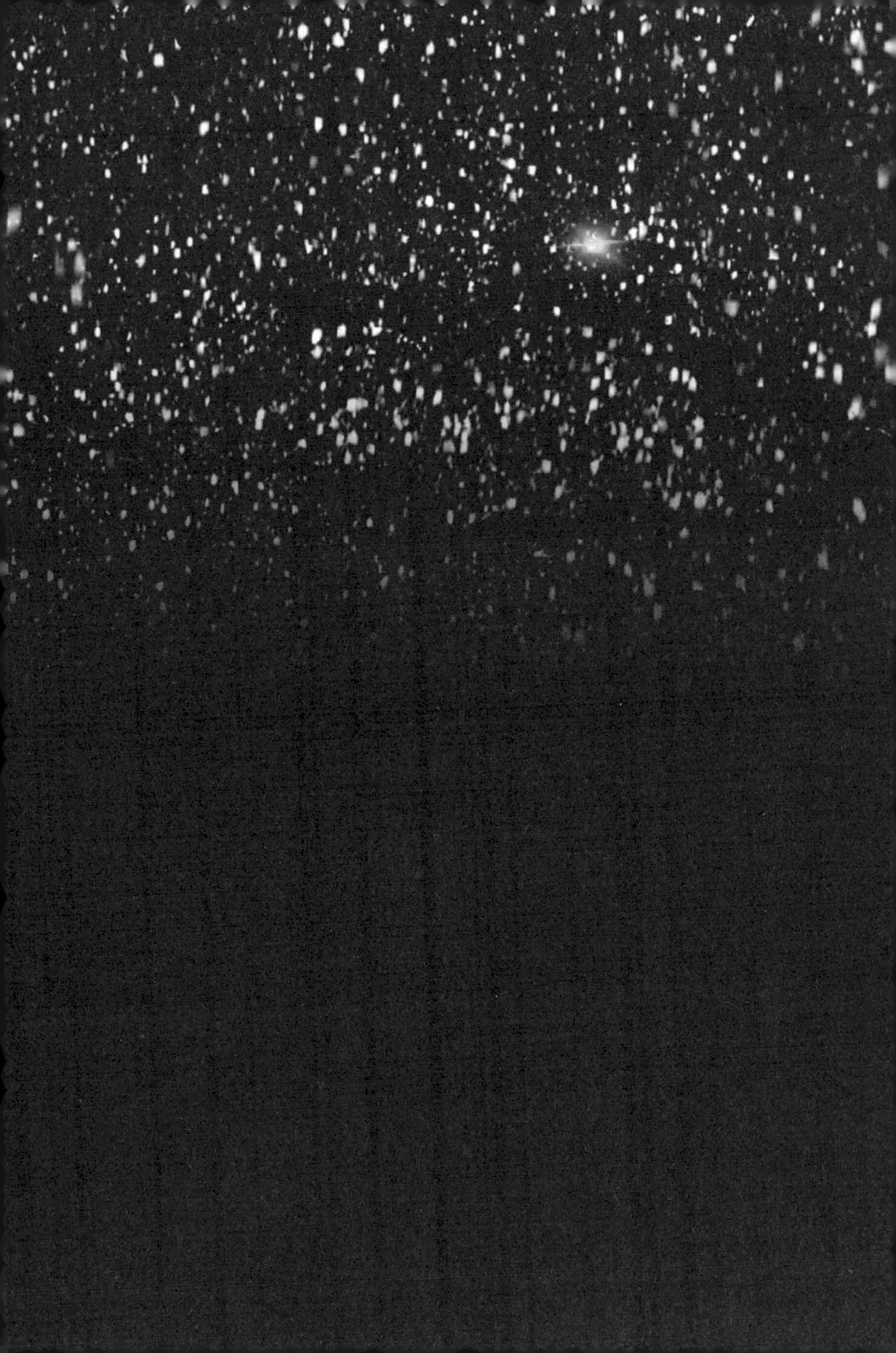

OBLIVION ROUGE

VOLUME 1

THE HAKKINEN

STORY AND ART BY Pap Souleye Fall

ROCKPORT

CONTENTS

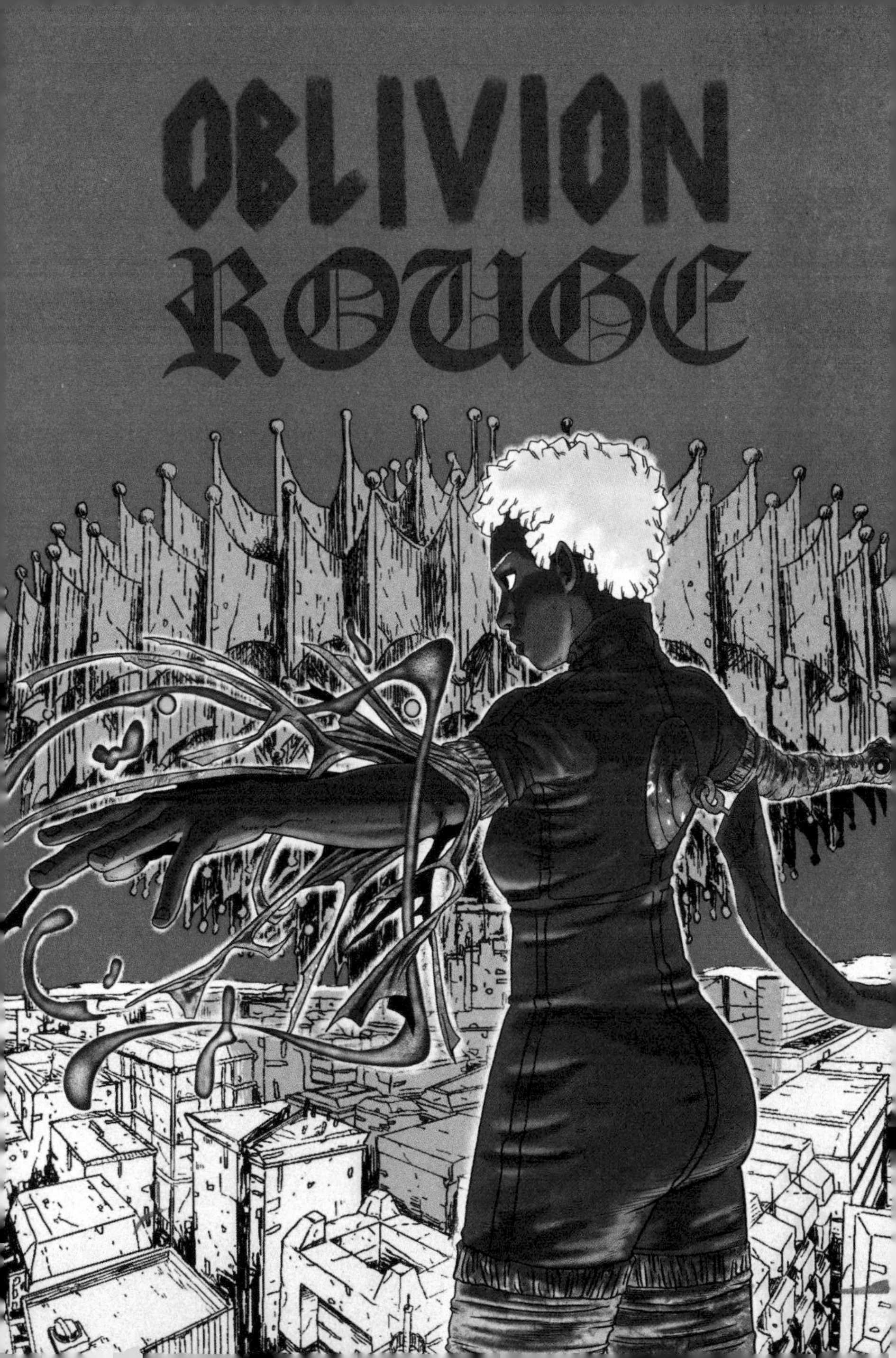
OBLIVION
ROUGE

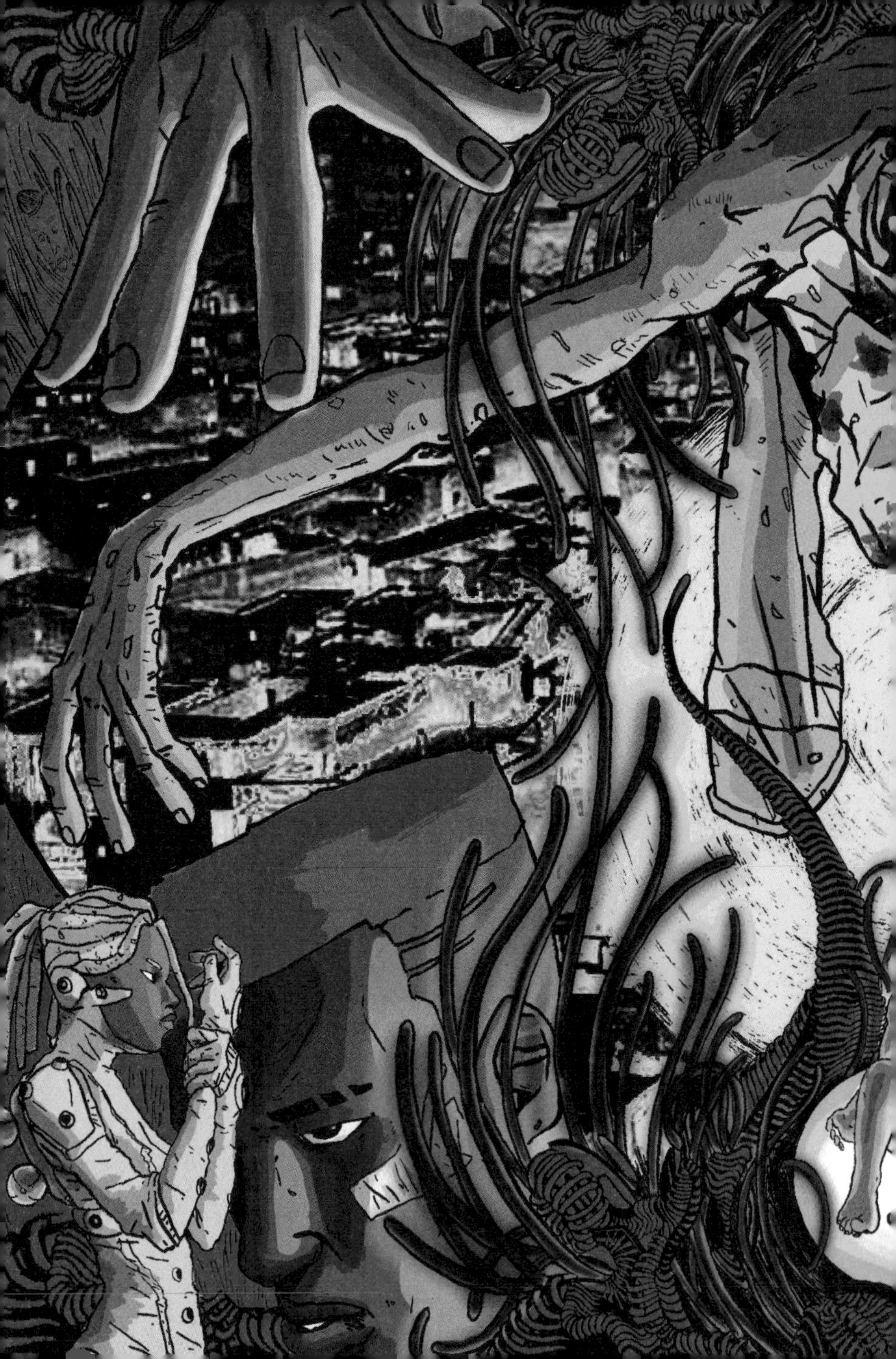

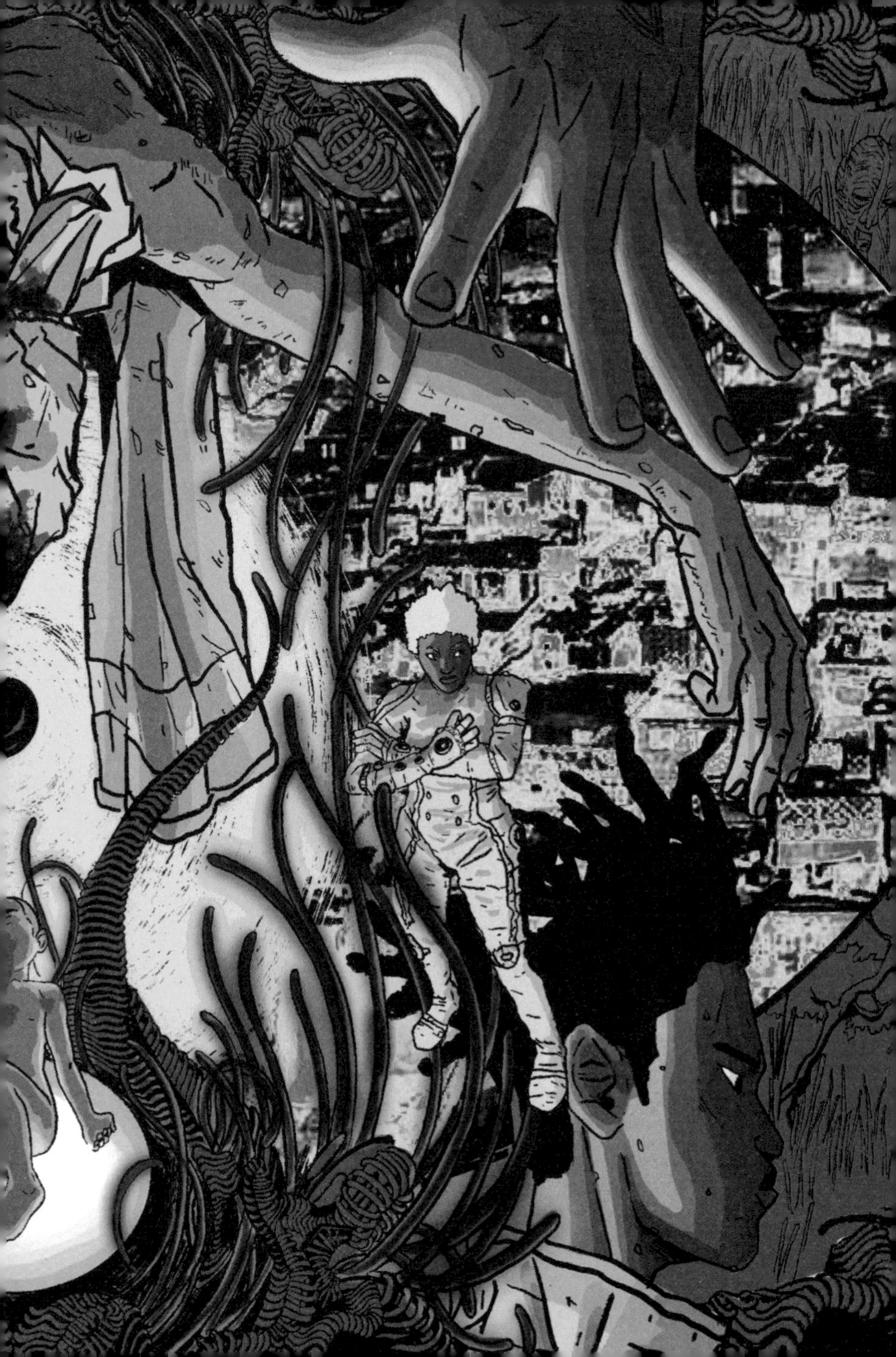

OBLIVION ROUGE

CHAPTER 1

In the Beginning, There Was Ata Emit - 0%

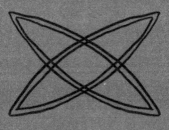

IN 2121, AFTER THE **LEUP PLAGUE**—A TUMOR-LIKE INFECTION THAT STARTS ON THE SKIN AND SOON CONSUMES THE HOST—HAS TAKEN CONTROL OF THE QAFURIAN CONTINENT, HUMANITY IS ON THE BRINK OF EXTINCTION. THE LAST COUNTRY REMAINING UNAFFECTED BY THE PLAGUE, **GALLOUM**, HAS SHUT ITS BORDERS. GALLOUM IS DELUGED BY ASYLUM SEEKERS FLEEING THE LEUP PLAGUE.
IN RESPONSE, GALLOUM'S REBEL ARMY, **THE HELLS,** ROUNDS UP AND EXECUTES IMMIGRANTS CROSSING **EUMEK**: A SMALL REGION ON THE BORDER BETWEEN LIAM AND GALLOUM. AN UNKNOWN MILITARY ORGANIZATION CALLED **THE HAKKINEN** APPEARS, THEIR ORIGIN A MYSTERY. SEEKING PEACE AND ERADICATION OF THE LEUP PLAGUE, THE HAKKINEN INTERVENE ON BEHALF OF THE PEOPLE OF EUMEK.

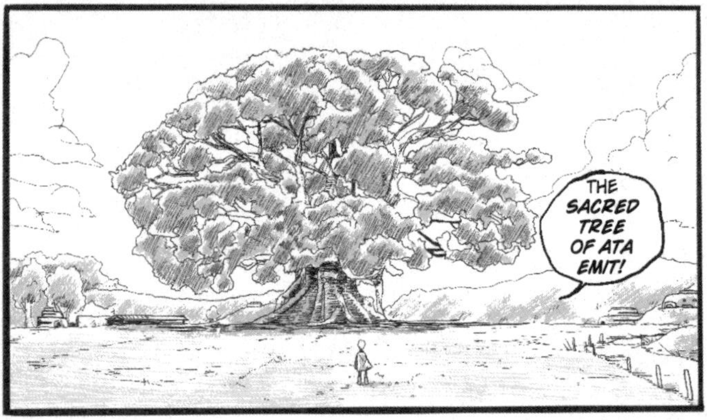
THE SACRED TREE OF ATA EMIT!

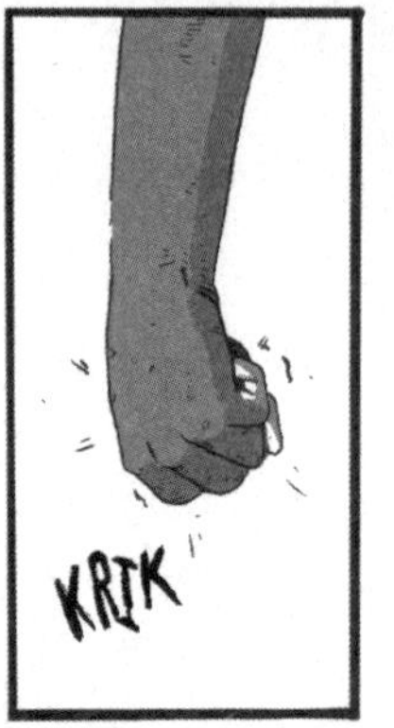
KRIK

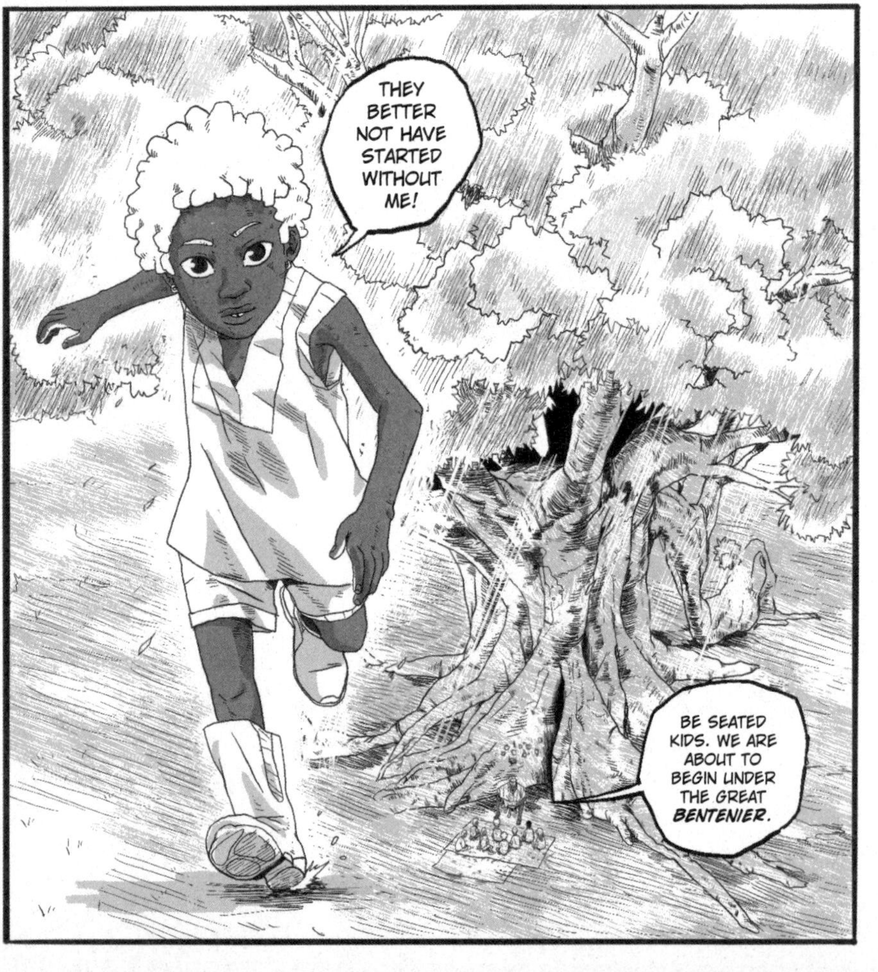
THEY BETTER NOT HAVE STARTED WITHOUT ME!
BE SEATED KIDS. WE ARE ABOUT TO BEGIN UNDER THE GREAT *BENTENIER*.

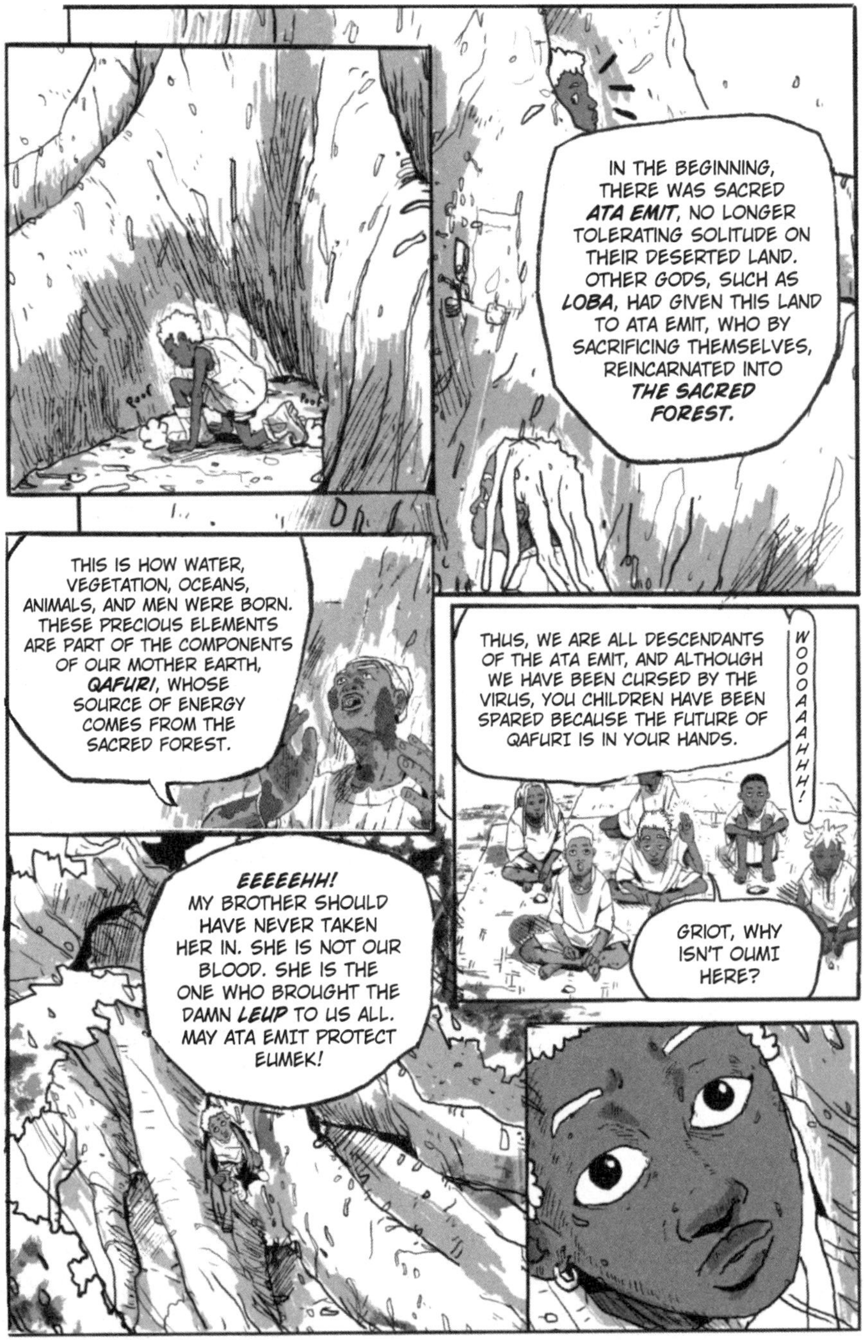
Poof
Poof
IN THE BEGINNING, THERE WAS SACRED ATA EMIT, NO LONGER TOLERATING SOLITUDE ON THEIR DESERTED LAND. OTHER GODS, SUCH AS LOBA, HAD GIVEN THIS LAND TO ATA EMIT, WHO BY SACRIFICING THEMSELVES, REINCARNATED INTO THE SACRED FOREST.
THIS IS HOW WATER, VEGETATION, OCEANS, ANIMALS, AND MEN WERE BORN. THESE PRECIOUS ELEMENTS ARE PART OF THE COMPONENTS OF OUR MOTHER EARTH, QAFURI, WHOSE SOURCE OF ENERGY COMES FROM THE SACRED FOREST.
THUS, WE ARE ALL DESCENDANTS OF THE ATA EMIT, AND ALTHOUGH WE HAVE BEEN CURSED BY THE VIRUS, YOU CHILDREN HAVE BEEN SPARED BECAUSE THE FUTURE OF QAFURI IS IN YOUR HANDS.
WOOOAAAHHH!
GRIOT, WHY ISN'T OUMI HERE?
EEEEEHH! MY BROTHER SHOULD HAVE NEVER TAKEN HER IN. SHE IS NOT OUR BLOOD. SHE IS THE ONE WHO BROUGHT THE DAMN LEUP TO US ALL. MAY ATA EMIT PROTECT ELIMEK!

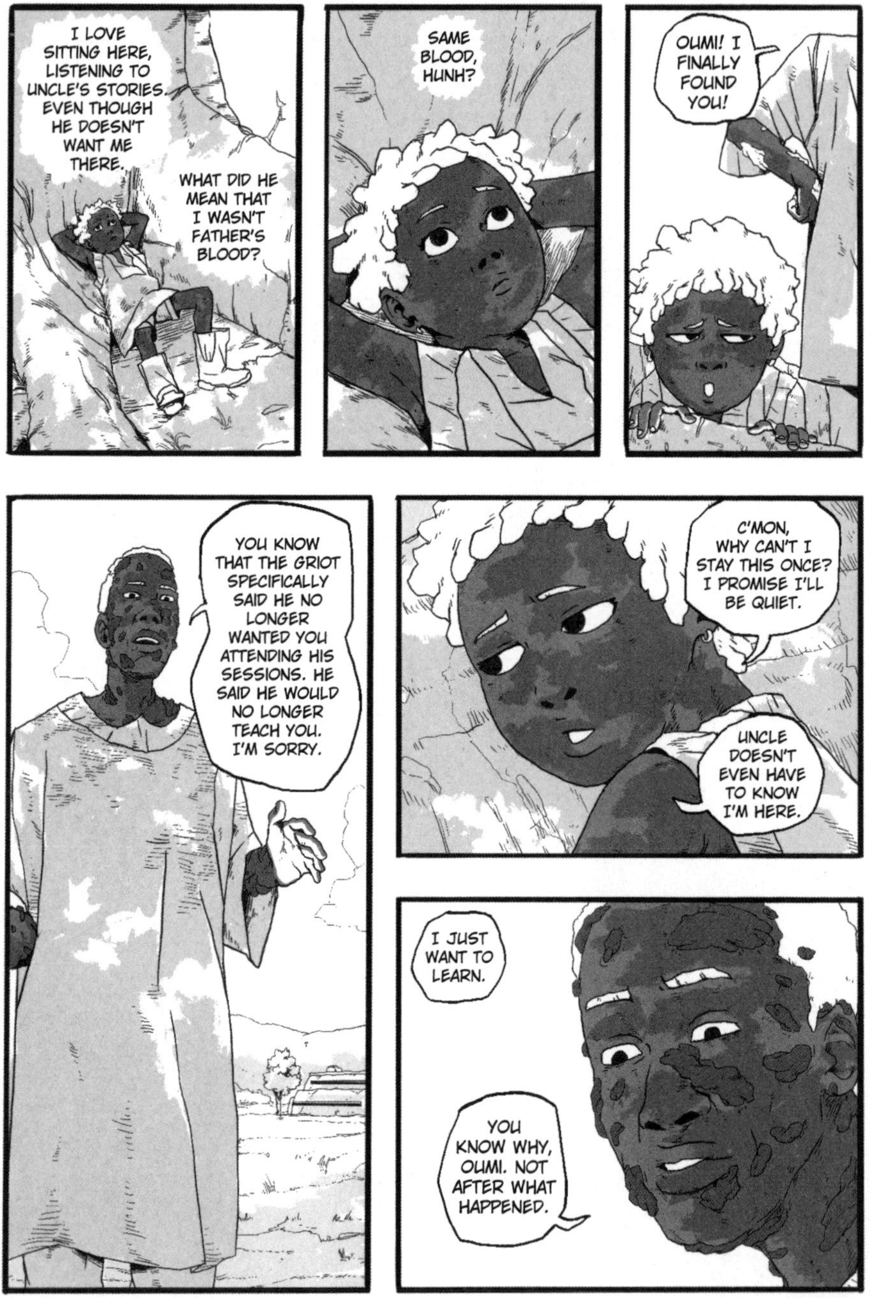
I LOVE SITTING HERE, LISTENING TO UNCLE'S STORIES. EVEN THOUGH HE DOESN'T WANT ME THERE.
WHAT DID HE MEAN THAT I WASN'T FATHER'S BLOOD?
SAME BLOOD, HUNH?
OUMI! I FINALLY FOUND YOU!
YOU KNOW THAT THE GRIOT SPECIFICALLY SAID HE NO LONGER WANTED YOU ATTENDING HIS SESSIONS. HE SAID HE WOULD NO LONGER TEACH YOU. I'M SORRY.
C'MON, WHY CAN'T I STAY THIS ONCE? I PROMISE I'LL BE QUIET.
UNCLE DOESN'T EVEN HAVE TO KNOW I'M HERE.
I JUST WANT TO LEARN.
YOU KNOW WHY, OUMI. NOT AFTER WHAT HAPPENED.

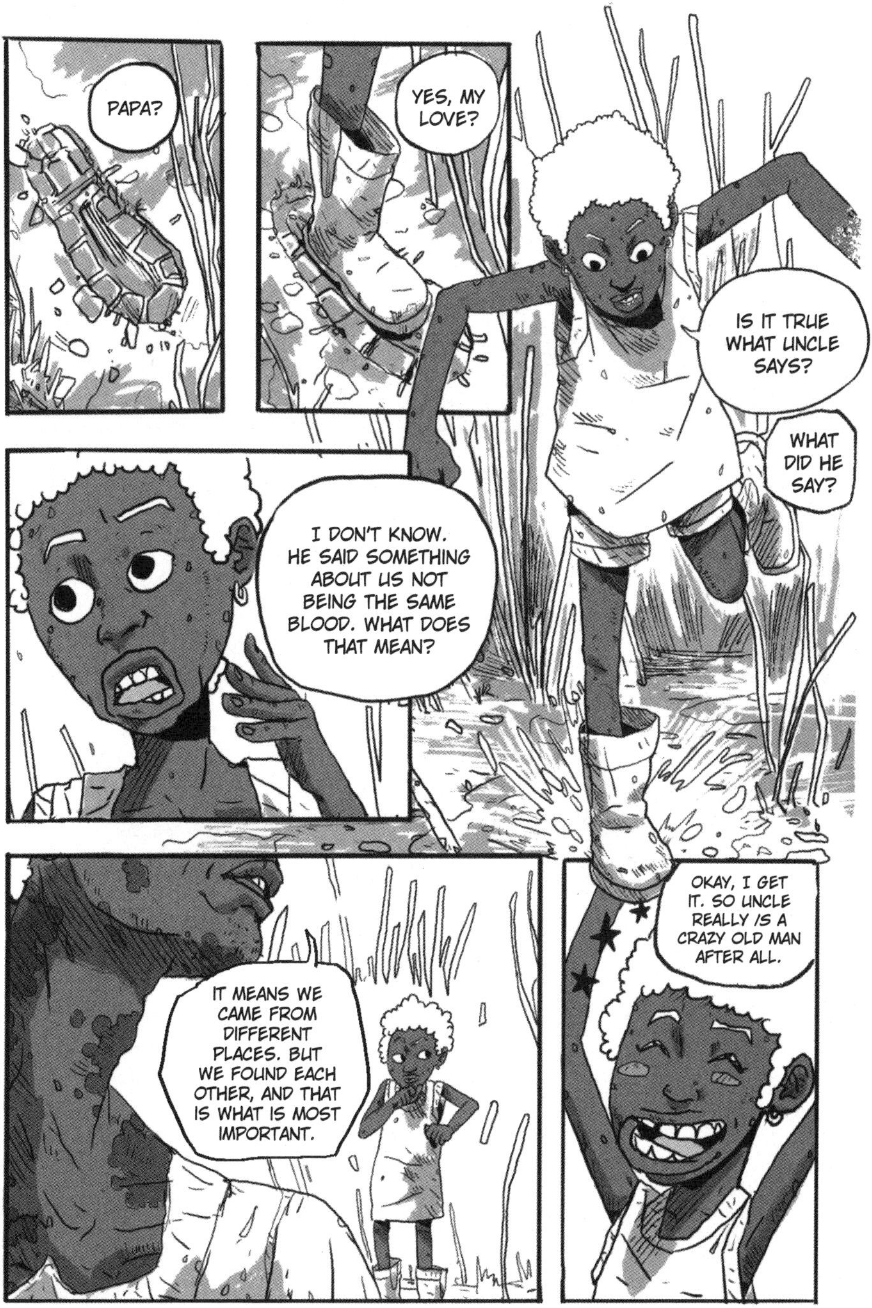
PAPA?
YES, MY LOVE?
IS IT TRUE WHAT UNCLE SAYS?
WHAT DID HE SAY?
I DON'T KNOW. HE SAID SOMETHING ABOUT US NOT BEING THE SAME BLOOD. WHAT DOES THAT MEAN?
IT MEANS WE CAME FROM DIFFERENT PLACES. BUT WE FOUND EACH OTHER, AND THAT IS WHAT IS MOST IMPORTANT.
OKAY, I GET IT. SO UNCLE REALLY IS A CRAZY OLD MAN AFTER ALL.

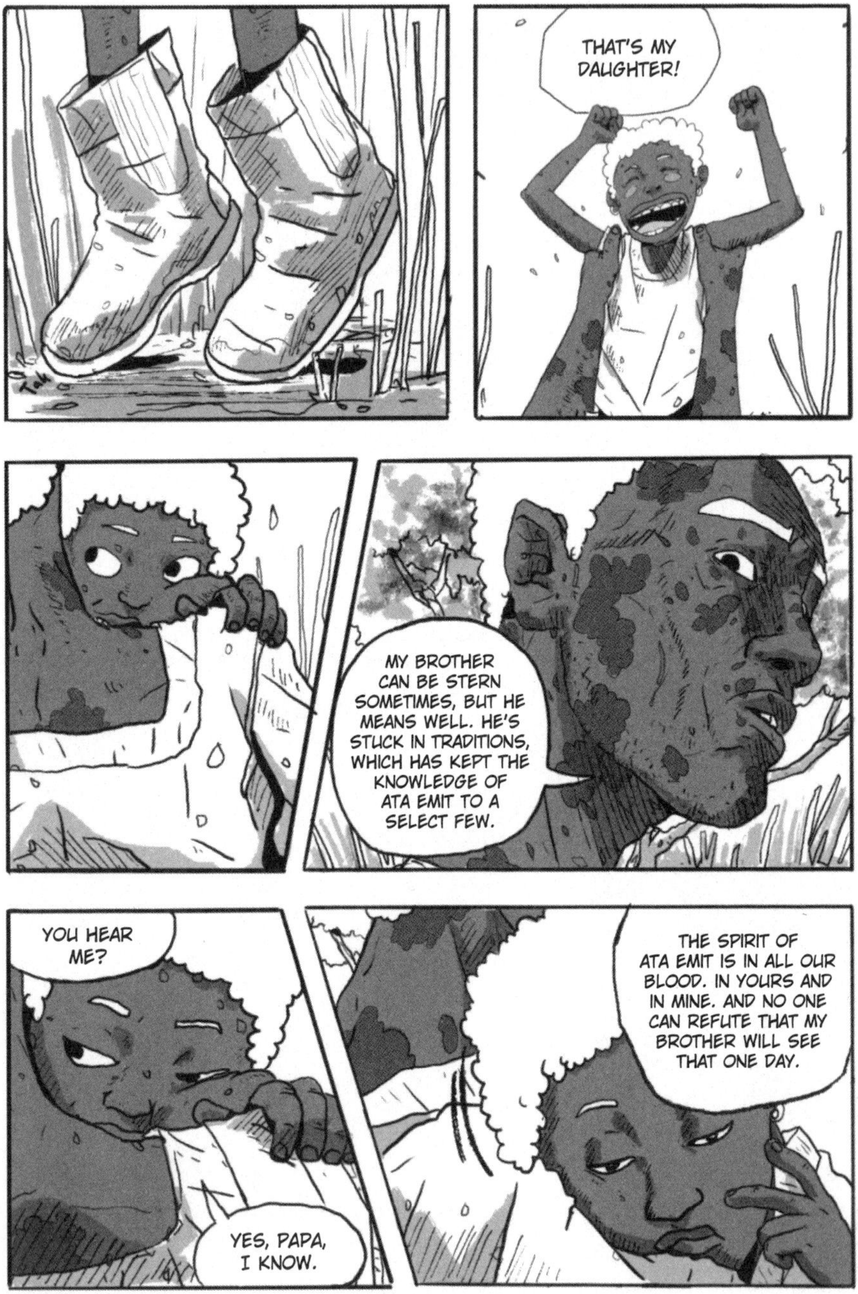
TAK
THAT'S MY DAUGHTER!
MY BROTHER CAN BE STERN SOMETIMES, BUT HE MEANS WELL. HE'S STUCK IN TRADITIONS, WHICH HAS KEPT THE KNOWLEDGE OF ATA EMIT TO A SELECT FEW.
YOU HEAR ME?
YES, PAPA, I KNOW.
THE SPIRIT OF ATA EMIT IS IN ALL OUR BLOOD. IN YOURS AND IN MINE. AND NO ONE CAN REFUTE THAT MY BROTHER WILL SEE THAT ONE DAY.

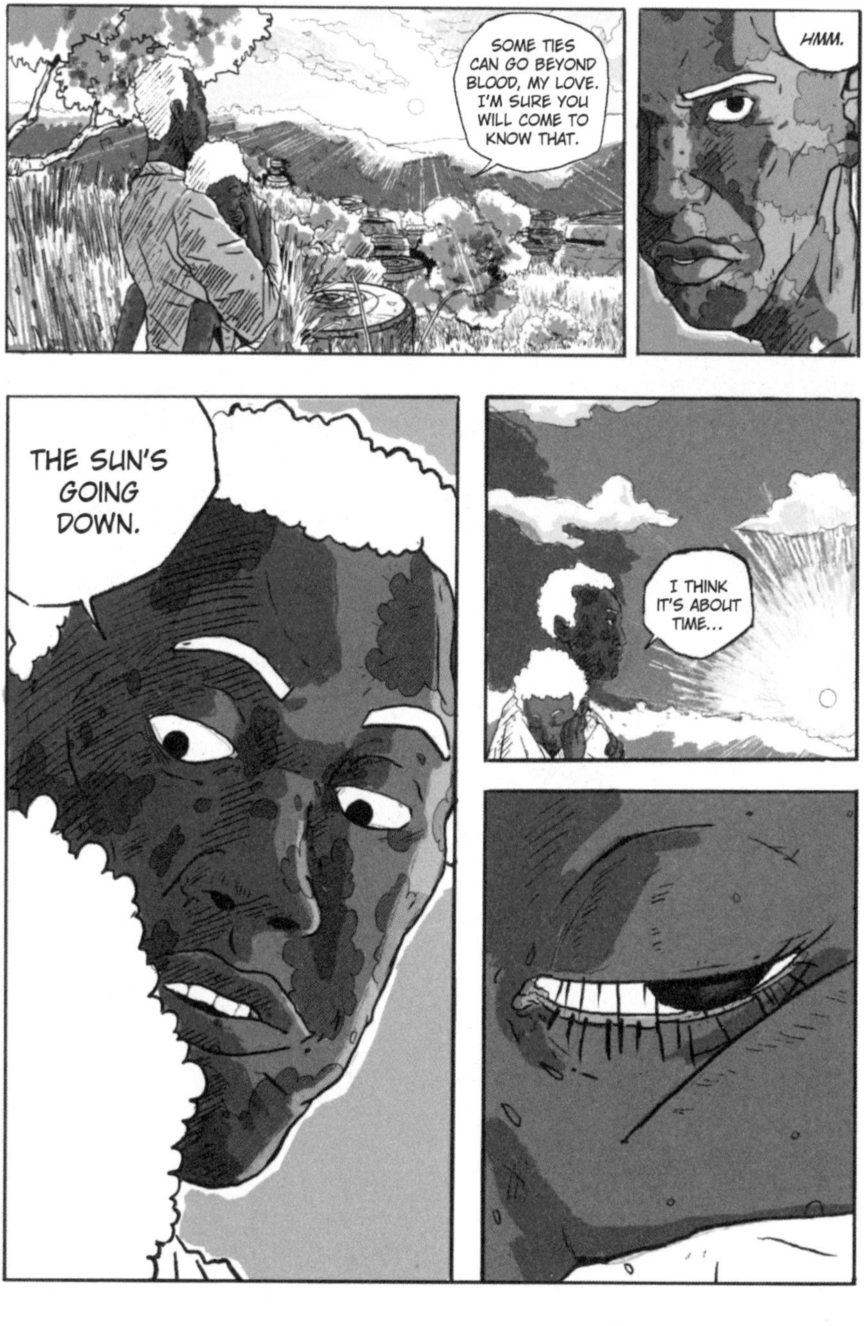
SOME TIES CAN GO BEYOND BLOOD, MY LOVE. I'M SURE YOU WILL COME TO KNOW THAT.
HMM.
THE SUN'S GOING DOWN.
I THINK IT'S ABOUT TIME...

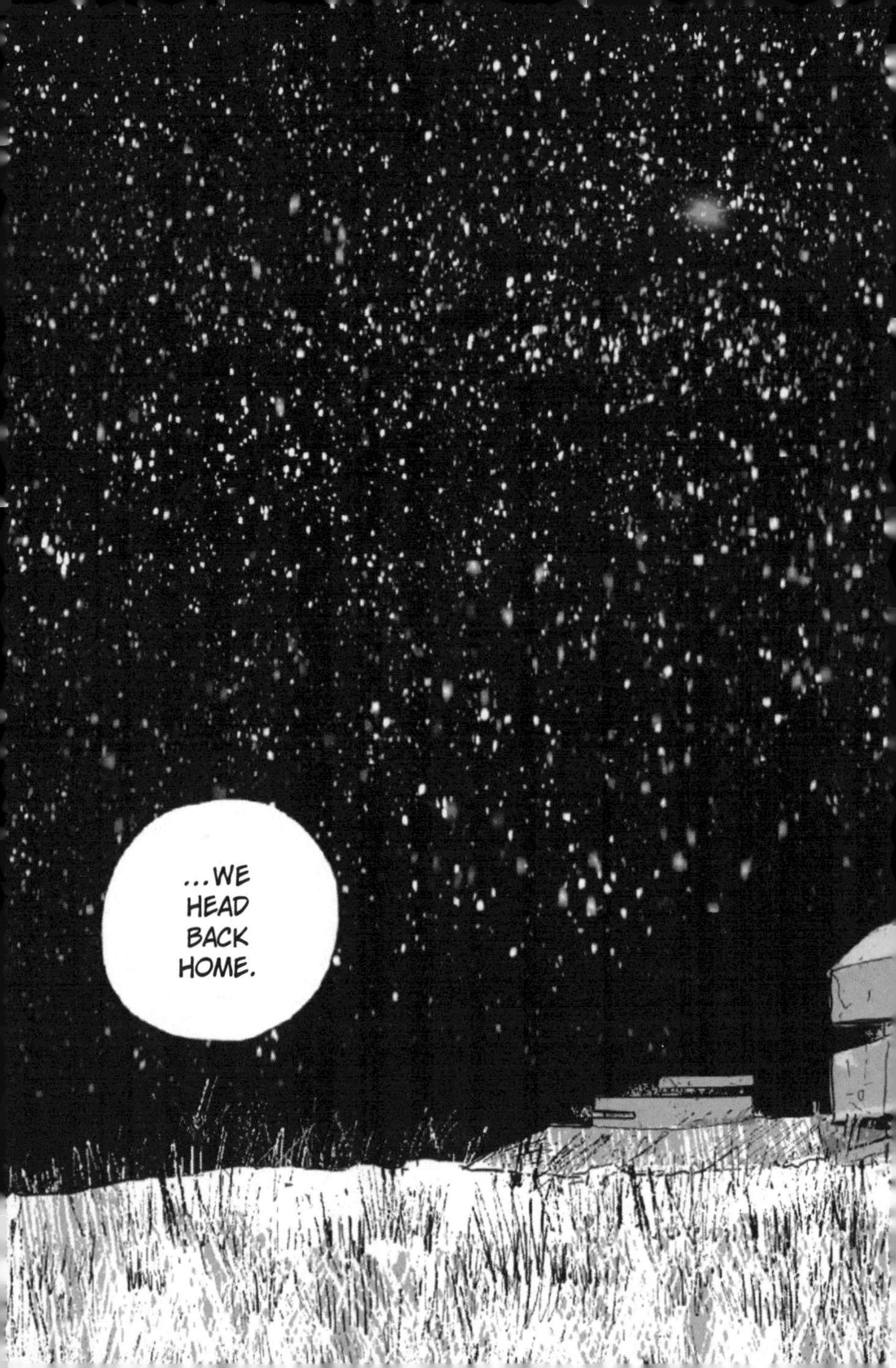
...WE HEAD BACK HOME.

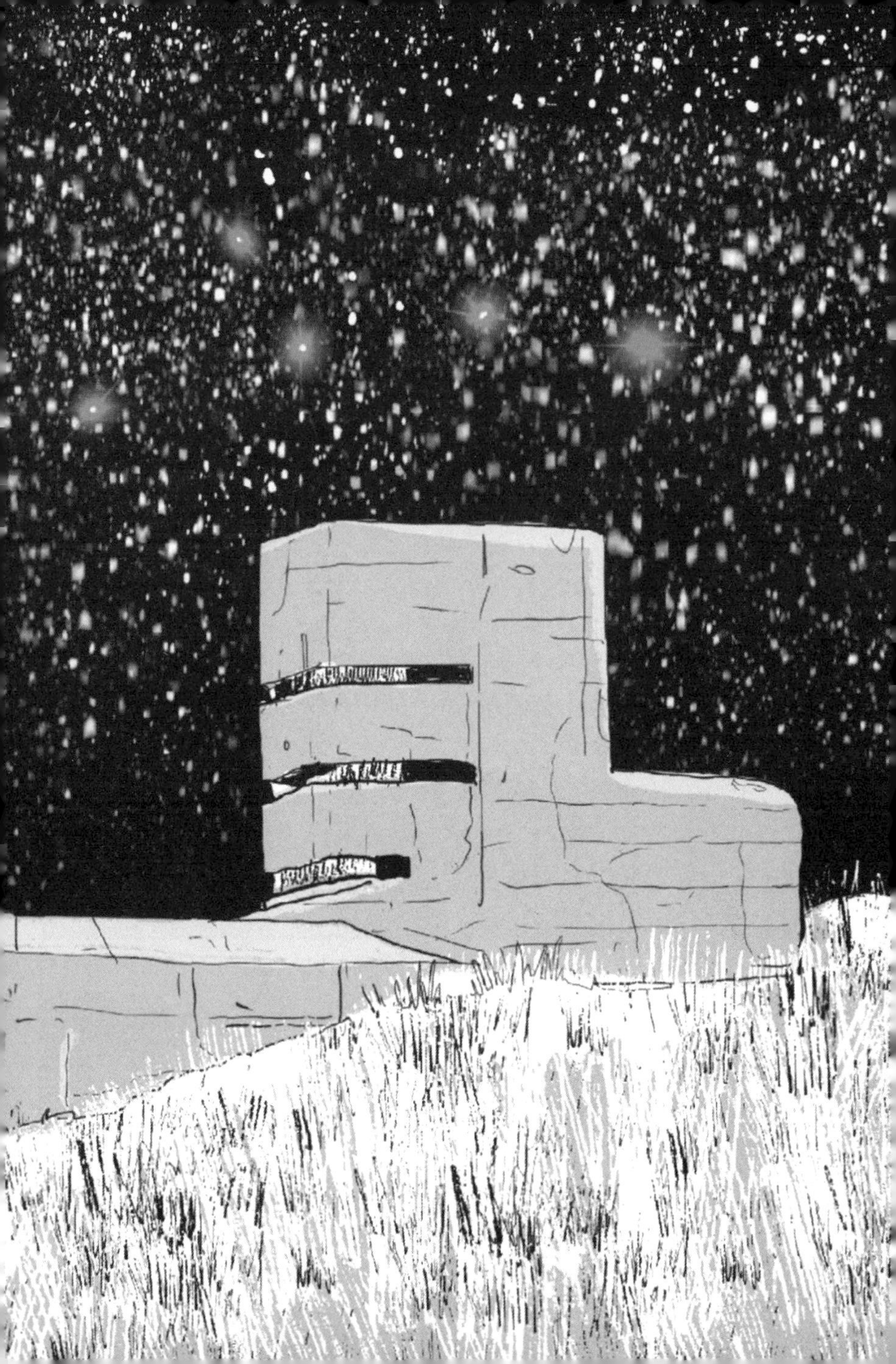

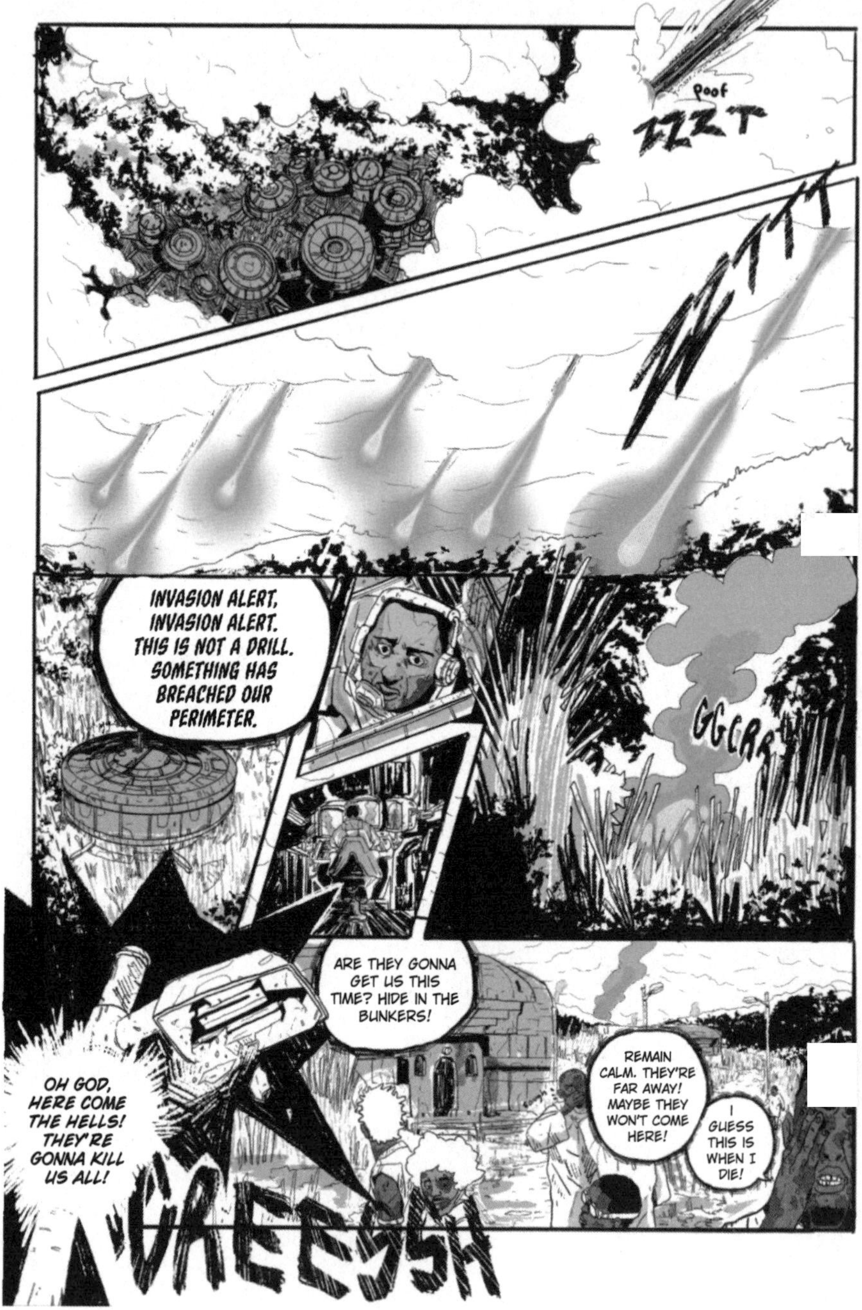
poof
ZZZT
INVASION ALERT, INVASION ALERT. THIS IS NOT A DRILL. SOMETHING HAS BREACHED OUR PERIMETER.
GGCRR
ARE THEY GONNA GET US THIS TIME? HIDE IN THE BUNKERS!
OH GOD, HERE COME THE HELLS! THEY'RE GONNA KILL US ALL!
REMAIN CALM. THEY'RE FAR AWAY! MAYBE THEY WON'T COME HERE!
I GUESS THIS IS WHEN I DIE!

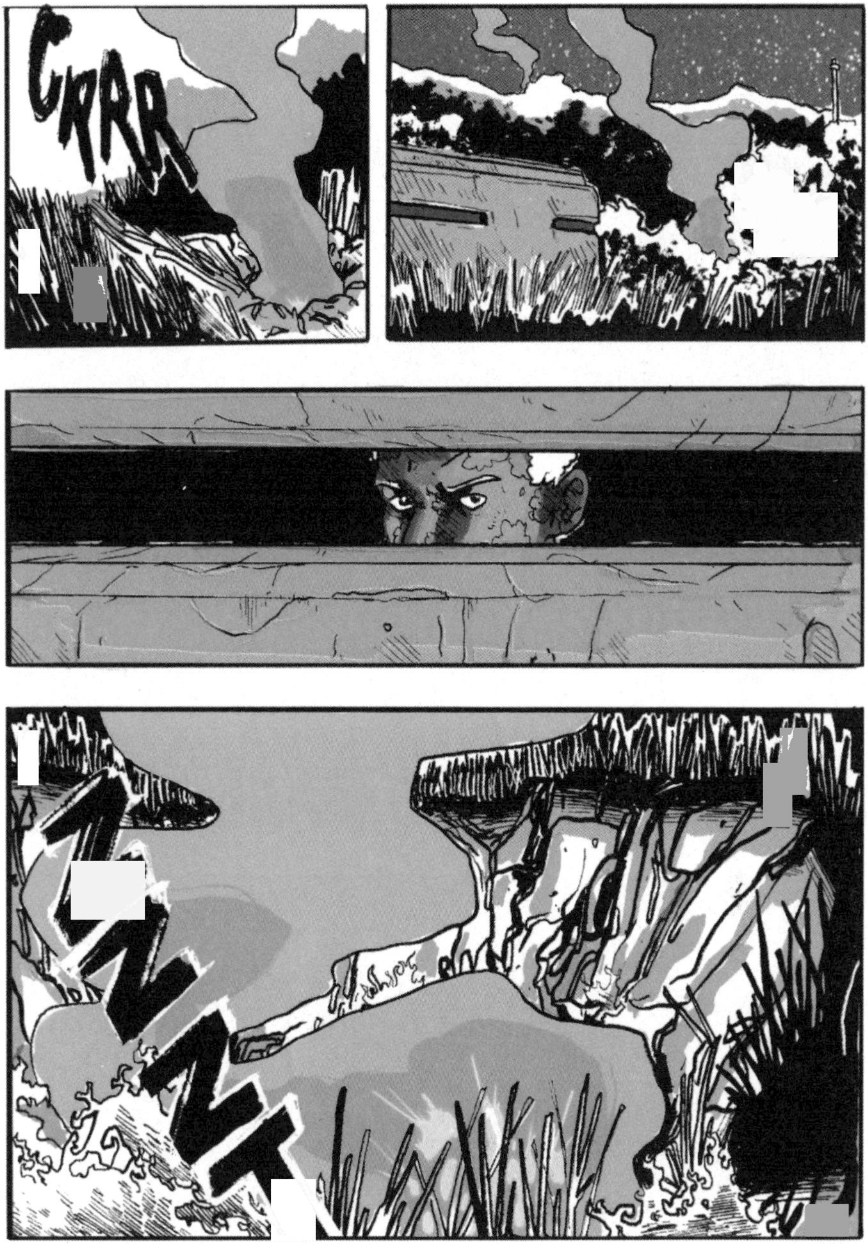
GRRR

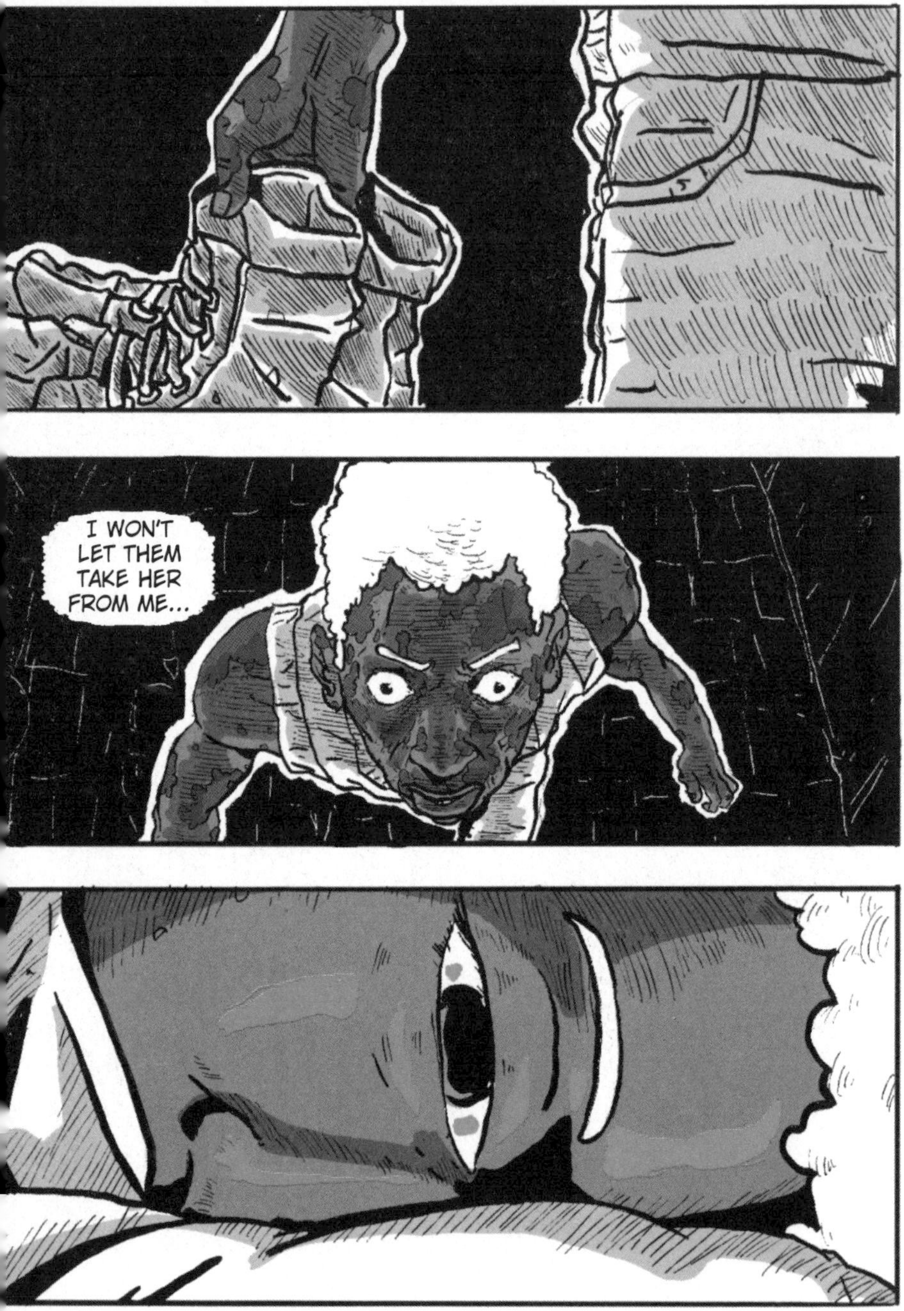
I WON'T LET THEM TAKE HER FROM ME...

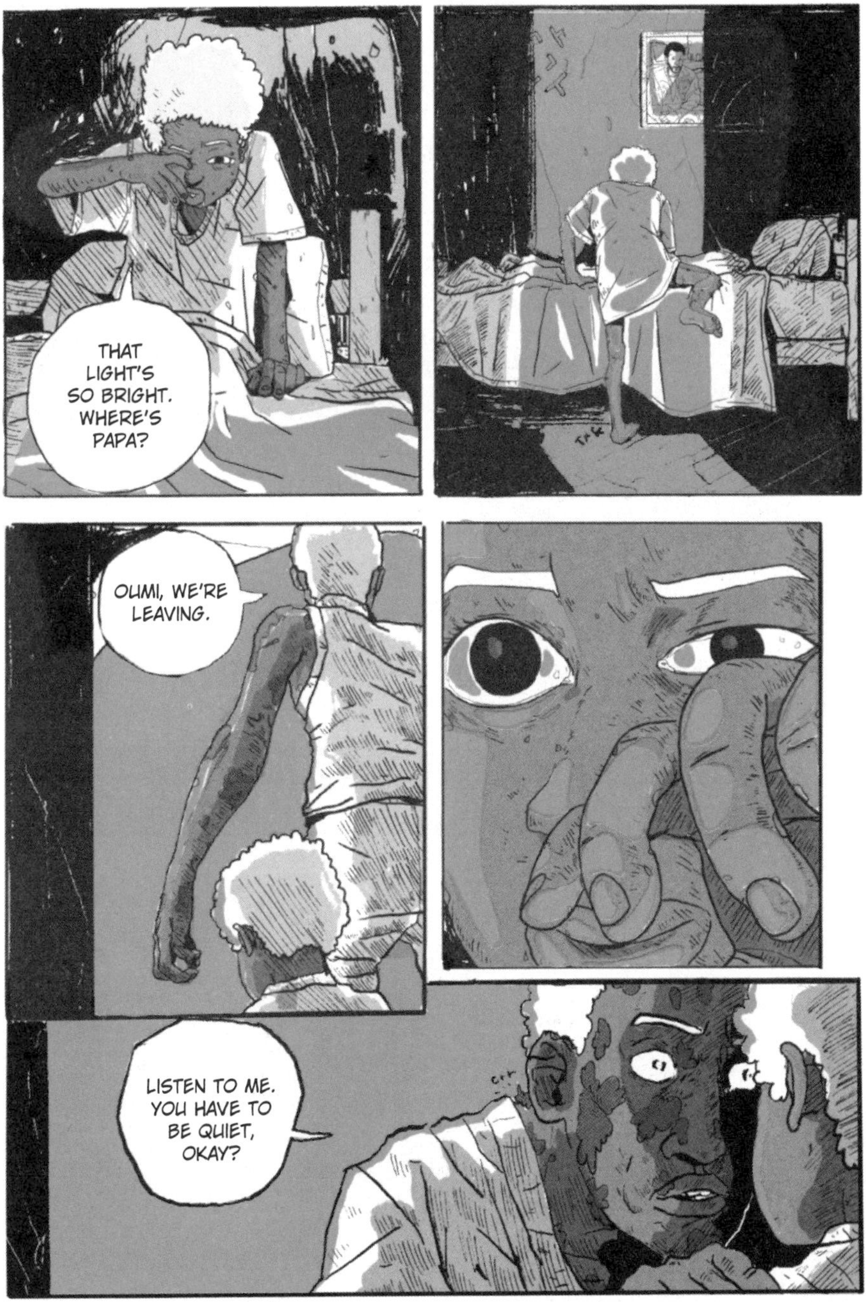
THAT LIGHT'S SO BRIGHT. WHERE'S PAPA?
OUMI, WE'RE LEAVING.
LISTEN TO ME. YOU HAVE TO BE QUIET, OKAY?

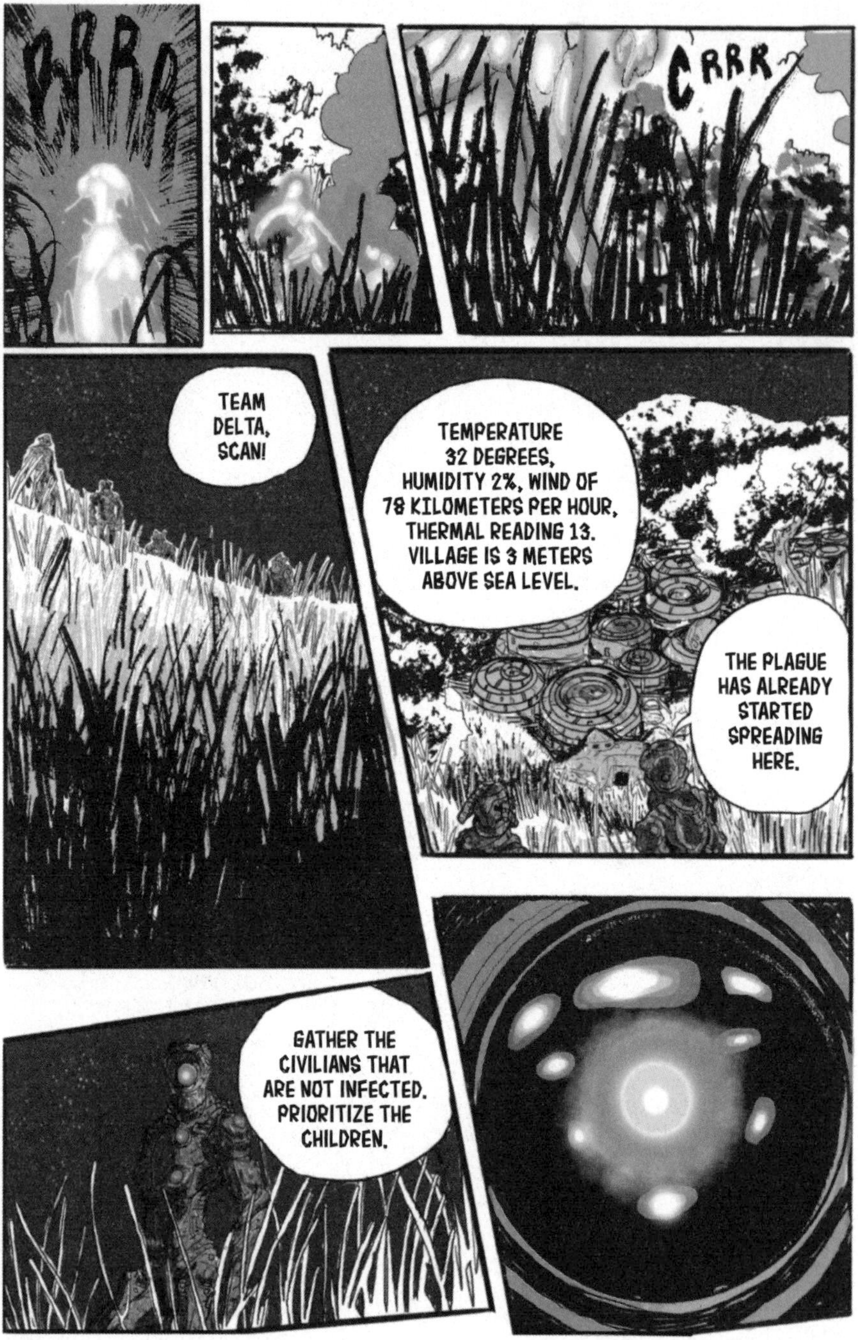
PRRR
CRRR
TEAM DELTA, SCAN!
TEMPERATURE 32 DEGREES, HUMIDITY 2%, WIND OF 78 KILOMETERS PER HOUR, THERMAL READING 13. VILLAGE IS 3 METERS ABOVE SEA LEVEL.
THE PLAGUE HAS ALREADY STARTED SPREADING HERE.
GATHER THE CIVILIANS THAT ARE NOT INFECTED. PRIORITIZE THE CHILDREN.

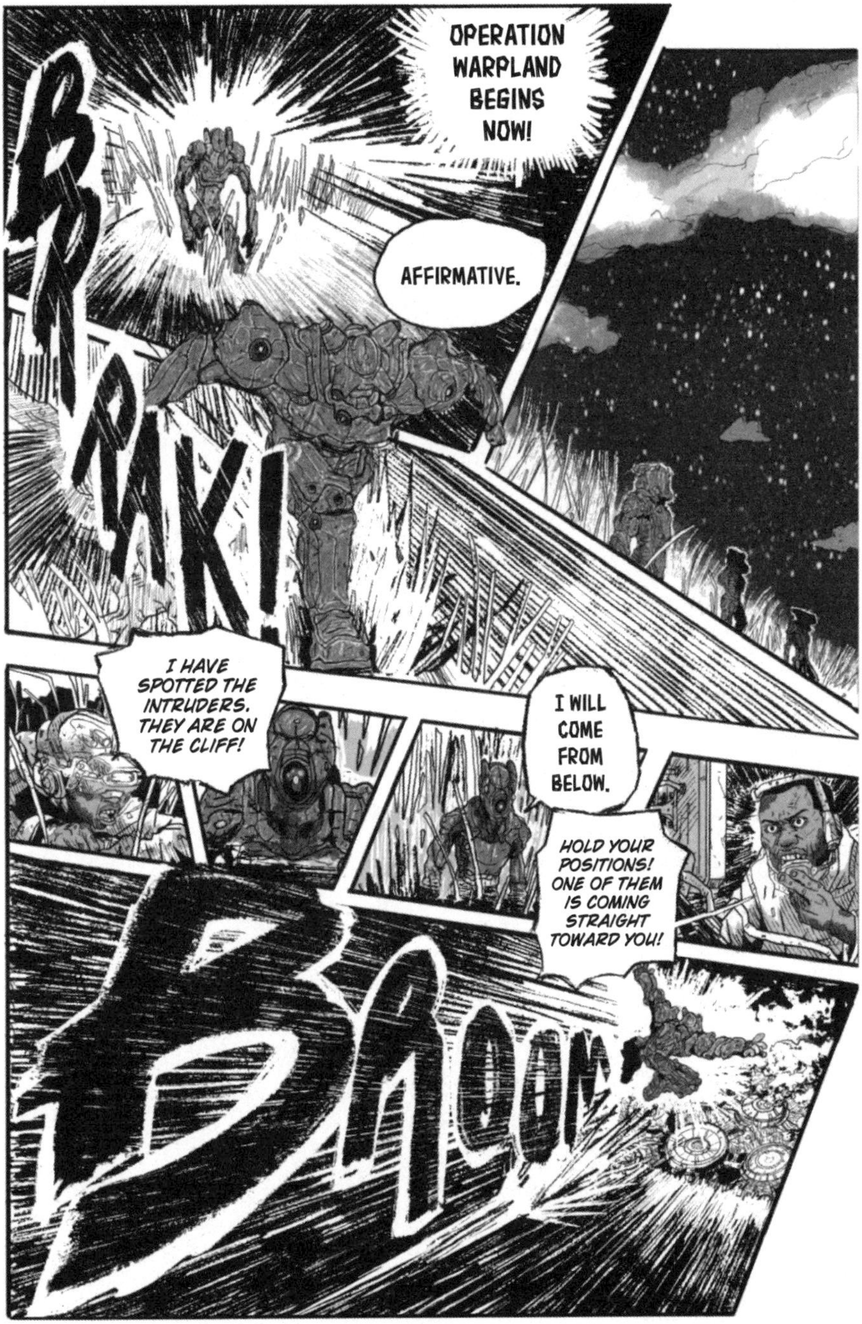
OPERATION WARPLAND BEGINS NOW!
AFFIRMATIVE.
I HAVE SPOTTED THE INTRUDERS. THEY ARE ON THE CLIFF!
I WILL COME FROM BELOW.
HOLD YOUR POSITIONS! ONE OF THEM IS COMING STRAIGHT TOWARD YOU!

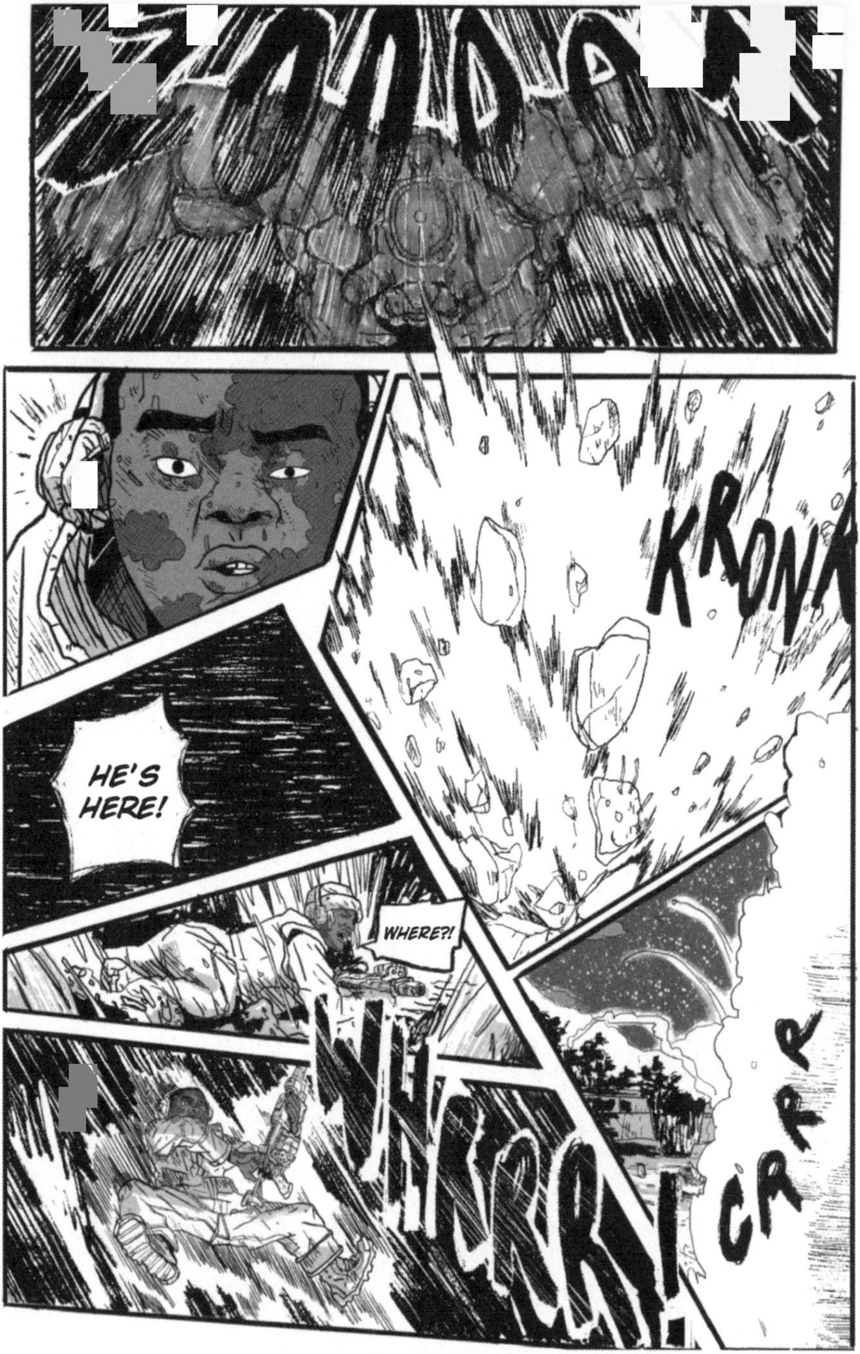
HE'S HERE!
WHERE?!
KRON

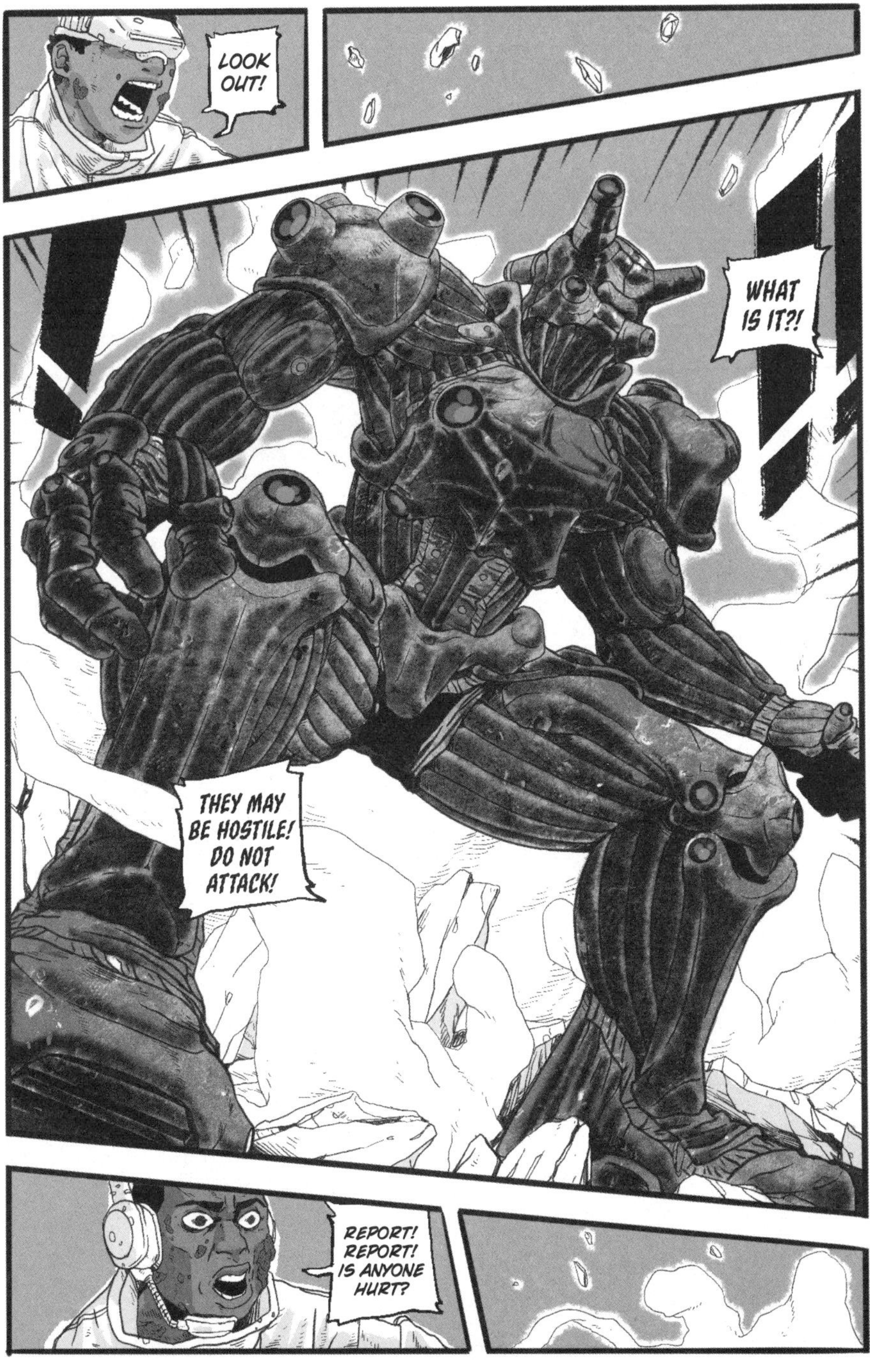
LOOK OUT!
WHAT IS IT?!
THEY MAY BE HOSTILE! DO NOT ATTACK!
REPORT! REPORT! IS ANYONE HURT?

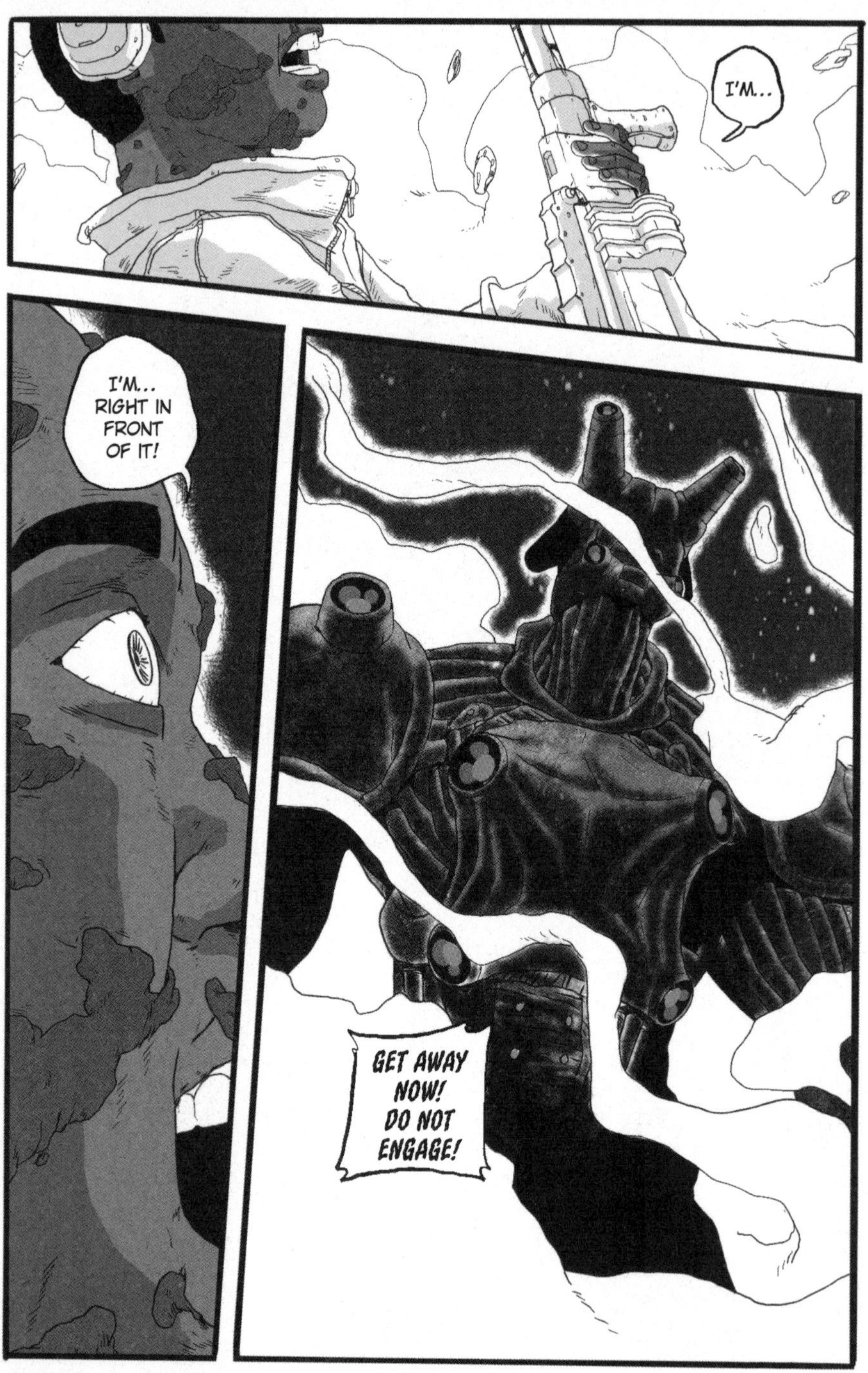
I'M...
I'M... RIGHT IN FRONT OF IT!
GET AWAY NOW! DO NOT ENGAGE!

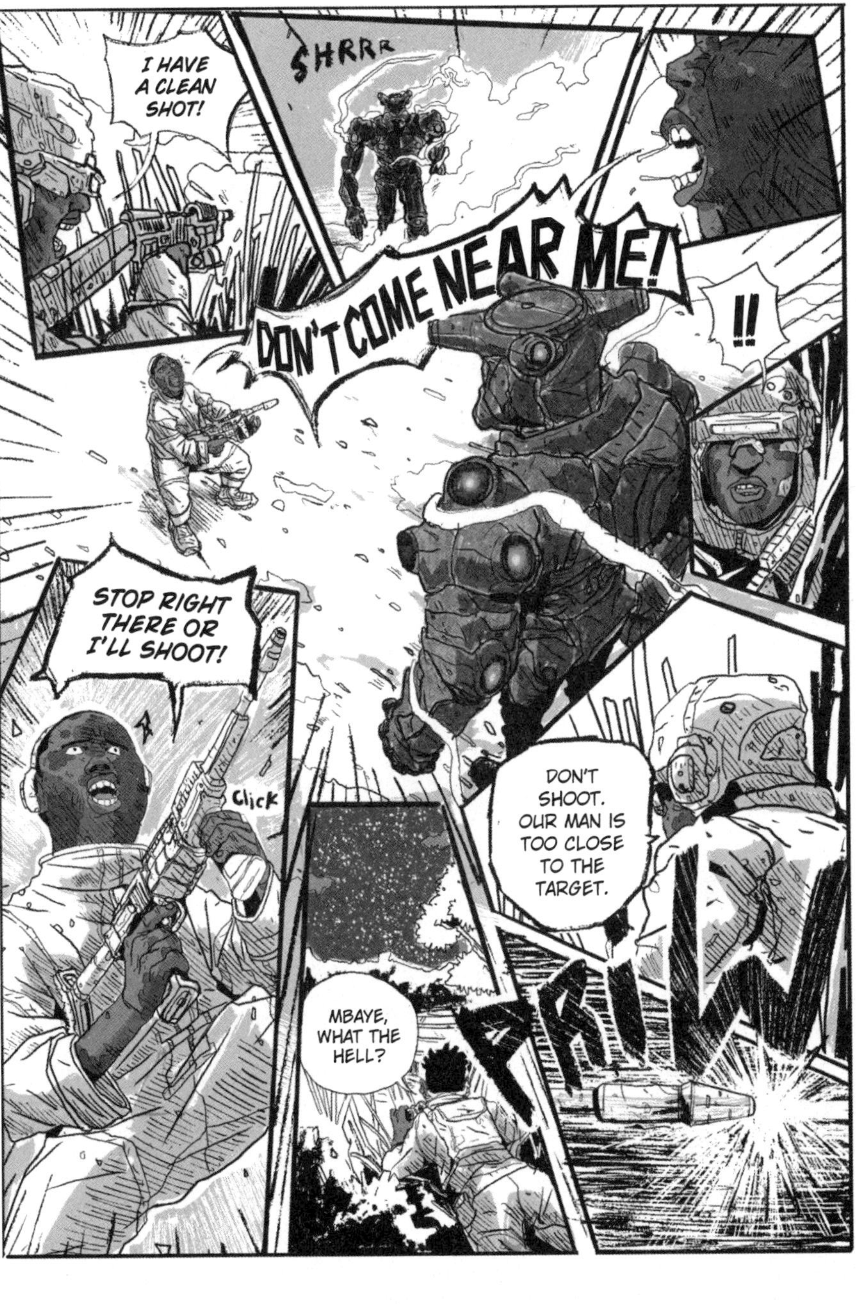
I HAVE A CLEAN SHOT!
SHRRR
DON'T COME NEAR ME!
!!
STOP RIGHT THERE OR I'LL SHOOT!
Click
MBAYE, WHAT THE HELL?
DON'T SHOOT. OUR MAN IS TOO CLOSE TO THE TARGET.
PRIIW

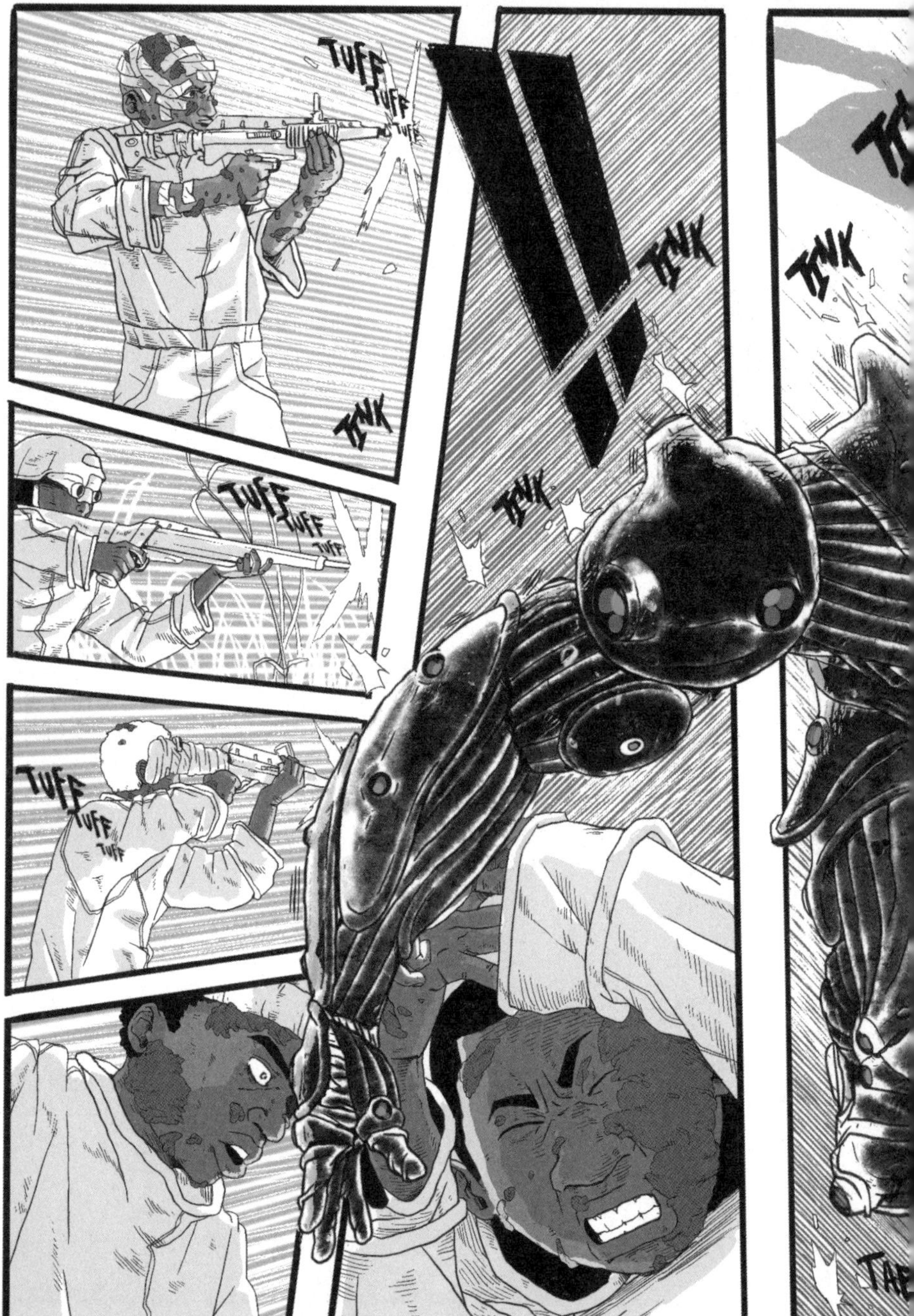
TUFF
TUFF
TUFF
TINK
TUFF
TUFF
TUFF
TUFF
TUFF
TUFF
TINK
TINK
TINK

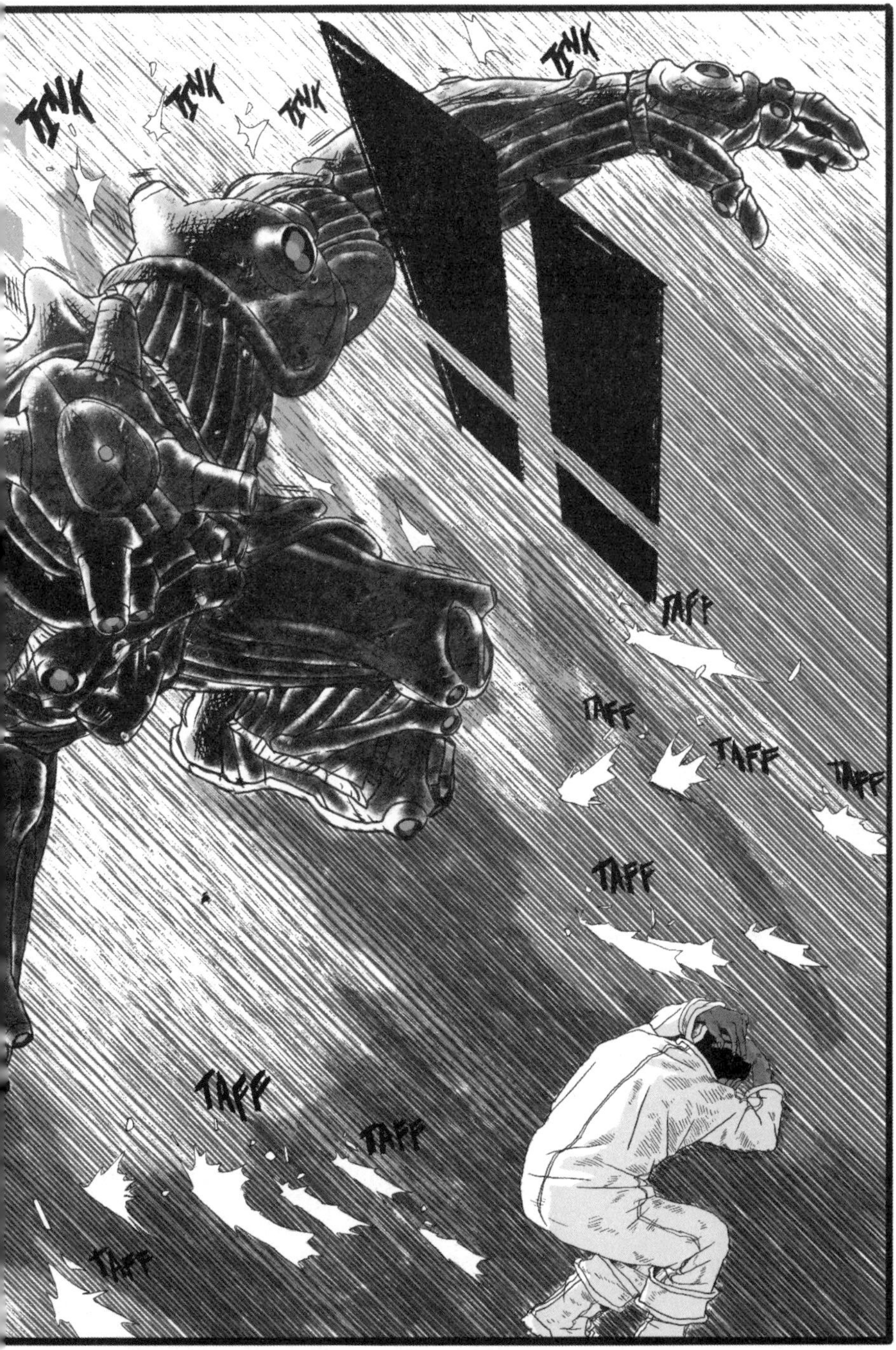
TINK
TINK
TINK
TINK
TAFF
TAFF
TAFF
TAFF
TAFF
TAFF
TAFF
TAFF

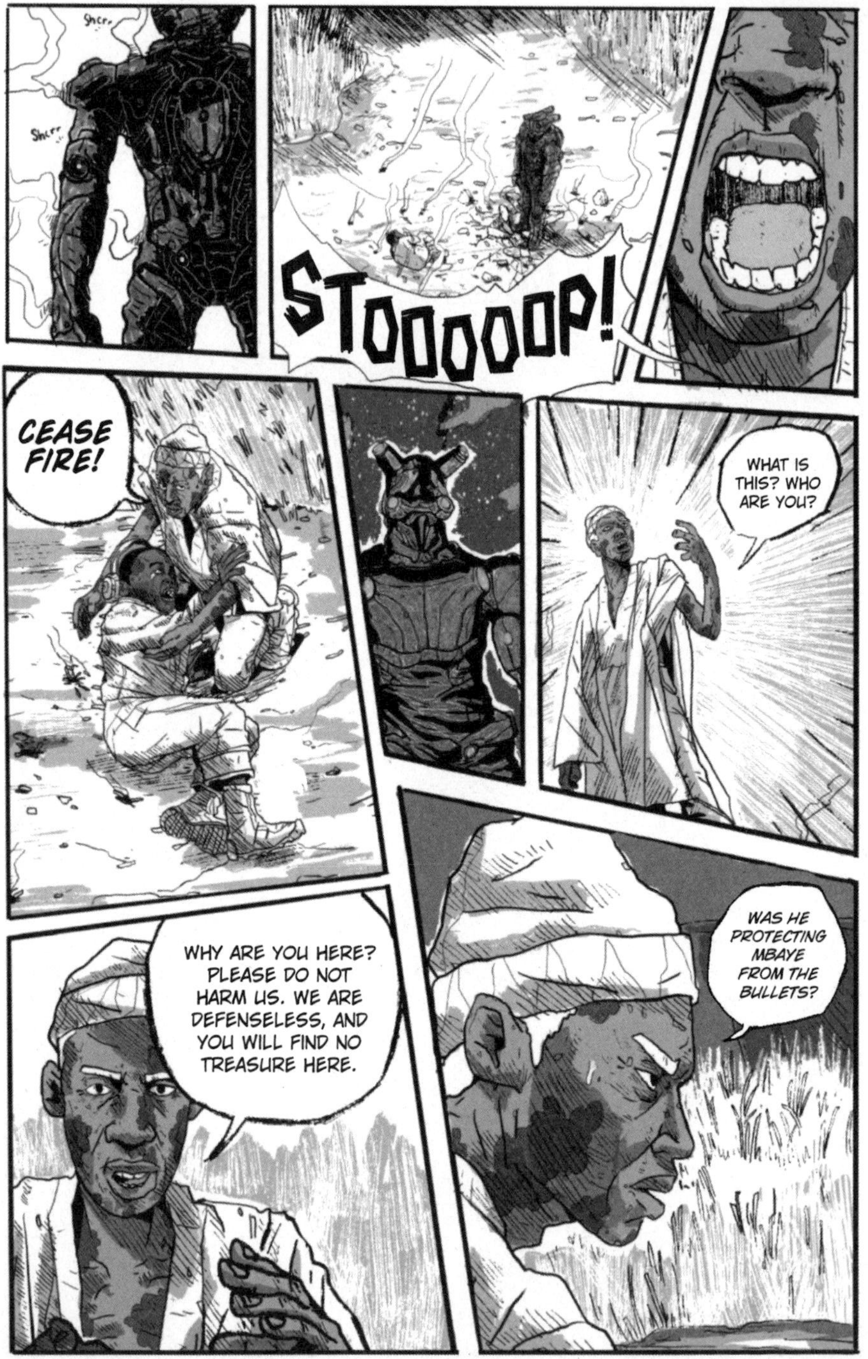
Shcrr
Shcrr
STOOOOOP!
CEASE FIRE!
WHAT IS THIS? WHO ARE YOU?
WHY ARE YOU HERE? PLEASE DO NOT HARM US. WE ARE DEFENSELESS, AND YOU WILL FIND NO TREASURE HERE.
WAS HE PROTECTING MBAYE FROM THE BULLETS?

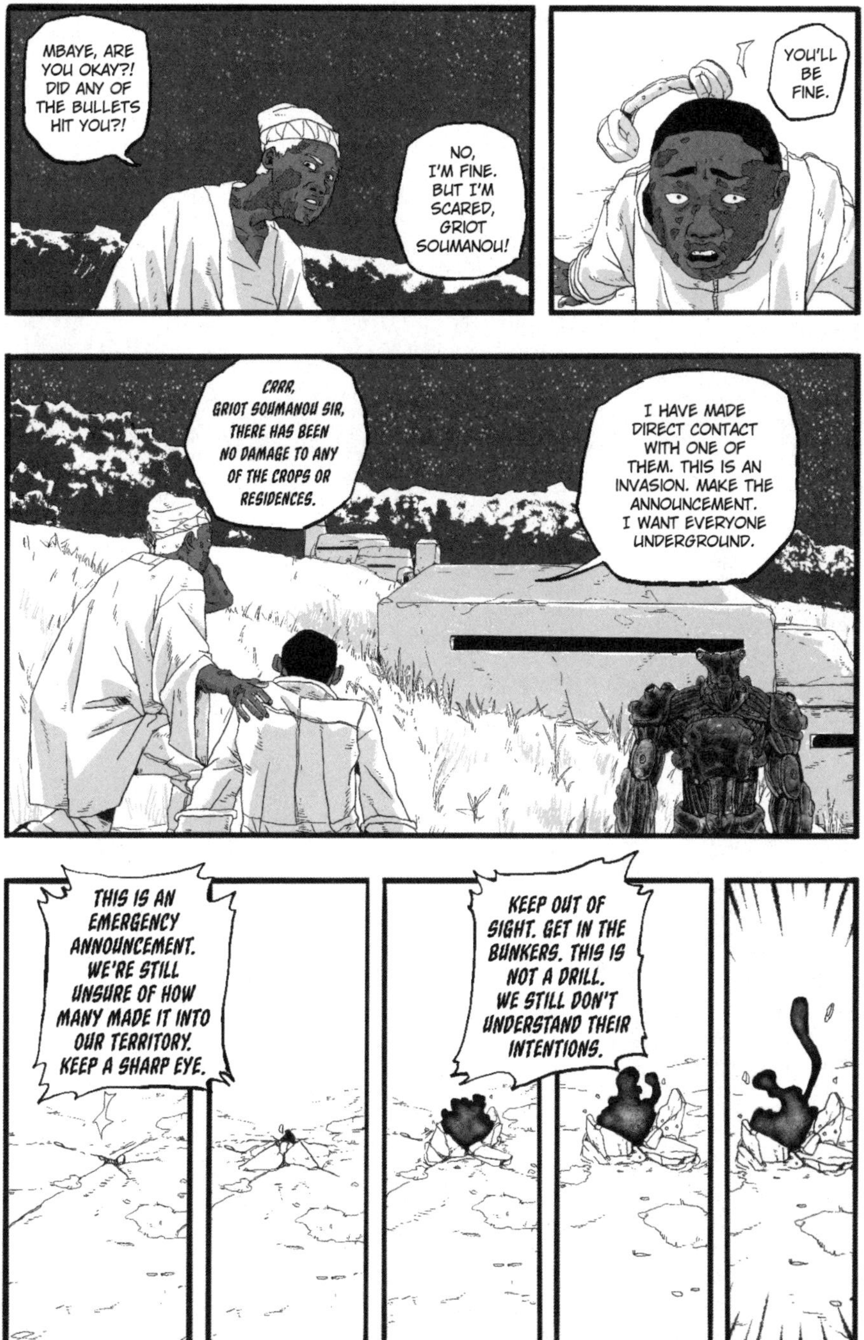
MBAYE, ARE YOU OKAY?! DID ANY OF THE BULLETS HIT YOU?!
NO, I'M FINE. BUT I'M SCARED, GRIOT SOUMANOU!
YOU'LL BE FINE.
CRRR, GRIOT SOUMANOU SIR, THERE HAS BEEN NO DAMAGE TO ANY OF THE CROPS OR RESIDENCES.
I HAVE MADE DIRECT CONTACT WITH ONE OF THEM. THIS IS AN INVASION. MAKE THE ANNOUNCEMENT. I WANT EVERYONE UNDERGROUND.
THIS IS AN EMERGENCY ANNOUNCEMENT. WE'RE STILL UNSURE OF HOW MANY MADE IT INTO OUR TERRITORY. KEEP A SHARP EYE.
KEEP OUT OF SIGHT. GET IN THE BUNKERS. THIS IS NOT A DRILL. WE STILL DON'T UNDERSTAND THEIR INTENTIONS.

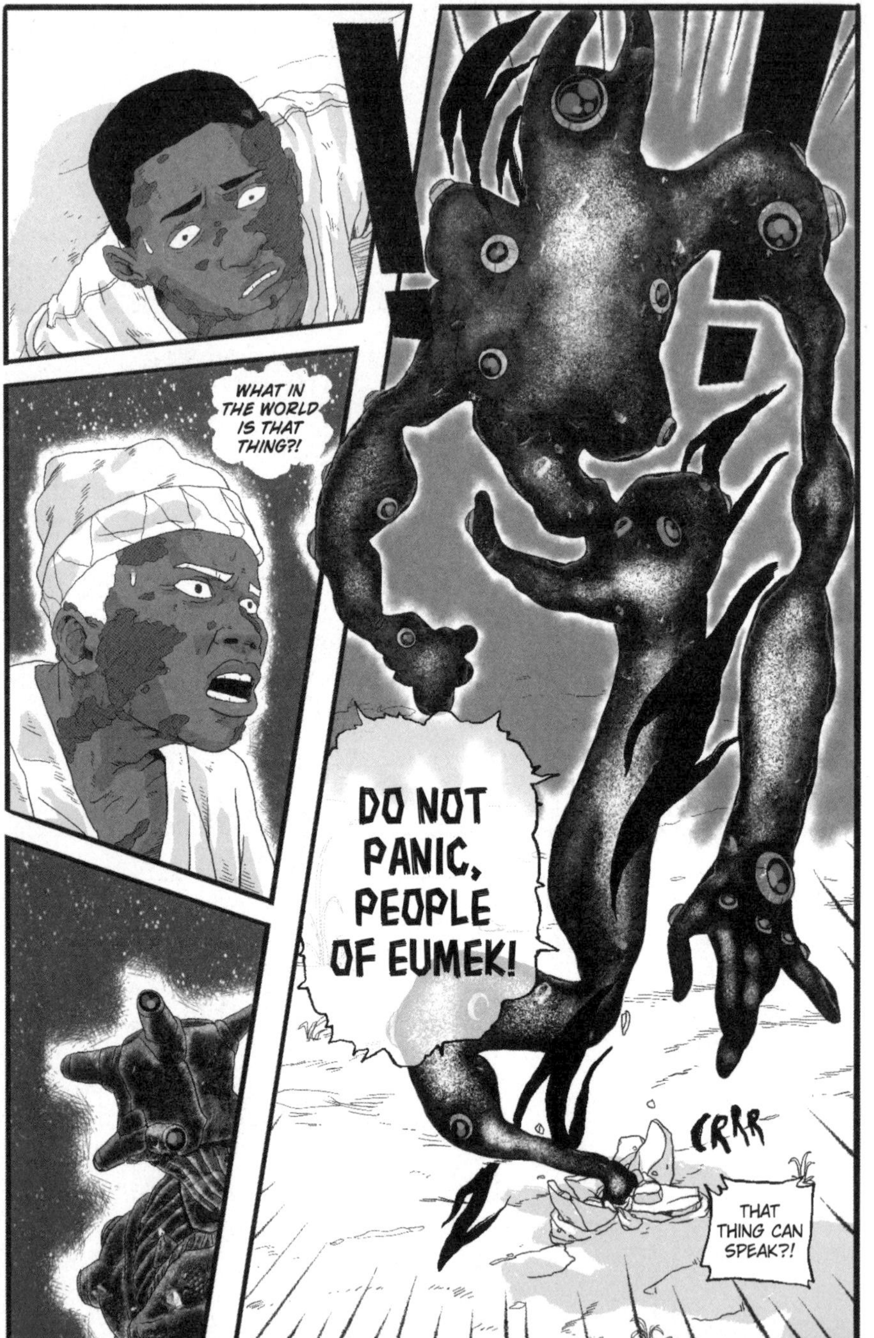
WHAT IN THE WORLD IS THAT THING?!
DO NOT PANIC, PEOPLE OF EUMEK!
CRRR
THAT THING CAN SPEAK?!

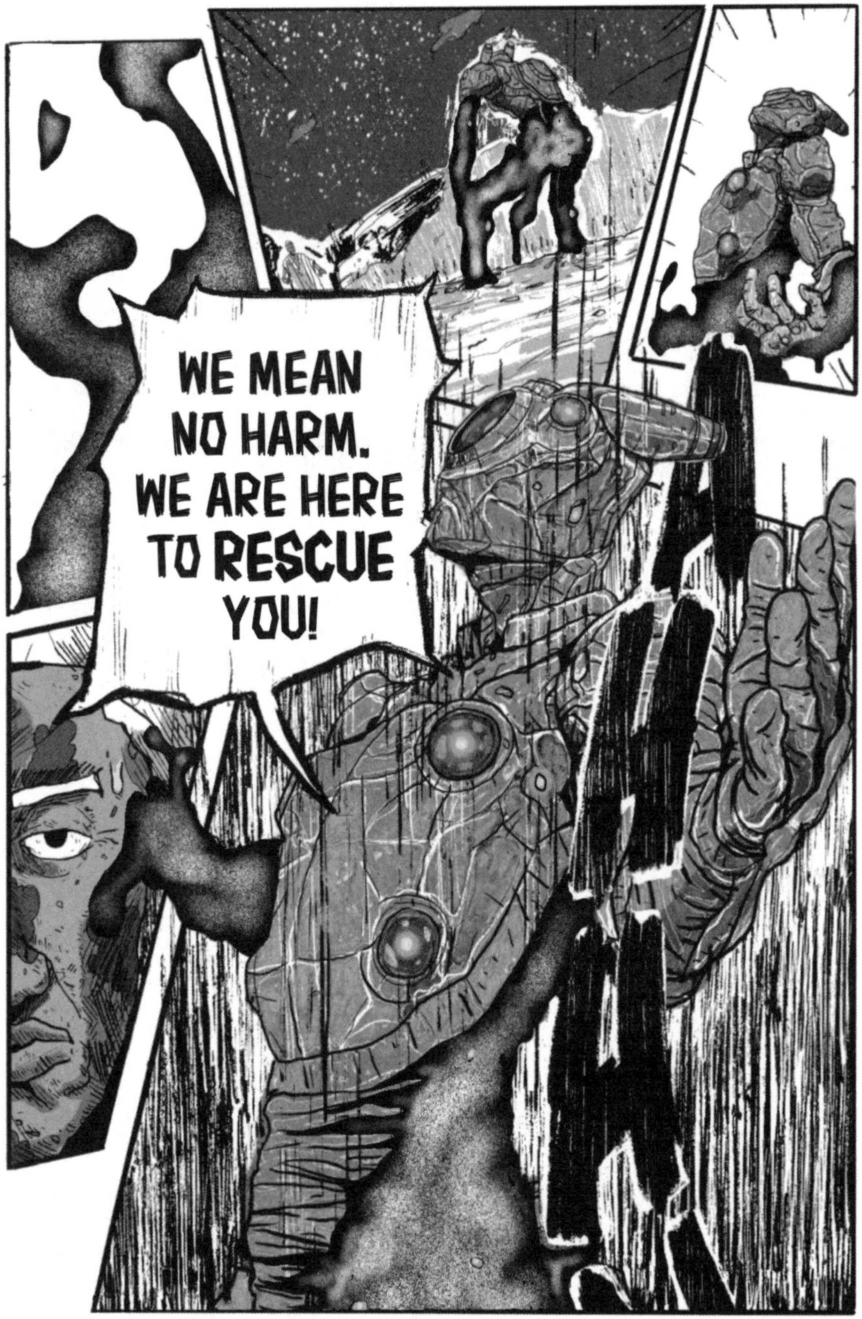
WE MEAN NO HARM. WE ARE HERE TO RESCUE YOU!

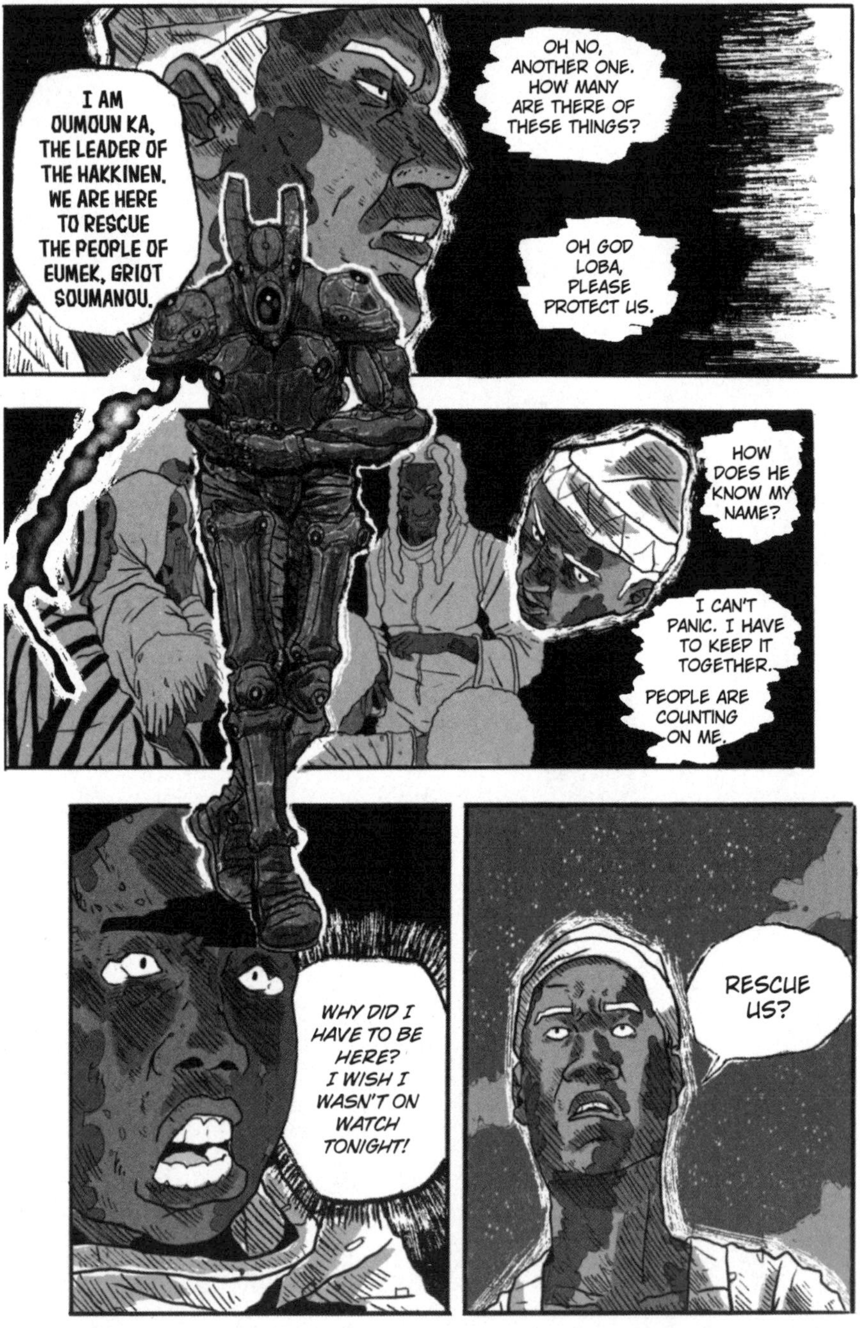
I AM OUMOUN KA, THE LEADER OF THE HAKKINEN. WE ARE HERE TO RESCUE THE PEOPLE OF EUMEK, GRIOT SOUMANOU.
OH NO, ANOTHER ONE. HOW MANY ARE THERE OF THESE THINGS?
OH GOD LOBA, PLEASE PROTECT US.
HOW DOES HE KNOW MY NAME?
I CAN'T PANIC. I HAVE TO KEEP IT TOGETHER.
PEOPLE ARE COUNTING ON ME.
WHY DID I HAVE TO BE HERE? I WISH I WASN'T ON WATCH TONIGHT!
RESCUE US?

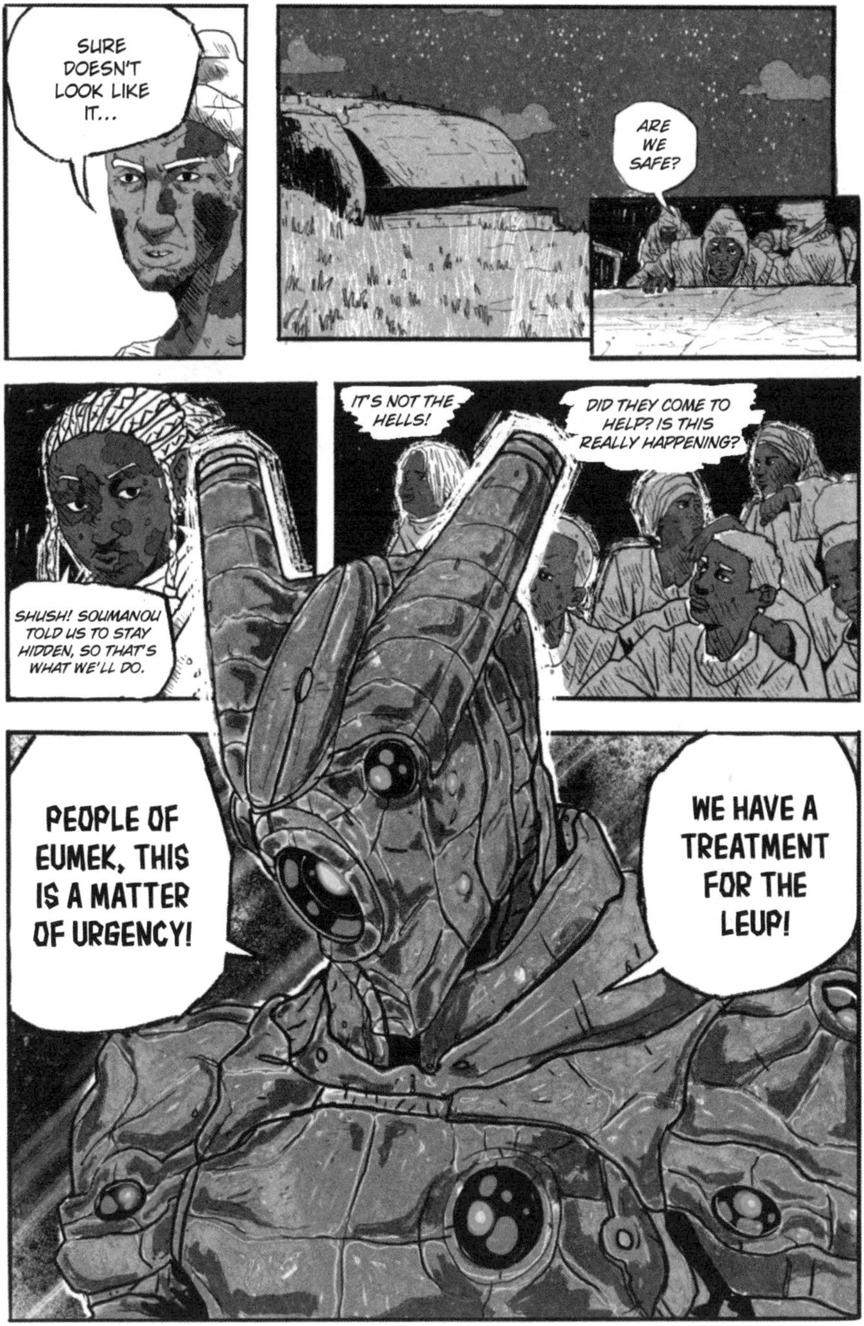
SURE DOESN'T LOOK LIKE IT...
ARE WE SAFE?
SHUSH! SOUMANOU TOLD US TO STAY HIDDEN, SO THAT'S WHAT WE'LL DO.
IT'S NOT THE HELLS!
DID THEY COME TO HELP? IS THIS REALLY HAPPENING?
PEOPLE OF EUMEK, THIS IS A MATTER OF URGENCY!
WE HAVE A TREATMENT FOR THE LEUP!

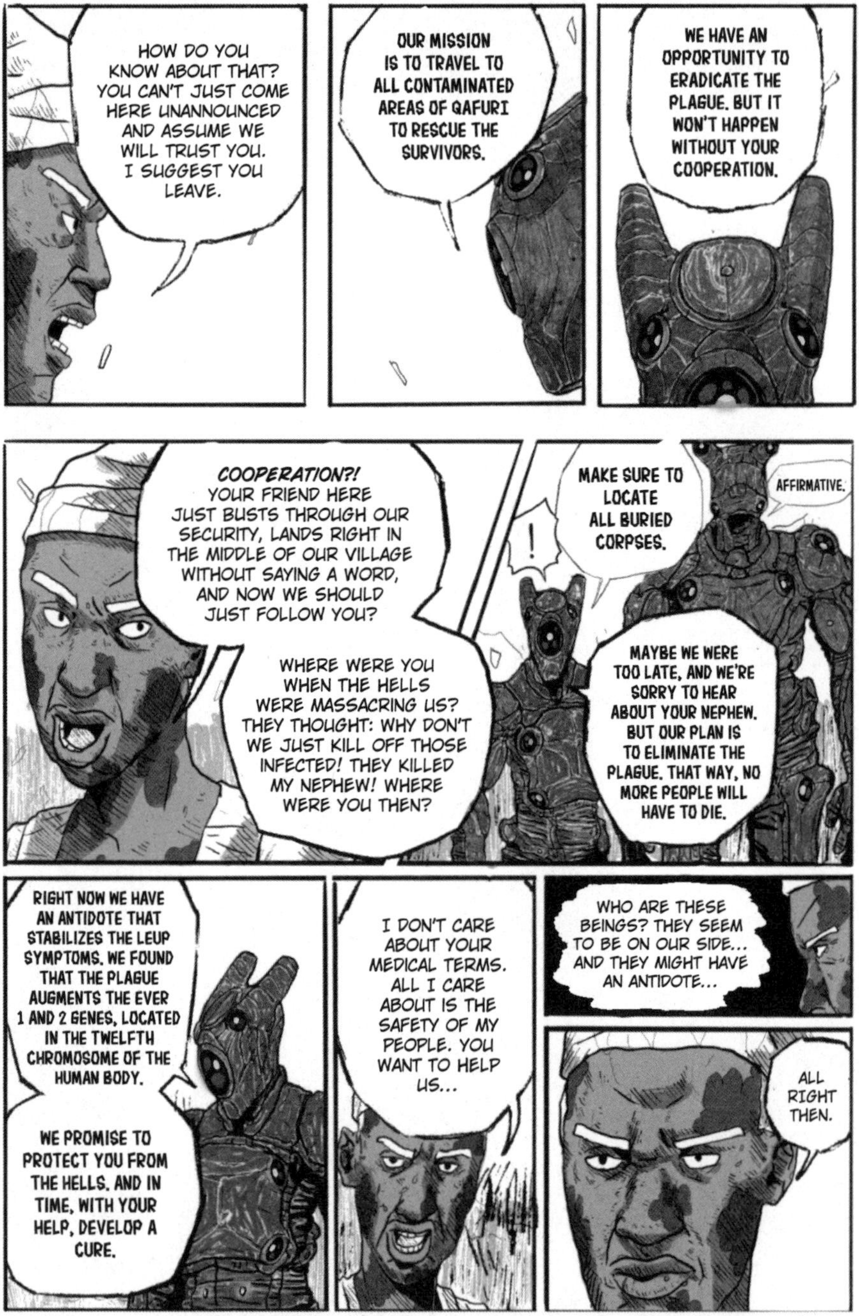
HOW DO YOU KNOW ABOUT THAT? YOU CAN'T JUST COME HERE UNANNOUNCED AND ASSUME WE WILL TRUST YOU. I SUGGEST YOU LEAVE.
OUR MISSION IS TO TRAVEL TO ALL CONTAMINATED AREAS OF QAFURI TO RESCUE THE SURVIVORS.
WE HAVE AN OPPORTUNITY TO ERADICATE THE PLAGUE. BUT IT WON'T HAPPEN WITHOUT YOUR COOPERATION.
COOPERATION?! YOUR FRIEND HERE JUST BUSTS THROUGH OUR SECURITY, LANDS RIGHT IN THE MIDDLE OF OUR VILLAGE WITHOUT SAYING A WORD, AND NOW WE SHOULD JUST FOLLOW YOU?
WHERE WERE YOU WHEN THE HELLS WERE MASSACRING US? THEY THOUGHT: WHY DON'T WE JUST KILL OFF THOSE INFECTED! THEY KILLED MY NEPHEW! WHERE WERE YOU THEN?
!
MAKE SURE TO LOCATE ALL BURIED CORPSES.
AFFIRMATIVE.
MAYBE WE WERE TOO LATE, AND WE'RE SORRY TO HEAR ABOUT YOUR NEPHEW. BUT OUR PLAN IS TO ELIMINATE THE PLAGUE. THAT WAY, NO MORE PEOPLE WILL HAVE TO DIE.
RIGHT NOW WE HAVE AN ANTIDOTE THAT STABILIZES THE LEUP SYMPTOMS. WE FOUND THAT THE PLAGUE AUGMENTS THE EVER 1 AND 2 GENES, LOCATED IN THE TWELFTH CHROMOSOME OF THE HUMAN BODY.
WE PROMISE TO PROTECT YOU FROM THE HELLS. AND IN TIME, WITH YOUR HELP, DEVELOP A CURE.
I DON'T CARE ABOUT YOUR MEDICAL TERMS. ALL I CARE ABOUT IS THE SAFETY OF MY PEOPLE. YOU WANT TO HELP US...
WHO ARE THESE BEINGS? THEY SEEM TO BE ON OUR SIDE... AND THEY MIGHT HAVE AN ANTIDOTE...
ALL RIGHT THEN.

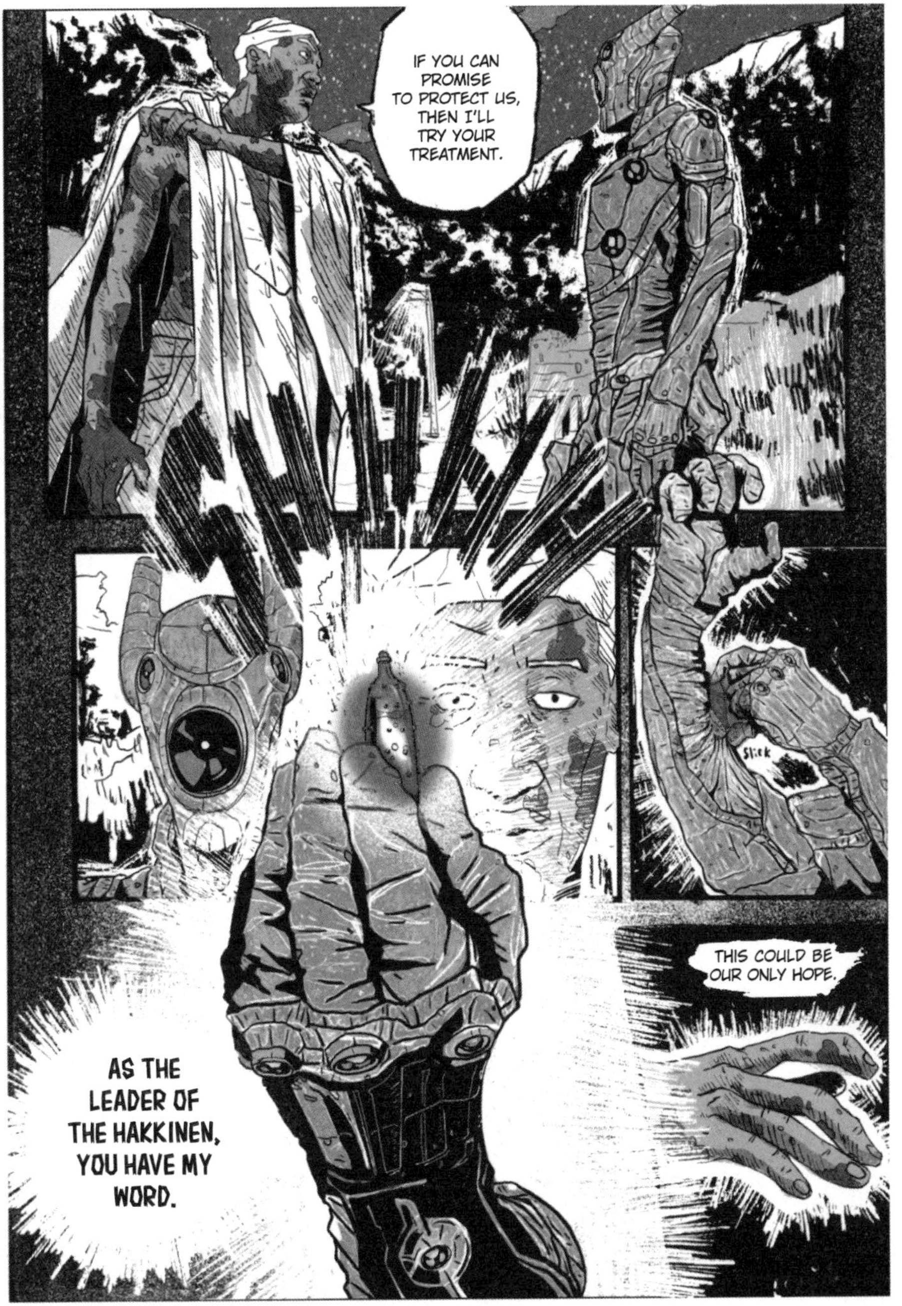
IF YOU CAN PROMISE TO PROTECT US, THEN I'LL TRY YOUR TREATMENT.
Slick
AS THE LEADER OF THE HAKKINEN, YOU HAVE MY WORD.
THIS COULD BE OUR ONLY HOPE.

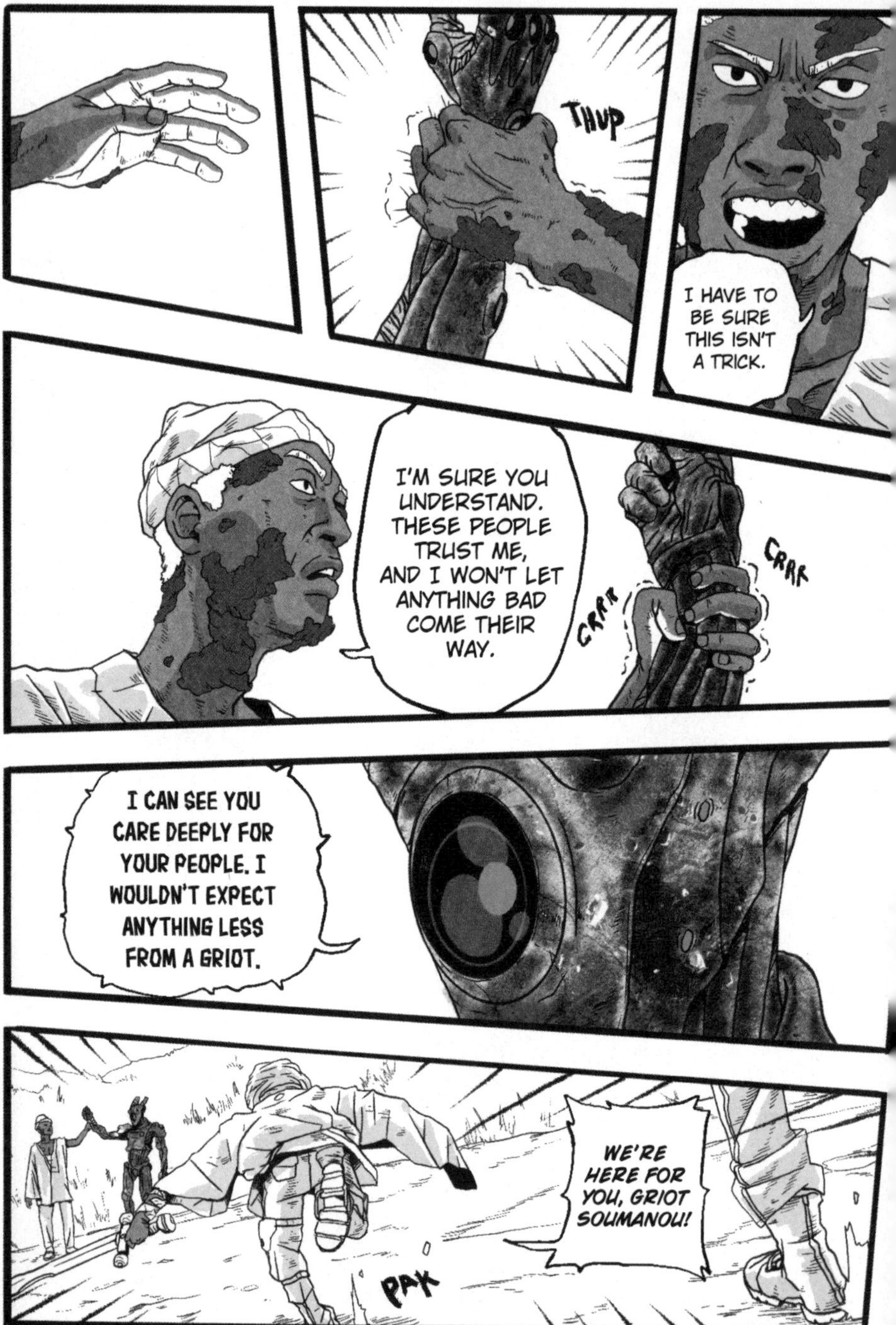
THUP
I HAVE TO BE SURE THIS ISN'T A TRICK.
I'M SURE YOU UNDERSTAND. THESE PEOPLE TRUST ME, AND I WON'T LET ANYTHING BAD COME THEIR WAY.
CRRR
CRRR
I CAN SEE YOU CARE DEEPLY FOR YOUR PEOPLE. I WOULDN'T EXPECT ANYTHING LESS FROM A GRIOT.
WE'RE HERE FOR YOU, GRIOT SOUMANOU!
PAK

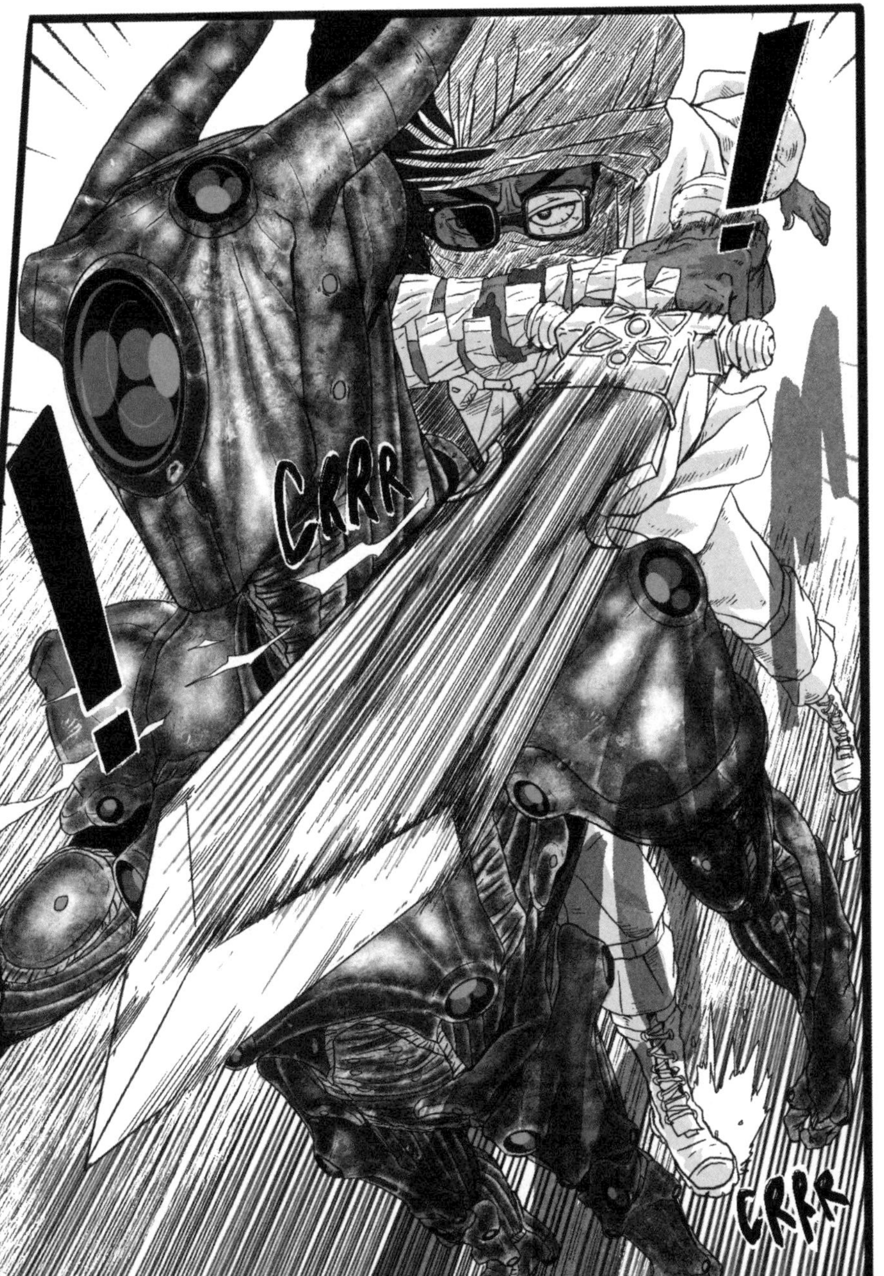
!
!
CRRR
CRRR

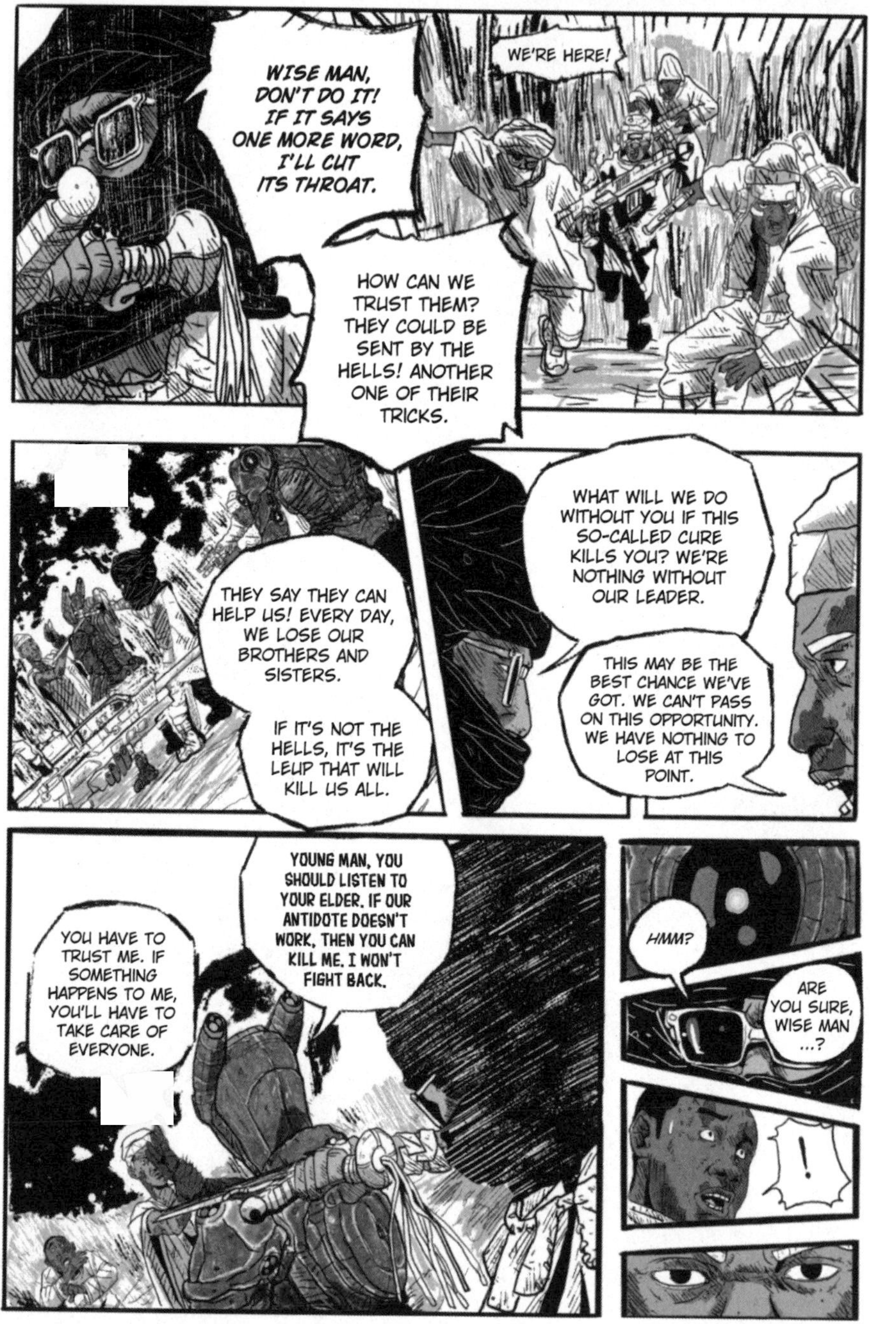
WISE MAN, DON'T DO IT! IF IT SAYS ONE MORE WORD, I'LL CUT ITS THROAT.
WE'RE HERE!
HOW CAN WE TRUST THEM? THEY COULD BE SENT BY THE HELLS! ANOTHER ONE OF THEIR TRICKS.
THEY SAY THEY CAN HELP US! EVERY DAY, WE LOSE OUR BROTHERS AND SISTERS.
IF IT'S NOT THE HELLS, IT'S THE LEUP THAT WILL KILL US ALL.
WHAT WILL WE DO WITHOUT YOU IF THIS SO-CALLED CURE KILLS YOU? WE'RE NOTHING WITHOUT OUR LEADER.
THIS MAY BE THE BEST CHANCE WE'VE GOT. WE CAN'T PASS ON THIS OPPORTUNITY. WE HAVE NOTHING TO LOSE AT THIS POINT.
YOU HAVE TO TRUST ME. IF SOMETHING HAPPENS TO ME, YOU'LL HAVE TO TAKE CARE OF EVERYONE.
YOUNG MAN, YOU SHOULD LISTEN TO YOUR ELDER. IF OUR ANTIDOTE DOESN'T WORK, THEN YOU CAN KILL ME. I WON'T FIGHT BACK.
HMM?
ARE YOU SURE, WISE MAN ...?
!

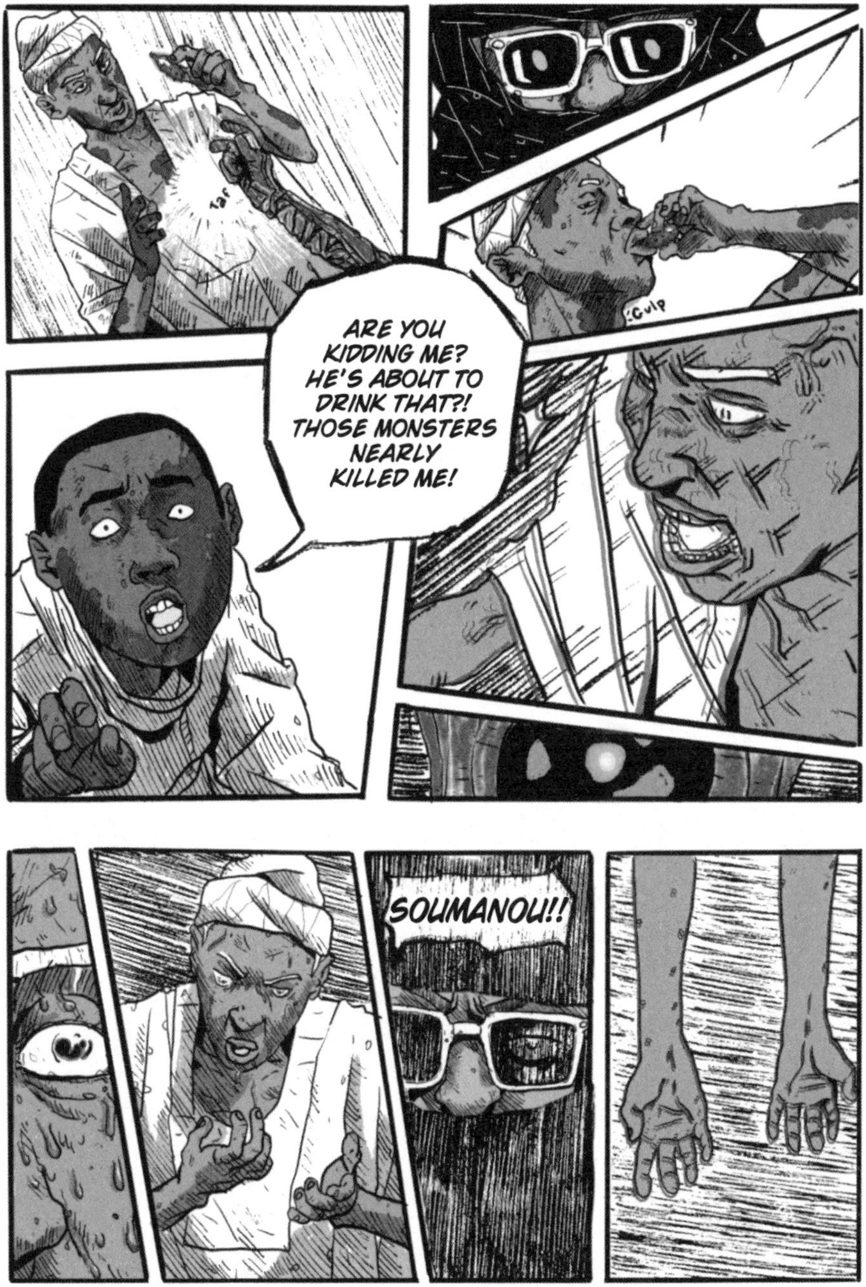
tac
Gulp
ARE YOU KIDDING ME? HE'S ABOUT TO DRINK THAT?! THOSE MONSTERS NEARLY KILLED ME!
SOUMANOU!!

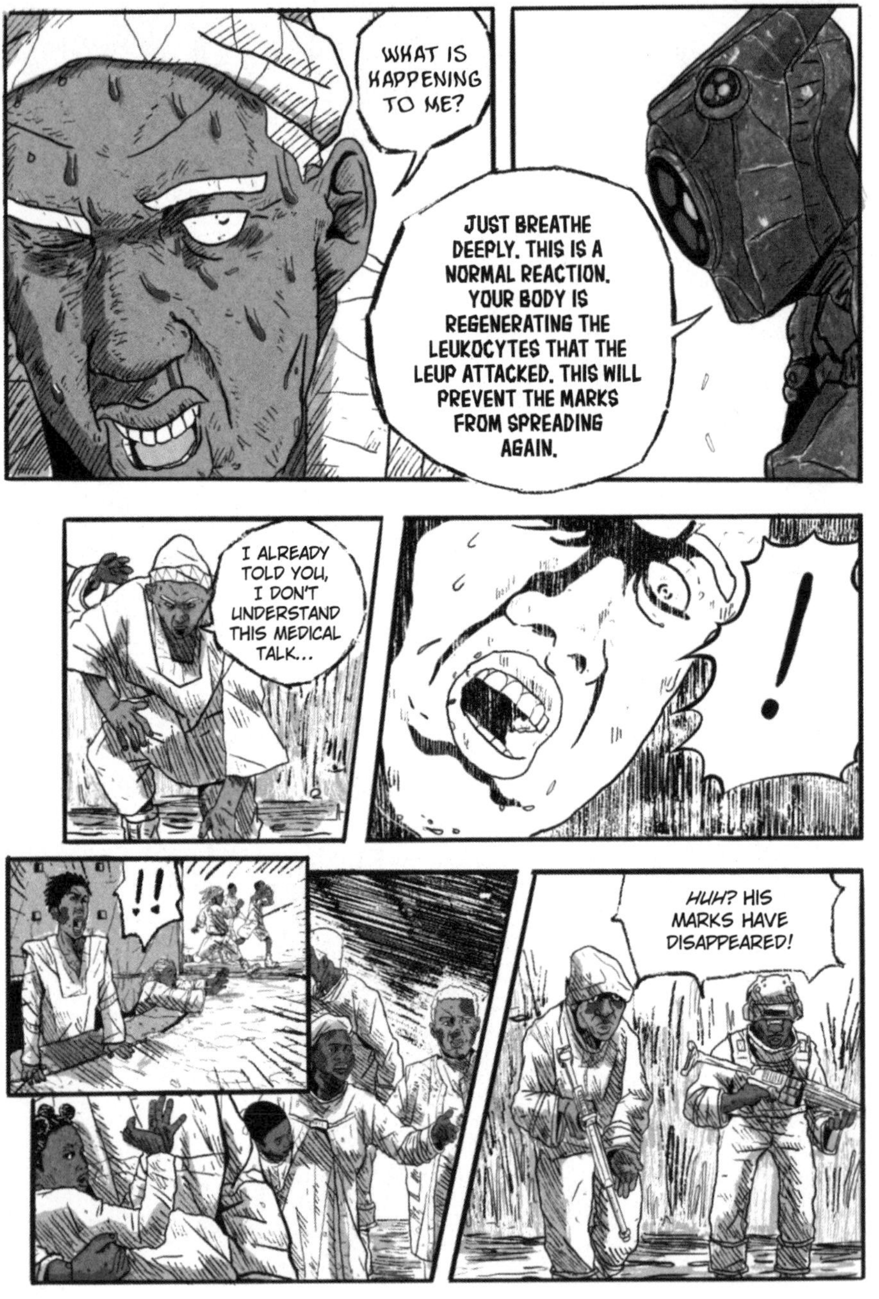

WHAT IS HAPPENING TO ME?
JUST BREATHE DEEPLY. THIS IS A NORMAL REACTION. YOUR BODY IS REGENERATING THE LEUKOCYTES THAT THE LEUP ATTACKED. THIS WILL PREVENT THE MARKS FROM SPREADING AGAIN.
I ALREADY TOLD YOU, I DON'T UNDERSTAND THIS MEDICAL TALK...
!
!!
HUH? HIS MARKS HAVE DISAPPEARED!

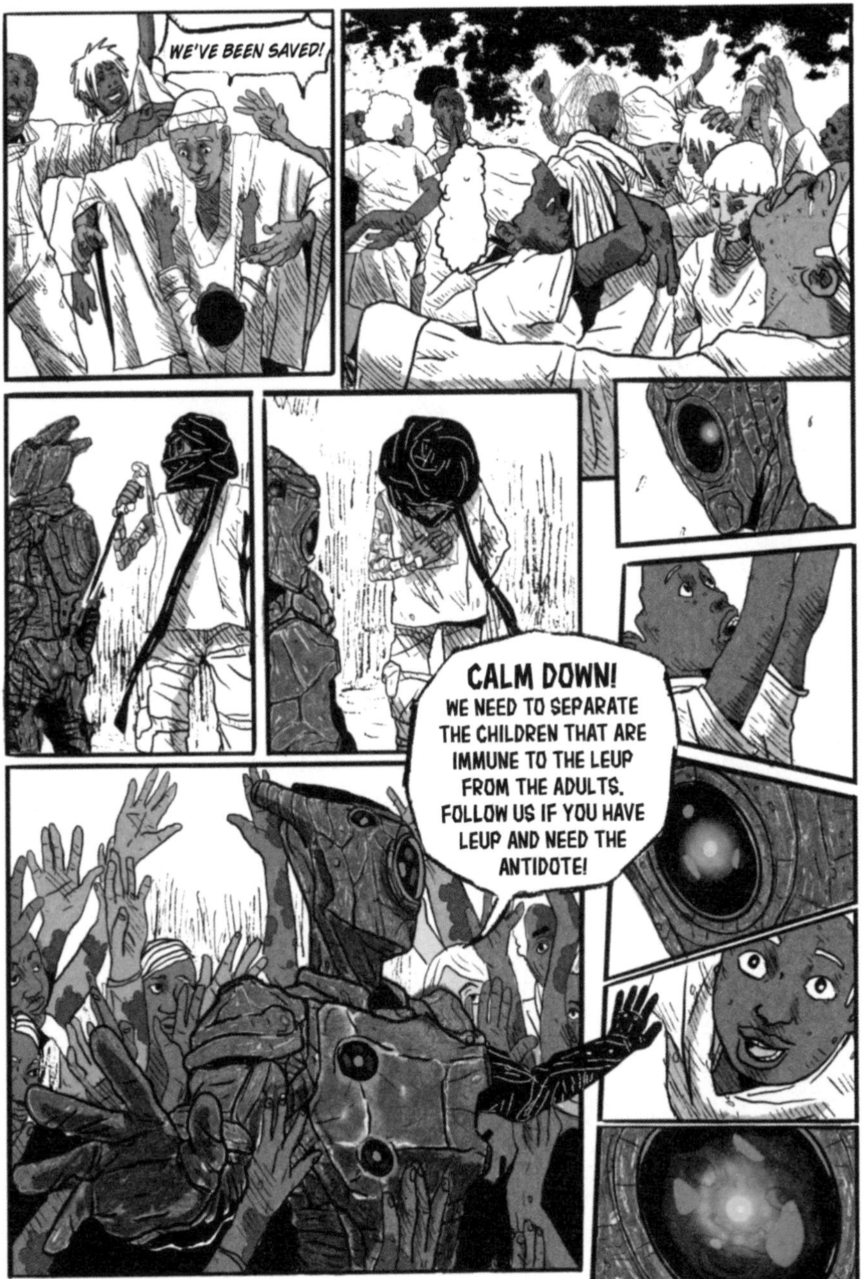
WE'VE BEEN SAVED!
CALM DOWN! WE NEED TO SEPARATE THE CHILDREN THAT ARE IMMUNE TO THE LEUP FROM THE ADULTS. FOLLOW US IF YOU HAVE LEUP AND NEED THE ANTIDOTE!

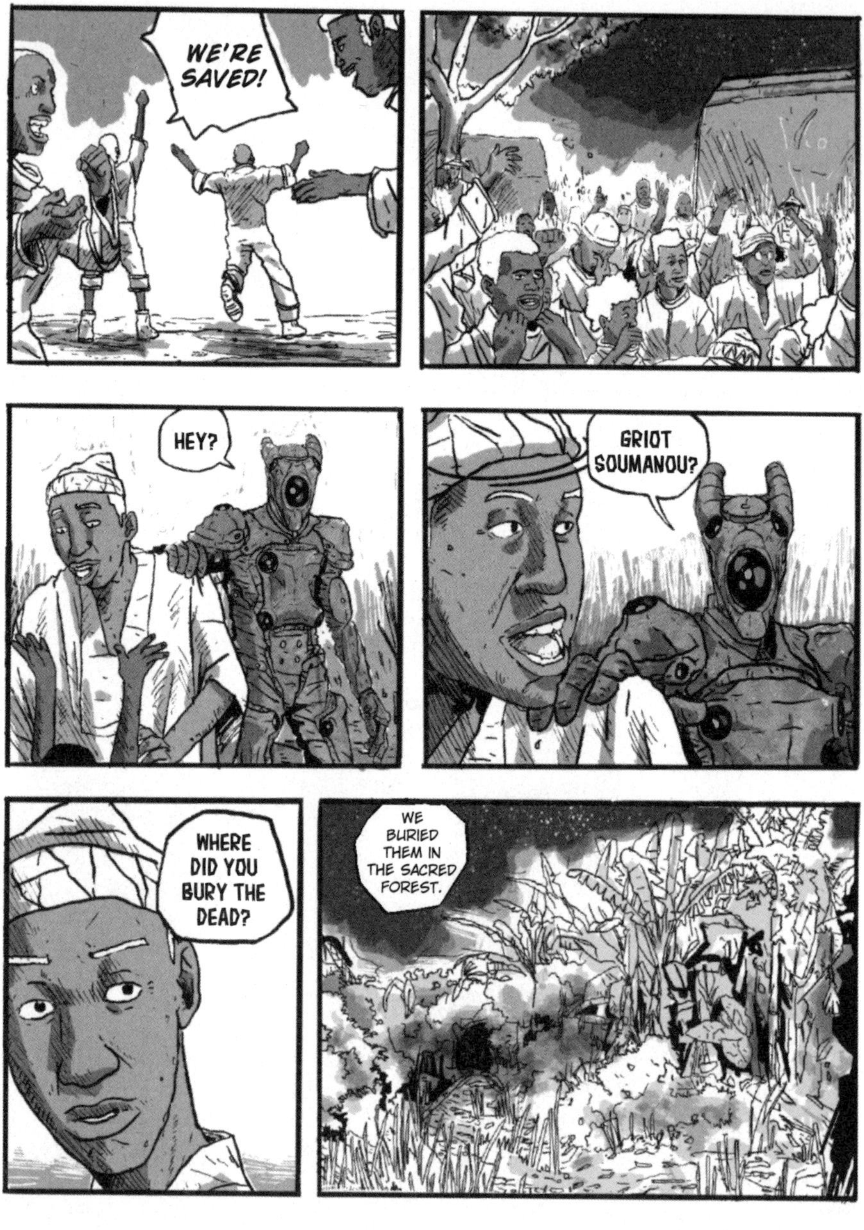
WE'RE SAVED!
HEY?
GRIOT SOUMANOU?
WHERE DID YOU BURY THE DEAD?
WE BURIED THEM IN THE SACRED FOREST.

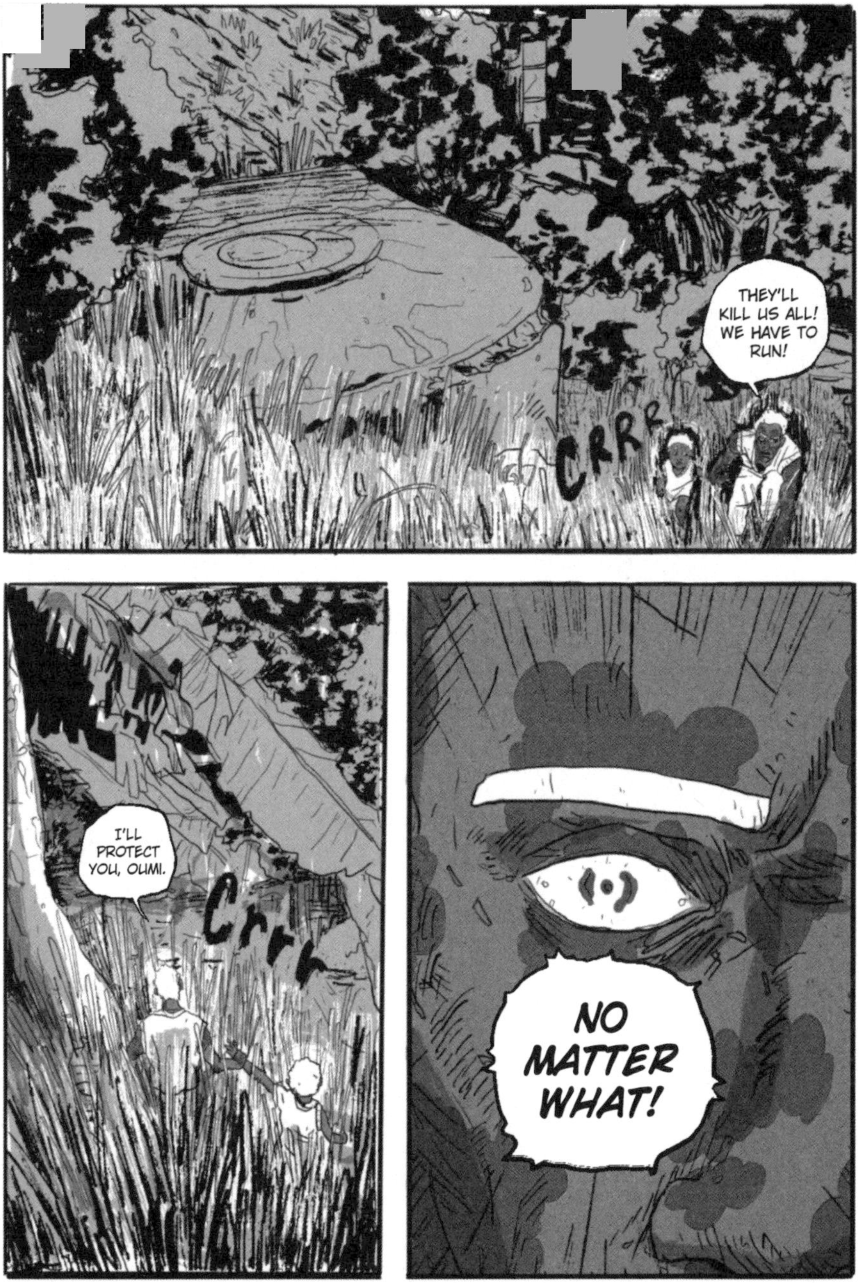
THEY'LL KILL US ALL! WE HAVE TO RUN!
CRRR
I'LL PROTECT YOU, OUMI.
CRRR
NO MATTER WHAT!

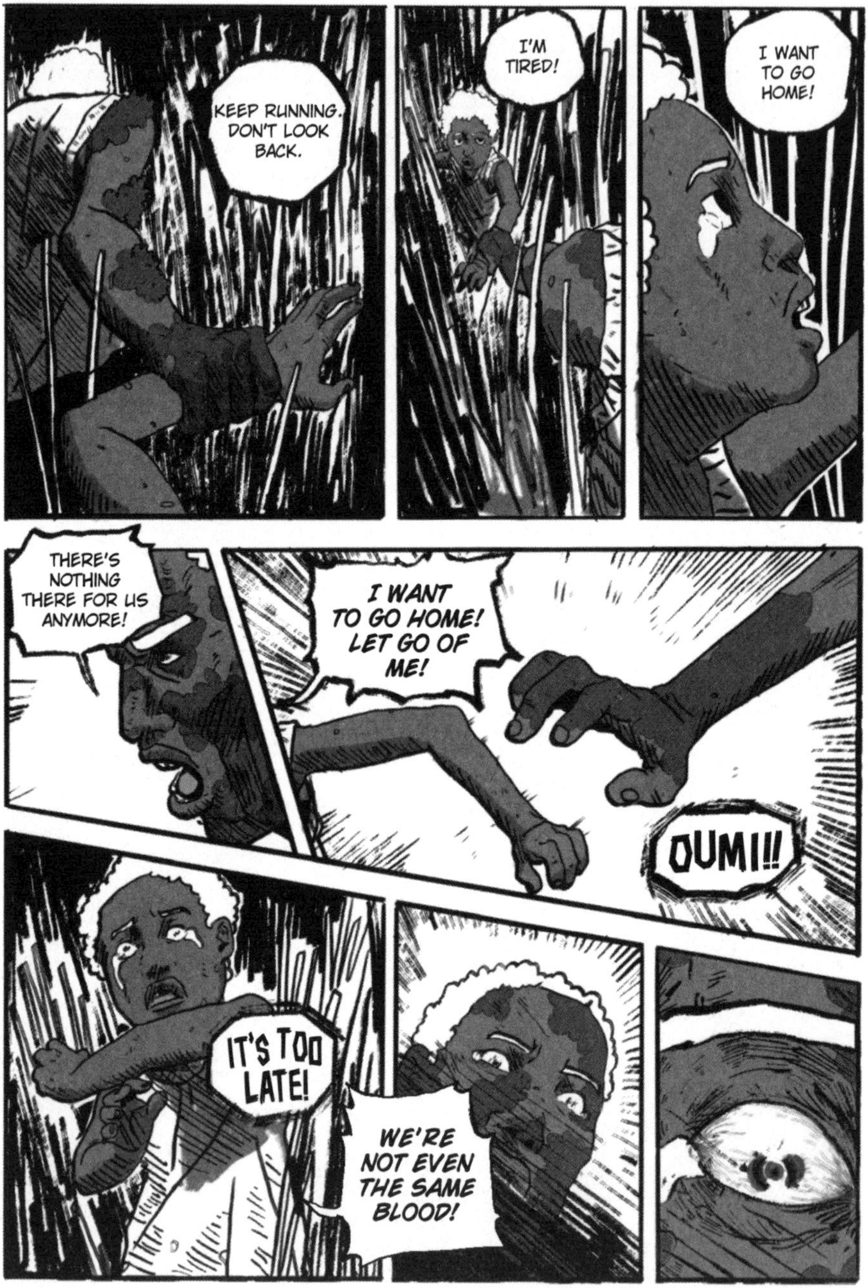
KEEP RUNNING. DON'T LOOK BACK.
I'M TIRED!
I WANT TO GO HOME!
THERE'S NOTHING THERE FOR US ANYMORE!
I WANT TO GO HOME! LET GO OF ME!
OUMI!!
IT'S TOO LATE!
WE'RE NOT EVEN THE SAME BLOOD!

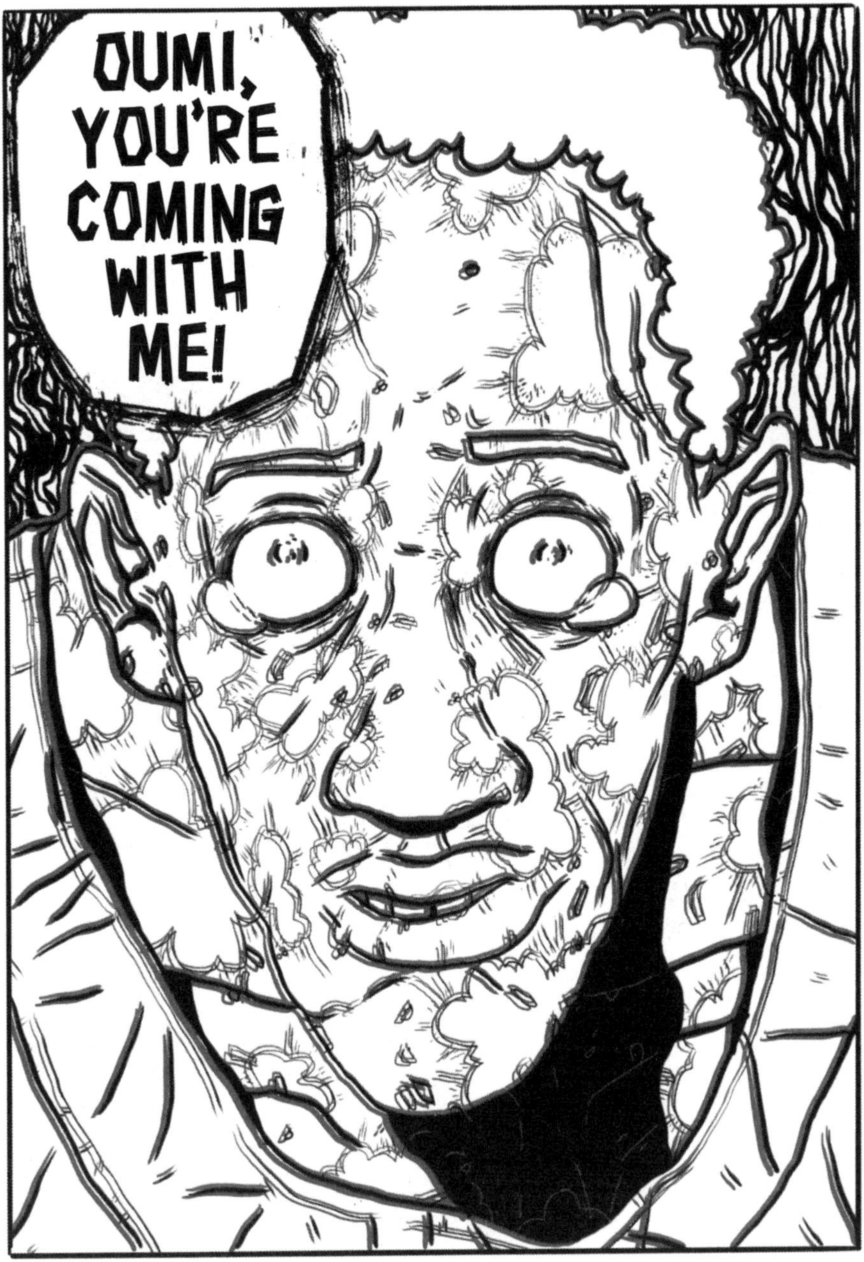
OUMI, YOU'RE COMING WITH ME!

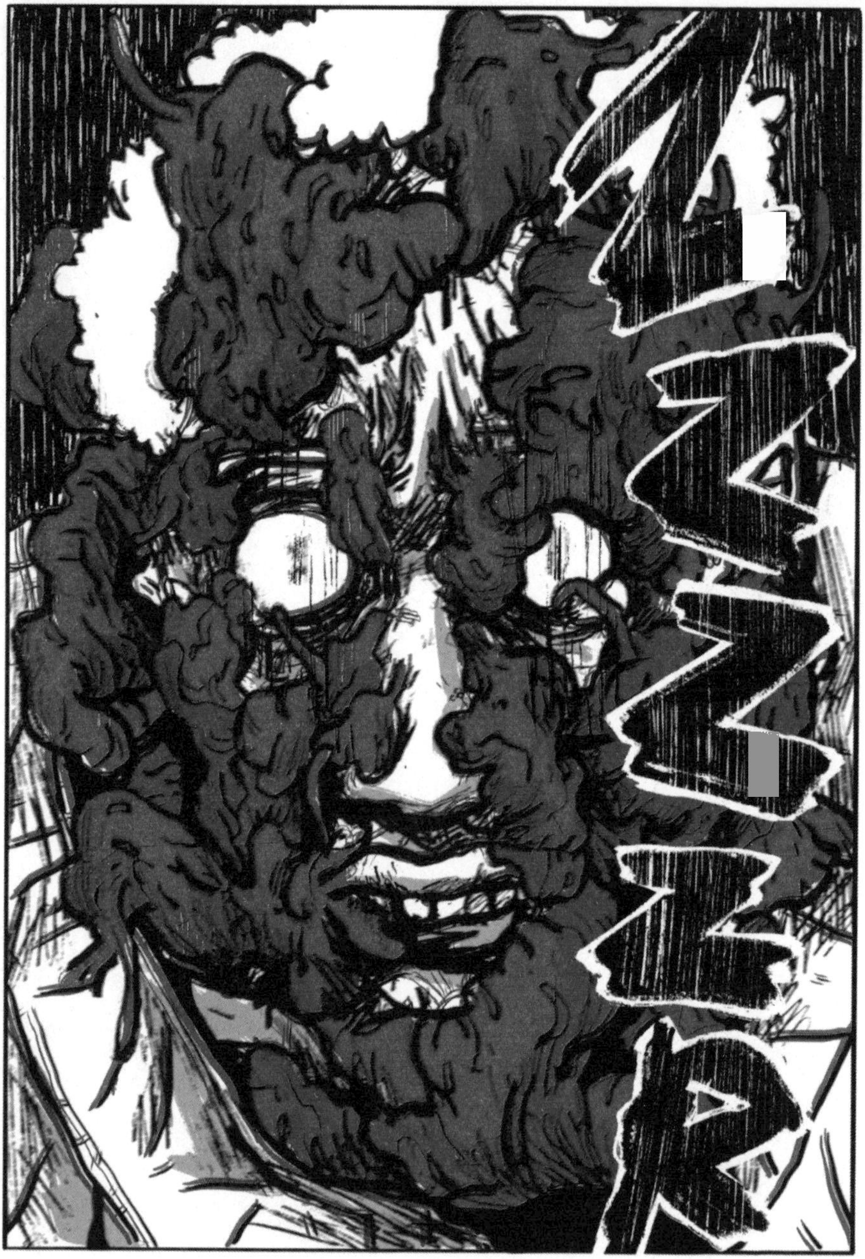

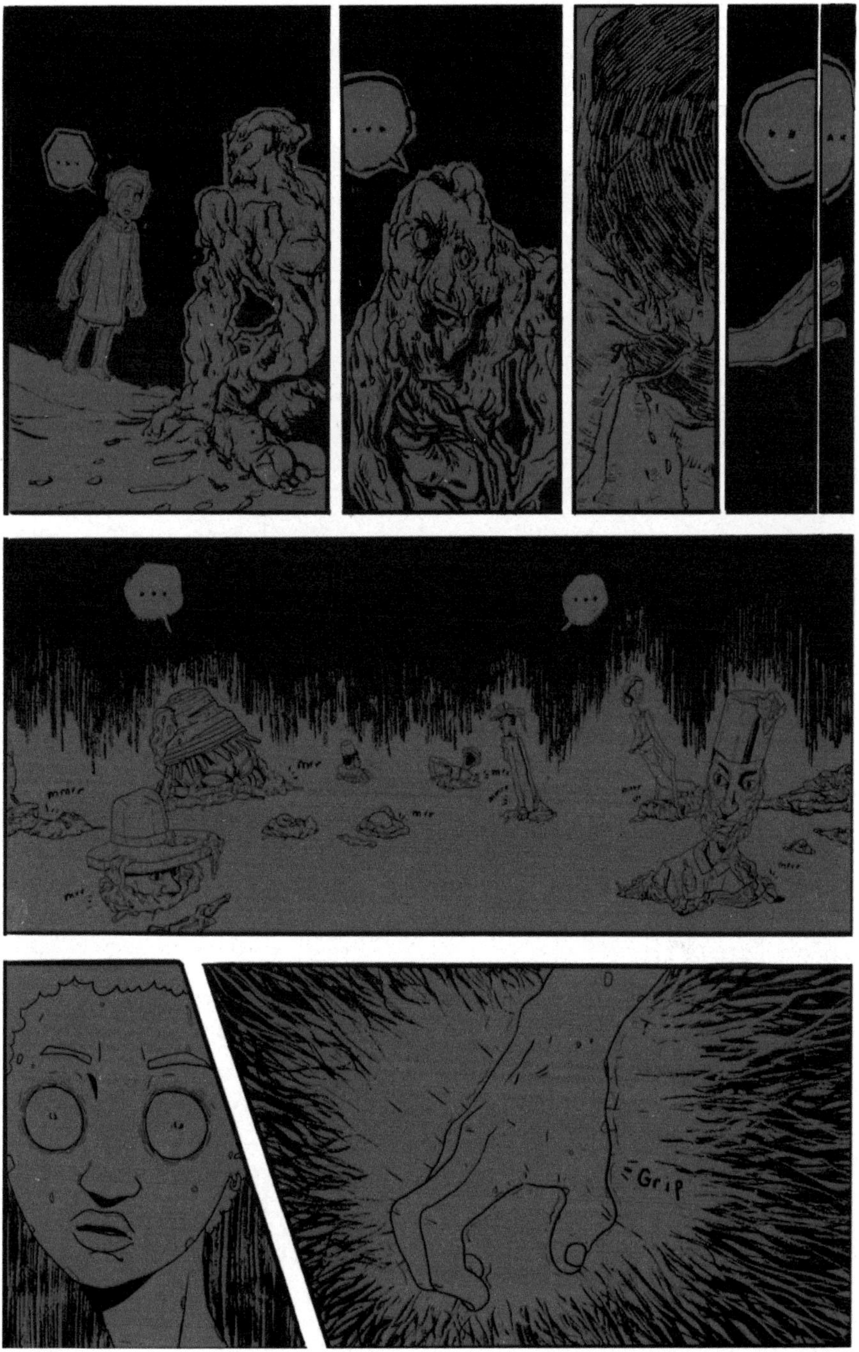

...
...
...
...
...
Grip

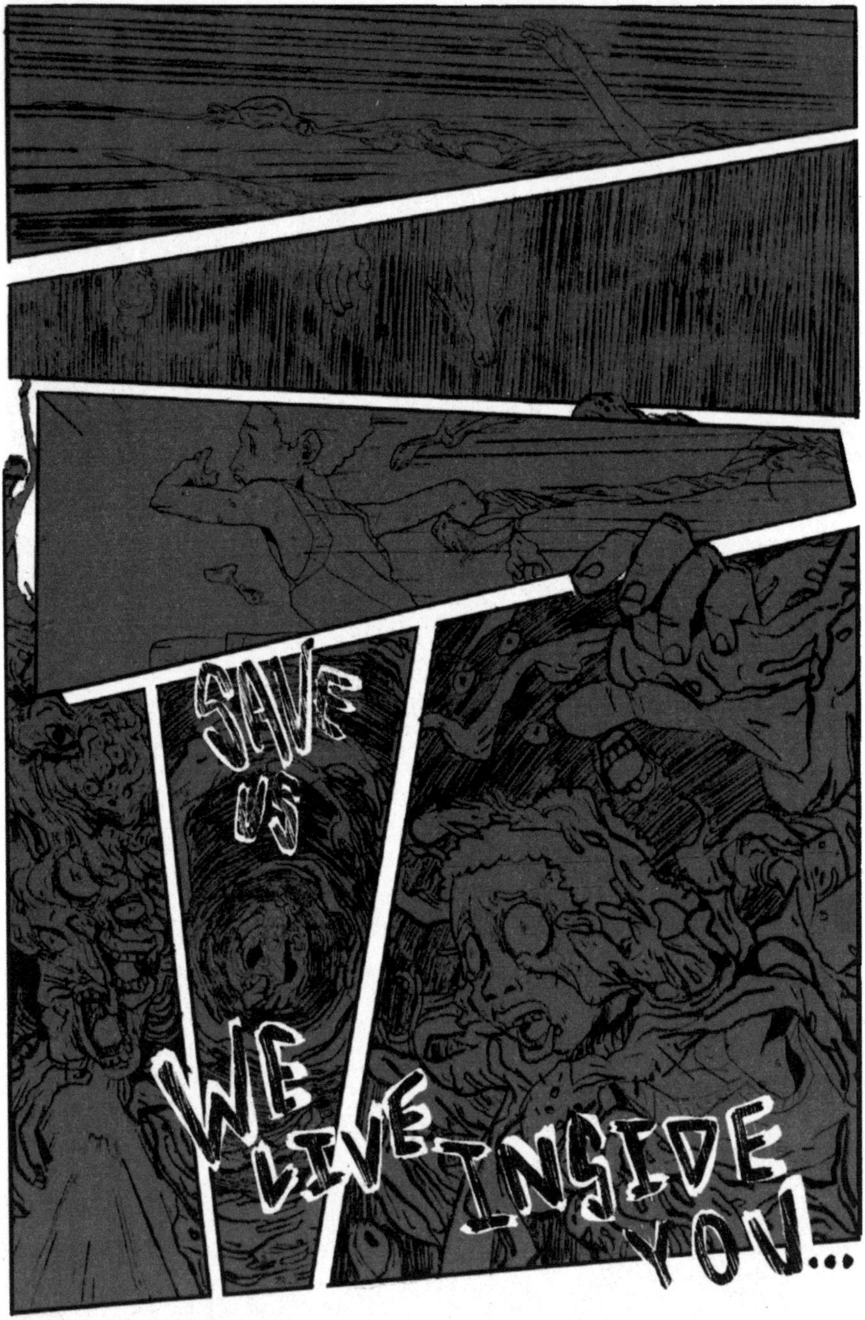
SAVE US
WE LIVE INSIDE YOU...

OBLIVION ROUGE

CHAPTER 2
Young Hakkinen - 0%

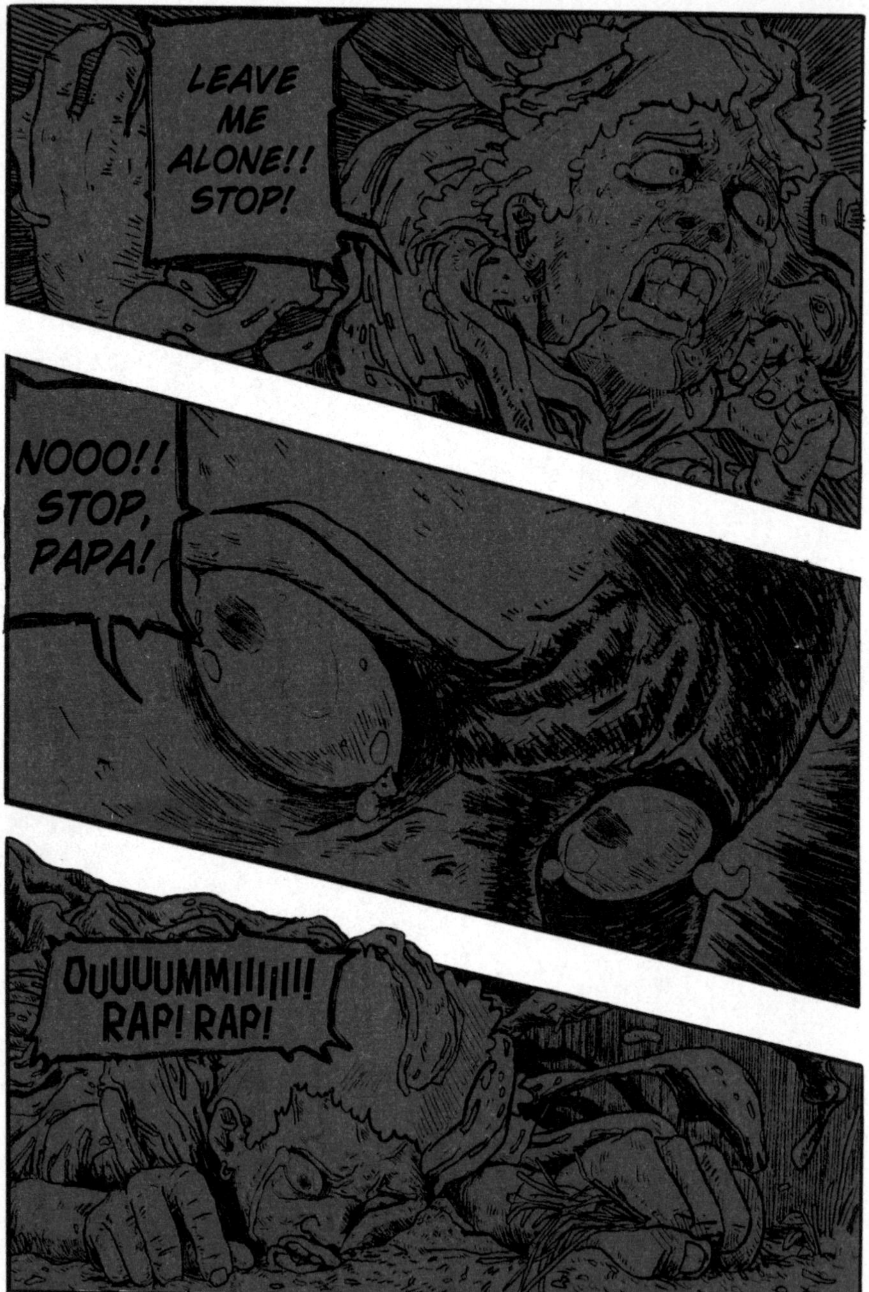
LEAVE ME ALONE!! STOP!
NOOO!! STOP, PAPA!
OUUUUMMIIIIIII! RAP! RAP!

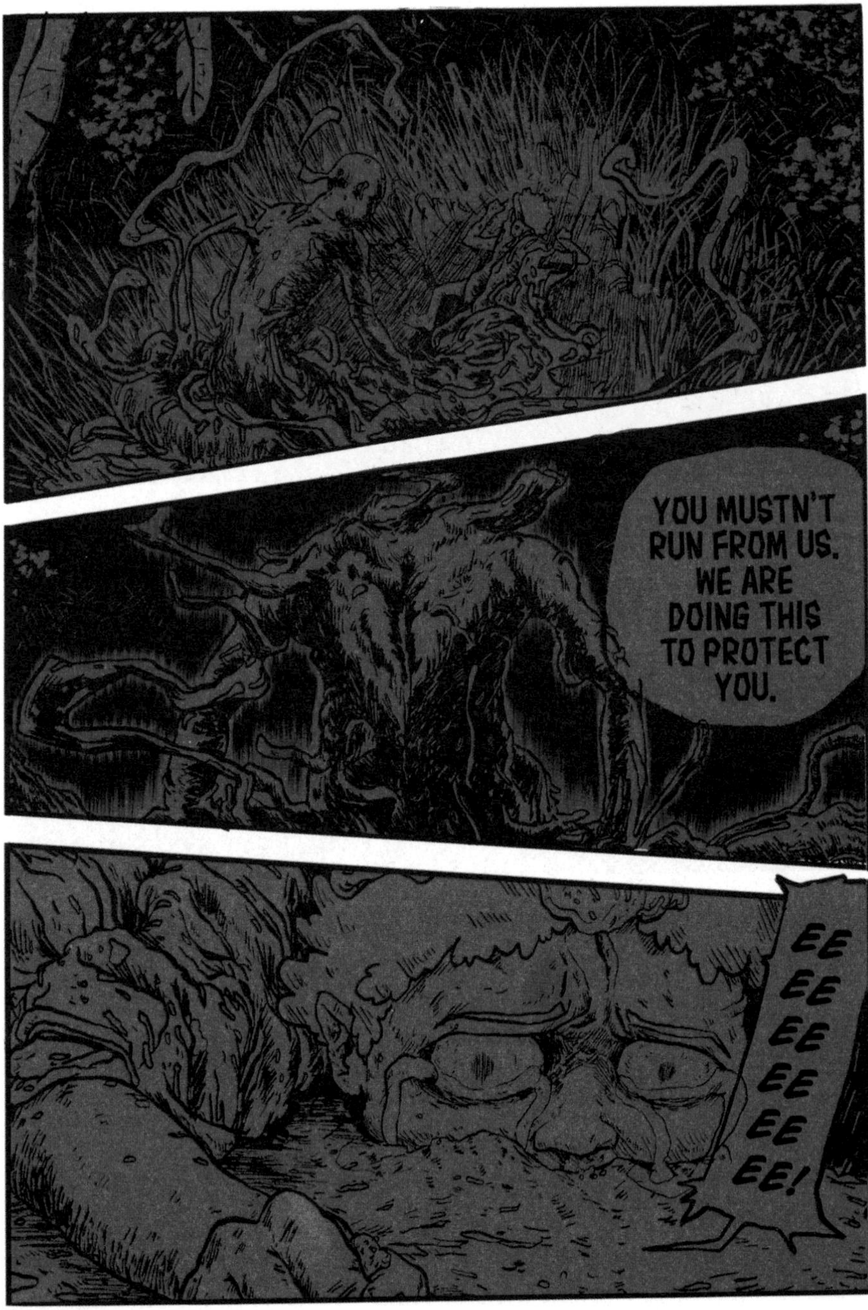
YOU MUSTN'T RUN FROM US. WE ARE DOING THIS TO PROTECT YOU.
EEEEEEEEEEEE!

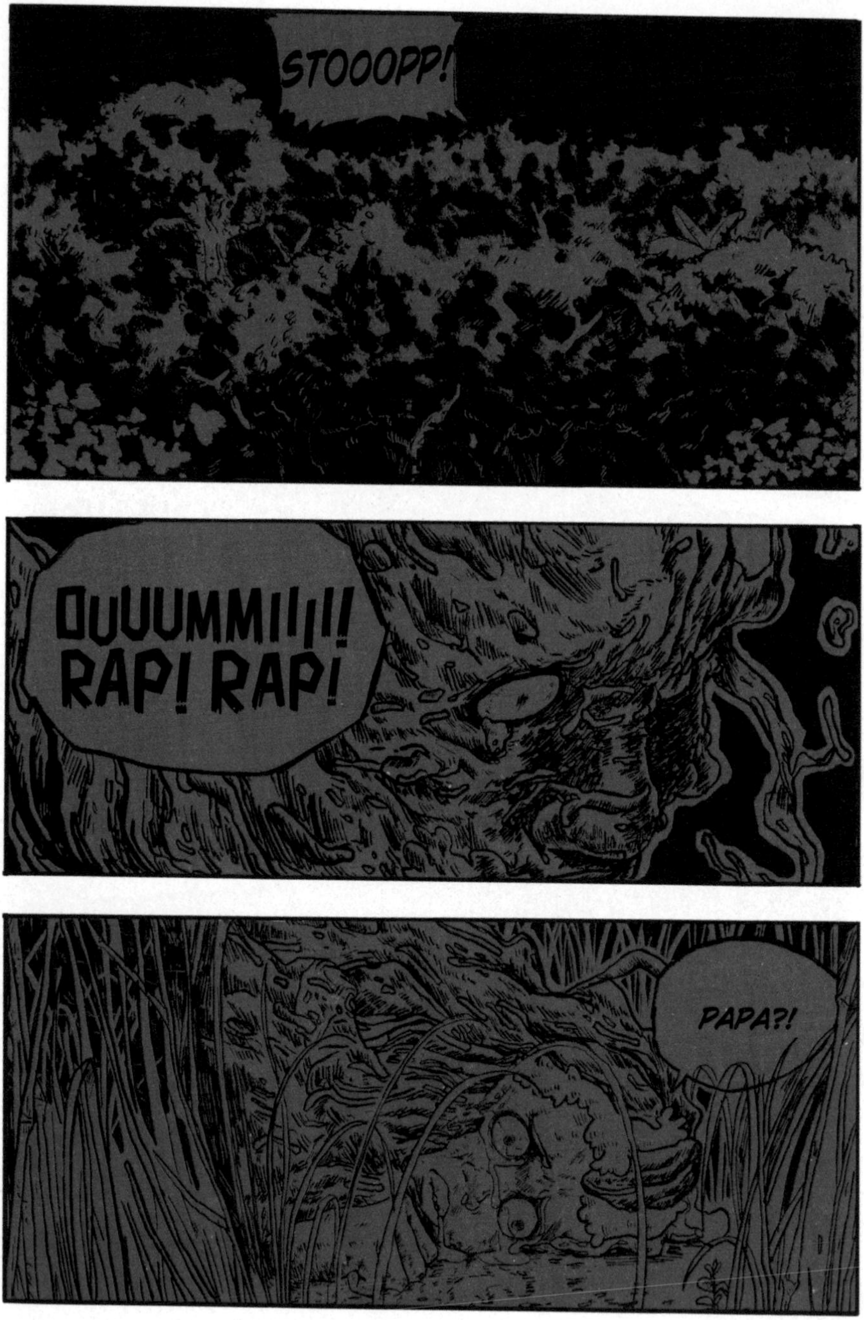
STOOOPP!
OUUUMMIIII!
RAP! RAP!
PAPA?!

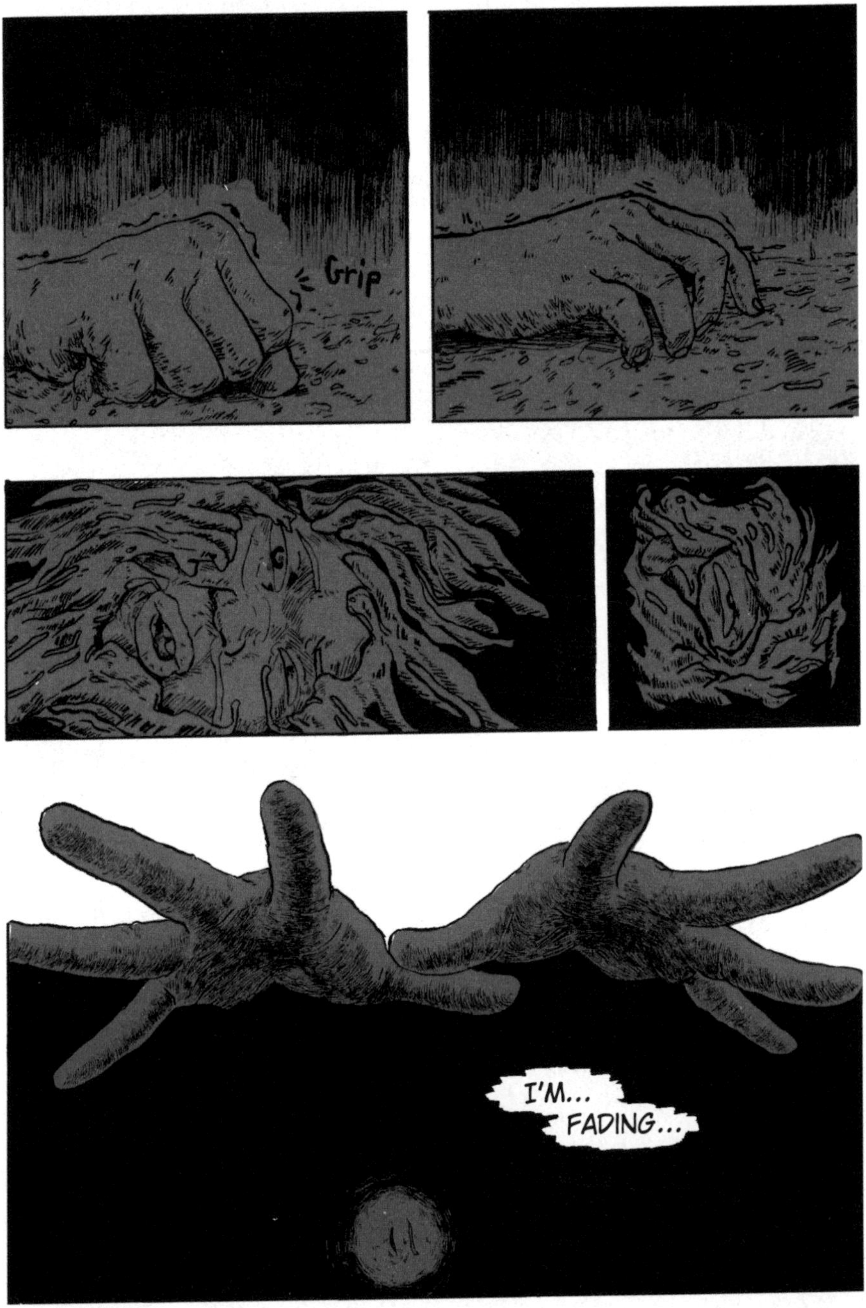
Grip
I'M... FADING...

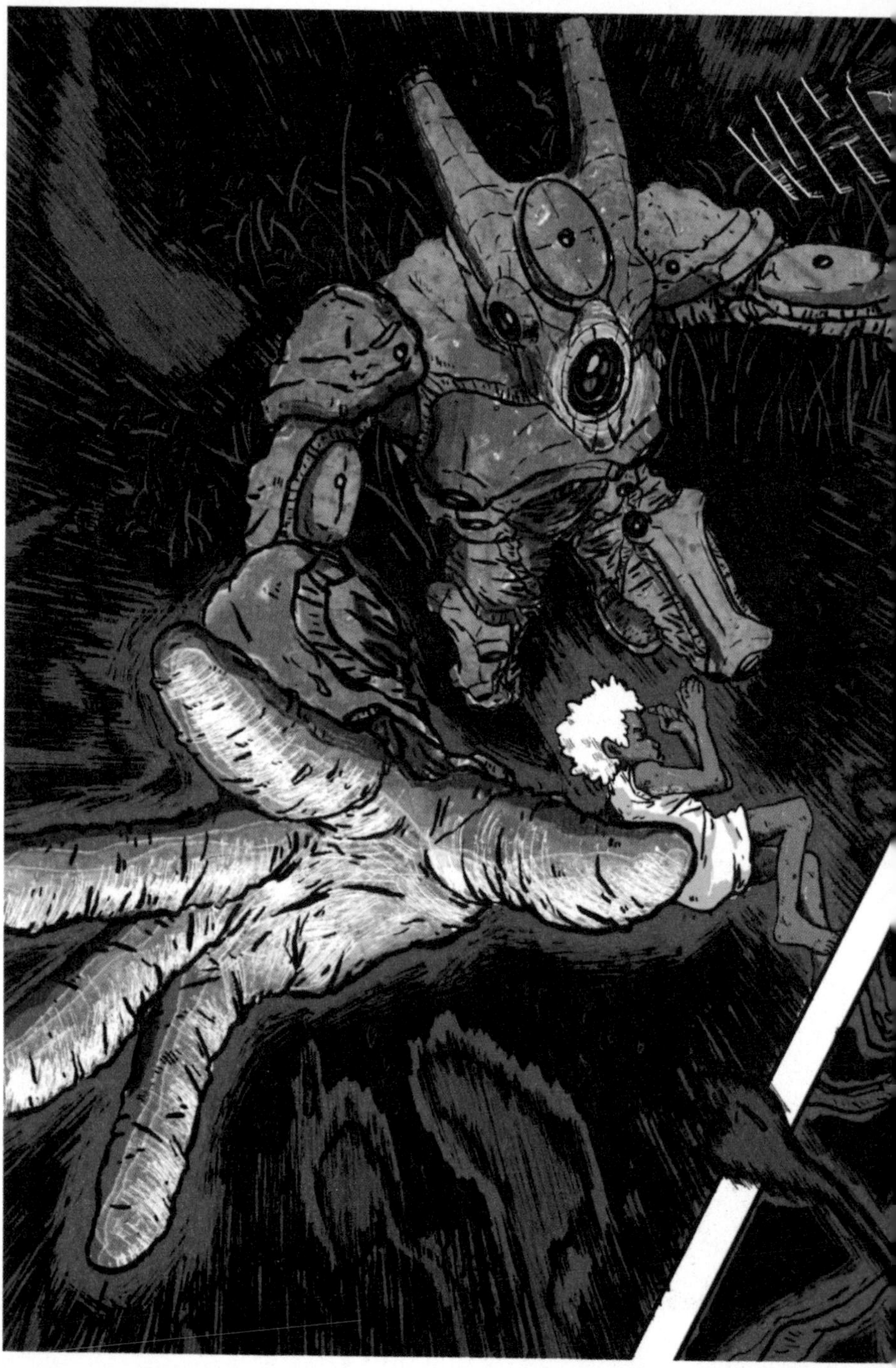

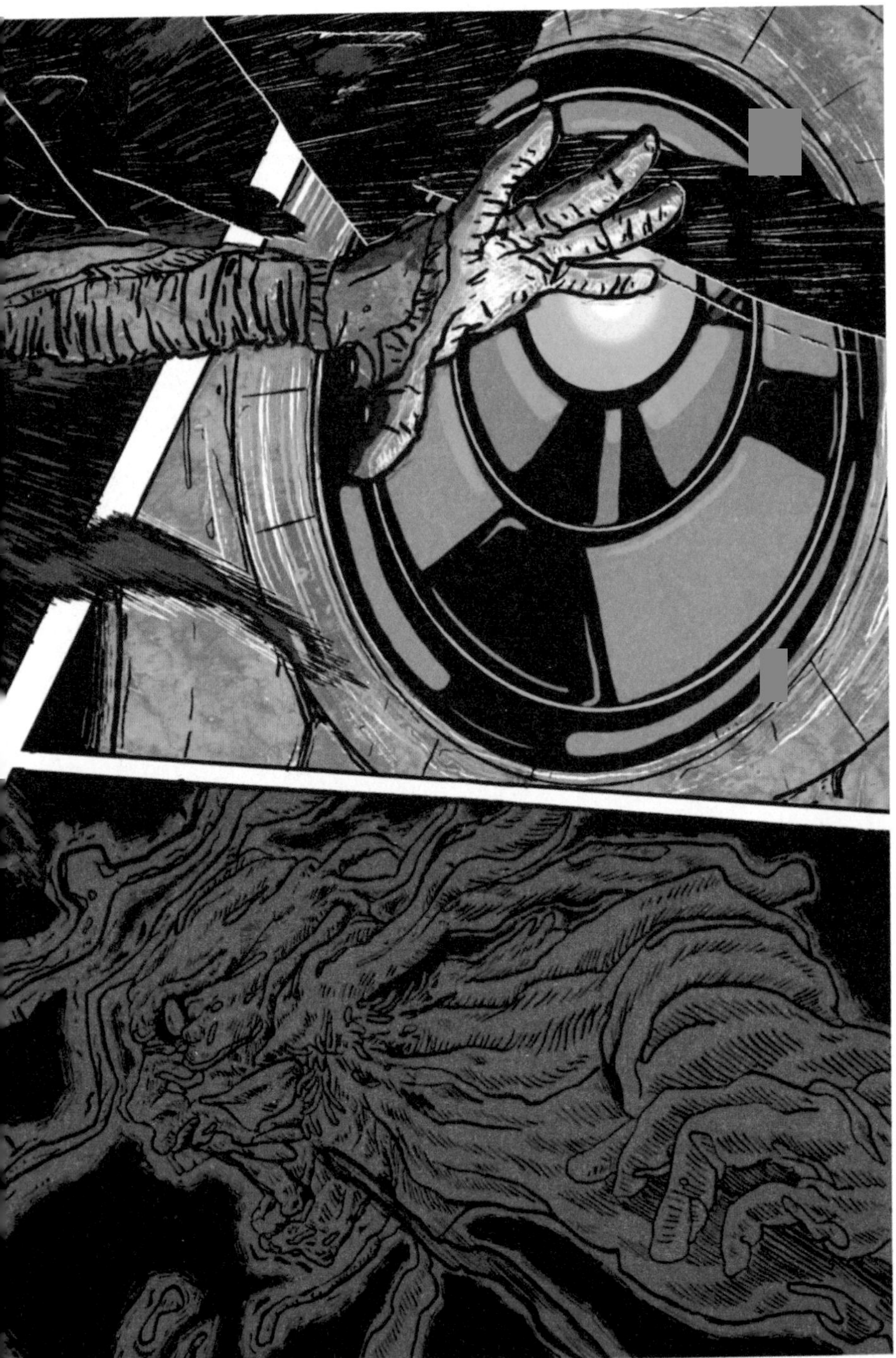

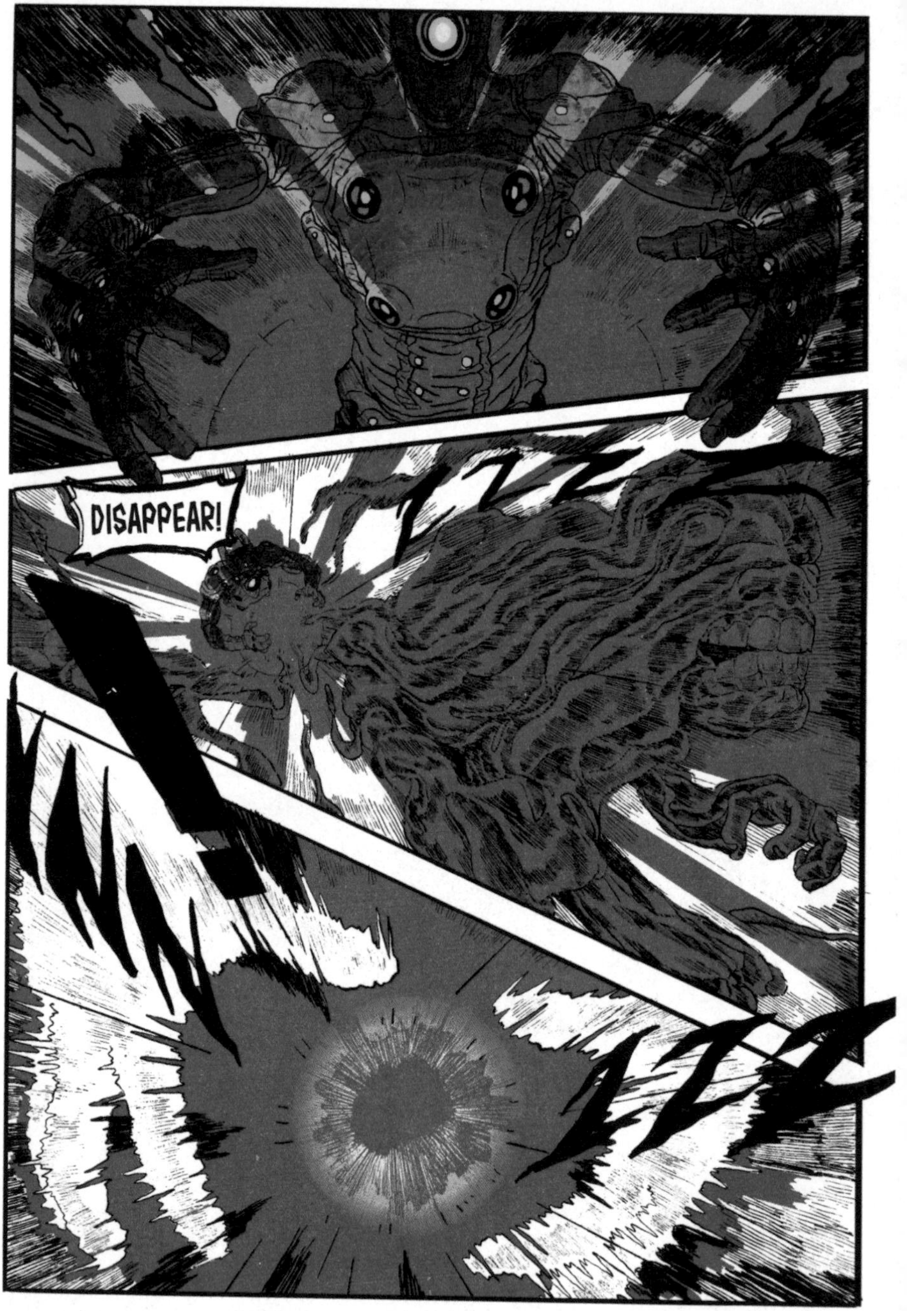
DISAPPEAR!

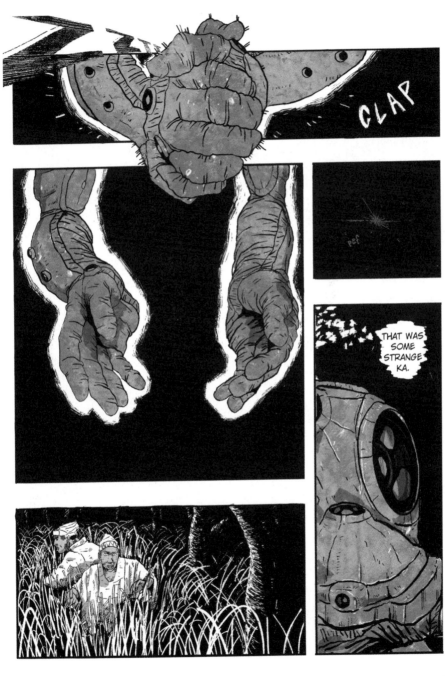

CLAP

THAT WAS SOME STRANGE KA.

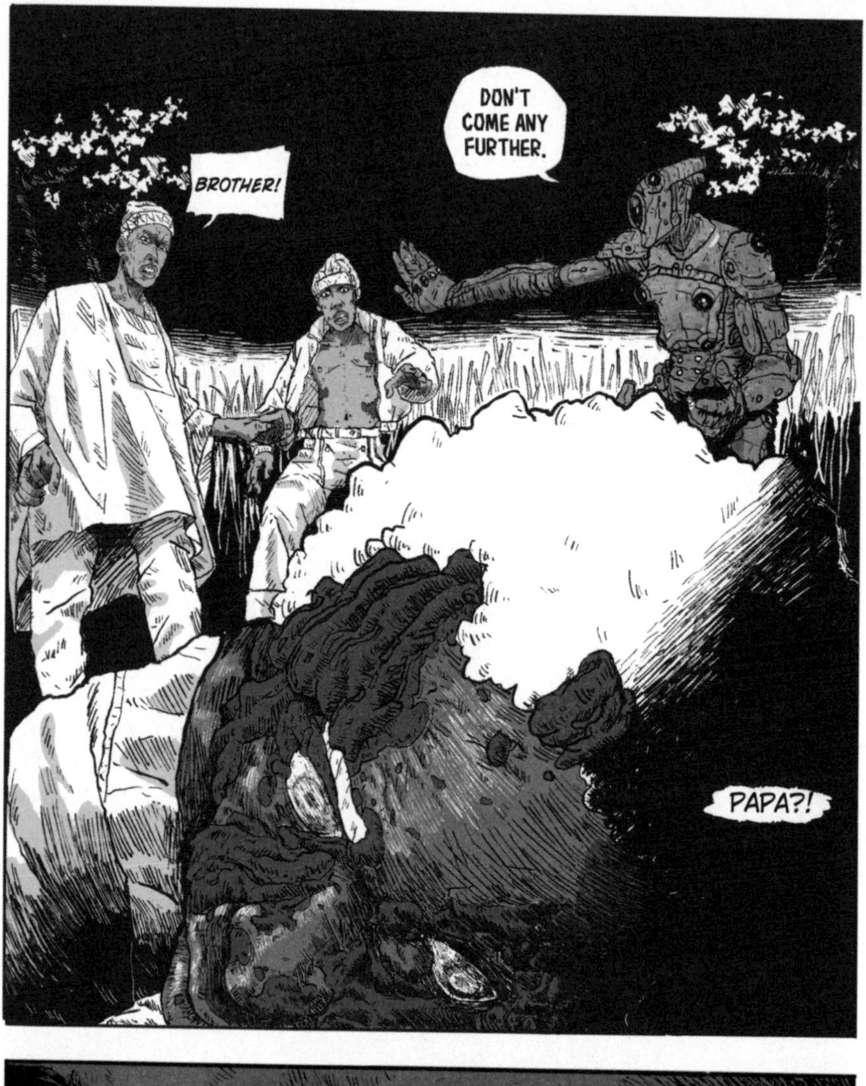
BROTHER!
DON'T COME ANY FURTHER.
PAPA?!

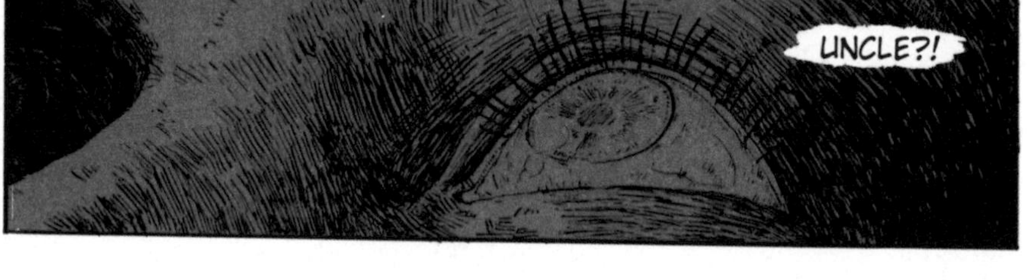
UNCLE?!

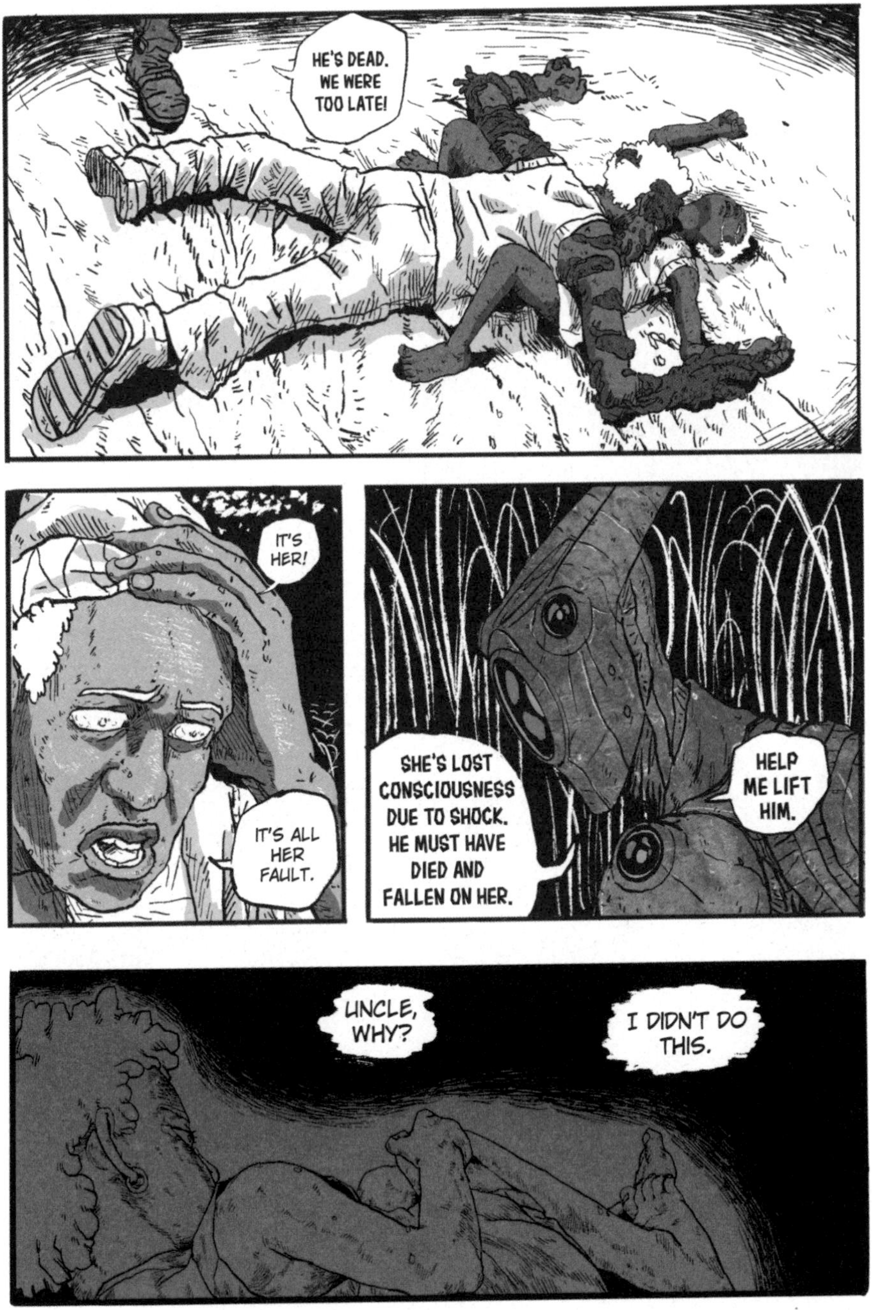
HE'S DEAD. WE WERE TOO LATE!
IT'S HER!
IT'S ALL HER FAULT.
SHE'S LOST CONSCIOUSNESS DUE TO SHOCK. HE MUST HAVE DIED AND FALLEN ON HER.
HELP ME LIFT HIM.
UNCLE, WHY?
I DIDN'T DO THIS.

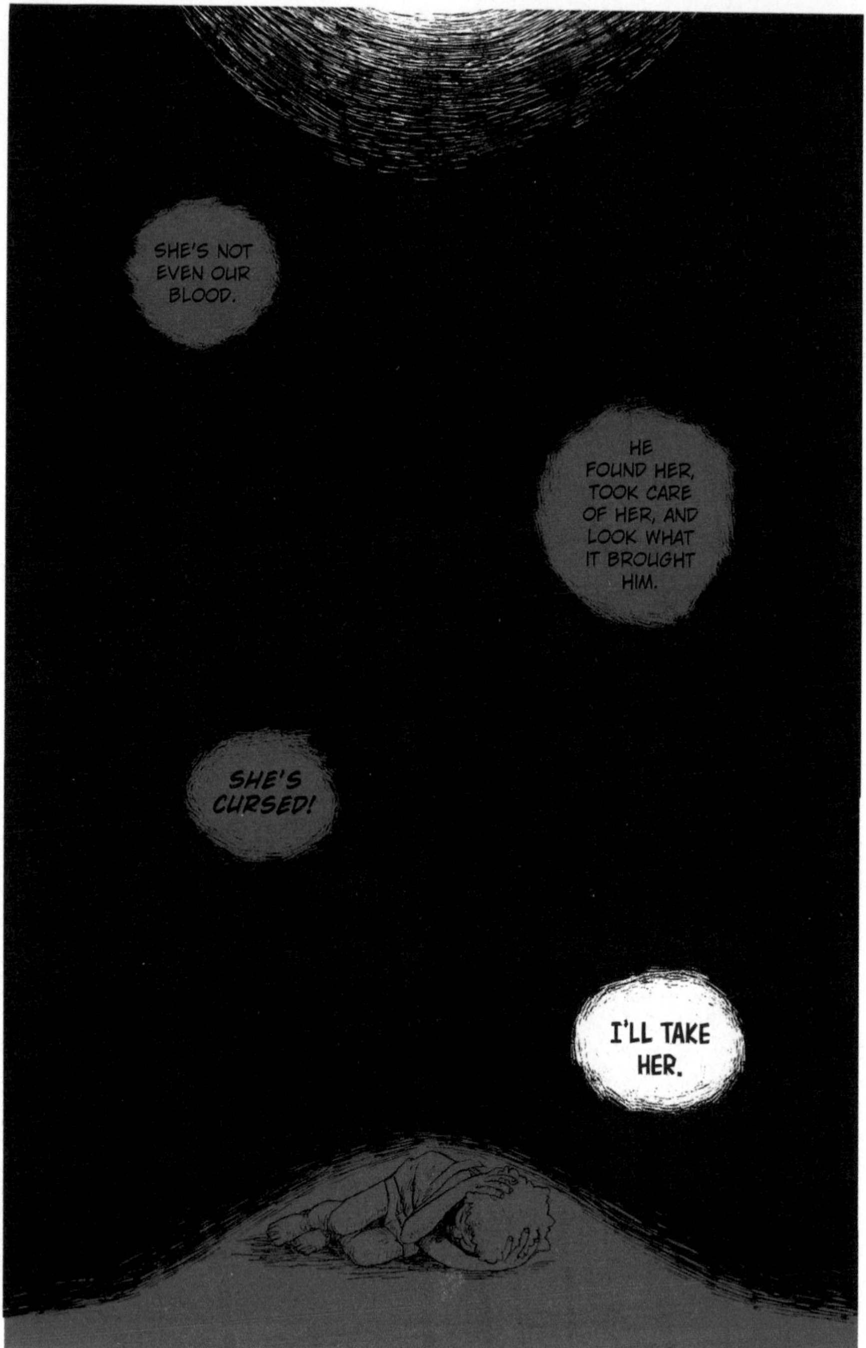
SHE'S NOT EVEN OUR BLOOD.
HE FOUND HER, TOOK CARE OF HER, AND LOOK WHAT IT BROUGHT HIM.
SHE'S CURSED!
I'LL TAKE HER.

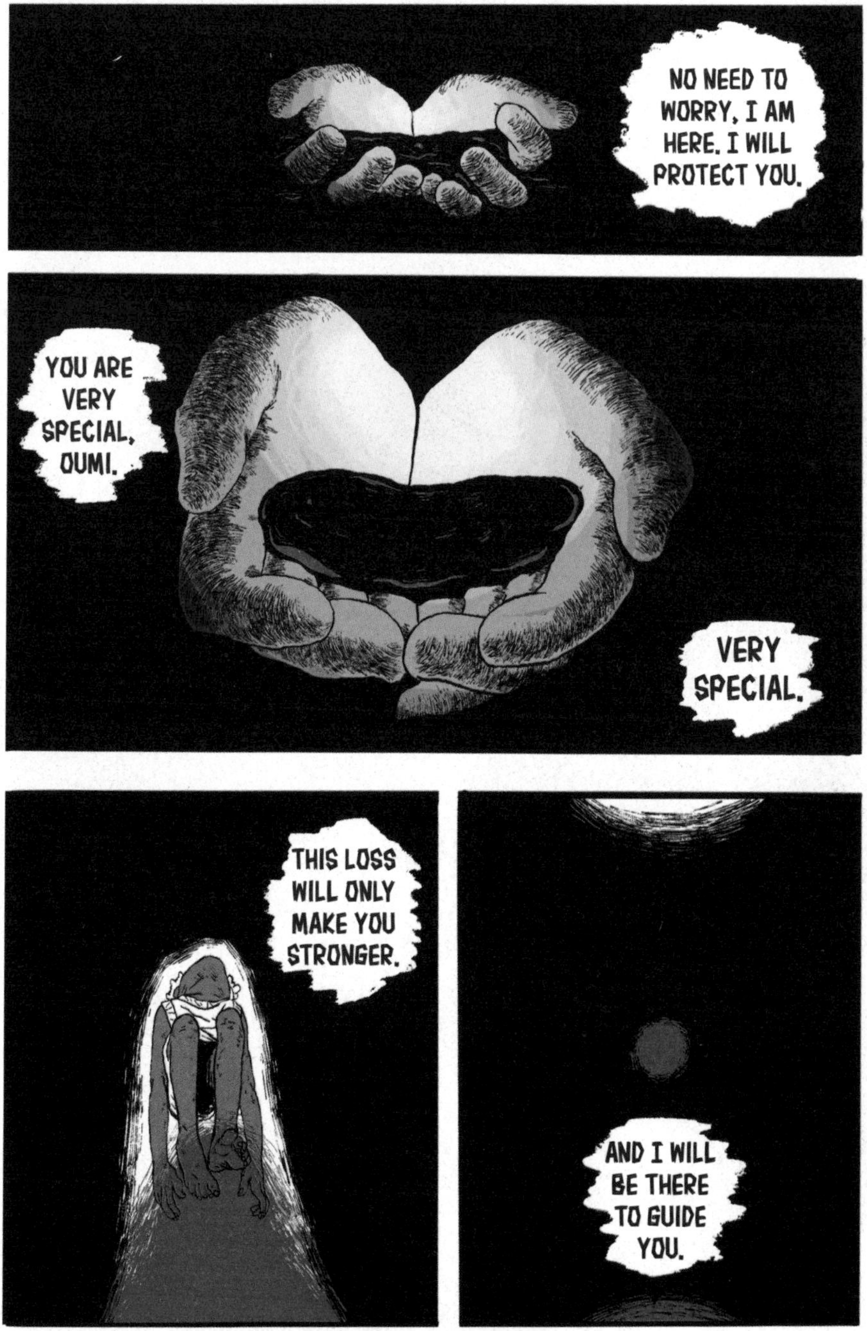
NO NEED TO WORRY, I AM HERE. I WILL PROTECT YOU.
YOU ARE VERY SPECIAL, OUMI.
VERY SPECIAL.
THIS LOSS WILL ONLY MAKE YOU STRONGER.
AND I WILL BE THERE TO GUIDE YOU.

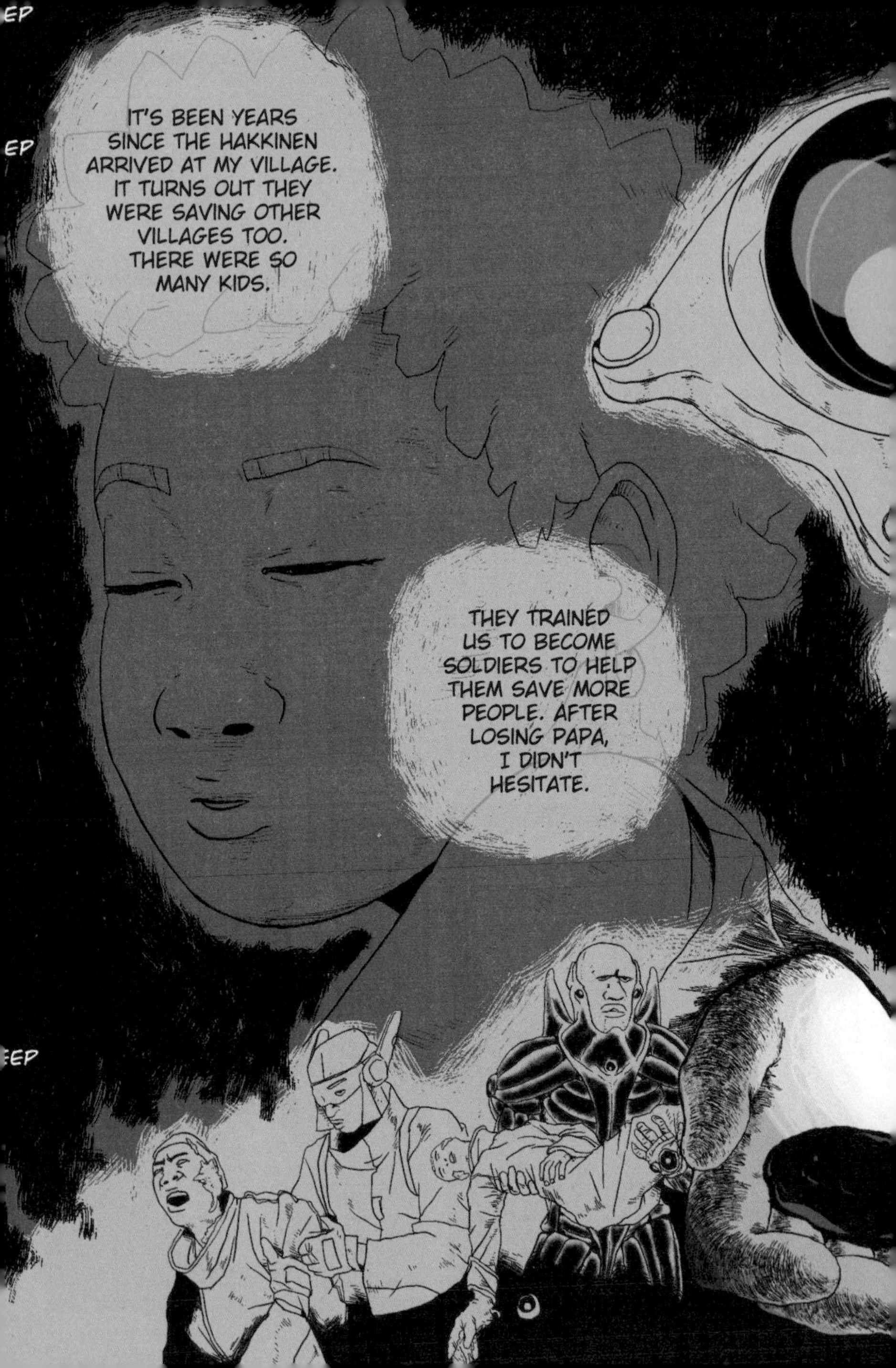
EP
EP
IT'S BEEN YEARS SINCE THE HAKKINEN ARRIVED AT MY VILLAGE. IT TURNS OUT THEY WERE SAVING OTHER VILLAGES TOO. THERE WERE SO MANY KIDS.
THEY TRAINED US TO BECOME SOLDIERS TO HELP THEM SAVE MORE PEOPLE. AFTER LOSING PAPA, I DIDN'T HESITATE.
EP

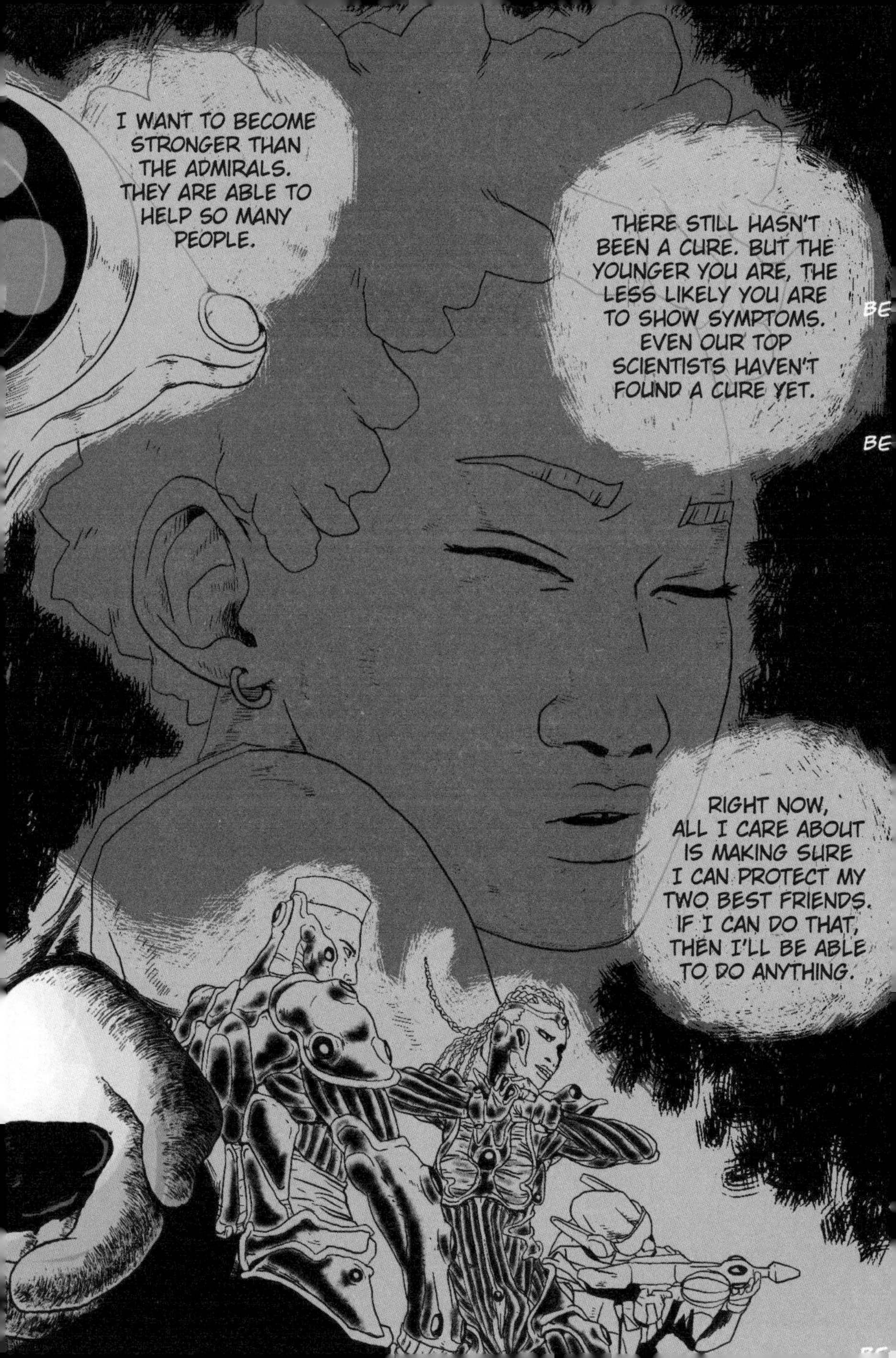
I WANT TO BECOME STRONGER THAN THE ADMIRALS. THEY ARE ABLE TO HELP SO MANY PEOPLE.
THERE STILL HASN'T BEEN A CURE. BUT THE YOUNGER YOU ARE, THE LESS LIKELY YOU ARE TO SHOW SYMPTOMS. EVEN OUR TOP SCIENTISTS HAVEN'T FOUND A CURE YET.
RIGHT NOW, ALL I CARE ABOUT IS MAKING SURE I CAN PROTECT MY TWO BEST FRIENDS. IF I CAN DO THAT, THEN I'LL BE ABLE TO DO ANYTHING.

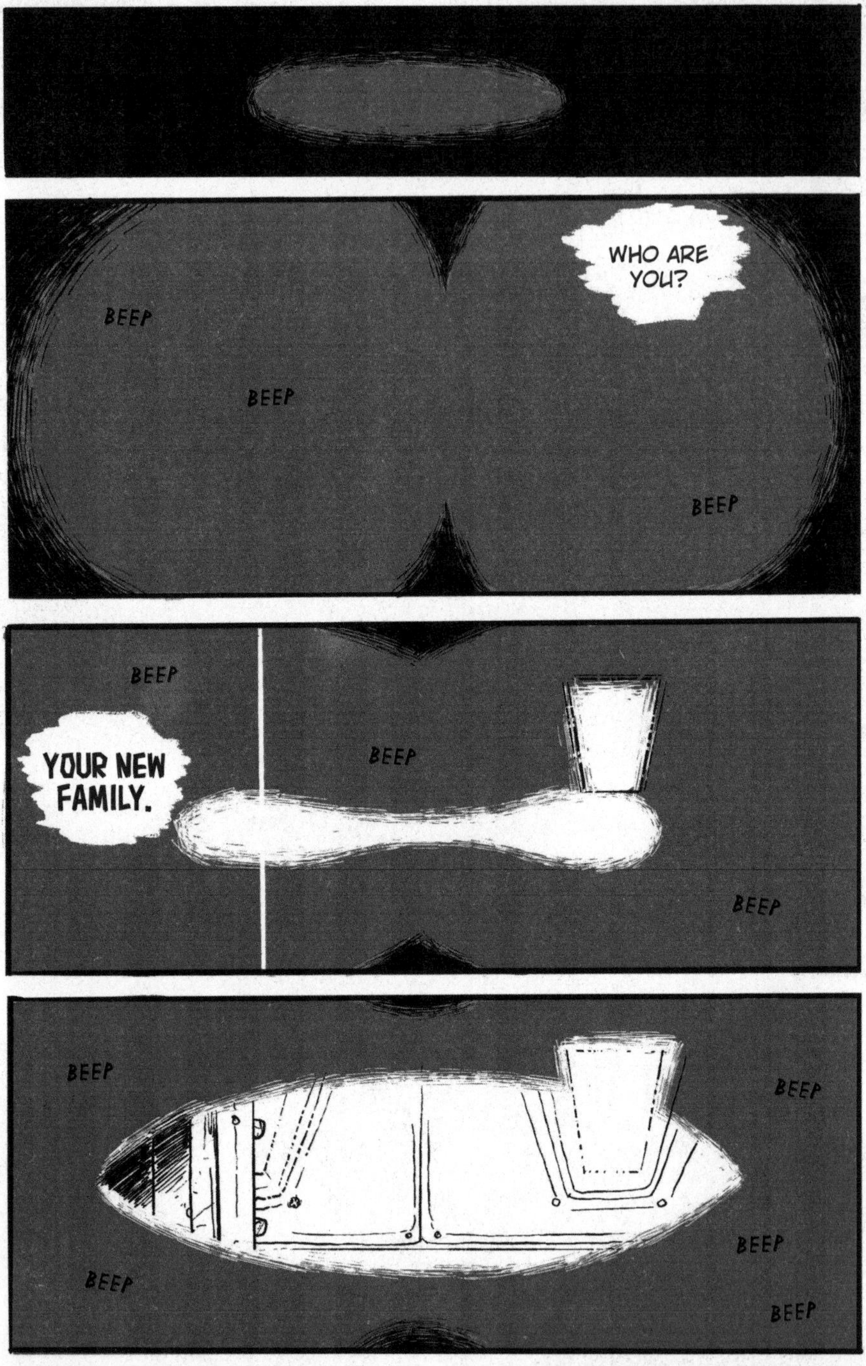
WHO ARE YOU?
BEEP
BEEP
BEEP
BEEP
YOUR NEW FAMILY.
BEEP
BEEP
BEEP
BEEP
BEEP
BEEP
BEEP

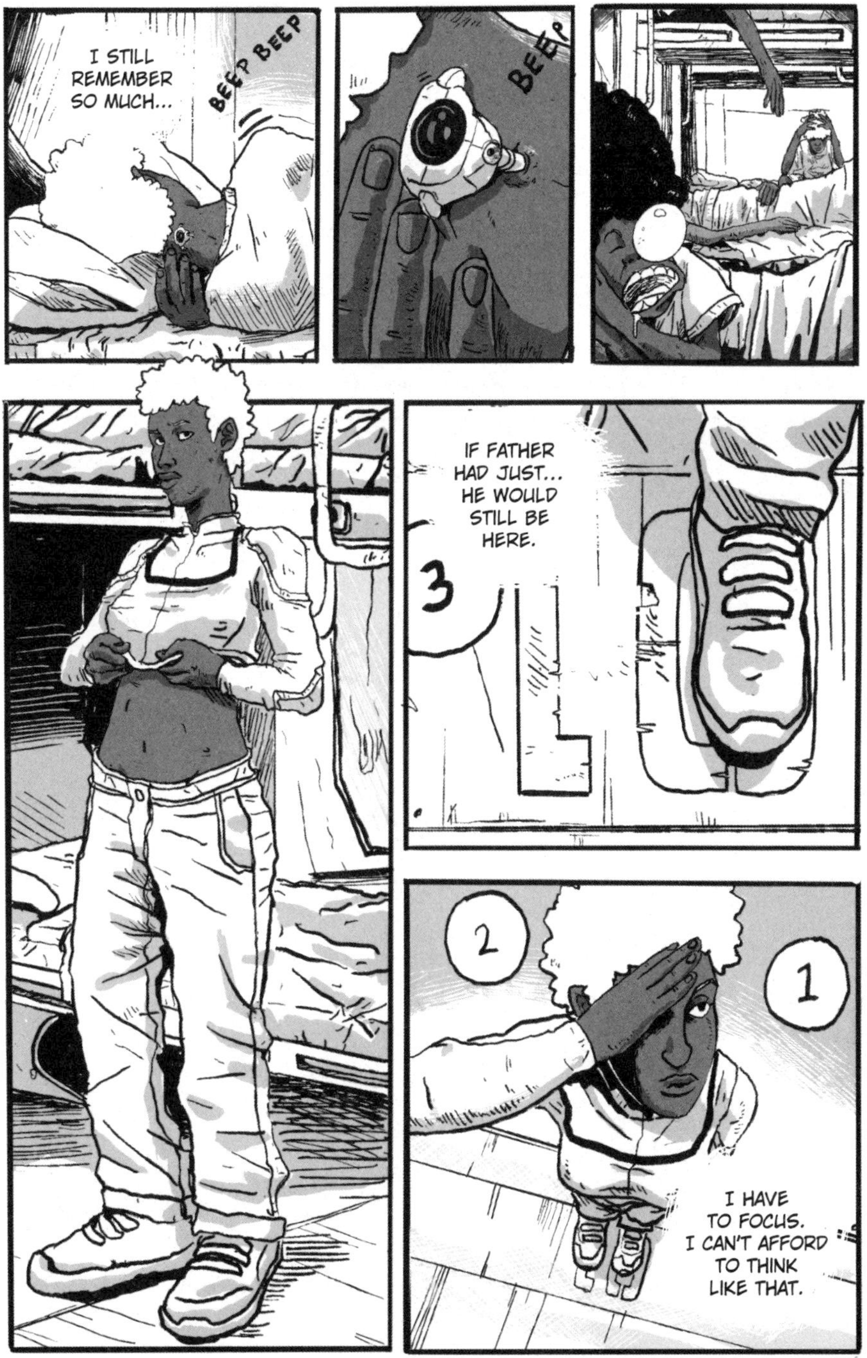
I STILL REMEMBER SO MUCH...
BEEP BEEP
BEEP
IF FATHER HAD JUST... HE WOULD STILL BE HERE.
3
2
1
I HAVE TO FOCUS. I CAN'T AFFORD TO THINK LIKE THAT.

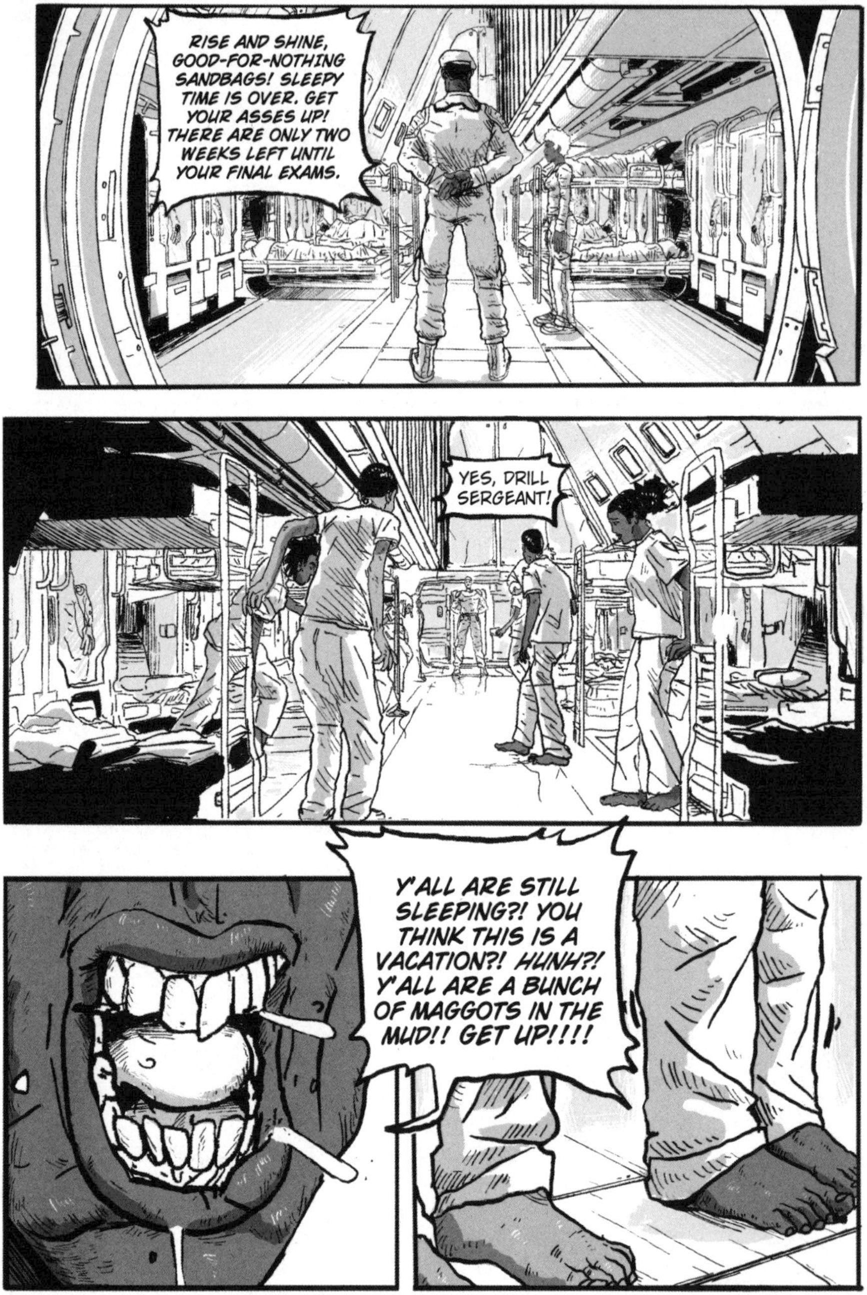
RISE AND SHINE, GOOD-FOR-NOTHING SANDBAGS! SLEEPY TIME IS OVER. GET YOUR ASSES UP! THERE ARE ONLY TWO WEEKS LEFT UNTIL YOUR FINAL EXAMS.
YES, DRILL SERGEANT!
Y'ALL ARE STILL SLEEPING?! YOU THINK THIS IS A VACATION?! HUNH?! Y'ALL ARE A BUNCH OF MAGGOTS IN THE MUD!! GET UP!!!!

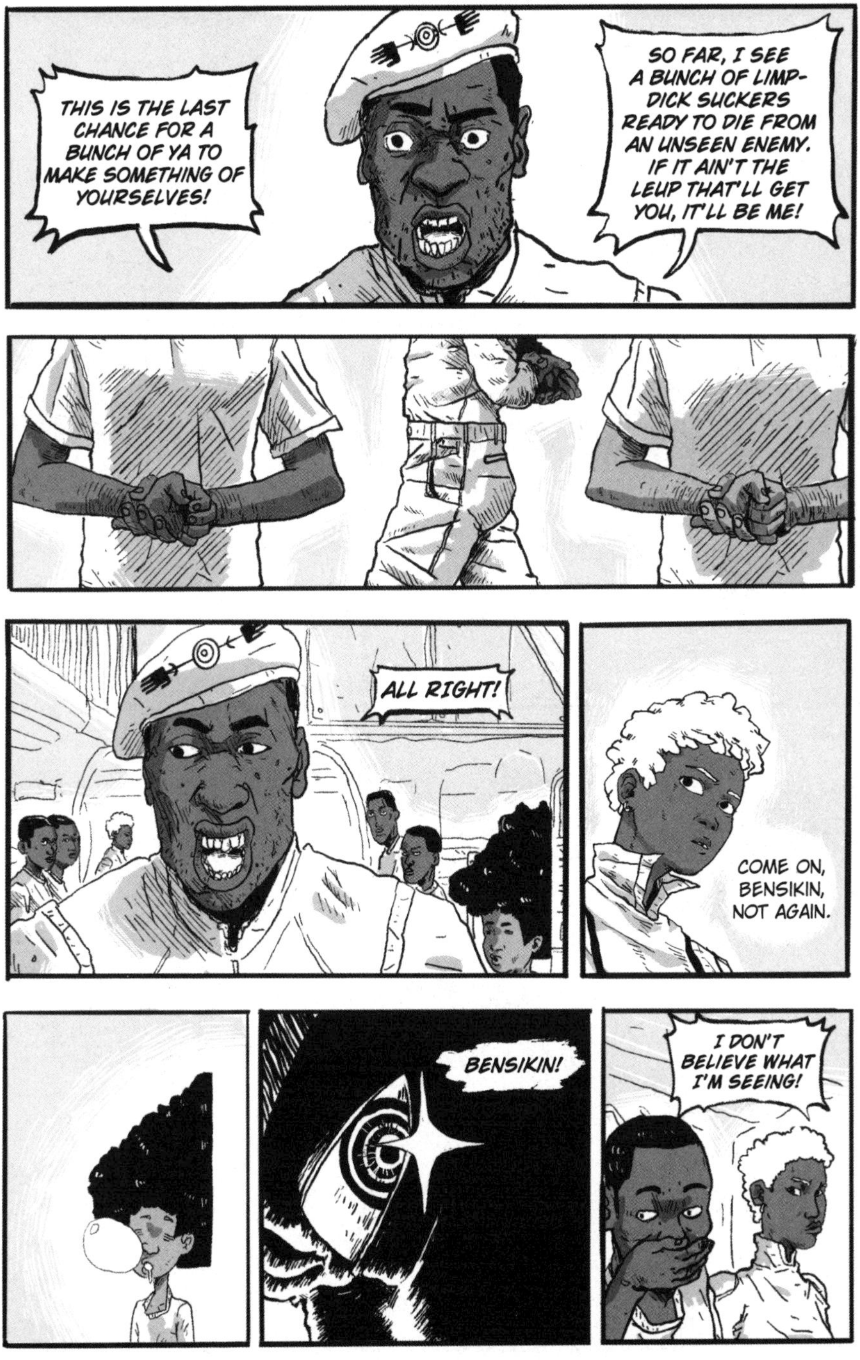
THIS IS THE LAST CHANCE FOR A BUNCH OF YA TO MAKE SOMETHING OF YOURSELVES!
SO FAR, I SEE A BUNCH OF LIMP-DICK SUCKERS READY TO DIE FROM AN UNSEEN ENEMY. IF IT AIN'T THE LEUP THAT'LL GET YOU, IT'LL BE ME!
ALL RIGHT!
COME ON, BENSIKIN, NOT AGAIN.
BENSIKIN!
I DON'T BELIEVE WHAT I'M SEEING!

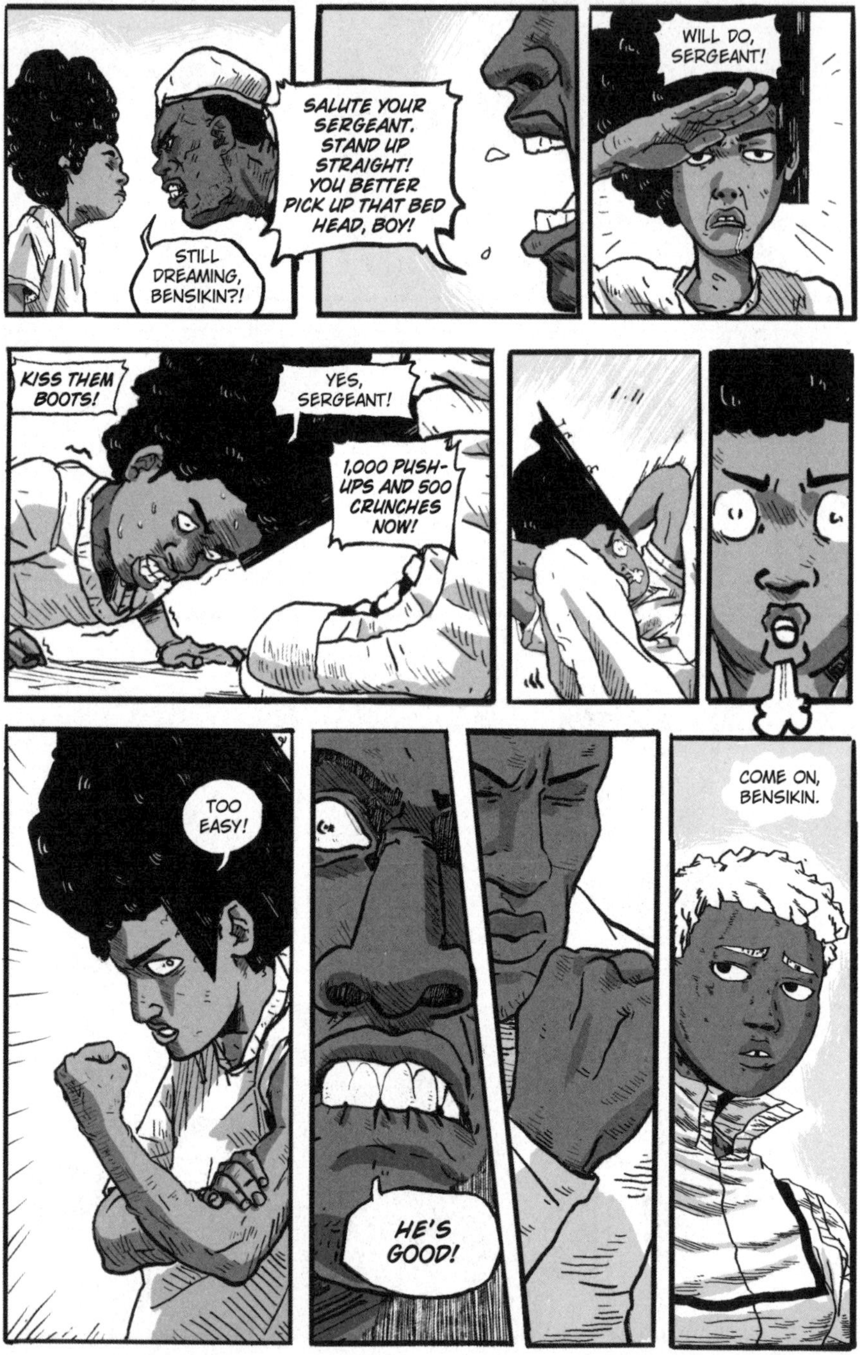
STILL DREAMING, BENSIKIN?!
SALUTE YOUR SERGEANT. STAND UP STRAIGHT! YOU BETTER PICK UP THAT BED HEAD, BOY!
WILL DO, SERGEANT!
KISS THEM BOOTS!
YES, SERGEANT!
1,000 PUSH-UPS AND 500 CRUNCHES NOW!
TOO EASY!
HE'S GOOD!
COME ON, BENSIKIN.

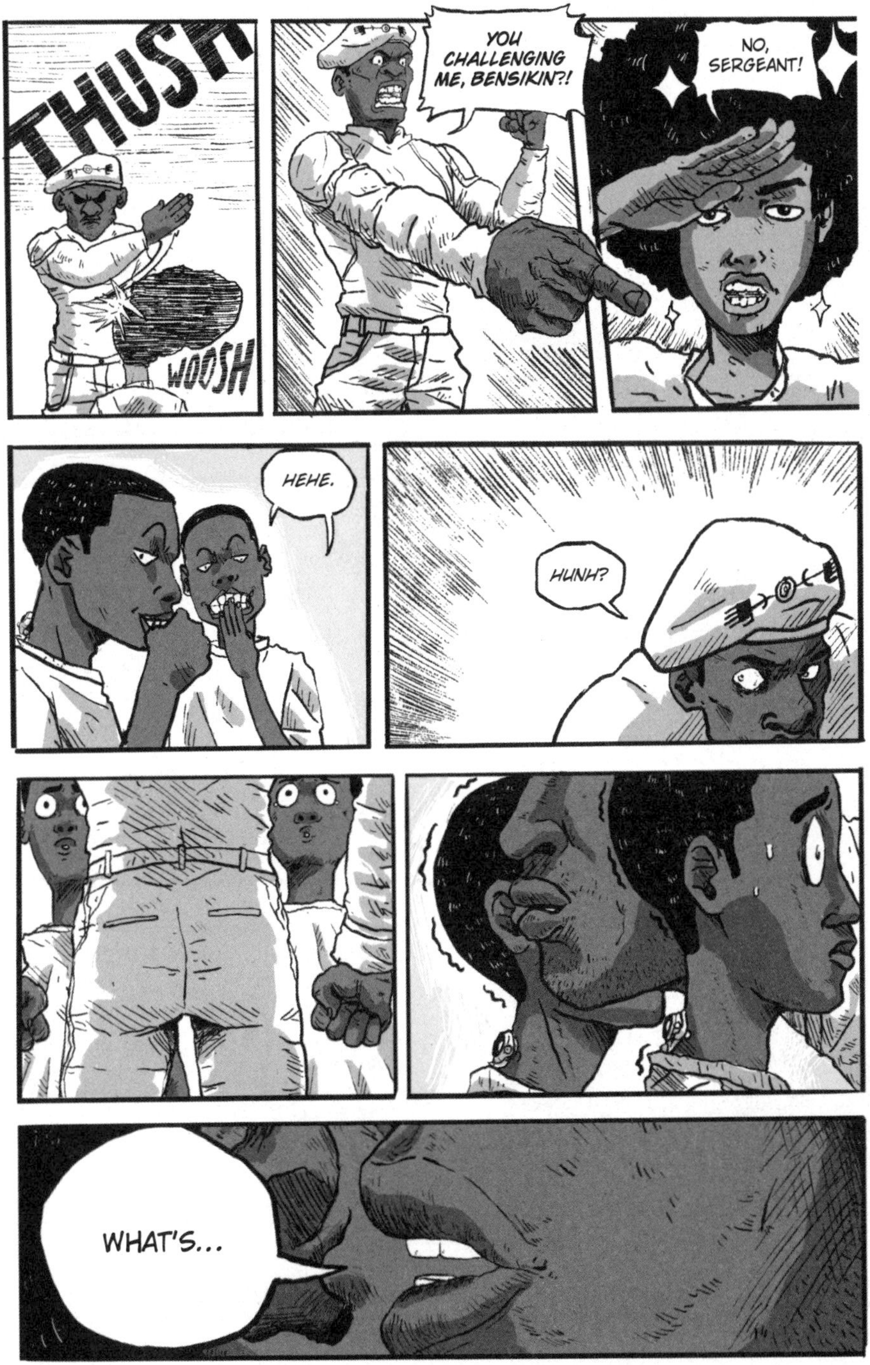
THUSH
WOOSH
YOU CHALLENGING ME, BENSIKIN?!
NO, SERGEANT!
HEHE.
HUNH?
WHAT'S...

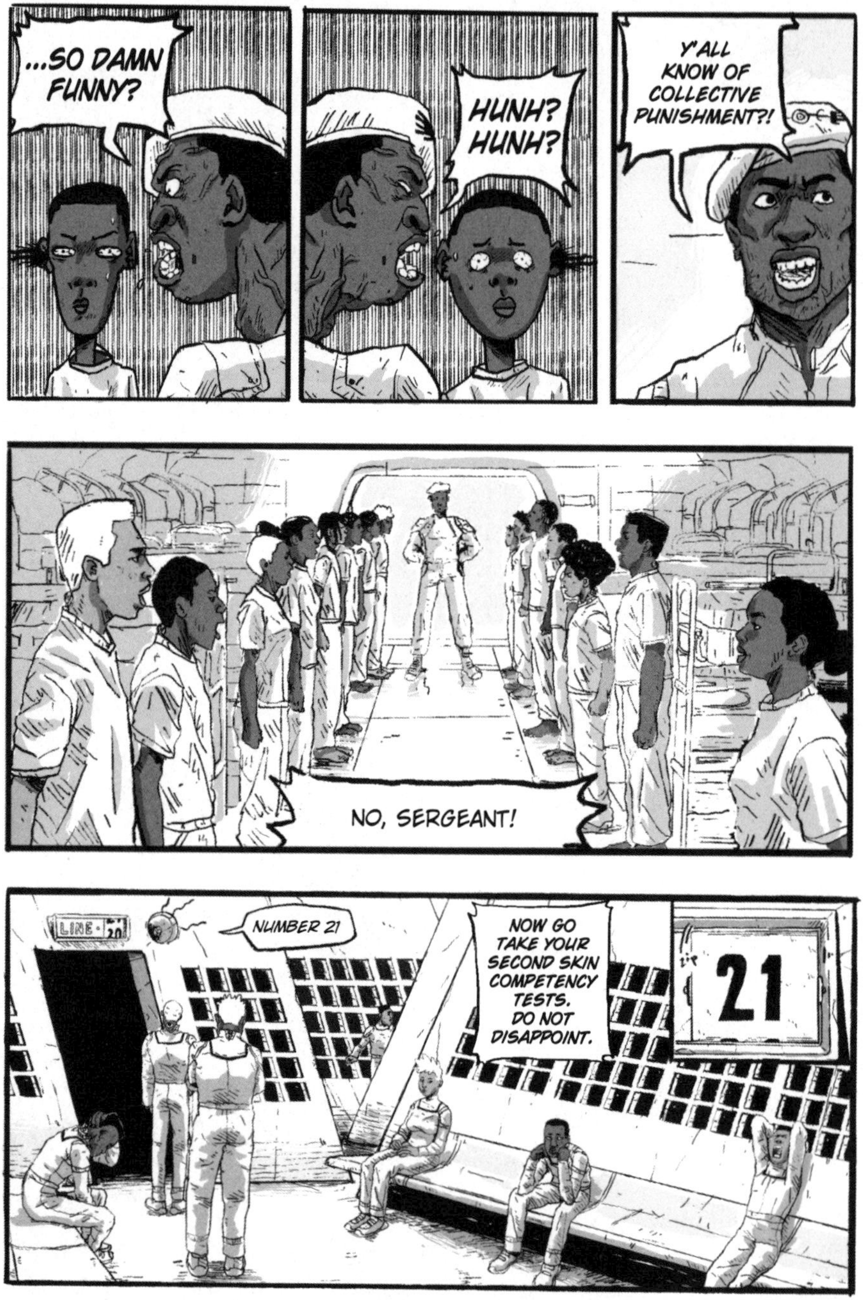
...SO DAMN FUNNY?
HUNH? HUNH?
Y'ALL KNOW OF COLLECTIVE PUNISHMENT?!
NO, SERGEANT!
LINE·20
NUMBER 21
NOW GO TAKE YOUR SECOND SKIN COMPETENCY TESTS. DO NOT DISAPPOINT.
21

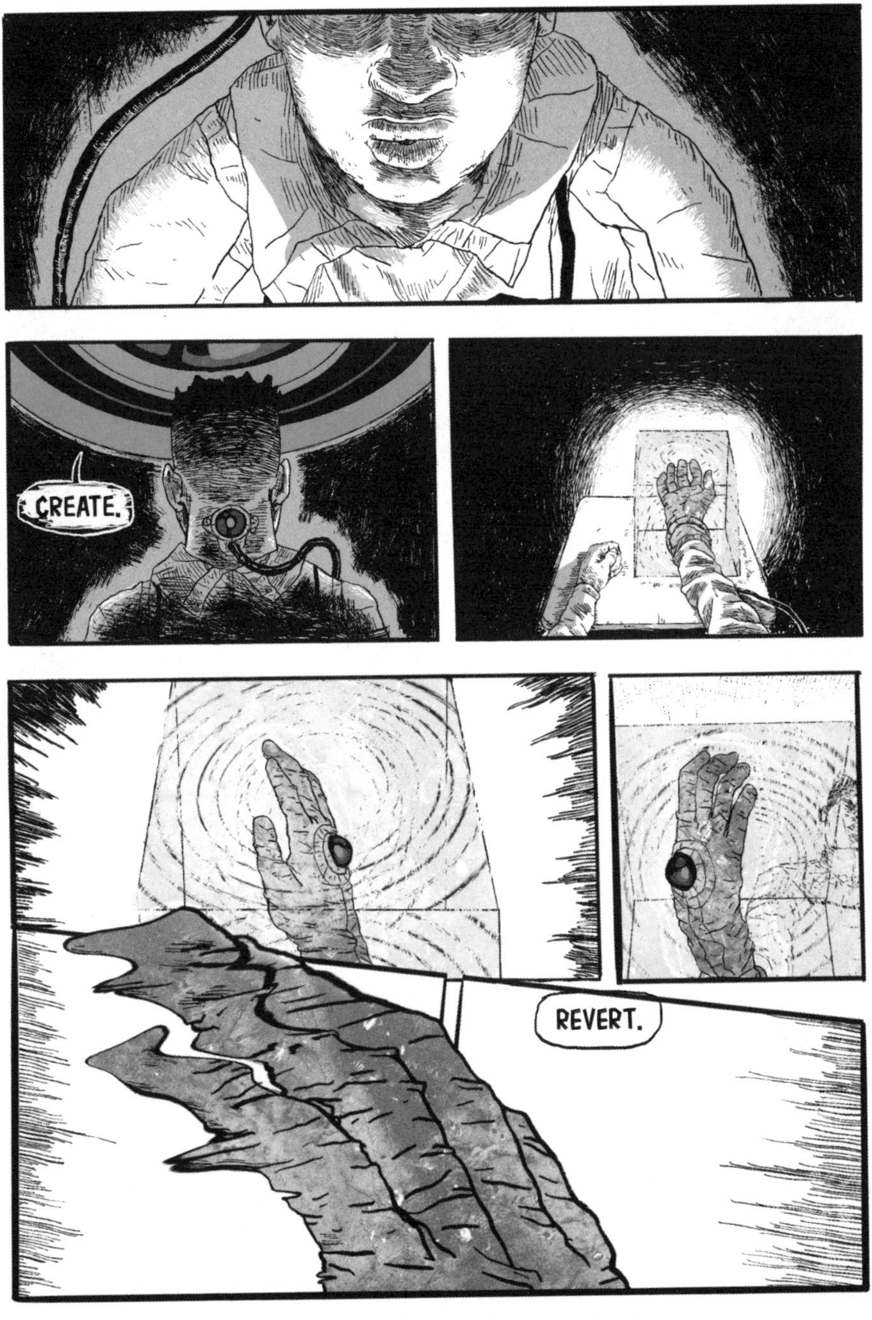
CREATE.
REVERT.

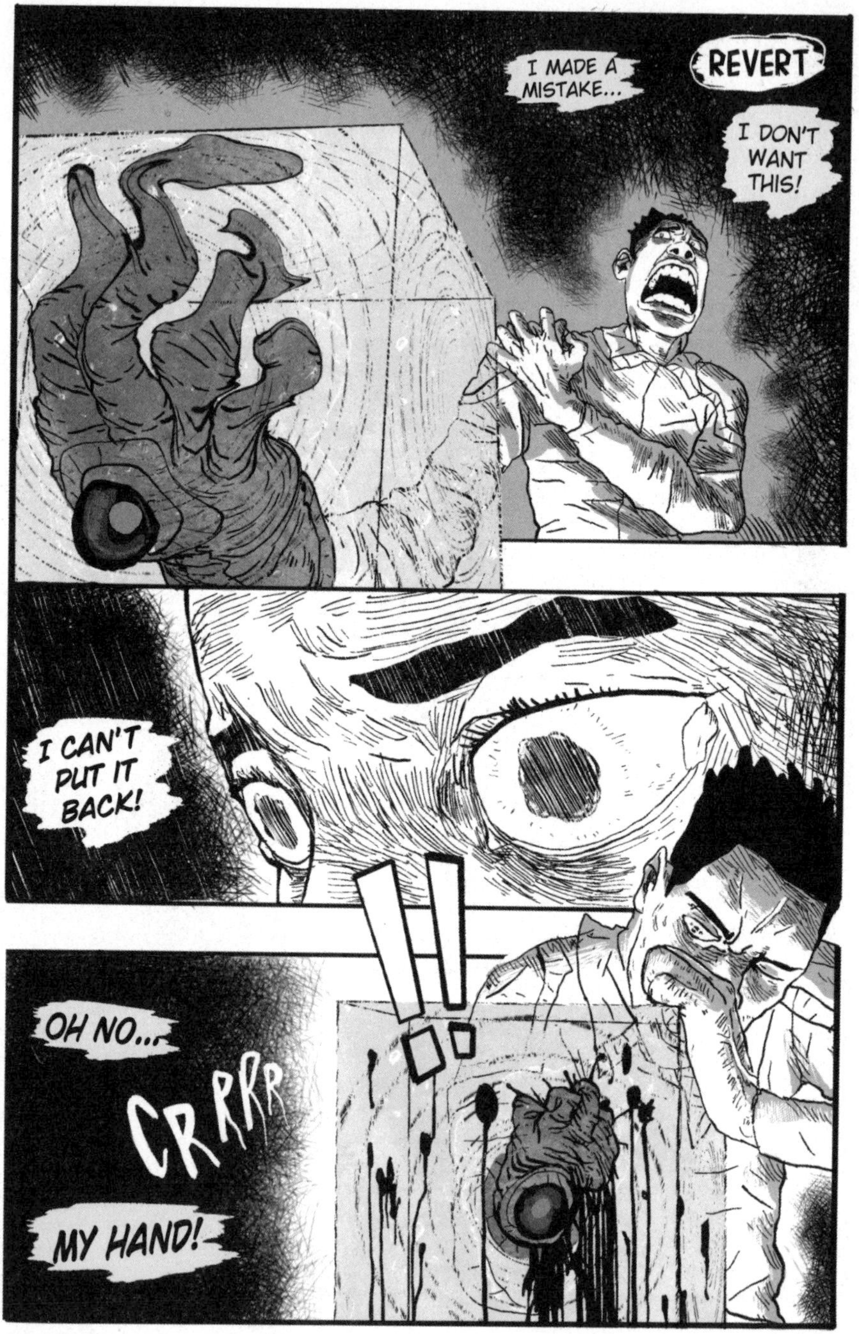
I MADE A MISTAKE...
REVERT
I DON'T WANT THIS!
I CAN'T PUT IT BACK!
OH NO...
CRRRR
MY HAND!

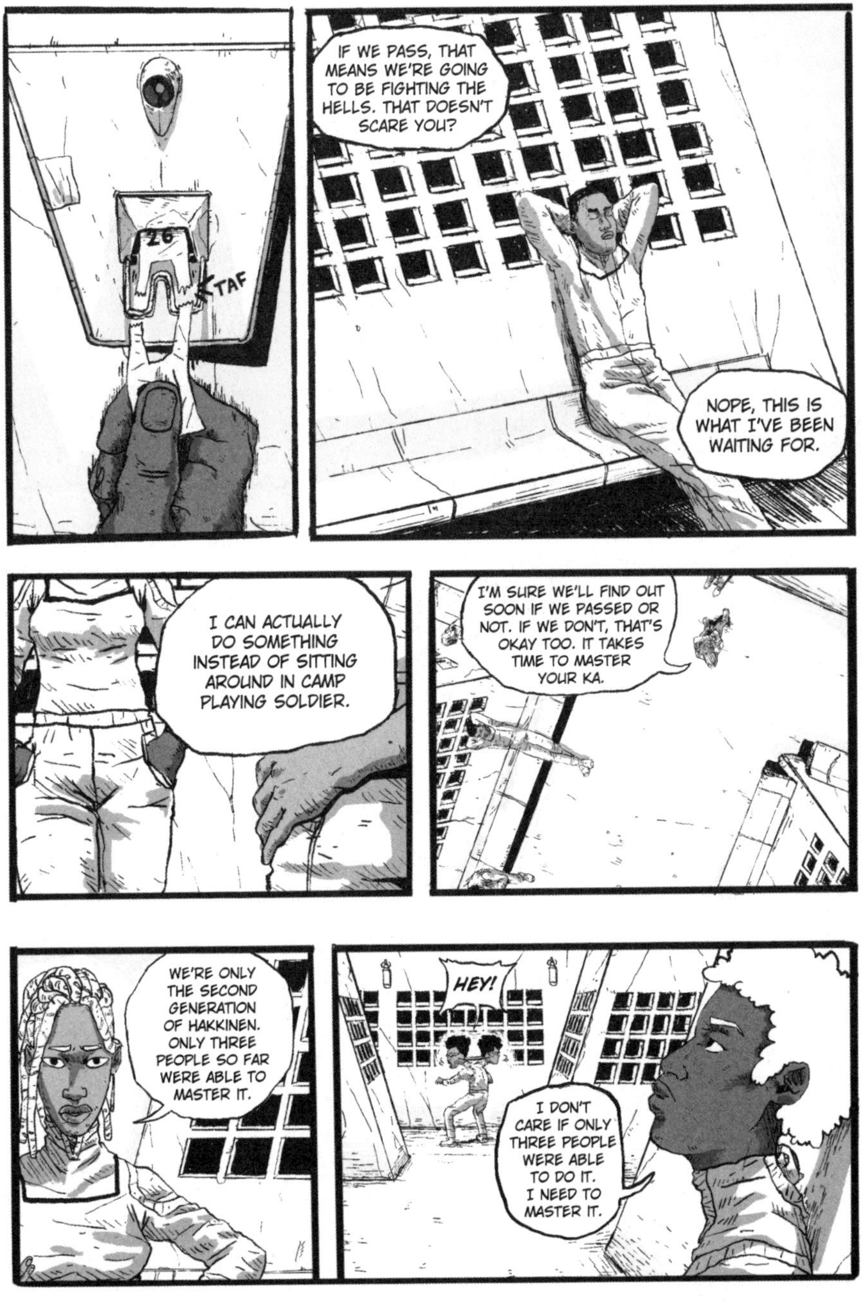
26
TAF
IF WE PASS, THAT MEANS WE'RE GOING TO BE FIGHTING THE HELLS. THAT DOESN'T SCARE YOU?
NOPE, THIS IS WHAT I'VE BEEN WAITING FOR.
I CAN ACTUALLY DO SOMETHING INSTEAD OF SITTING AROUND IN CAMP PLAYING SOLDIER.
I'M SURE WE'LL FIND OUT SOON IF WE PASSED OR NOT. IF WE DON'T, THAT'S OKAY TOO. IT TAKES TIME TO MASTER YOUR KA.
WE'RE ONLY THE SECOND GENERATION OF HAKKINEN. ONLY THREE PEOPLE SO FAR WERE ABLE TO MASTER IT.
HEY!
I DON'T CARE IF ONLY THREE PEOPLE WERE ABLE TO DO IT. I NEED TO MASTER IT.

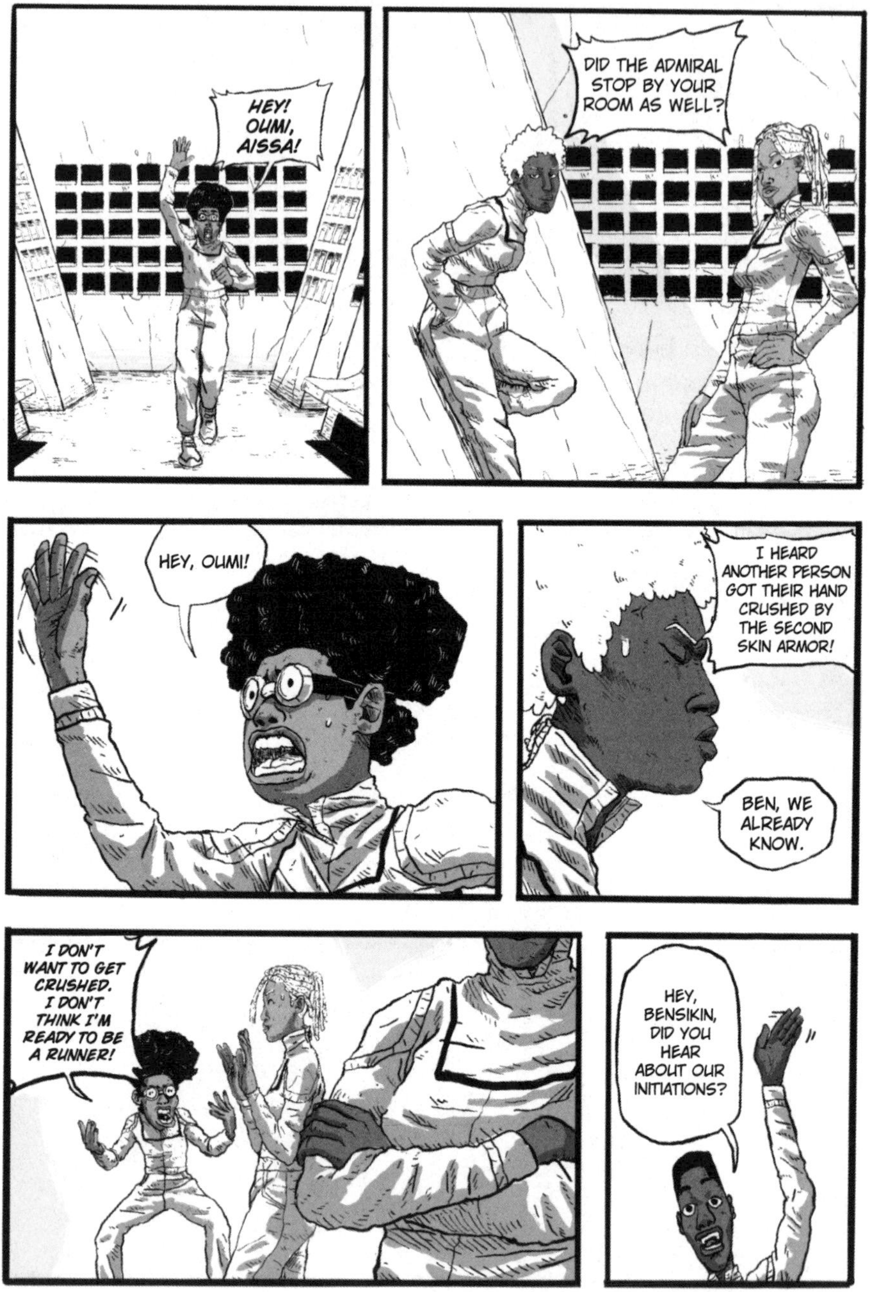
HEY! OUMI, AISSA!
DID THE ADMIRAL STOP BY YOUR ROOM AS WELL?
HEY, OUMI!
I HEARD ANOTHER PERSON GOT THEIR HAND CRUSHED BY THE SECOND SKIN ARMOR!
BEN, WE ALREADY KNOW.
I DON'T WANT TO GET CRUSHED. I DON'T THINK I'M READY TO BE A RUNNER!
HEY, BENSIKIN, DID YOU HEAR ABOUT OUR INITIATIONS?

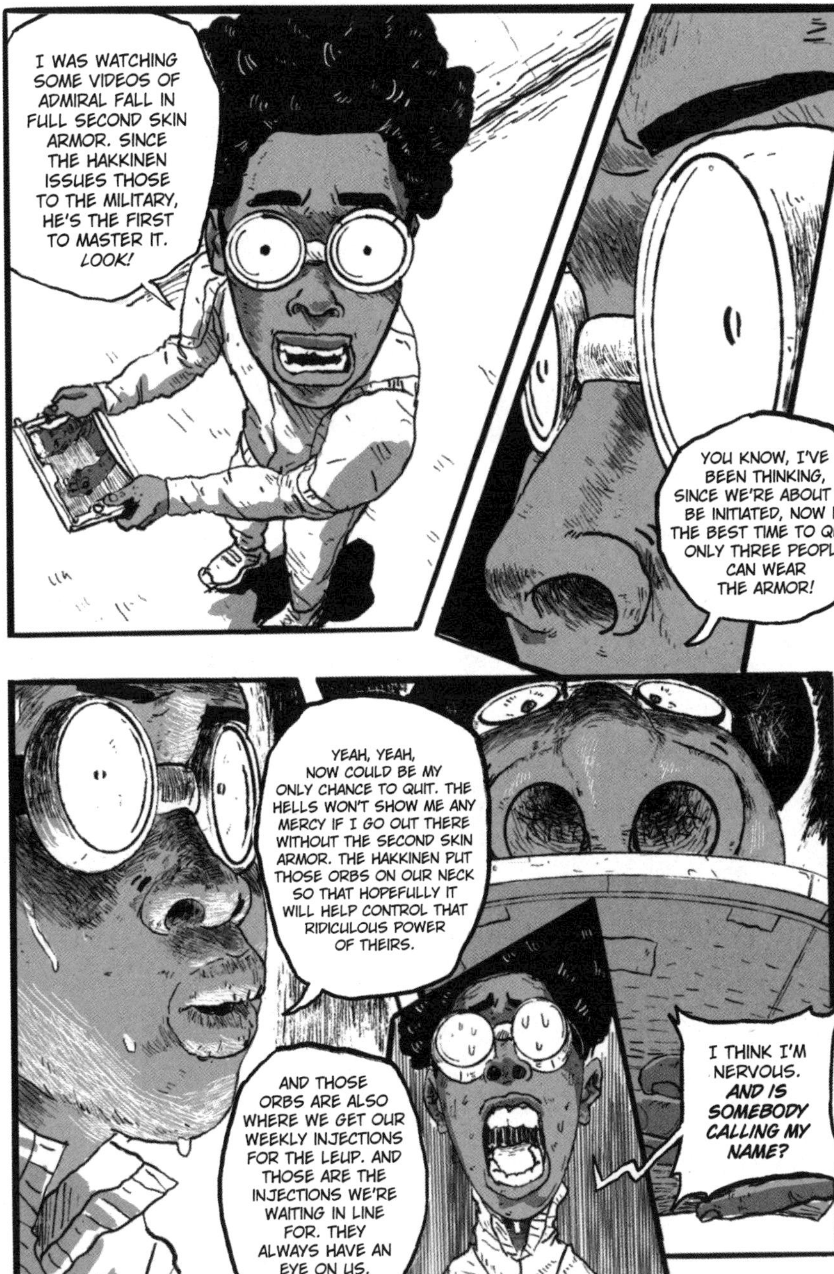
I WAS WATCHING SOME VIDEOS OF ADMIRAL FALL IN FULL SECOND SKIN ARMOR. SINCE THE HAKKINEN ISSUES THOSE TO THE MILITARY, HE'S THE FIRST TO MASTER IT. *LOOK!*
YOU KNOW, I'VE BEEN THINKING, SINCE WE'RE ABOUT TO BE INITIATED, NOW IS THE BEST TIME TO QUIT. ONLY THREE PEOPLE CAN WEAR THE ARMOR!
YEAH, YEAH, NOW COULD BE MY ONLY CHANCE TO QUIT. THE HELLS WON'T SHOW ME ANY MERCY IF I GO OUT THERE WITHOUT THE SECOND SKIN ARMOR. THE HAKKINEN PUT THOSE ORBS ON OUR NECK SO THAT HOPEFULLY IT WILL HELP CONTROL THAT RIDICULOUS POWER OF THEIRS.
AND THOSE ORBS ARE ALSO WHERE WE GET OUR WEEKLY INJECTIONS FOR THE LEUP. AND THOSE ARE THE INJECTIONS WE'RE WAITING IN LINE FOR. THEY ALWAYS HAVE AN EYE ON US.
I THINK I'M NERVOUS. ***AND IS SOMEBODY CALLING MY NAME?***

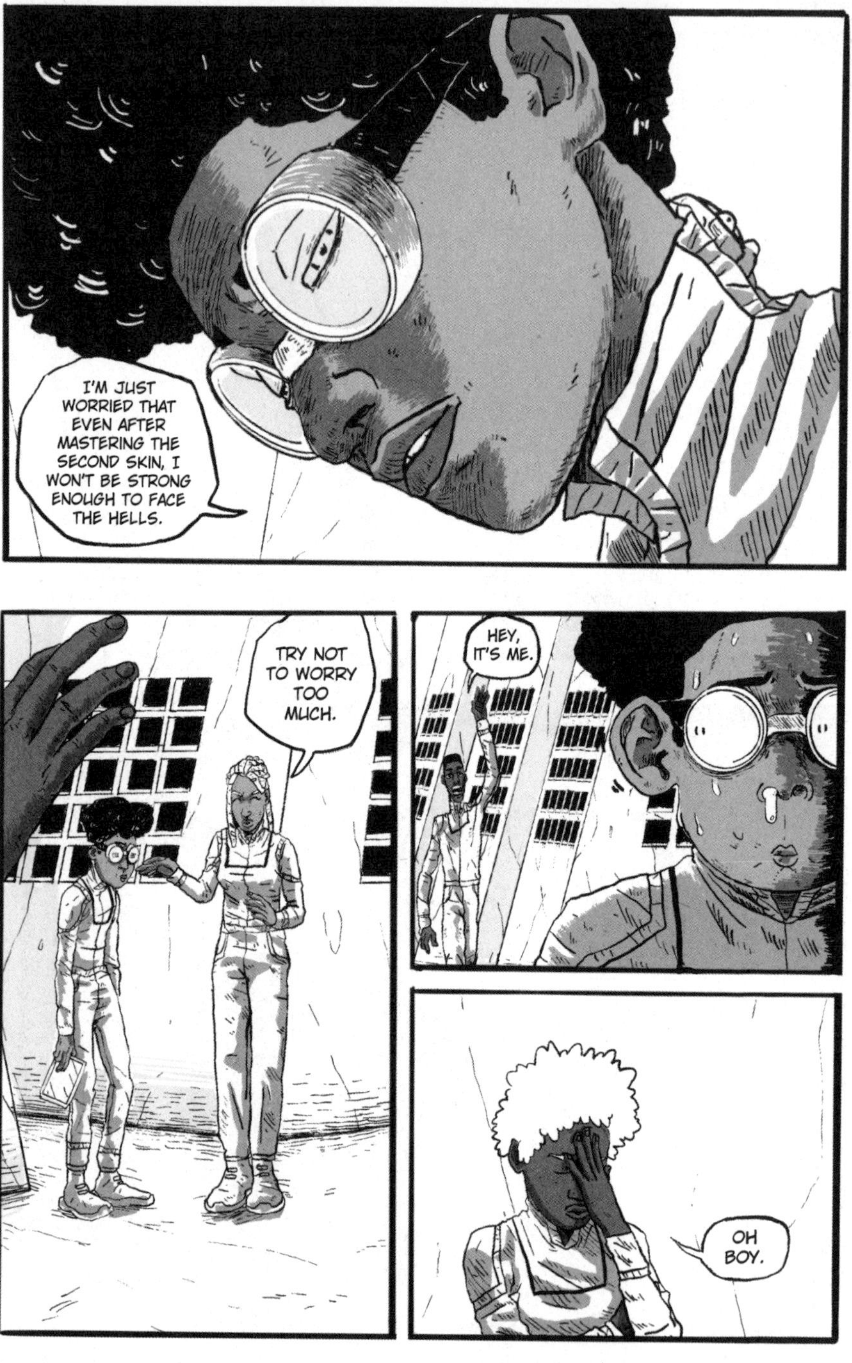
I'M JUST WORRIED THAT EVEN AFTER MASTERING THE SECOND SKIN, I WON'T BE STRONG ENOUGH TO FACE THE HELLS.
TRY NOT TO WORRY TOO MUCH.
HEY, IT'S ME.
OH BOY.

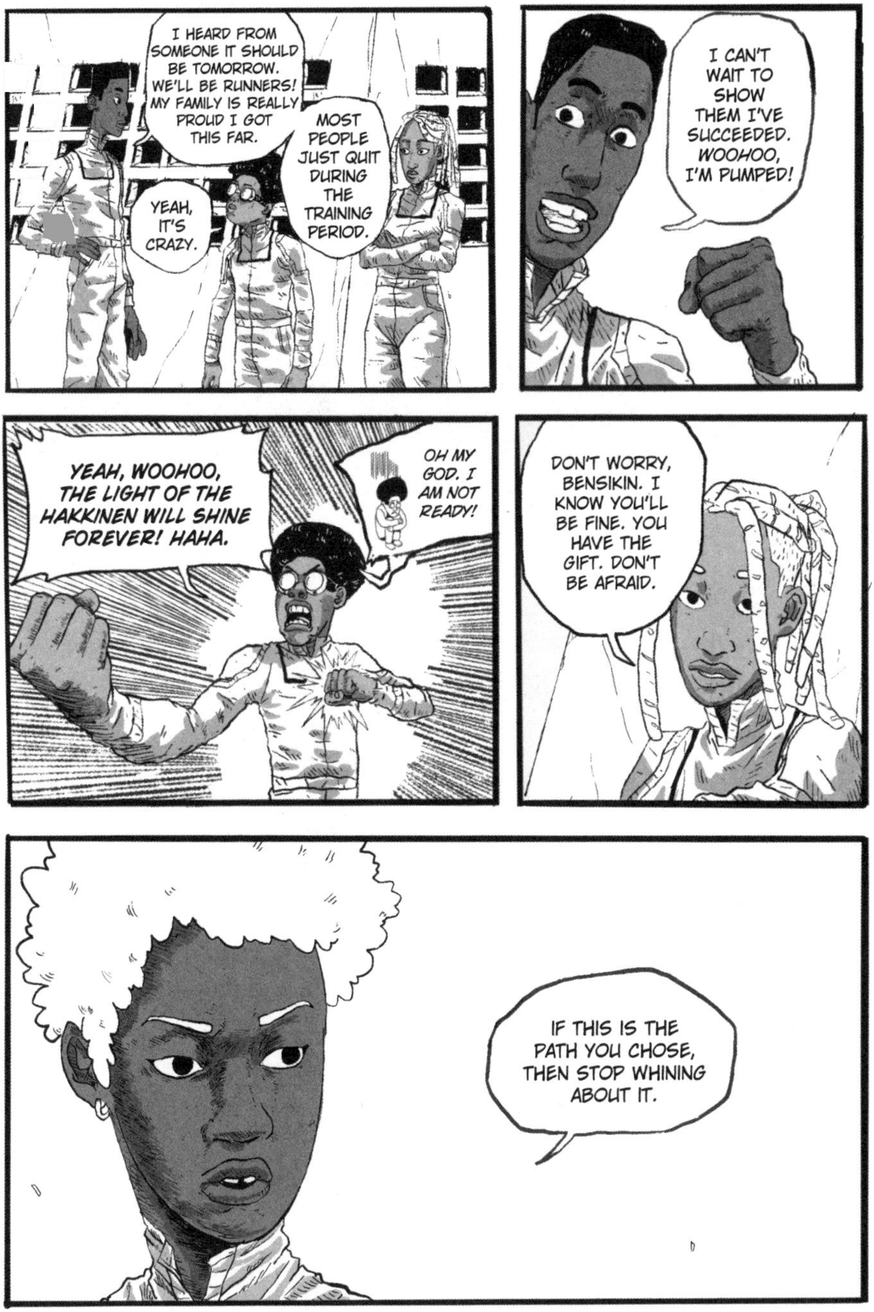
I HEARD FROM SOMEONE IT SHOULD BE TOMORROW. WE'LL BE RUNNERS! MY FAMILY IS REALLY PROUD I GOT THIS FAR.
YEAH, IT'S CRAZY.
MOST PEOPLE JUST QUIT DURING THE TRAINING PERIOD.
I CAN'T WAIT TO SHOW THEM I'VE SUCCEEDED. WOOHOO, I'M PUMPED!
YEAH, WOOHOO, THE LIGHT OF THE HAKKINEN WILL SHINE FOREVER! HAHA.
OH MY GOD. I AM NOT READY!
DON'T WORRY, BENSIKIN. I KNOW YOU'LL BE FINE. YOU HAVE THE GIFT. DON'T BE AFRAID.
IF THIS IS THE PATH YOU CHOSE, THEN STOP WHINING ABOUT IT.

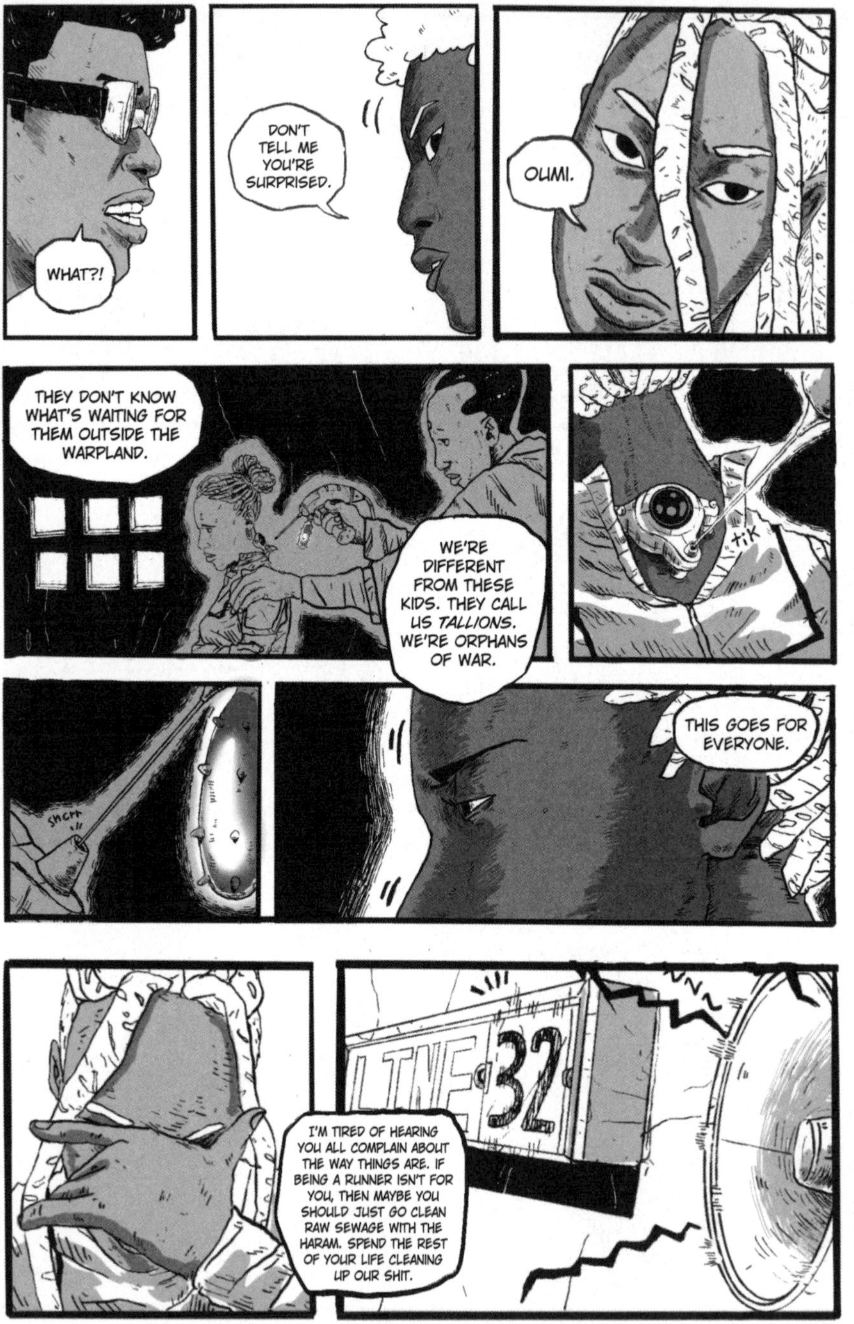
WHAT?!
DON'T TELL ME YOU'RE SURPRISED.
OUMI.
THEY DON'T KNOW WHAT'S WAITING FOR THEM OUTSIDE THE WARPLAND.
WE'RE DIFFERENT FROM THESE KIDS. THEY CALL US *TALLIONS*. WE'RE ORPHANS OF WAR.
tik
THIS GOES FOR EVERYONE.
I'M TIRED OF HEARING YOU ALL COMPLAIN ABOUT THE WAY THINGS ARE. IF BEING A RUNNER ISN'T FOR YOU, THEN MAYBE YOU SHOULD JUST GO CLEAN RAW SEWAGE WITH THE HARAM. SPEND THE REST OF YOUR LIFE CLEANING UP OUR SHIT.
LINE 32

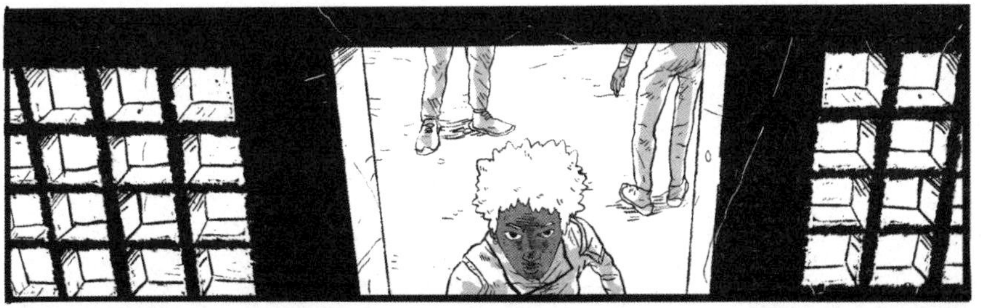

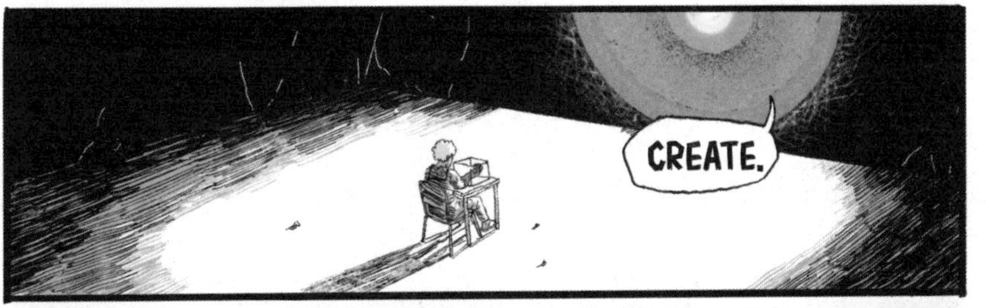
CREATE.

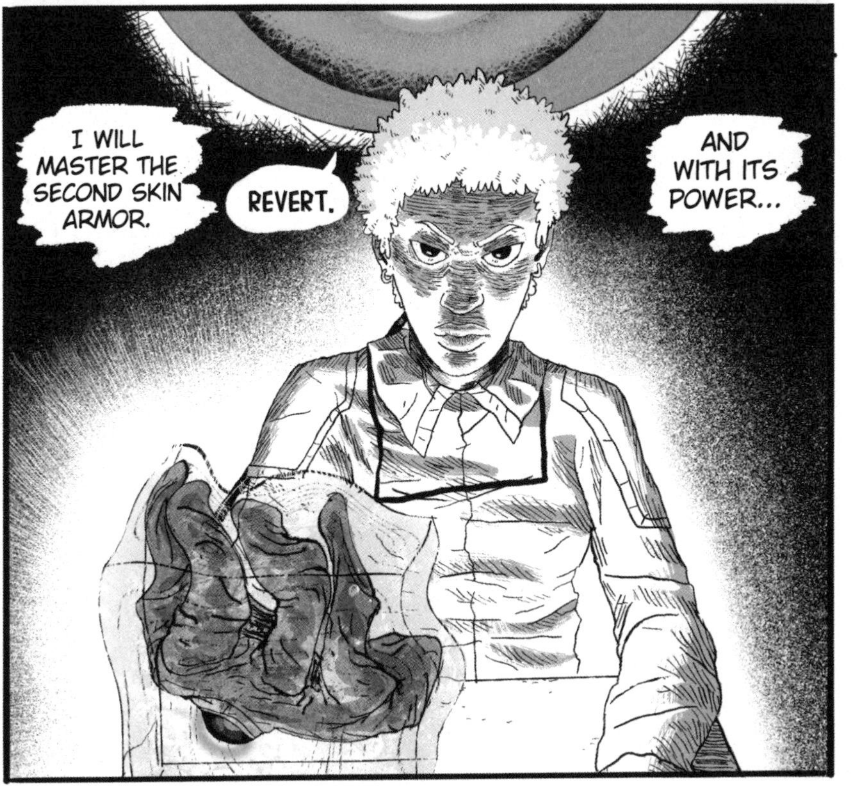
I WILL MASTER THE SECOND SKIN ARMOR.
REVERT.
AND WITH ITS POWER...

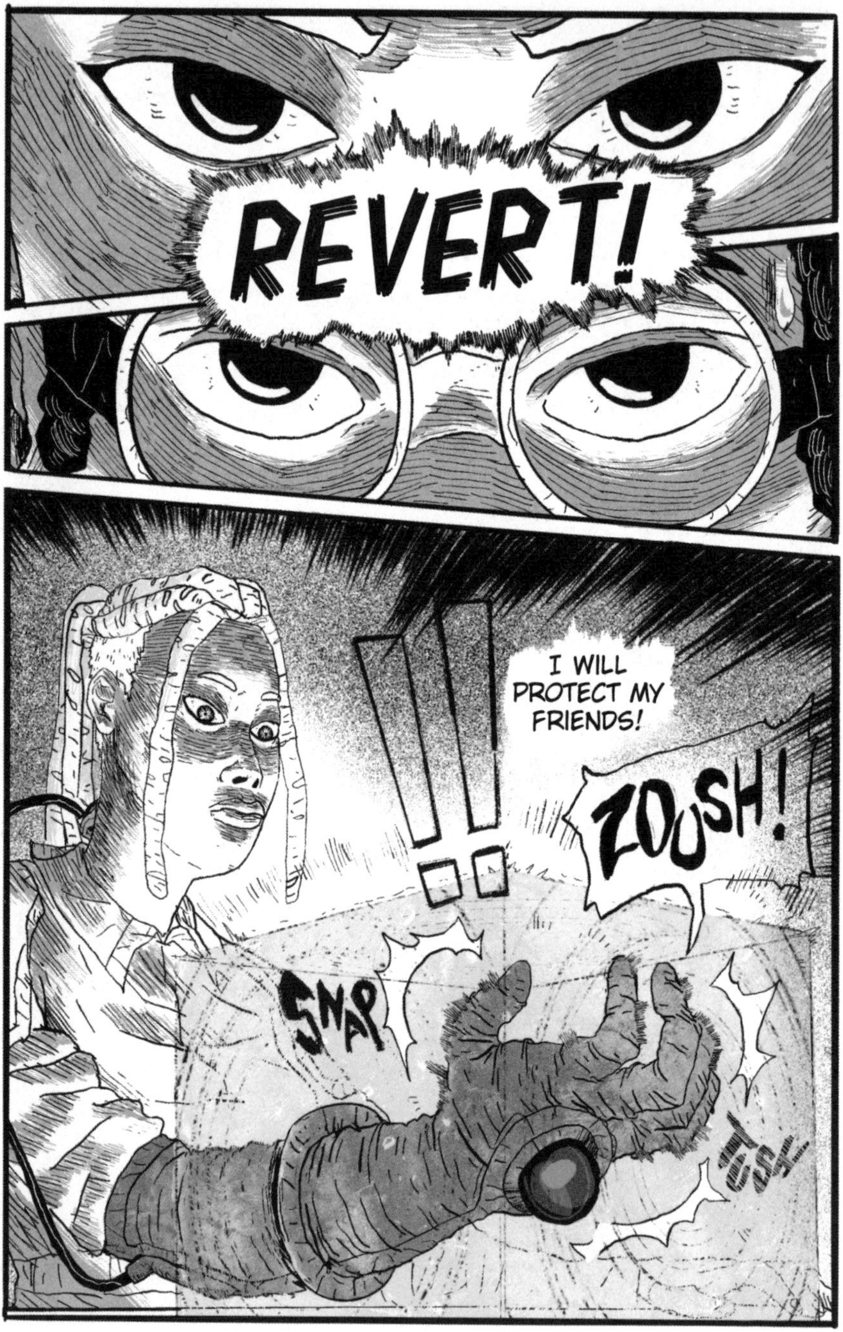
REVERT!
!!
I WILL PROTECT MY FRIENDS!
ZOUSH!
SNAP
TSK...

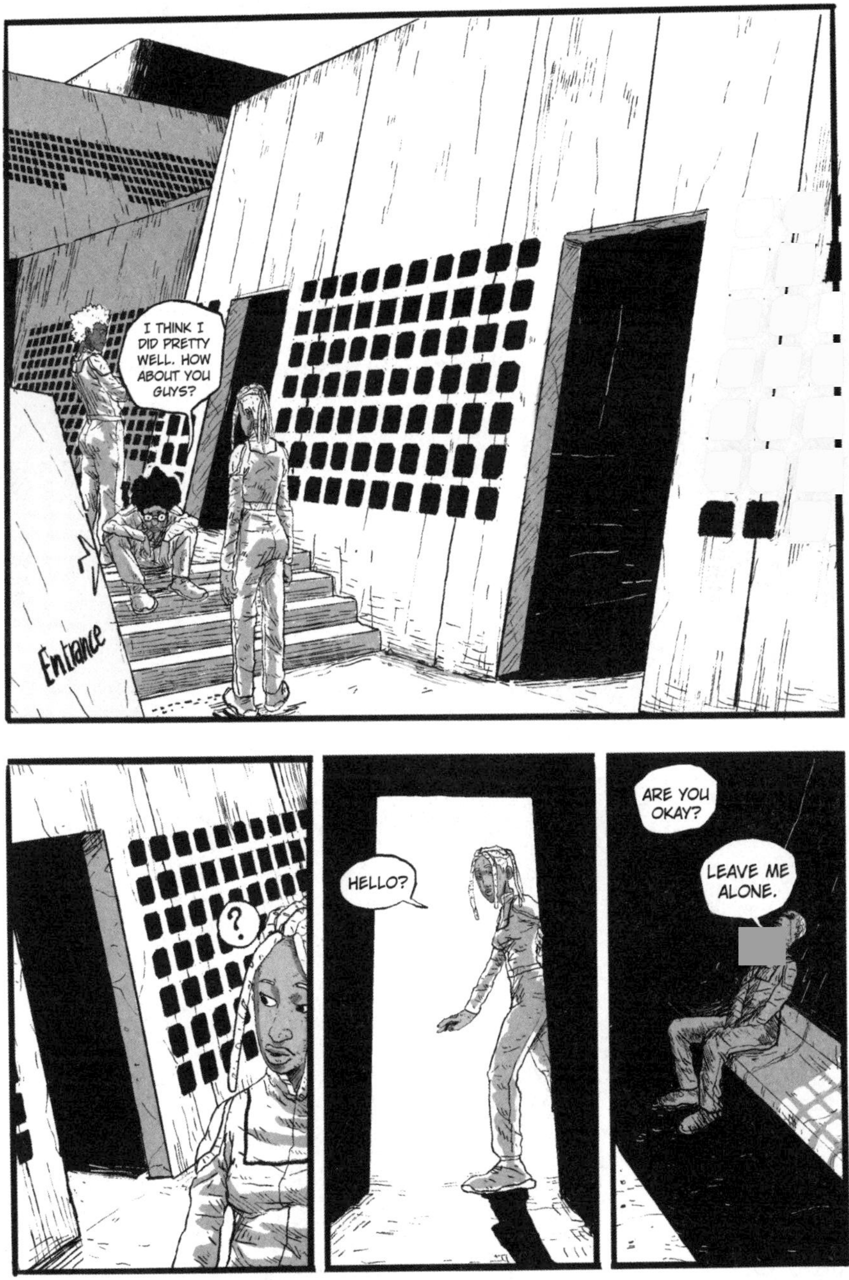
I THINK I DID PRETTY WELL. HOW ABOUT YOU GUYS?
Entrance
?
HELLO?
ARE YOU OKAY?
LEAVE ME ALONE.

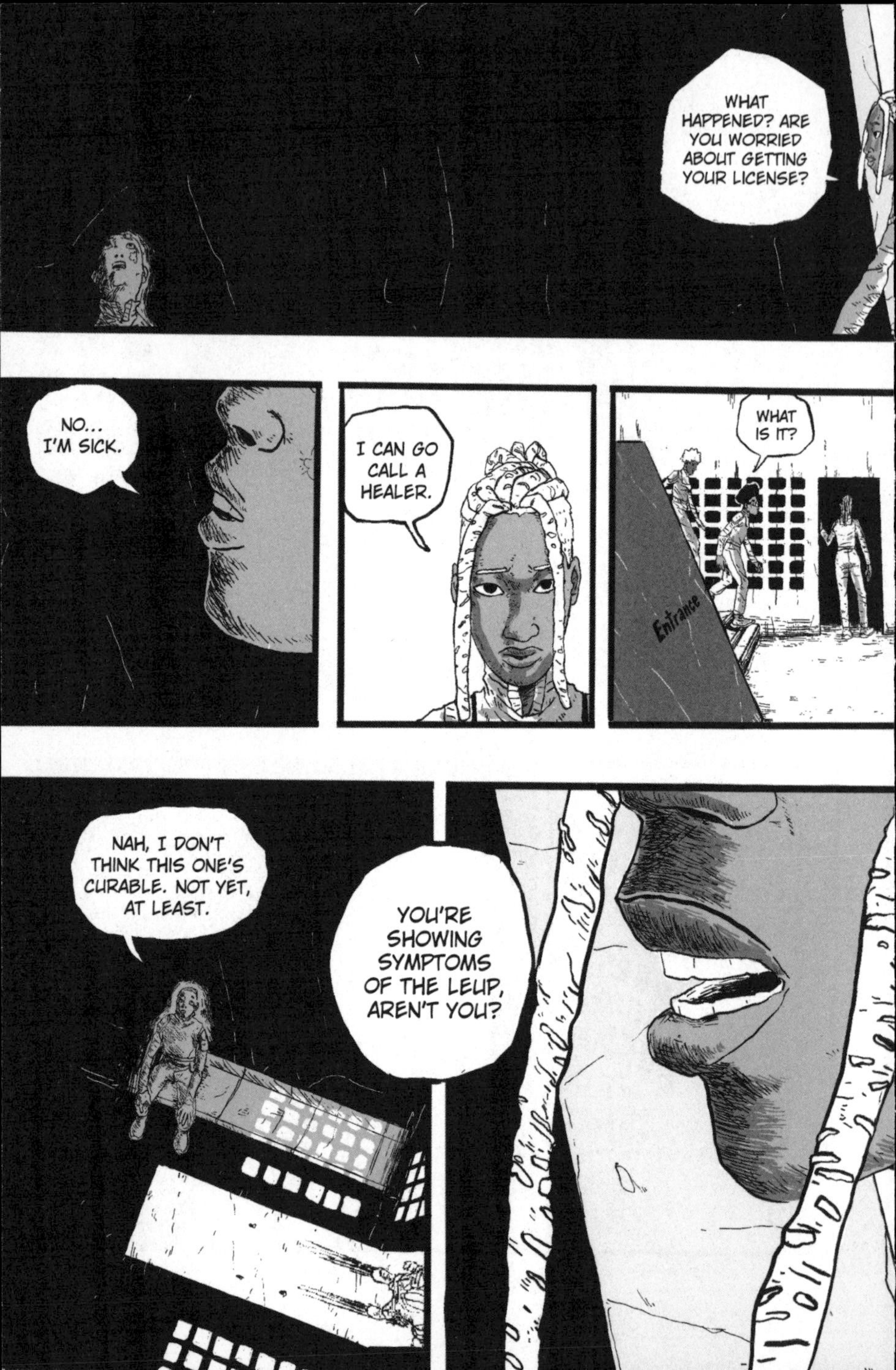
WHAT HAPPENED? ARE YOU WORRIED ABOUT GETTING YOUR LICENSE?
NO... I'M SICK.
I CAN GO CALL A HEALER.
WHAT IS IT?
Entrance
NAH, I DON'T THINK THIS ONE'S CURABLE. NOT YET, AT LEAST.
YOU'RE SHOWING SYMPTOMS OF THE LEUP, AREN'T YOU?

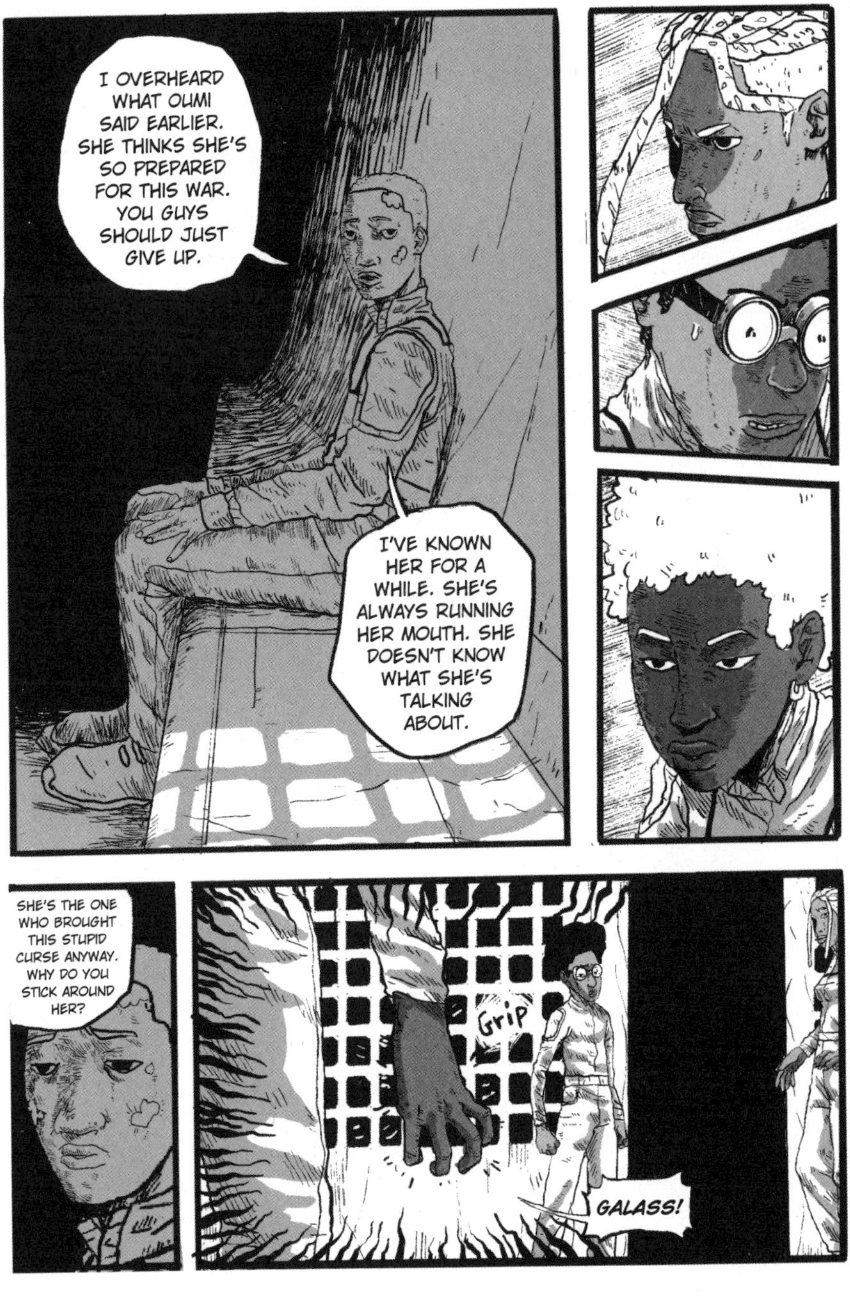
I OVERHEARD WHAT OUMI SAID EARLIER. SHE THINKS SHE'S SO PREPARED FOR THIS WAR. YOU GUYS SHOULD JUST GIVE UP.
I'VE KNOWN HER FOR A WHILE. SHE'S ALWAYS RUNNING HER MOUTH. SHE DOESN'T KNOW WHAT SHE'S TALKING ABOUT.
SHE'S THE ONE WHO BROUGHT THIS STUPID CURSE ANYWAY. WHY DO YOU STICK AROUND HER?
Grip
GALASS!

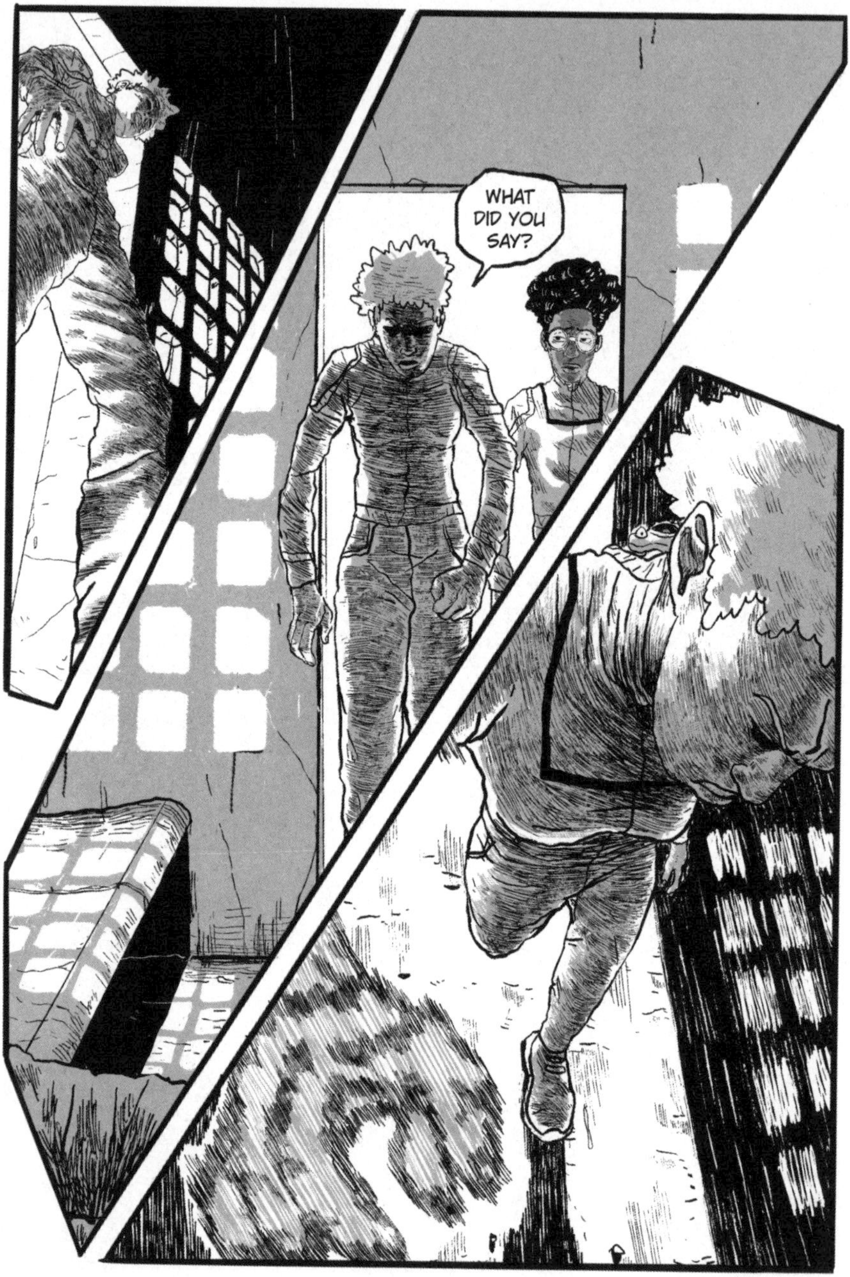
WHAT DID YOU SAY?

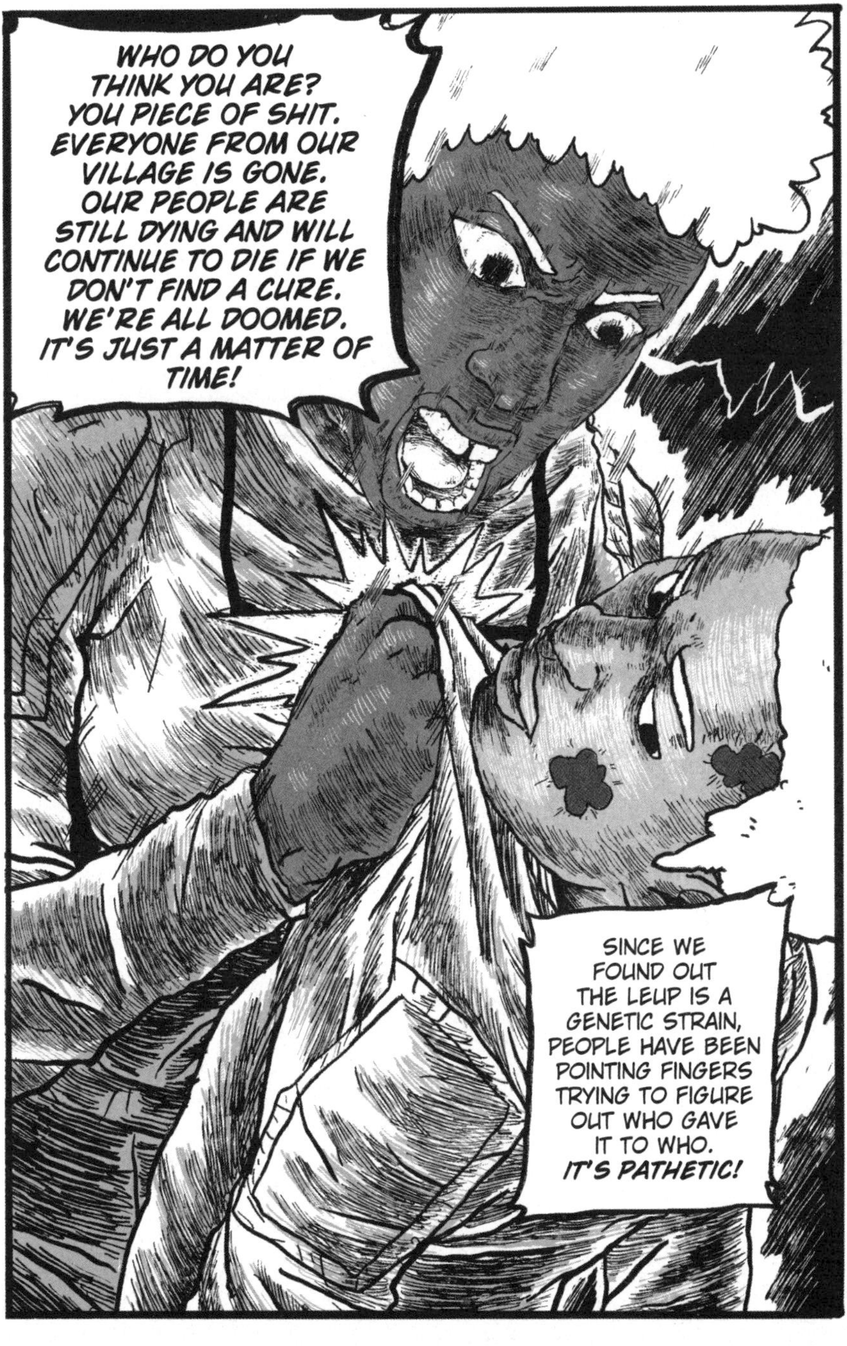
WHO DO YOU THINK YOU ARE? YOU PIECE OF SHIT. EVERYONE FROM OUR VILLAGE IS GONE. OUR PEOPLE ARE STILL DYING AND WILL CONTINUE TO DIE IF WE DON'T FIND A CURE. WE'RE ALL DOOMED. IT'S JUST A MATTER OF TIME!
SINCE WE FOUND OUT THE LEUP IS A GENETIC STRAIN, PEOPLE HAVE BEEN POINTING FINGERS TRYING TO FIGURE OUT WHO GAVE IT TO WHO. IT'S PATHETIC!

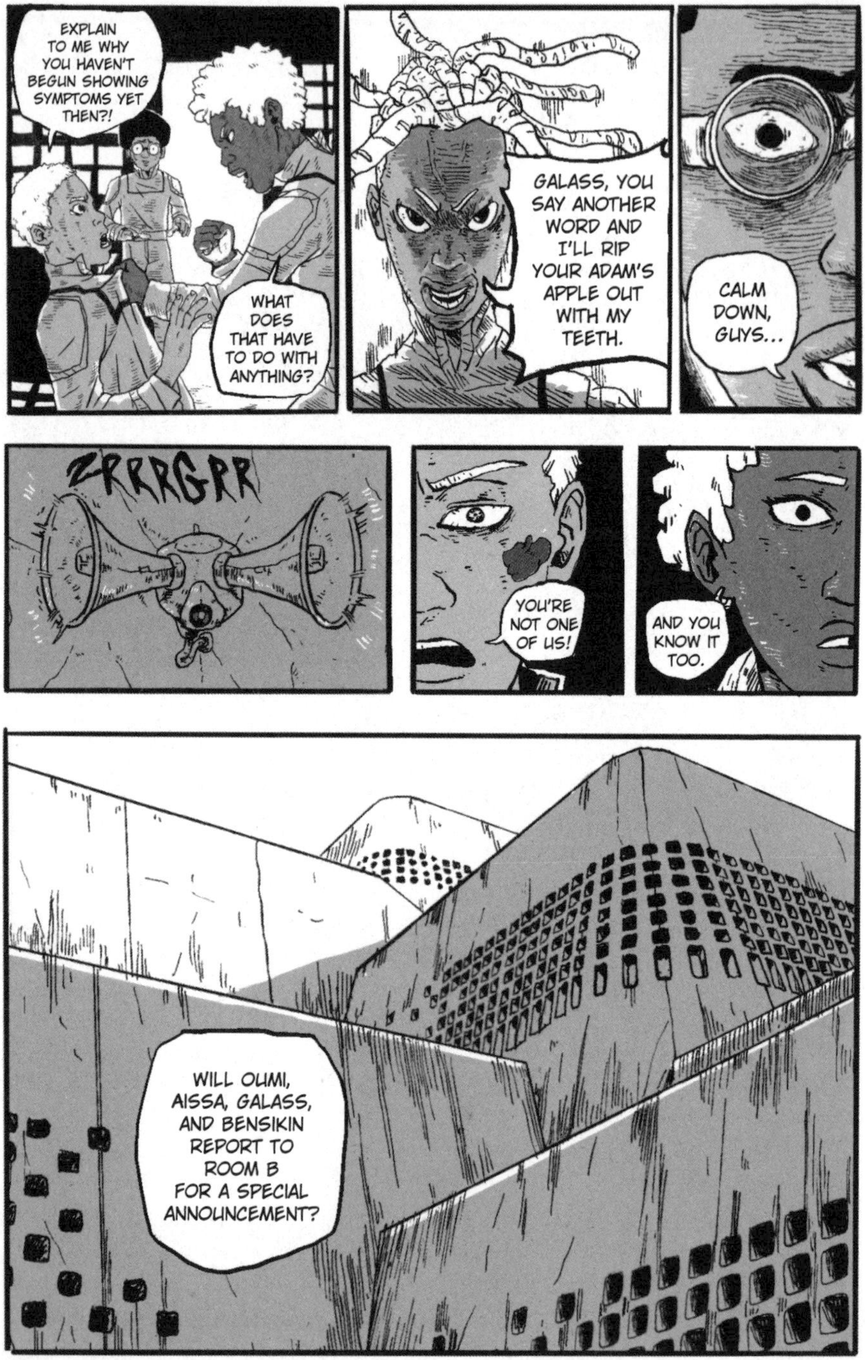
EXPLAIN TO ME WHY YOU HAVEN'T BEGUN SHOWING SYMPTOMS YET THEN?!
WHAT DOES THAT HAVE TO DO WITH ANYTHING?
GALASS, YOU SAY ANOTHER WORD AND I'LL RIP YOUR ADAM'S APPLE OUT WITH MY TEETH.
CALM DOWN, GUYS...
ZRRRGRR
YOU'RE NOT ONE OF US!
AND YOU KNOW IT TOO.
WILL OUMI, AISSA, GALASS, AND BENSIKIN REPORT TO ROOM B FOR A SPECIAL ANNOUNCEMENT?

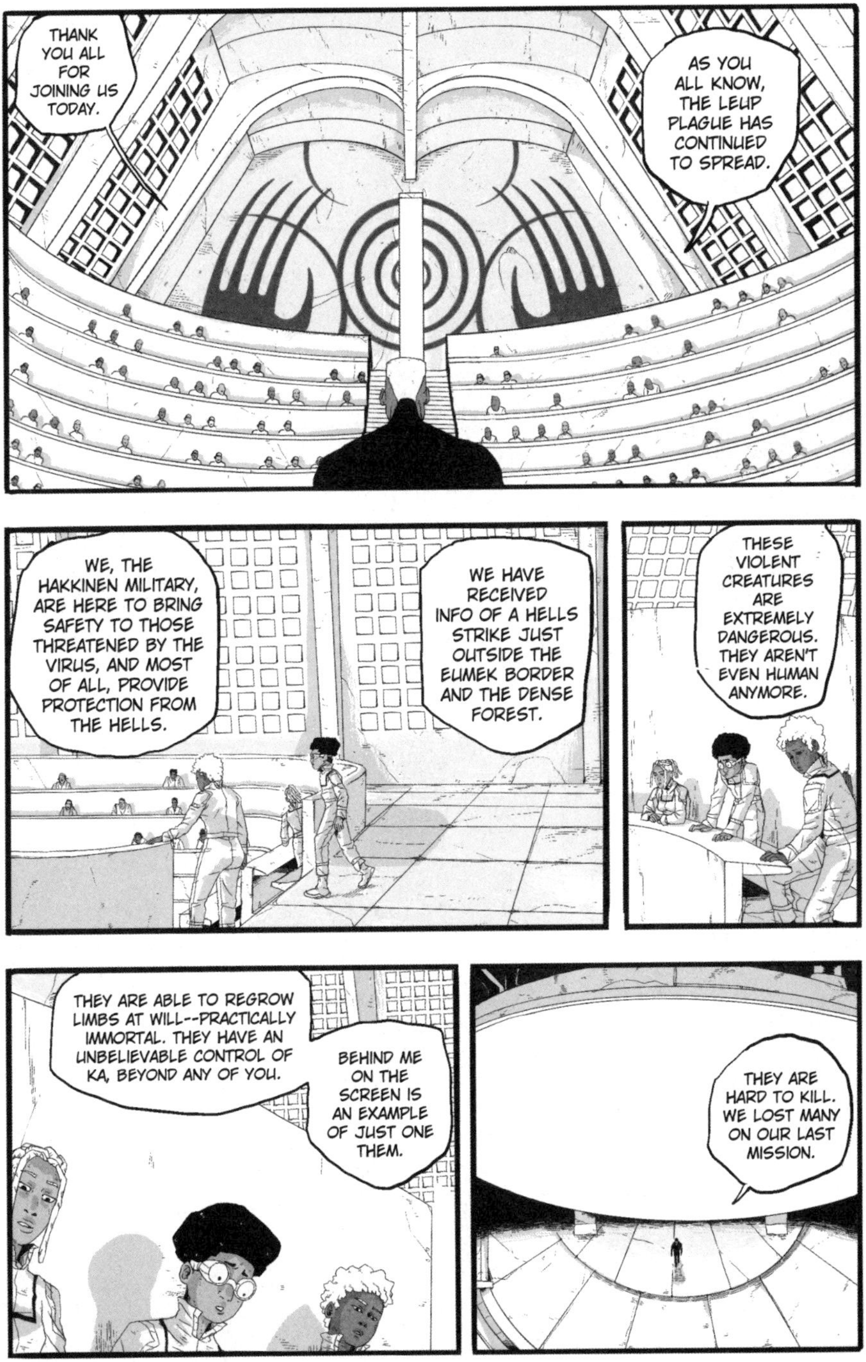

THANK YOU ALL FOR JOINING US TODAY.
AS YOU ALL KNOW, THE LEUP PLAGUE HAS CONTINUED TO SPREAD.
WE, THE HAKKINEN MILITARY, ARE HERE TO BRING SAFETY TO THOSE THREATENED BY THE VIRUS, AND MOST OF ALL, PROVIDE PROTECTION FROM THE HELLS.
WE HAVE RECEIVED INFO OF A HELLS STRIKE JUST OUTSIDE THE EUMEK BORDER AND THE DENSE FOREST.
THESE VIOLENT CREATURES ARE EXTREMELY DANGEROUS. THEY AREN'T EVEN HUMAN ANYMORE.
THEY ARE ABLE TO REGROW LIMBS AT WILL--PRACTICALLY IMMORTAL. THEY HAVE AN UNBELIEVABLE CONTROL OF KA, BEYOND ANY OF YOU.
BEHIND ME ON THE SCREEN IS AN EXAMPLE OF JUST ONE THEM.
THEY ARE HARD TO KILL. WE LOST MANY ON OUR LAST MISSION.

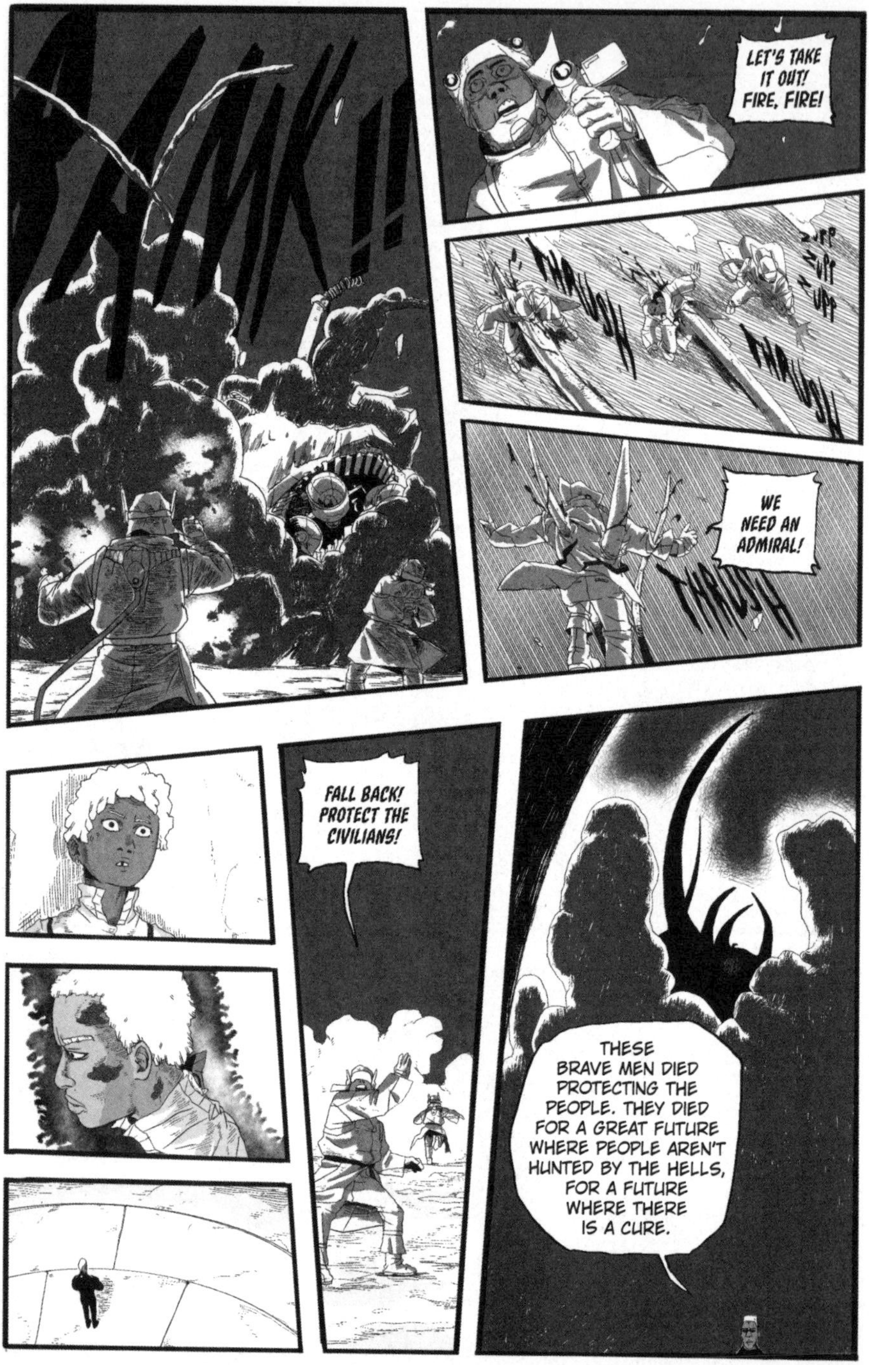
BANK!!
LET'S TAKE IT OUT! FIRE, FIRE!
THRUSH
ZUPP ZUPP ZUPP
THRUSH
WE NEED AN ADMIRAL!
THRUSH
FALL BACK! PROTECT THE CIVILIANS!
THESE BRAVE MEN DIED PROTECTING THE PEOPLE. THEY DIED FOR A GREAT FUTURE WHERE PEOPLE AREN'T HUNTED BY THE HELLS, FOR A FUTURE WHERE THERE IS A CURE.

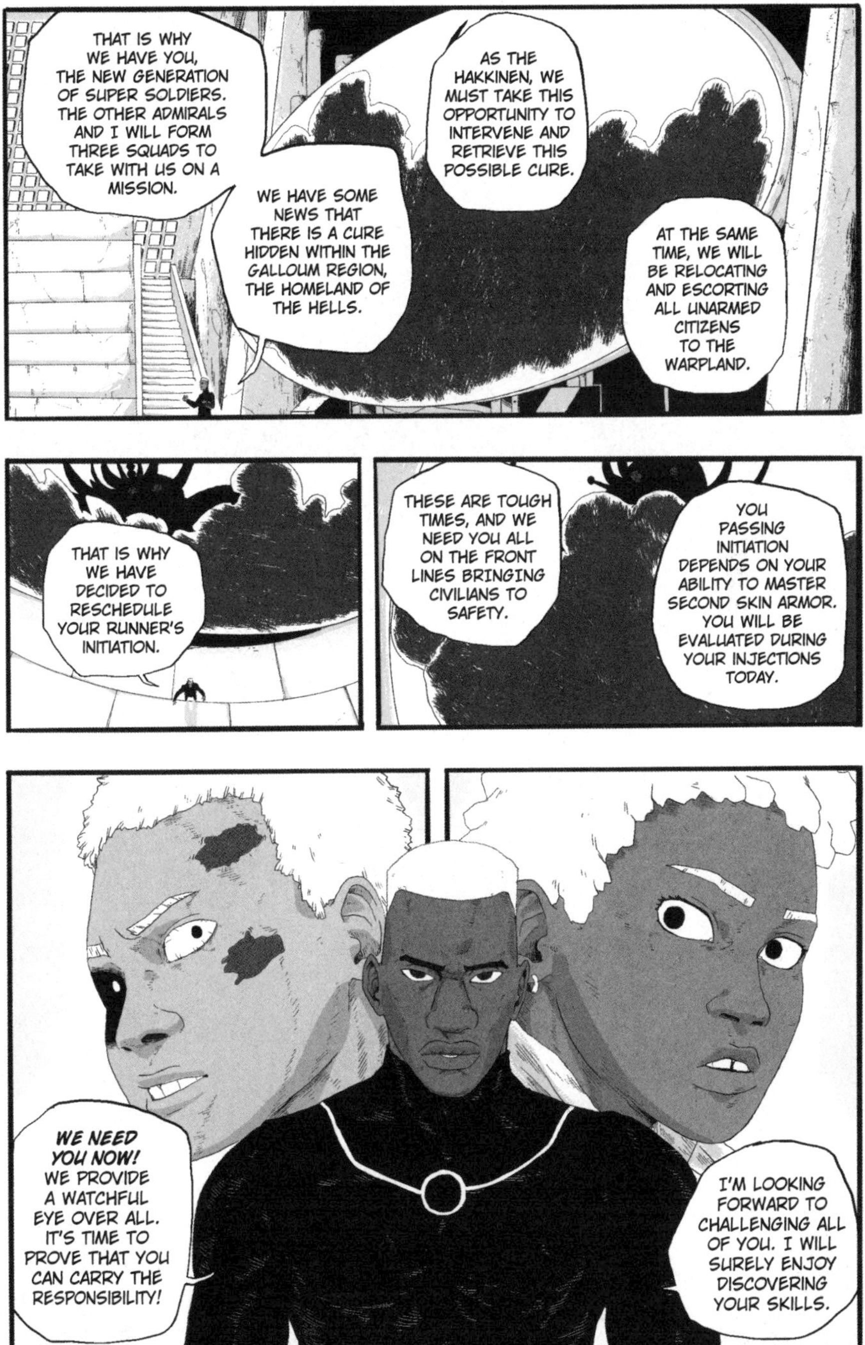
THAT IS WHY WE HAVE YOU, THE NEW GENERATION OF SUPER SOLDIERS. THE OTHER ADMIRALS AND I WILL FORM THREE SQUADS TO TAKE WITH US ON A MISSION.
WE HAVE SOME NEWS THAT THERE IS A CURE HIDDEN WITHIN THE GALLOUM REGION, THE HOMELAND OF THE HELLS.
AS THE HAKKINEN, WE MUST TAKE THIS OPPORTUNITY TO INTERVENE AND RETRIEVE THIS POSSIBLE CURE.
AT THE SAME TIME, WE WILL BE RELOCATING AND ESCORTING ALL UNARMED CITIZENS TO THE WARPLAND.
THAT IS WHY WE HAVE DECIDED TO RESCHEDULE YOUR RUNNER'S INITIATION.
THESE ARE TOUGH TIMES, AND WE NEED YOU ALL ON THE FRONT LINES BRINGING CIVILIANS TO SAFETY.
YOU PASSING INITIATION DEPENDS ON YOUR ABILITY TO MASTER SECOND SKIN ARMOR. YOU WILL BE EVALUATED DURING YOUR INJECTIONS TODAY.
WE NEED YOU NOW! WE PROVIDE A WATCHFUL EYE OVER ALL. IT'S TIME TO PROVE THAT YOU CAN CARRY THE RESPONSIBILITY!
I'M LOOKING FORWARD TO CHALLENGING ALL OF YOU. I WILL SURELY ENJOY DISCOVERING YOUR SKILLS.

OBLIVION ROUGE

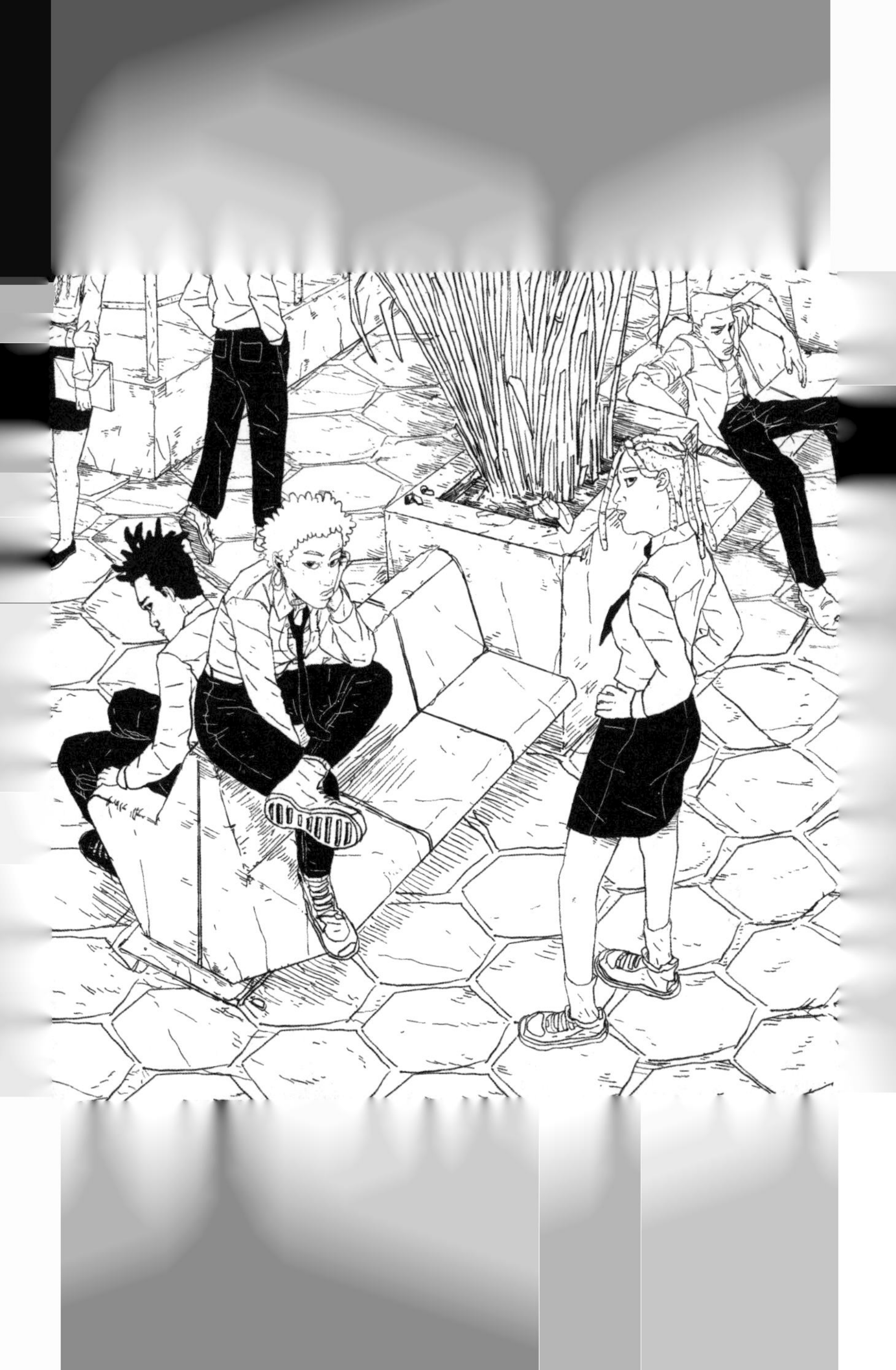

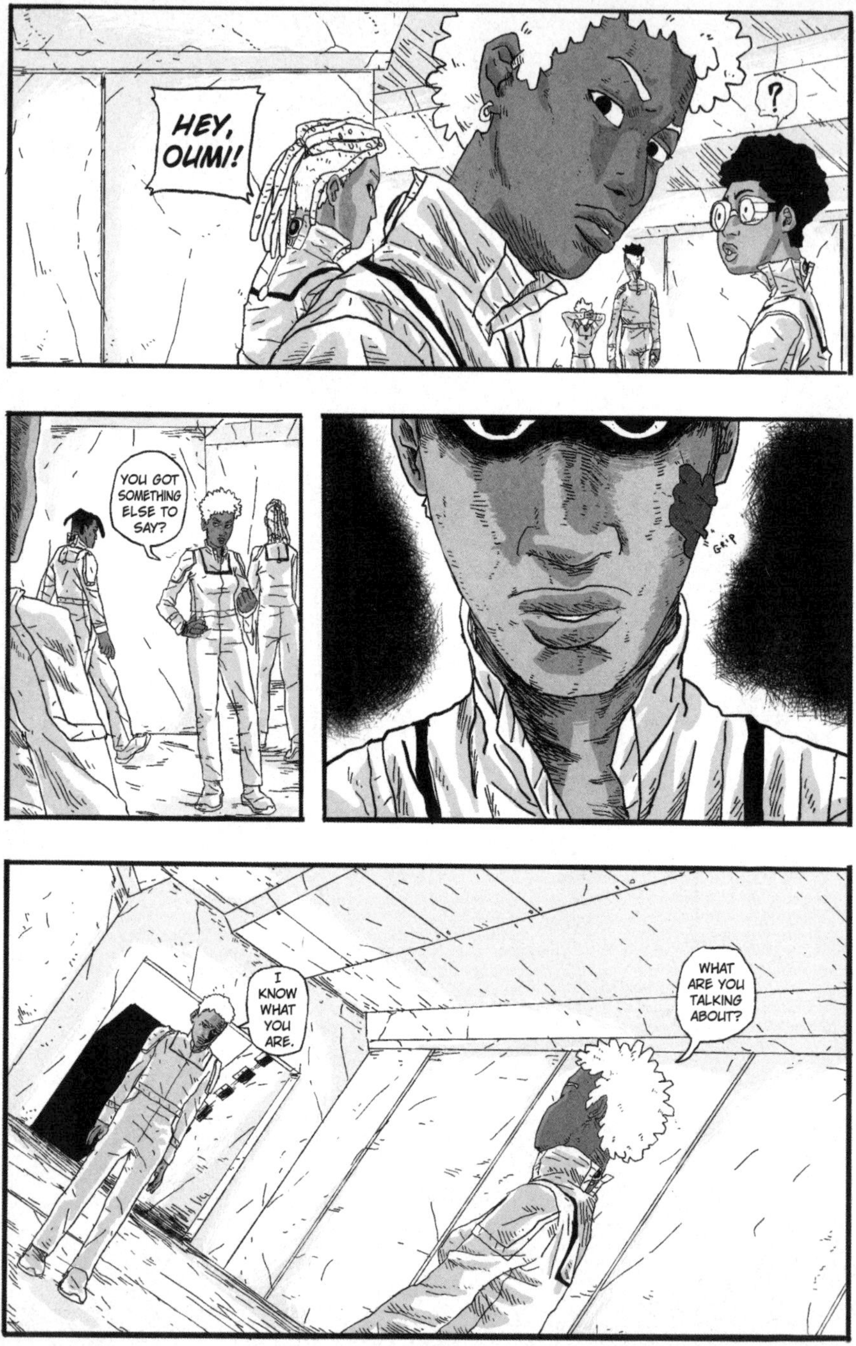
HEY, OUMI!
?
YOU GOT SOMETHING ELSE TO SAY?
GRIP
I KNOW WHAT YOU ARE.
WHAT ARE YOU TALKING ABOUT?

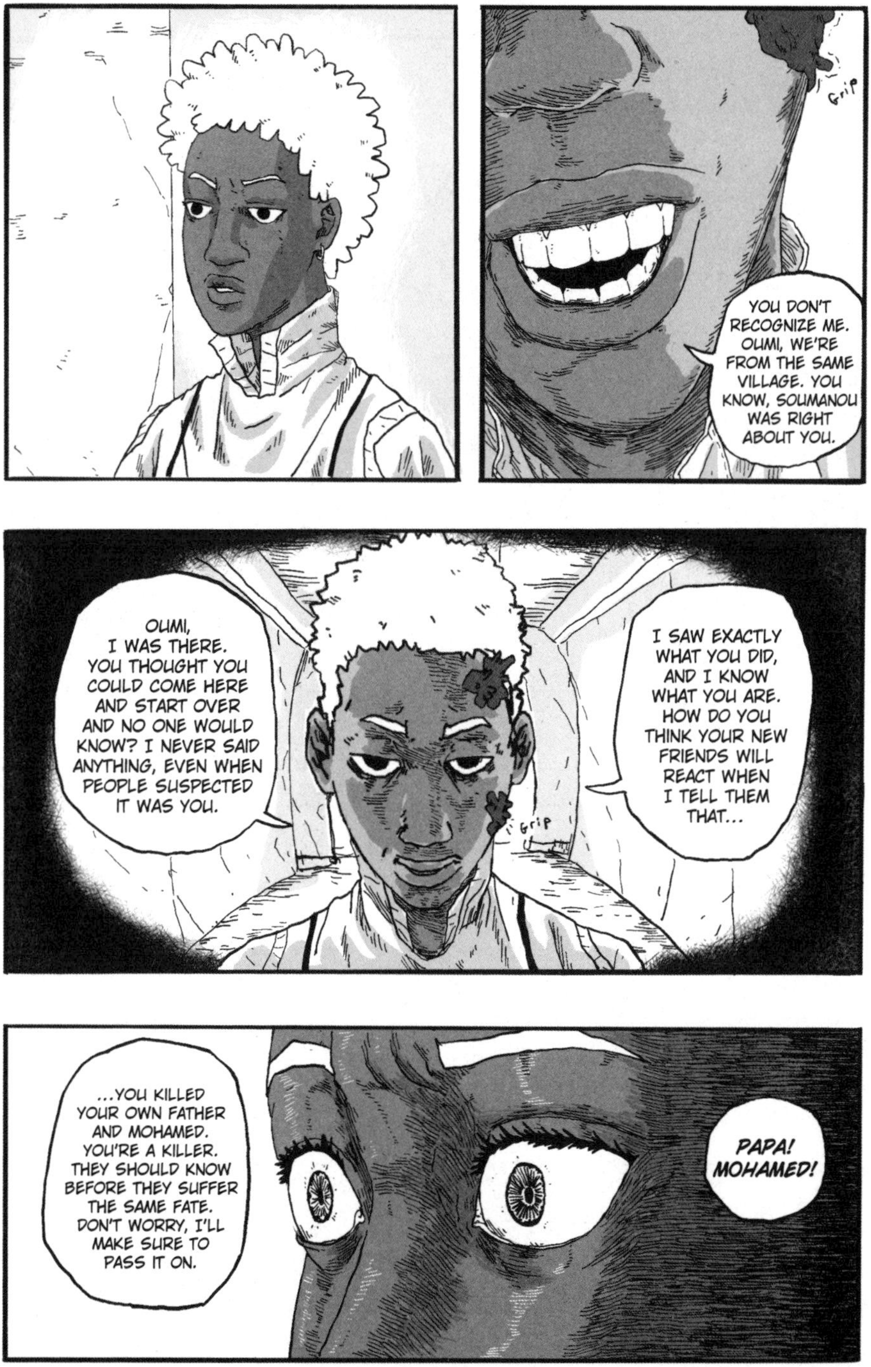
Grip
YOU DON'T RECOGNIZE ME. OUMI, WE'RE FROM THE SAME VILLAGE. YOU KNOW, SOUMANOU WAS RIGHT ABOUT YOU.
OUMI, I WAS THERE. YOU THOUGHT YOU COULD COME HERE AND START OVER AND NO ONE WOULD KNOW? I NEVER SAID ANYTHING, EVEN WHEN PEOPLE SUSPECTED IT WAS YOU.
Grip
I SAW EXACTLY WHAT YOU DID, AND I KNOW WHAT YOU ARE. HOW DO YOU THINK YOUR NEW FRIENDS WILL REACT WHEN I TELL THEM THAT...
...YOU KILLED YOUR OWN FATHER AND MOHAMED. YOU'RE A KILLER. THEY SHOULD KNOW BEFORE THEY SUFFER THE SAME FATE. DON'T WORRY, I'LL MAKE SURE TO PASS IT ON.
PAPA! MOHAMED!

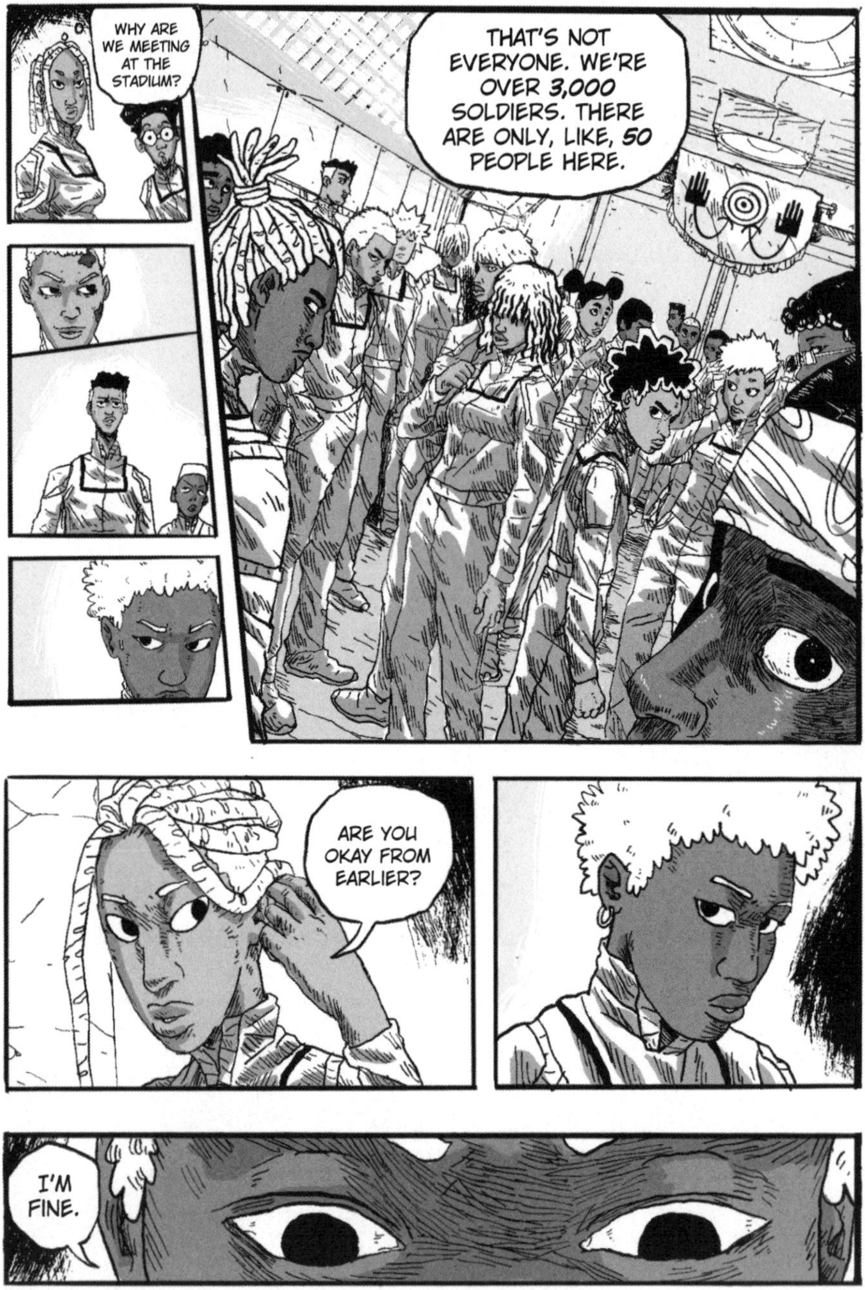

WHY ARE WE MEETING AT THE STADIUM?
THAT'S NOT EVERYONE. WE'RE OVER 3,000 SOLDIERS. THERE ARE ONLY, LIKE, 50 PEOPLE HERE.
ARE YOU OKAY FROM EARLIER?
I'M FINE.

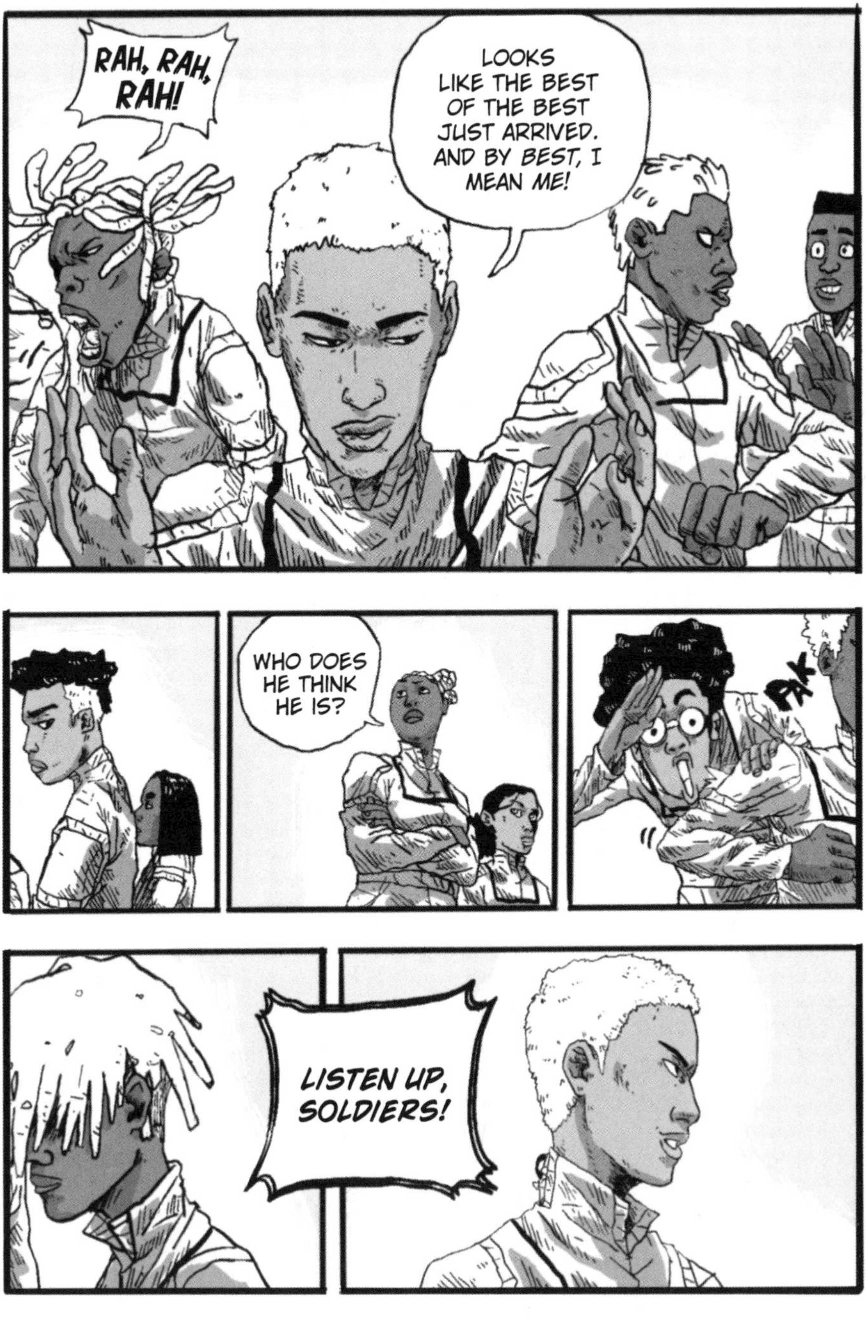
RAH, RAH, RAH!
LOOKS LIKE THE BEST OF THE BEST JUST ARRIVED. AND BY BEST, I MEAN ME!
WHO DOES HE THINK HE IS?
PAK
LISTEN UP, SOLDIERS!

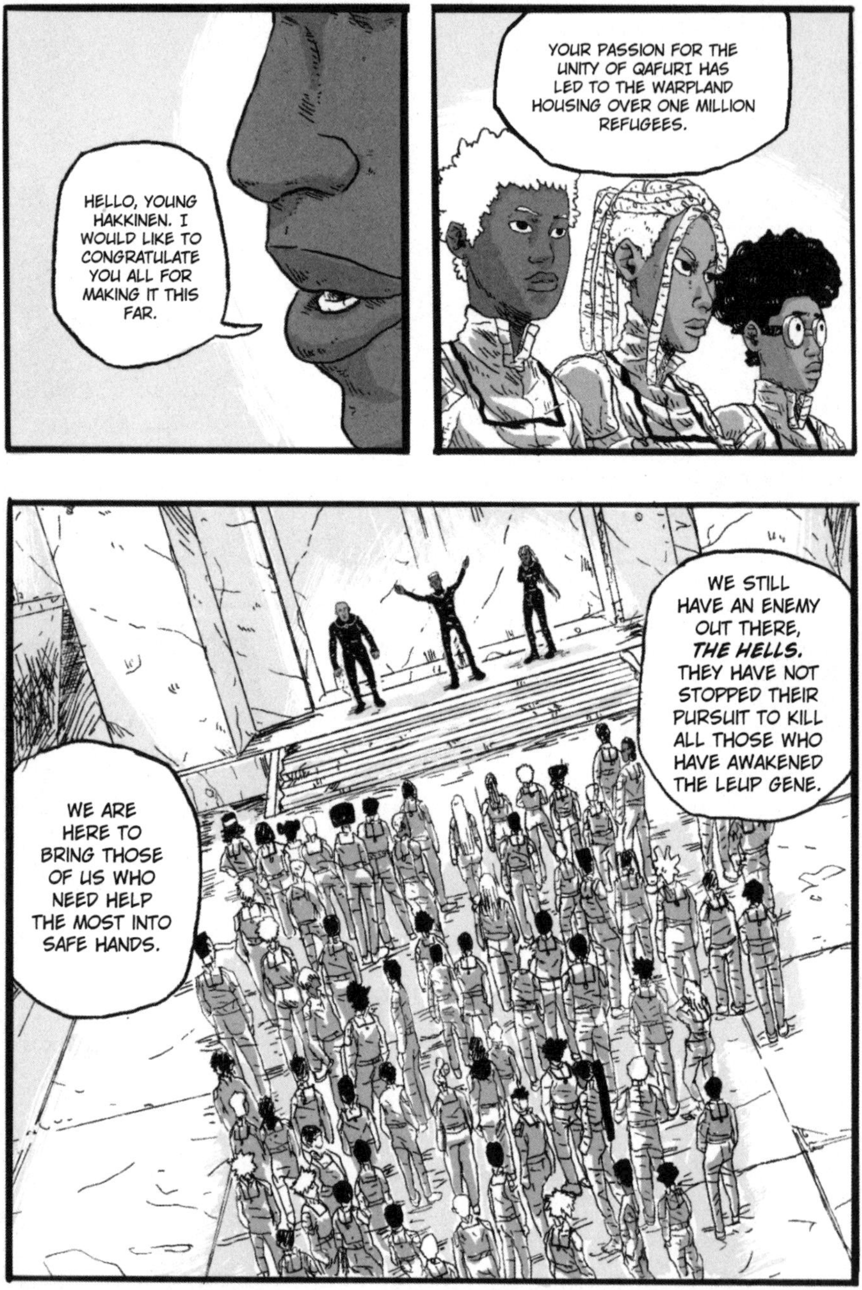
HELLO, YOUNG HAKKINEN. I WOULD LIKE TO CONGRATULATE YOU ALL FOR MAKING IT THIS FAR.
YOUR PASSION FOR THE UNITY OF QAFURI HAS LED TO THE WARPLAND HOUSING OVER ONE MILLION REFUGEES.
WE STILL HAVE AN ENEMY OUT THERE, ***THE HELLS.*** THEY HAVE NOT STOPPED THEIR PURSUIT TO KILL ALL THOSE WHO HAVE AWAKENED THE LEUP GENE.
WE ARE HERE TO BRING THOSE OF US WHO NEED HELP THE MOST INTO SAFE HANDS.

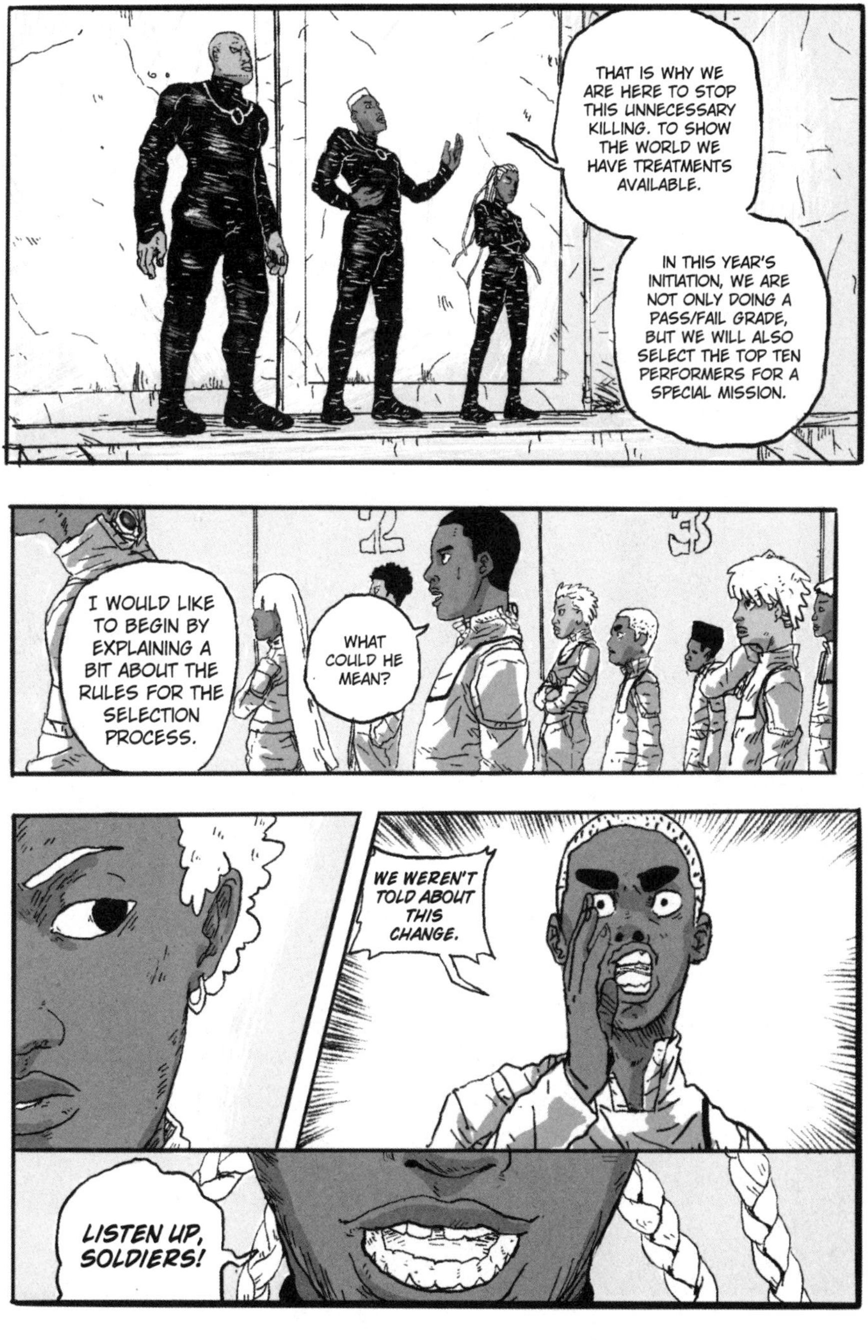
THAT IS WHY WE ARE HERE TO STOP THIS UNNECESSARY KILLING. TO SHOW THE WORLD WE HAVE TREATMENTS AVAILABLE.
IN THIS YEAR'S INITIATION, WE ARE NOT ONLY DOING A PASS/FAIL GRADE, BUT WE WILL ALSO SELECT THE TOP TEN PERFORMERS FOR A SPECIAL MISSION.
I WOULD LIKE TO BEGIN BY EXPLAINING A BIT ABOUT THE RULES FOR THE SELECTION PROCESS.
WHAT COULD HE MEAN?
WE WEREN'T TOLD ABOUT THIS CHANGE.
LISTEN UP, SOLDIERS!

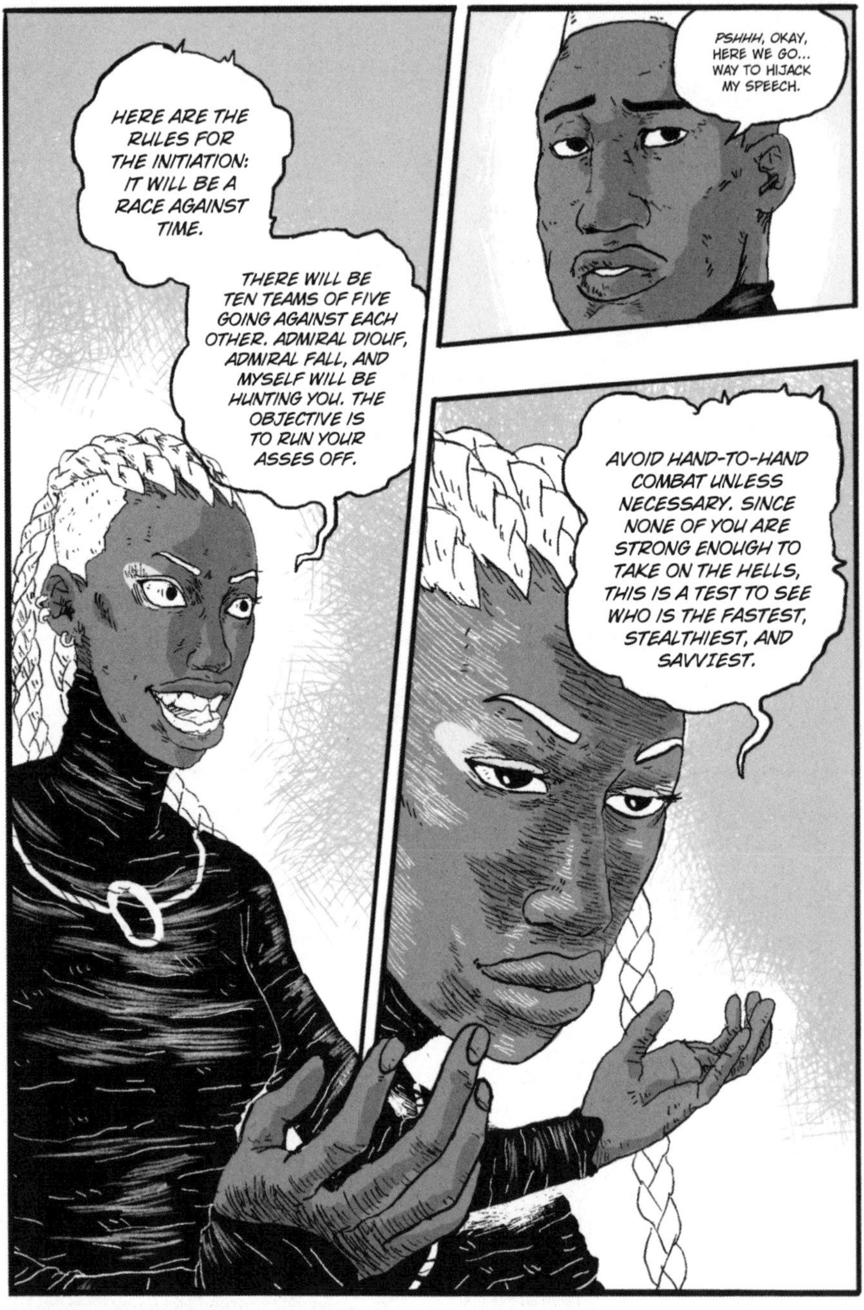
HERE ARE THE RULES FOR THE INITIATION: IT WILL BE A RACE AGAINST TIME.
THERE WILL BE TEN TEAMS OF FIVE GOING AGAINST EACH OTHER. ADMIRAL DIOUF, ADMIRAL FALL, AND MYSELF WILL BE HUNTING YOU. THE OBJECTIVE IS TO RUN YOUR ASSES OFF.
PSHHH, OKAY, HERE WE GO... WAY TO HIJACK MY SPEECH.
AVOID HAND-TO-HAND COMBAT UNLESS NECESSARY. SINCE NONE OF YOU ARE STRONG ENOUGH TO TAKE ON THE HELLS, THIS IS A TEST TO SEE WHO IS THE FASTEST, STEALTHIEST, AND SAVVIEST.

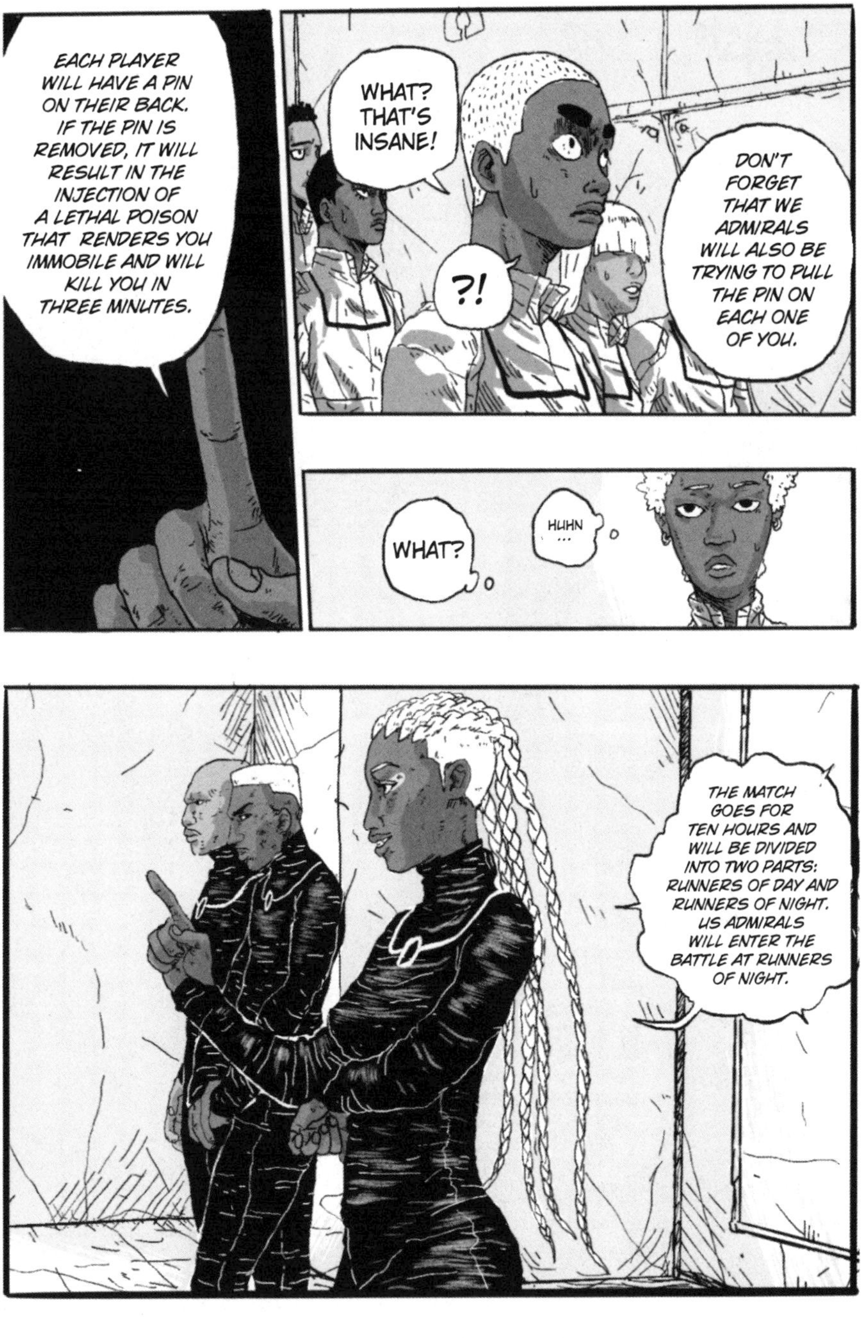
EACH PLAYER WILL HAVE A PIN ON THEIR BACK. IF THE PIN IS REMOVED, IT WILL RESULT IN THE INJECTION OF A LETHAL POISON THAT RENDERS YOU IMMOBILE AND WILL KILL YOU IN THREE MINUTES.
WHAT? THAT'S INSANE!
?!
DON'T FORGET THAT WE ADMIRALS WILL ALSO BE TRYING TO PULL THE PIN ON EACH ONE OF YOU.
WHAT?
HUHN ...
THE MATCH GOES FOR TEN HOURS AND WILL BE DIVIDED INTO TWO PARTS: RUNNERS OF DAY AND RUNNERS OF NIGHT. US ADMIRALS WILL ENTER THE BATTLE AT RUNNERS OF NIGHT.

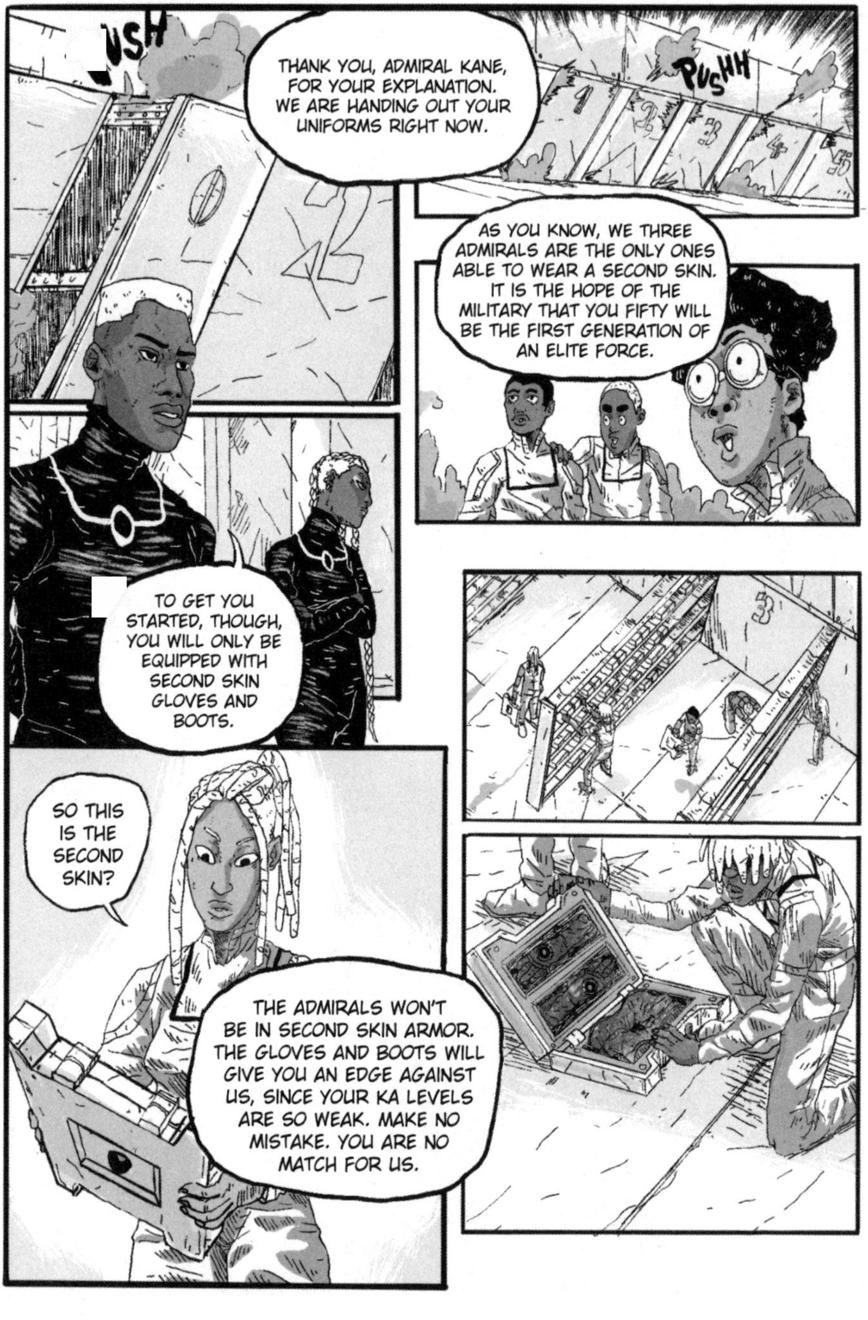
THANK YOU, ADMIRAL KANE, FOR YOUR EXPLANATION. WE ARE HANDING OUT YOUR UNIFORMS RIGHT NOW.
PUSHH
AS YOU KNOW, WE THREE ADMIRALS ARE THE ONLY ONES ABLE TO WEAR A SECOND SKIN. IT IS THE HOPE OF THE MILITARY THAT YOU FIFTY WILL BE THE FIRST GENERATION OF AN ELITE FORCE.
TO GET YOU STARTED, THOUGH, YOU WILL ONLY BE EQUIPPED WITH SECOND SKIN GLOVES AND BOOTS.
SO THIS IS THE SECOND SKIN?
THE ADMIRALS WON'T BE IN SECOND SKIN ARMOR. THE GLOVES AND BOOTS WILL GIVE YOU AN EDGE AGAINST US, SINCE YOUR KA LEVELS ARE SO WEAK. MAKE NO MISTAKE. YOU ARE NO MATCH FOR US.

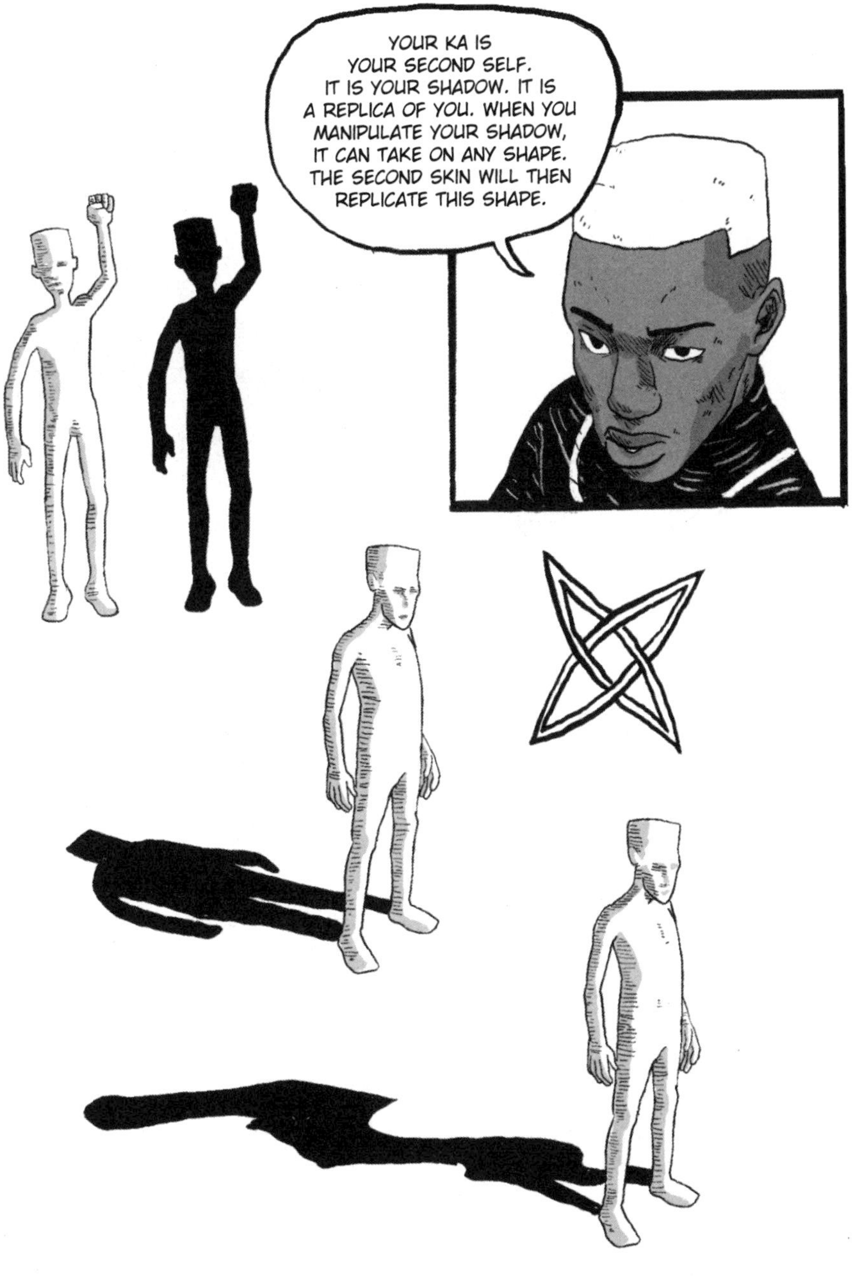
YOUR KA IS YOUR SECOND SELF. IT IS YOUR SHADOW. IT IS A REPLICA OF YOU. WHEN YOU MANIPULATE YOUR SHADOW, IT CAN TAKE ON ANY SHAPE. THE SECOND SKIN WILL THEN REPLICATE THIS SHAPE.

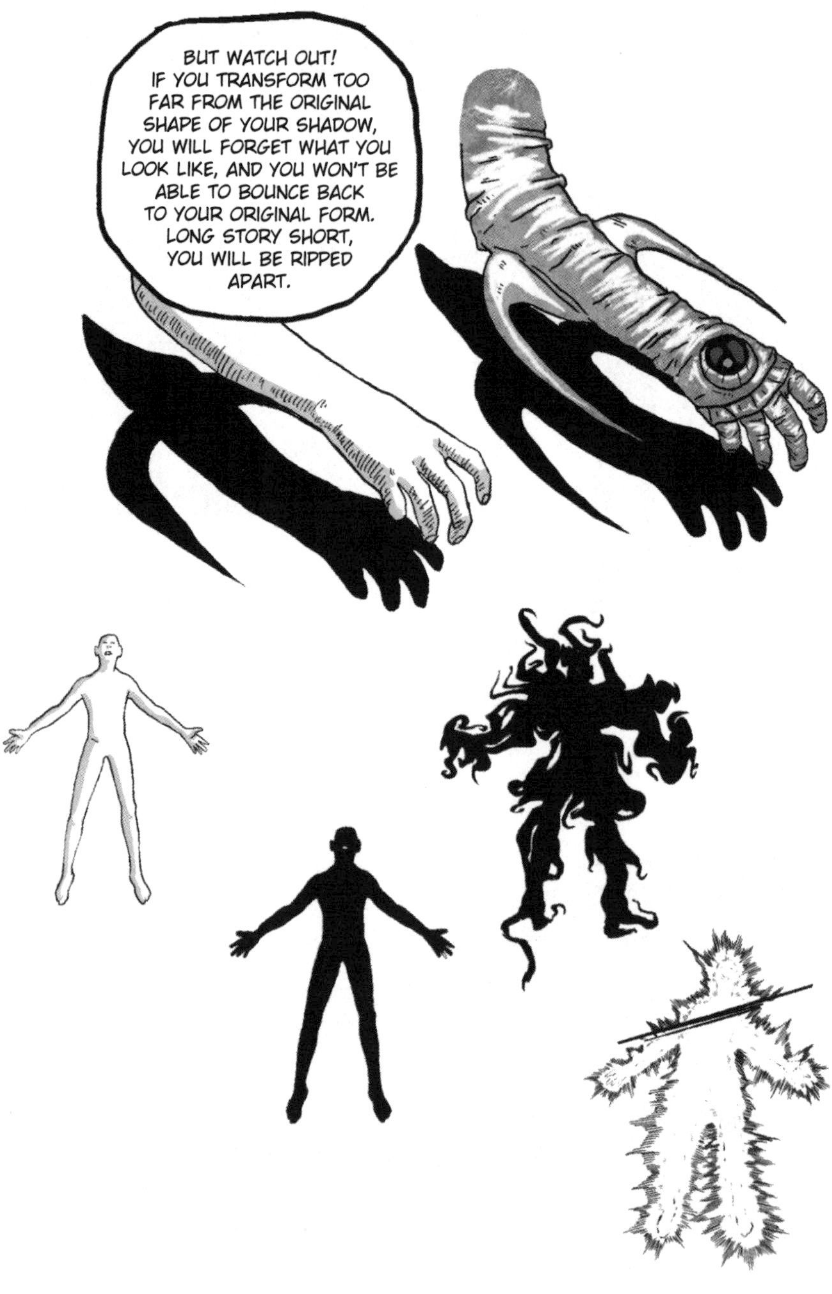
BUT WATCH OUT! IF YOU TRANSFORM TOO FAR FROM THE ORIGINAL SHAPE OF YOUR SHADOW, YOU WILL FORGET WHAT YOU LOOK LIKE, AND YOU WON'T BE ABLE TO BOUNCE BACK TO YOUR ORIGINAL FORM. LONG STORY SHORT, YOU WILL BE RIPPED APART.

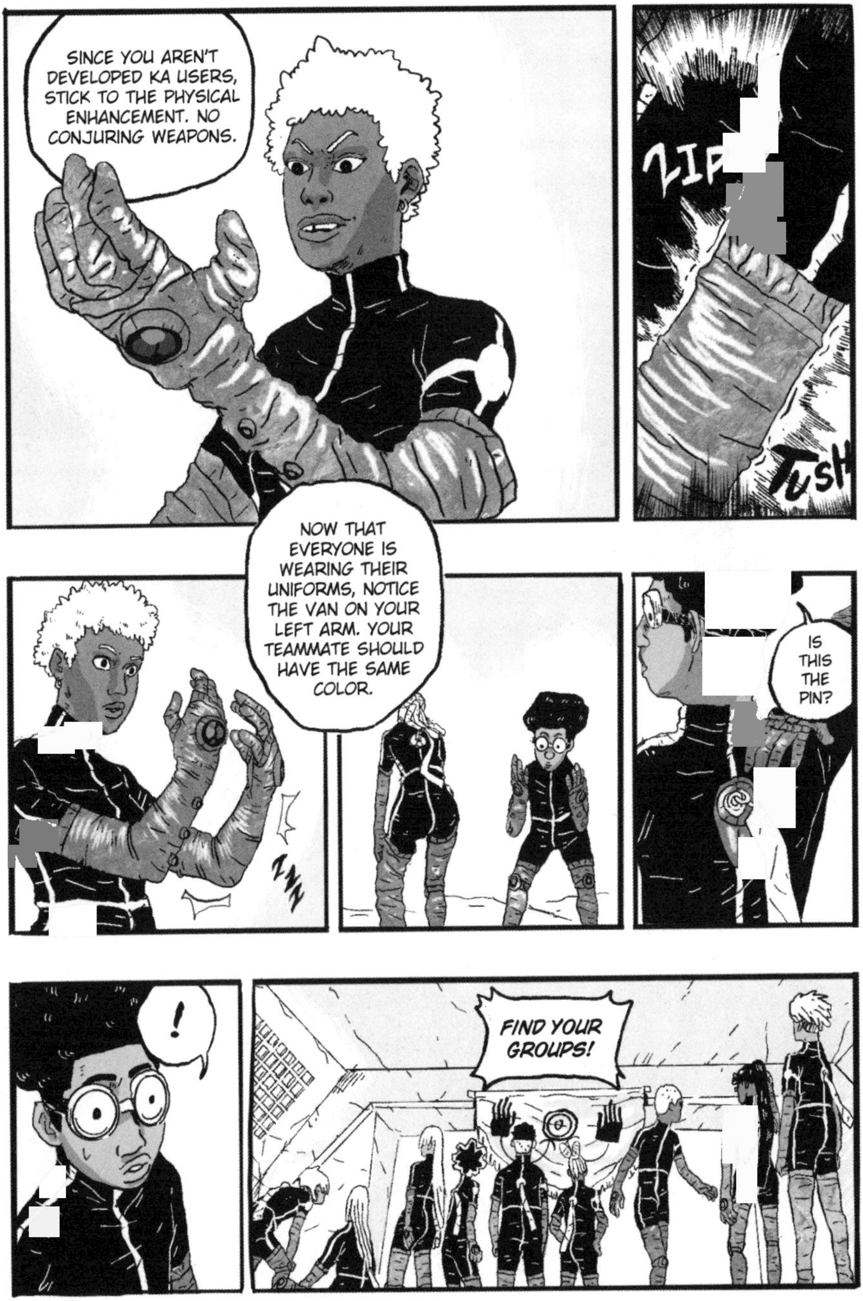
SINCE YOU AREN'T DEVELOPED KA USERS, STICK TO THE PHYSICAL ENHANCEMENT. NO CONJURING WEAPONS.
TUSH
NOW THAT EVERYONE IS WEARING THEIR UNIFORMS, NOTICE THE VAN ON YOUR LEFT ARM. YOUR TEAMMATE SHOULD HAVE THE SAME COLOR.
IS THIS THE PIN?
!
FIND YOUR GROUPS!

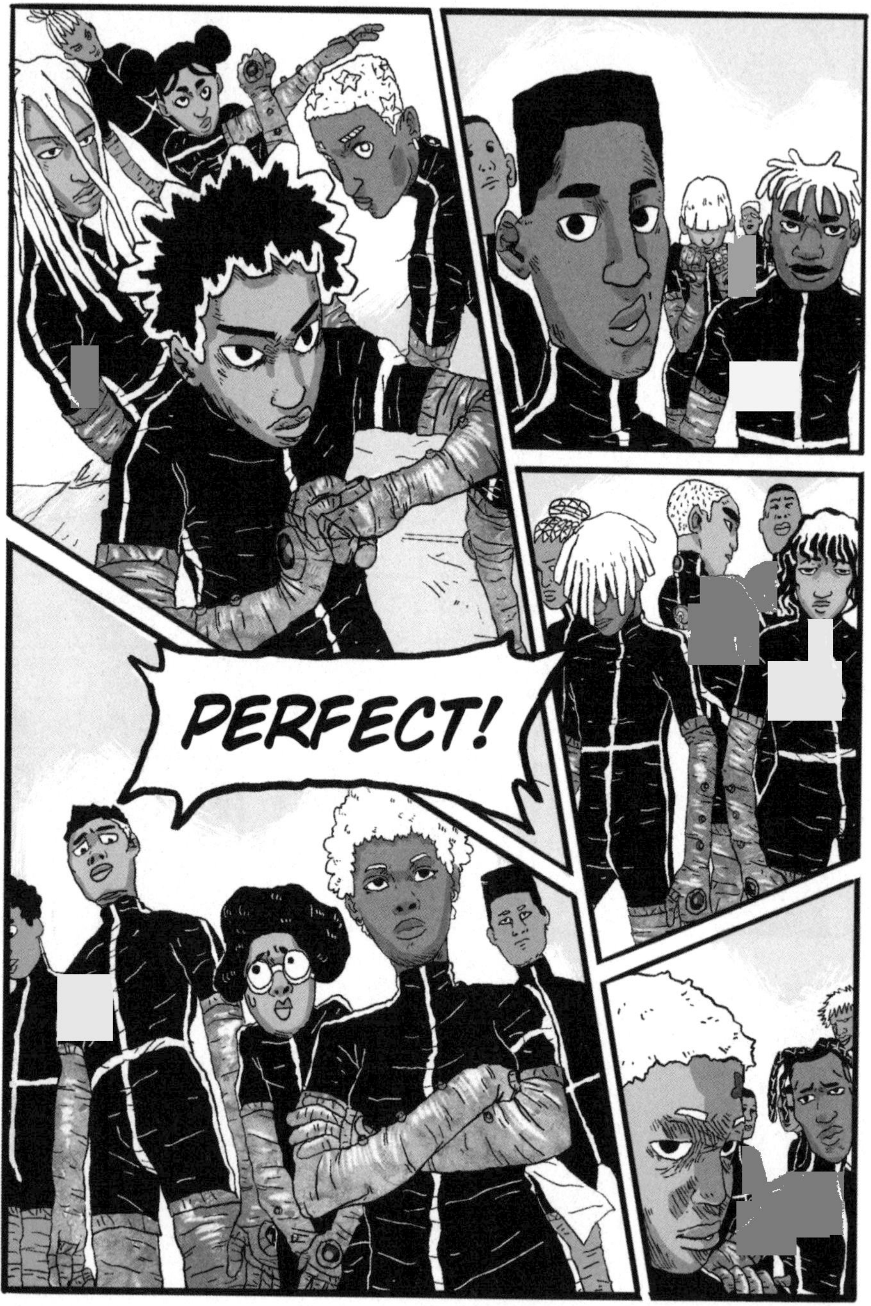
PERFECT!

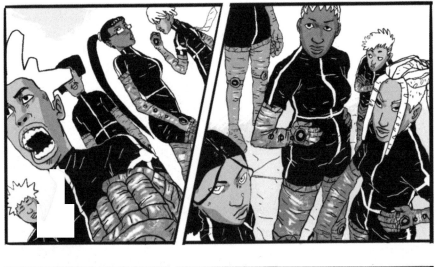

THE EXAMS WILL BEGIN...

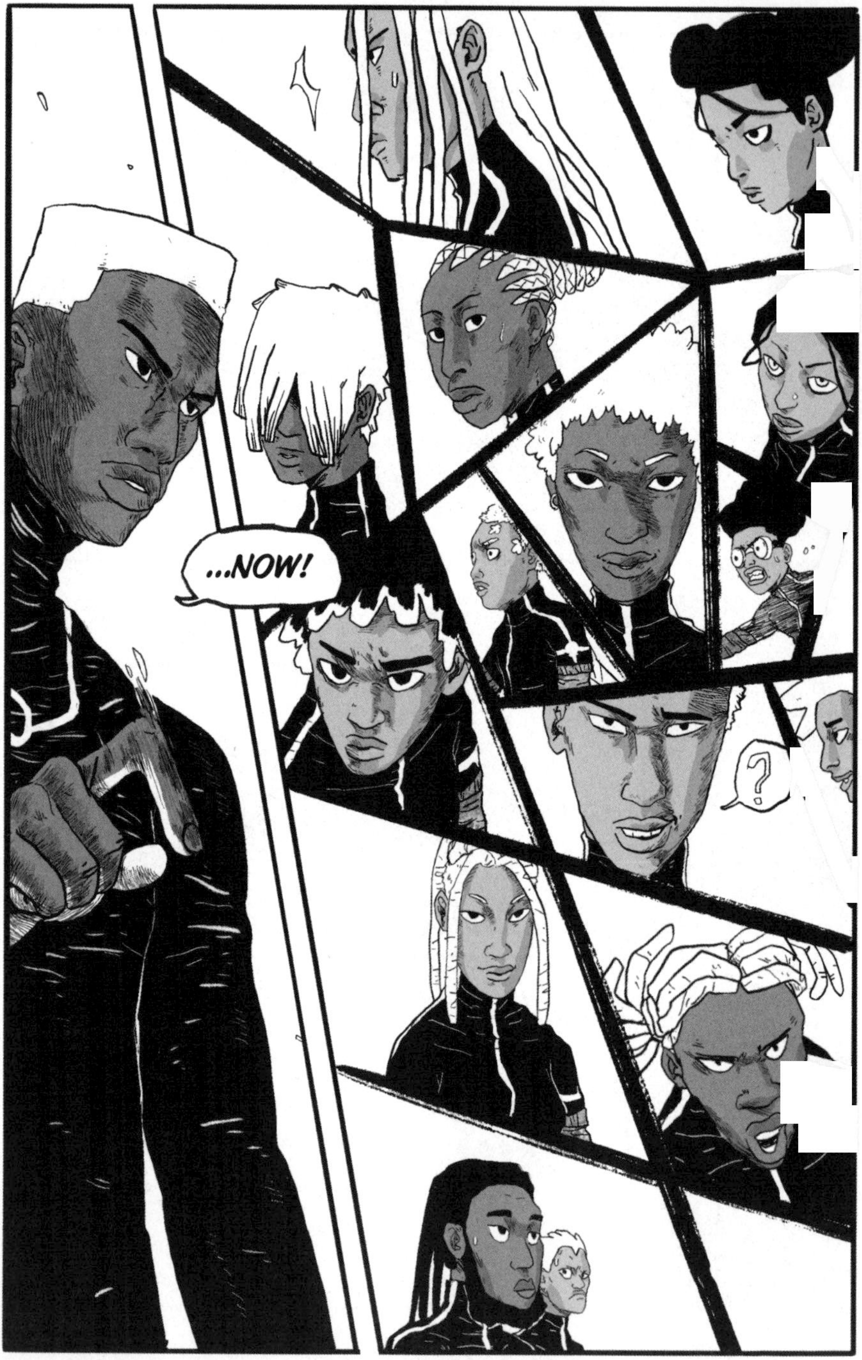
...NOW!
?

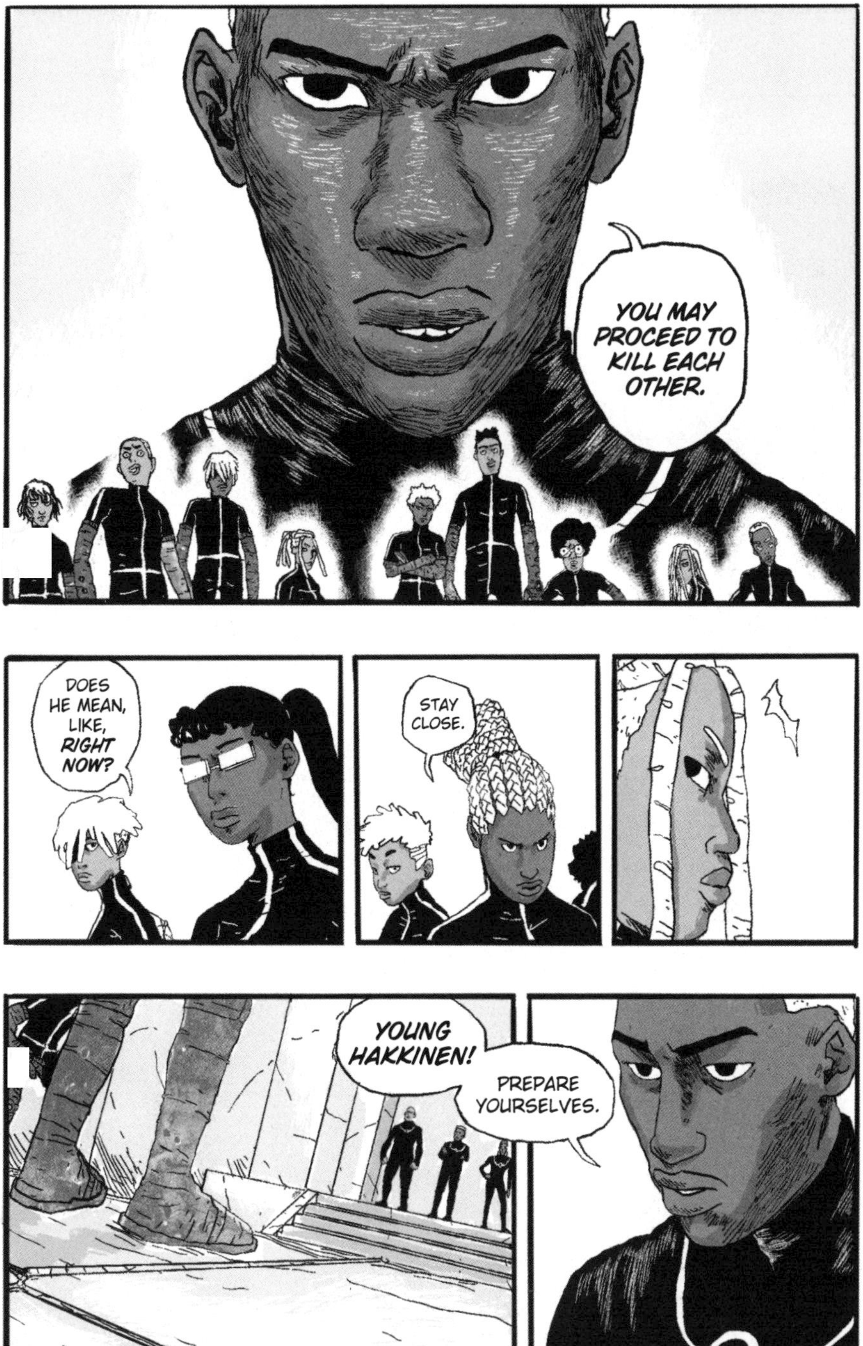
YOU MAY PROCEED TO KILL EACH OTHER.
DOES HE MEAN, LIKE, RIGHT NOW?
STAY CLOSE.
YOUNG HAKKINEN!
PREPARE YOURSELVES.

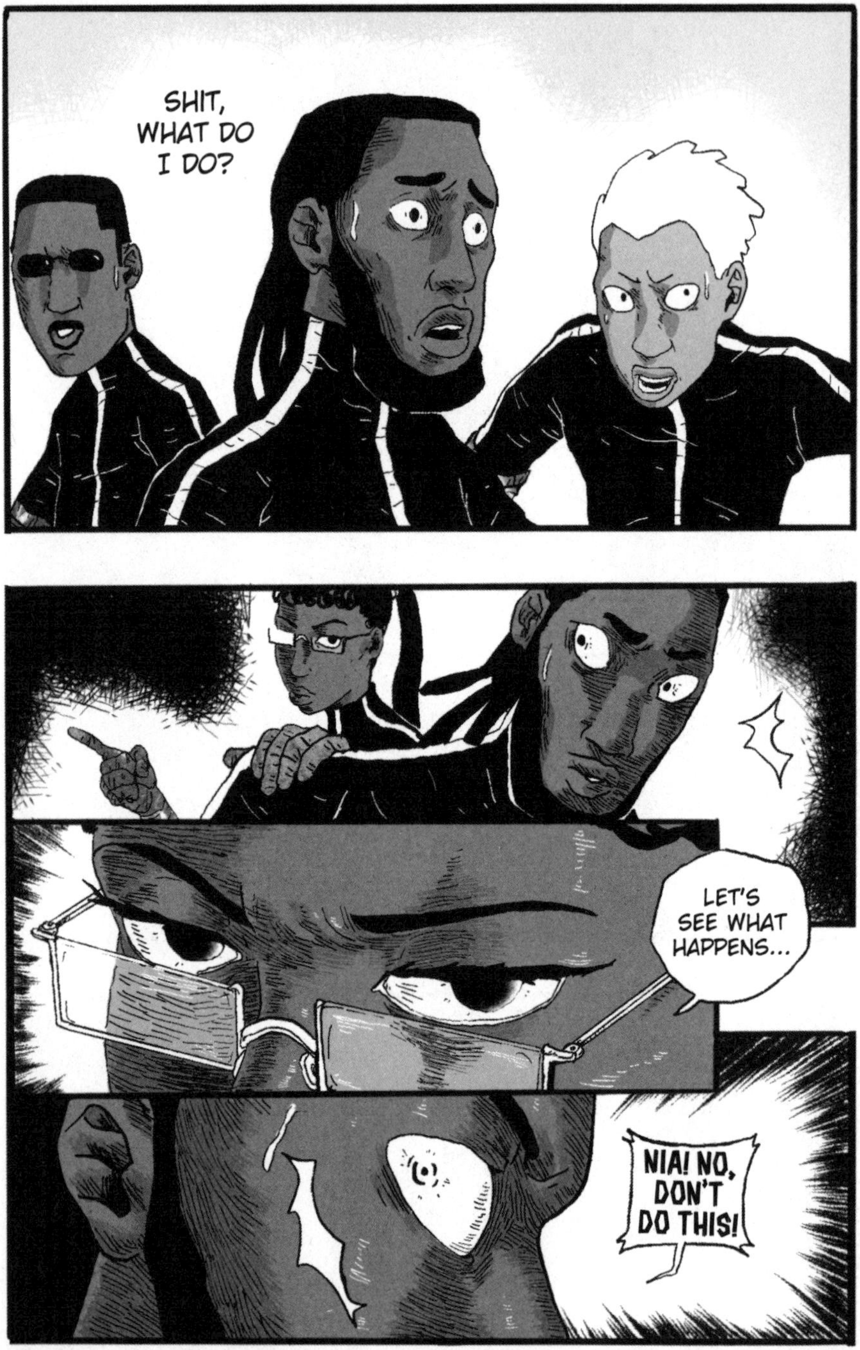
SHIT, WHAT DO I DO?
LET'S SEE WHAT HAPPENS...
NIA! NO, DON'T DO THIS!

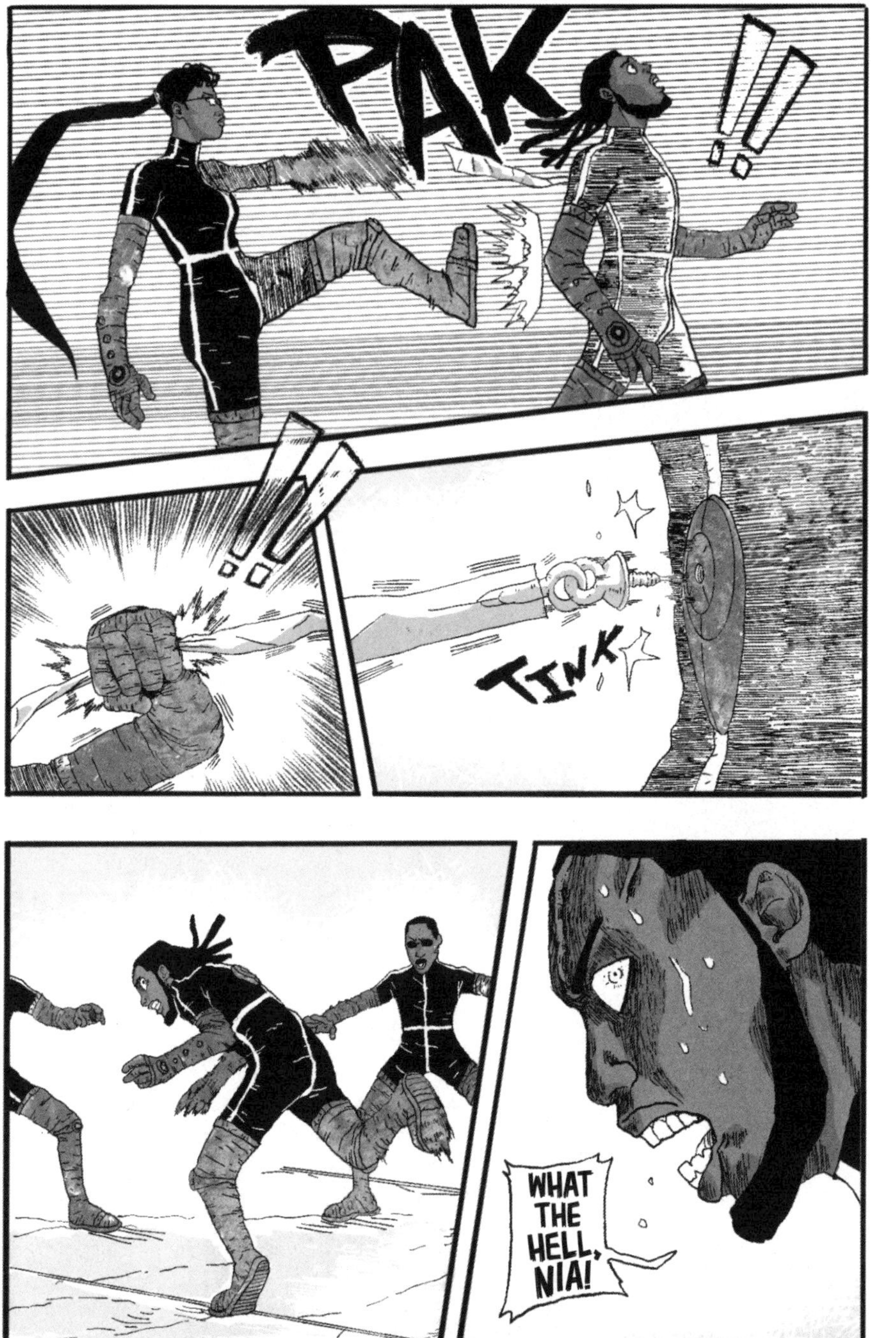
PAK
!!!
!!
TINK
WHAT THE HELL, NIA!

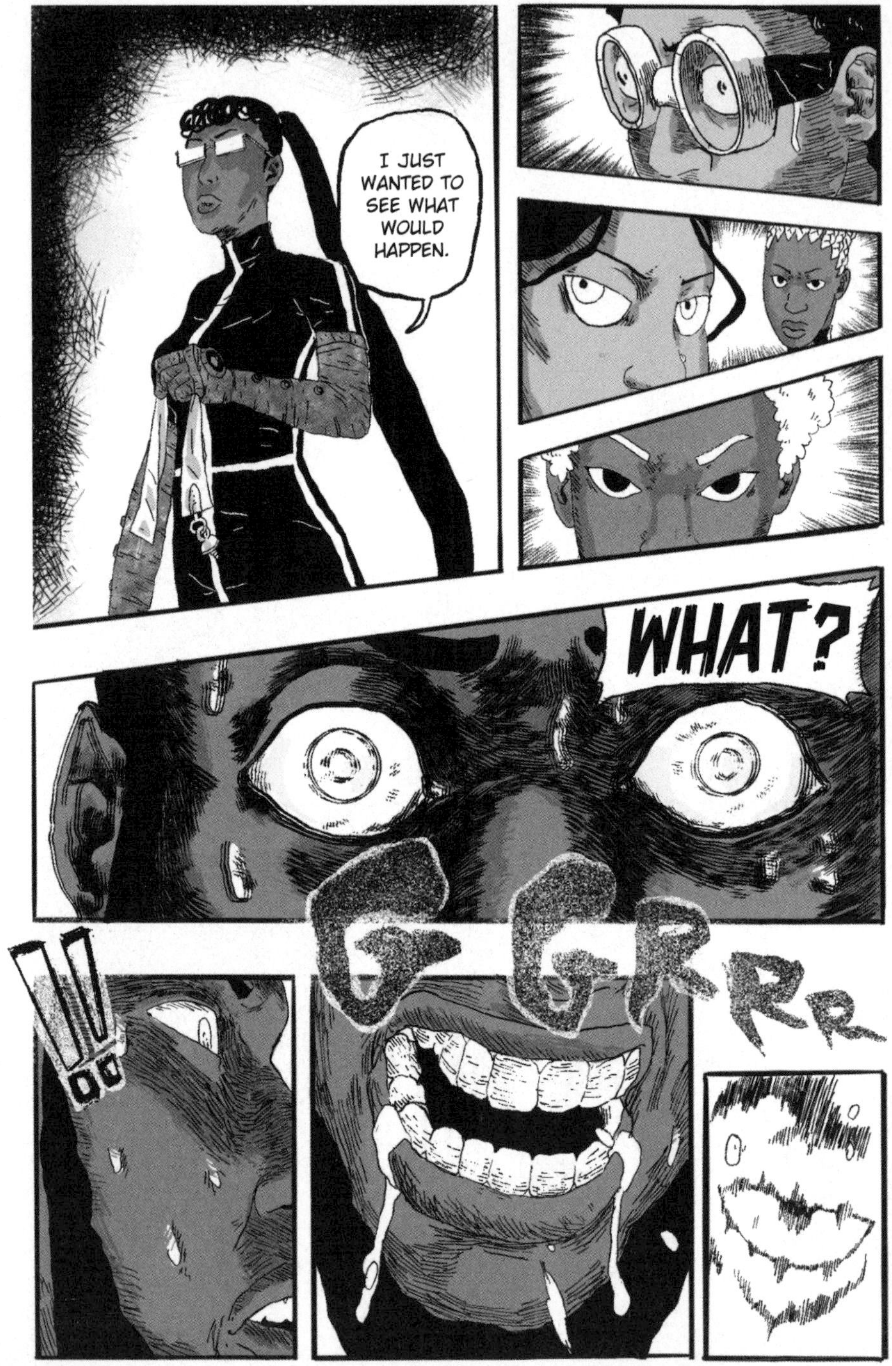
I JUST WANTED TO SEE WHAT WOULD HAPPEN.
WHAT?
!!
GGRRR

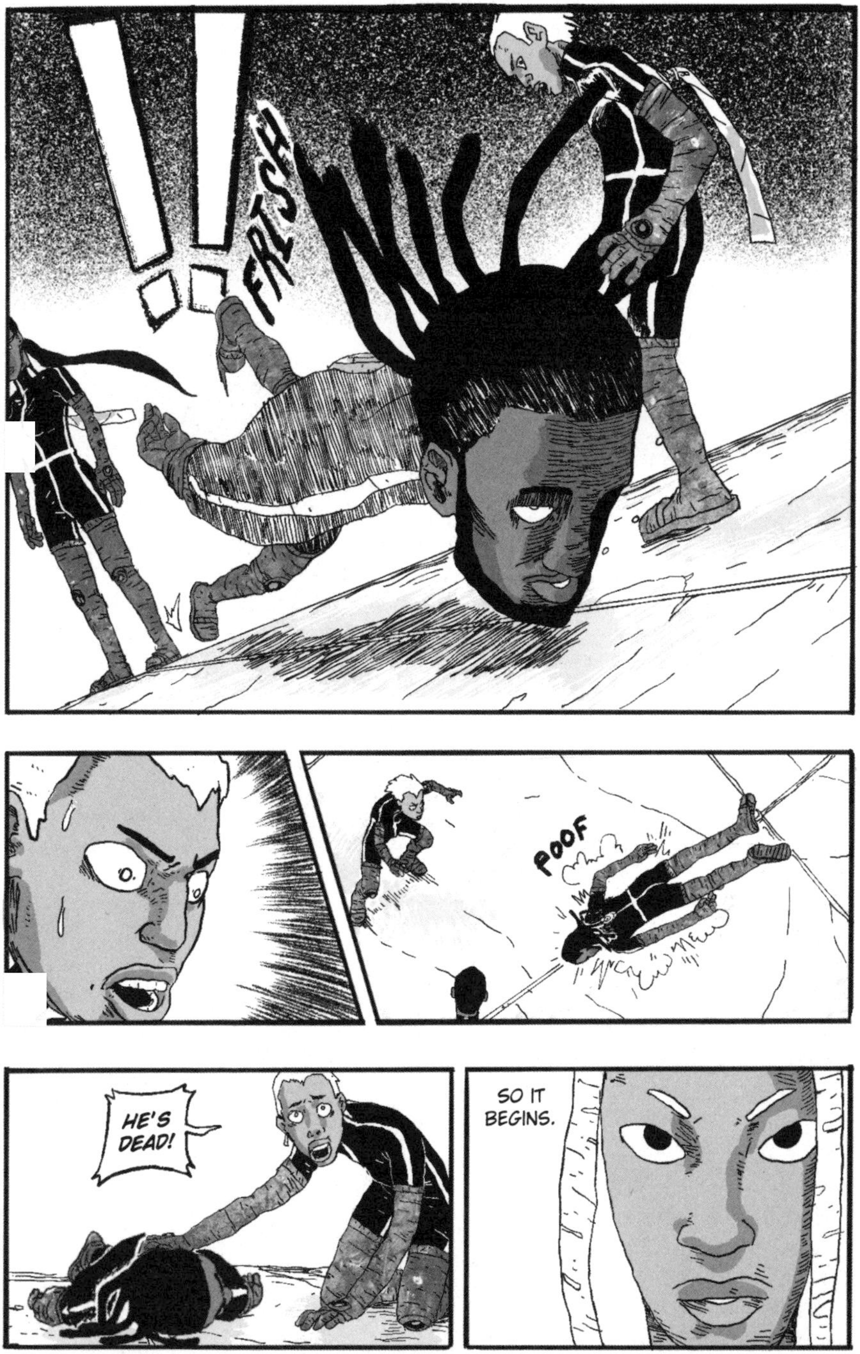
!!
FRTSH
POOF
HE'S DEAD!
SO IT BEGINS.

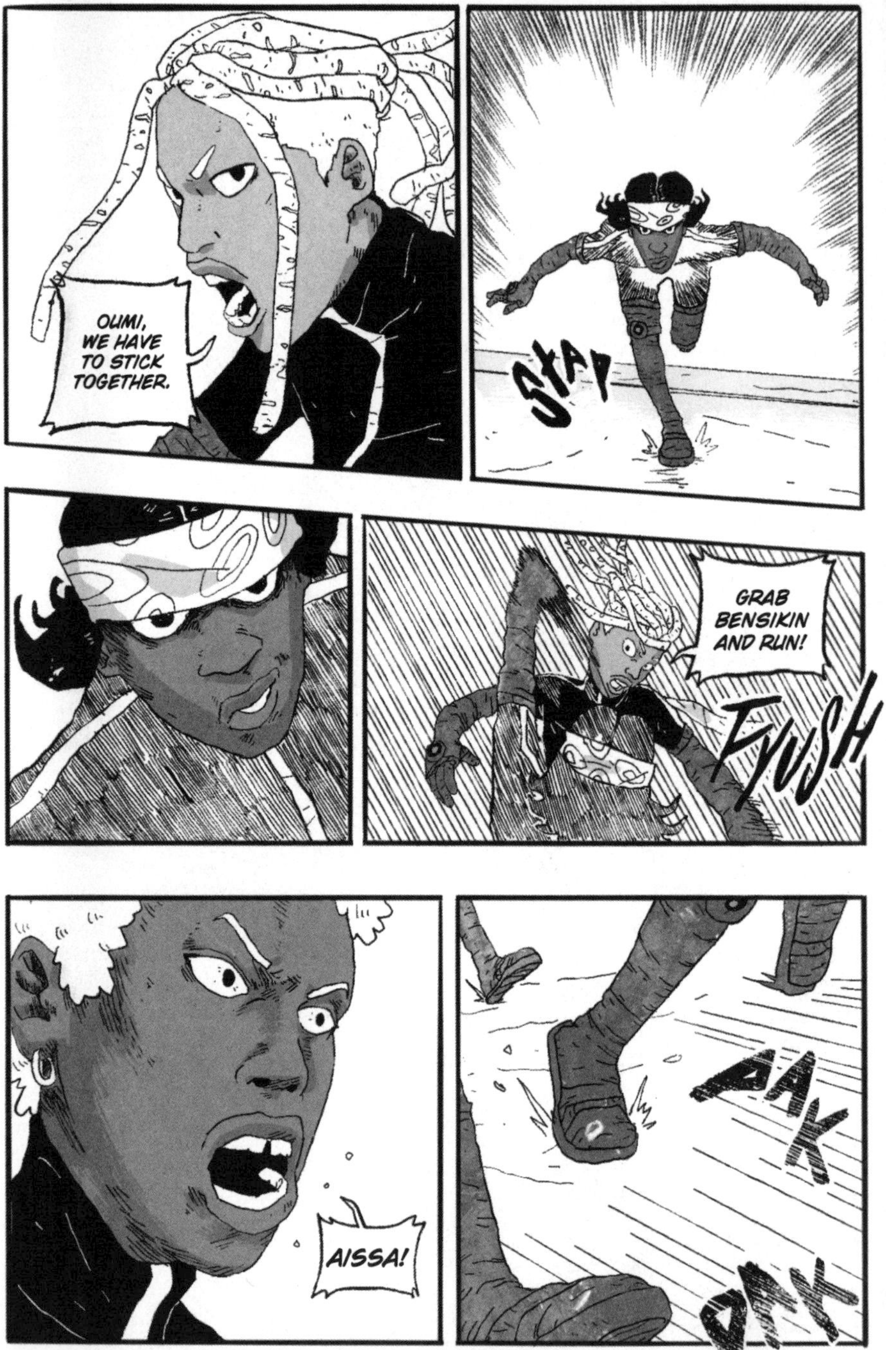
OUMI, WE HAVE TO STICK TOGETHER.
STAP
GRAB BENSIKIN AND RUN!
FYUSH
AISSA!
PAK
PAK

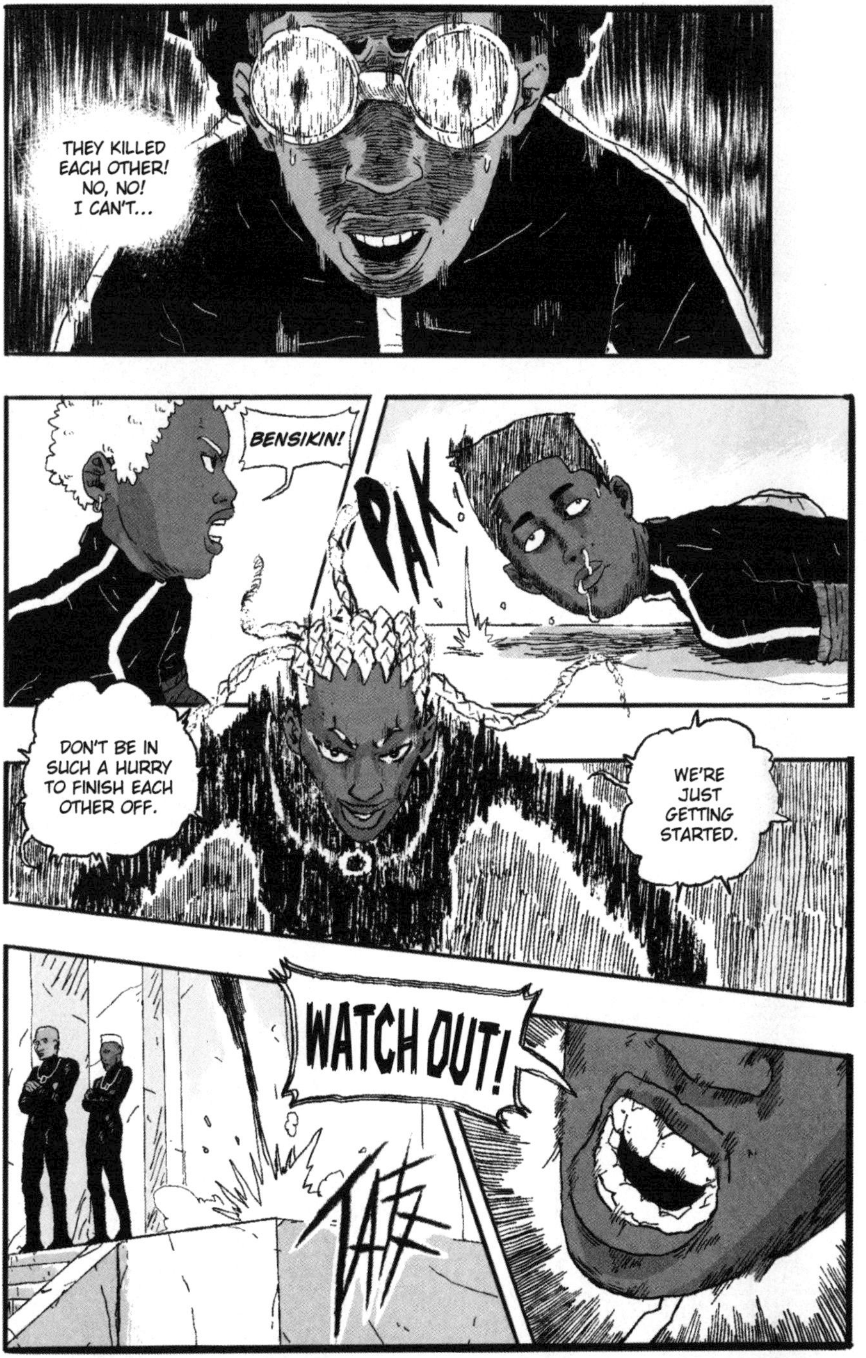
THEY KILLED EACH OTHER! NO, NO! I CAN'T...
BENSIKIN!
PAK
DON'T BE IN SUCH A HURRY TO FINISH EACH OTHER OFF.
WE'RE JUST GETTING STARTED.
WATCH OUT!

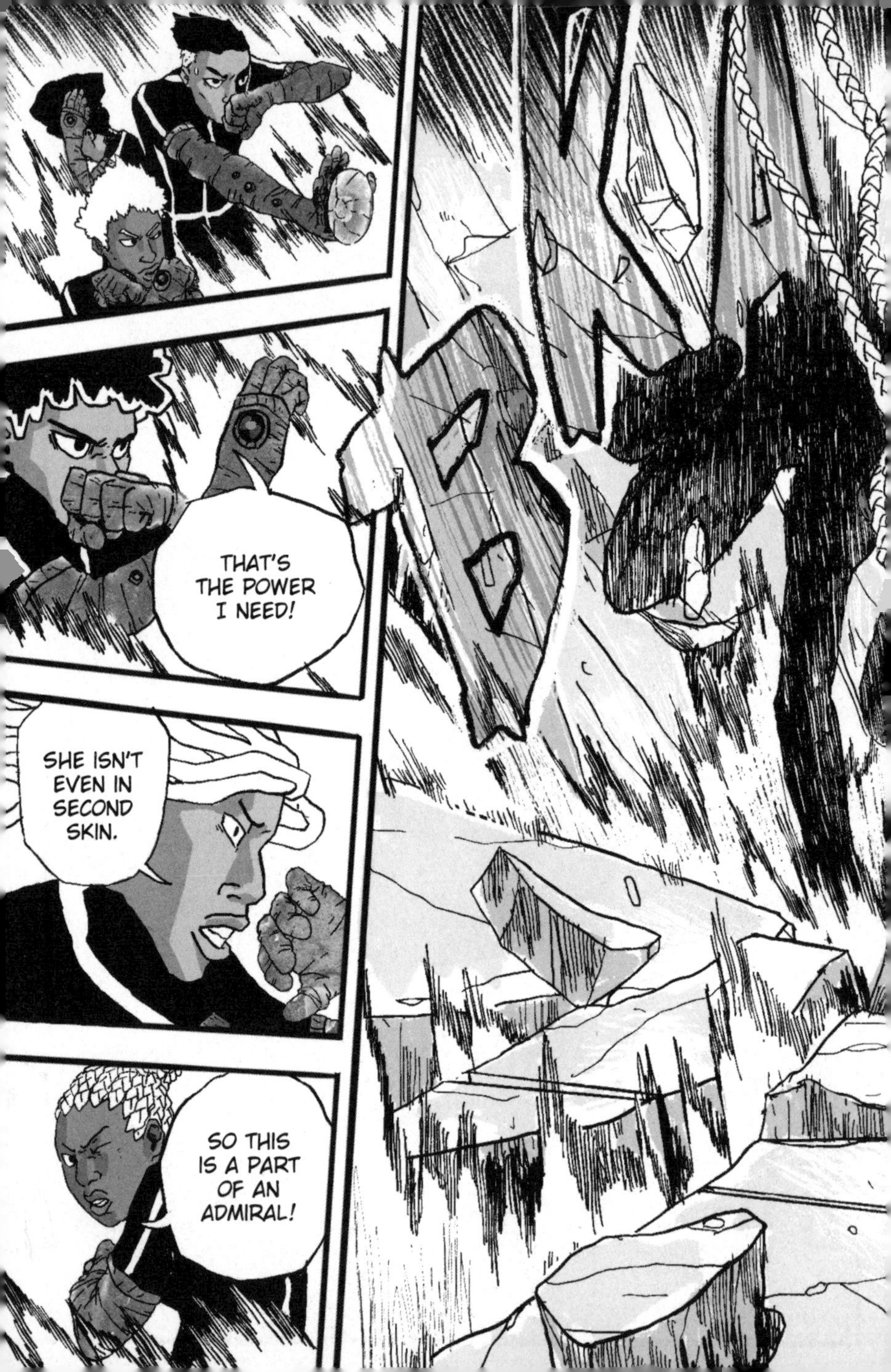
THAT'S THE POWER I NEED!
SHE ISN'T EVEN IN SECOND SKIN.
SO THIS IS A PART OF AN ADMIRAL!

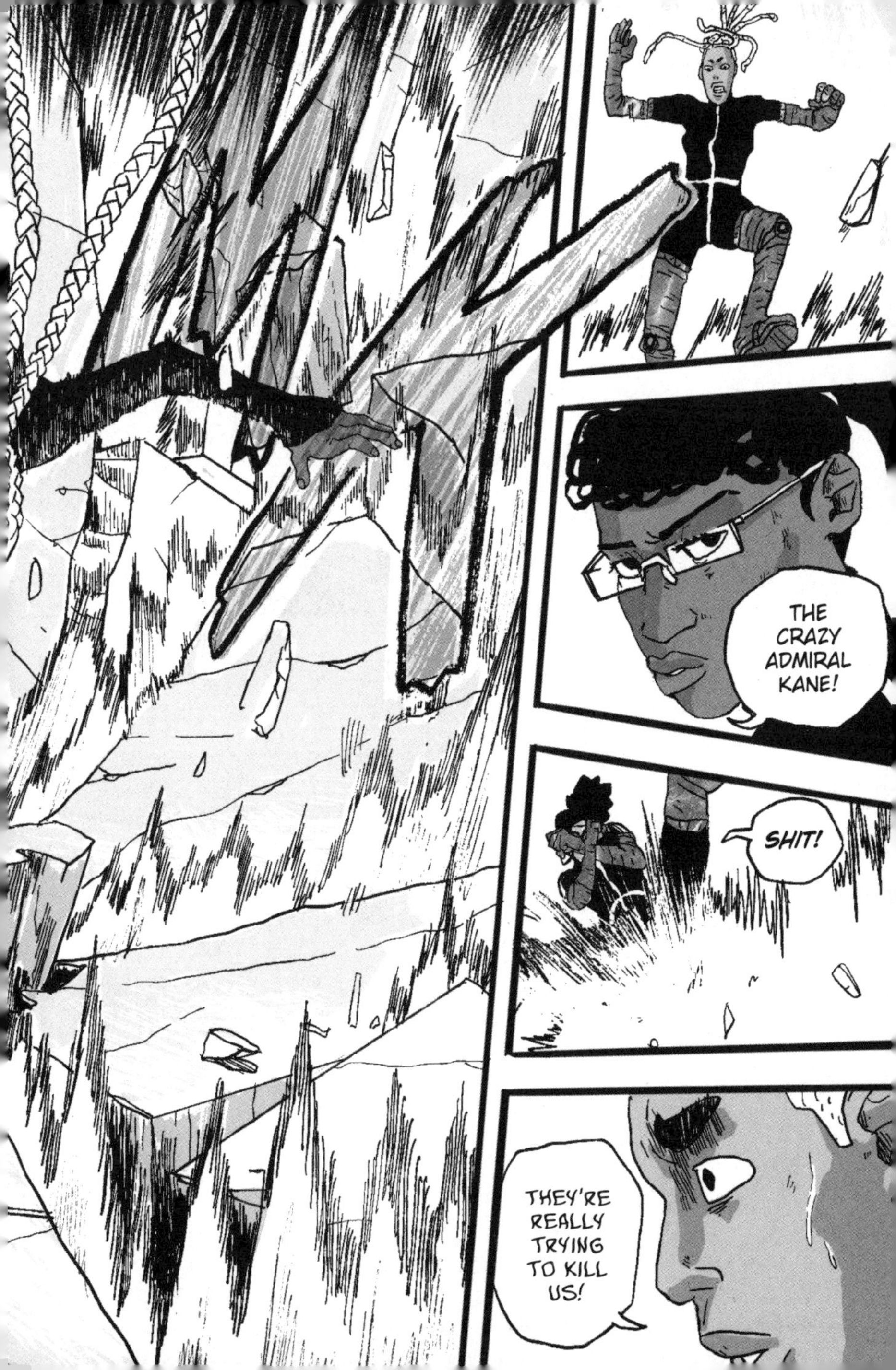
THE CRAZY ADMIRAL KANE!
SHIT!
THEY'RE REALLY TRYING TO KILL US!

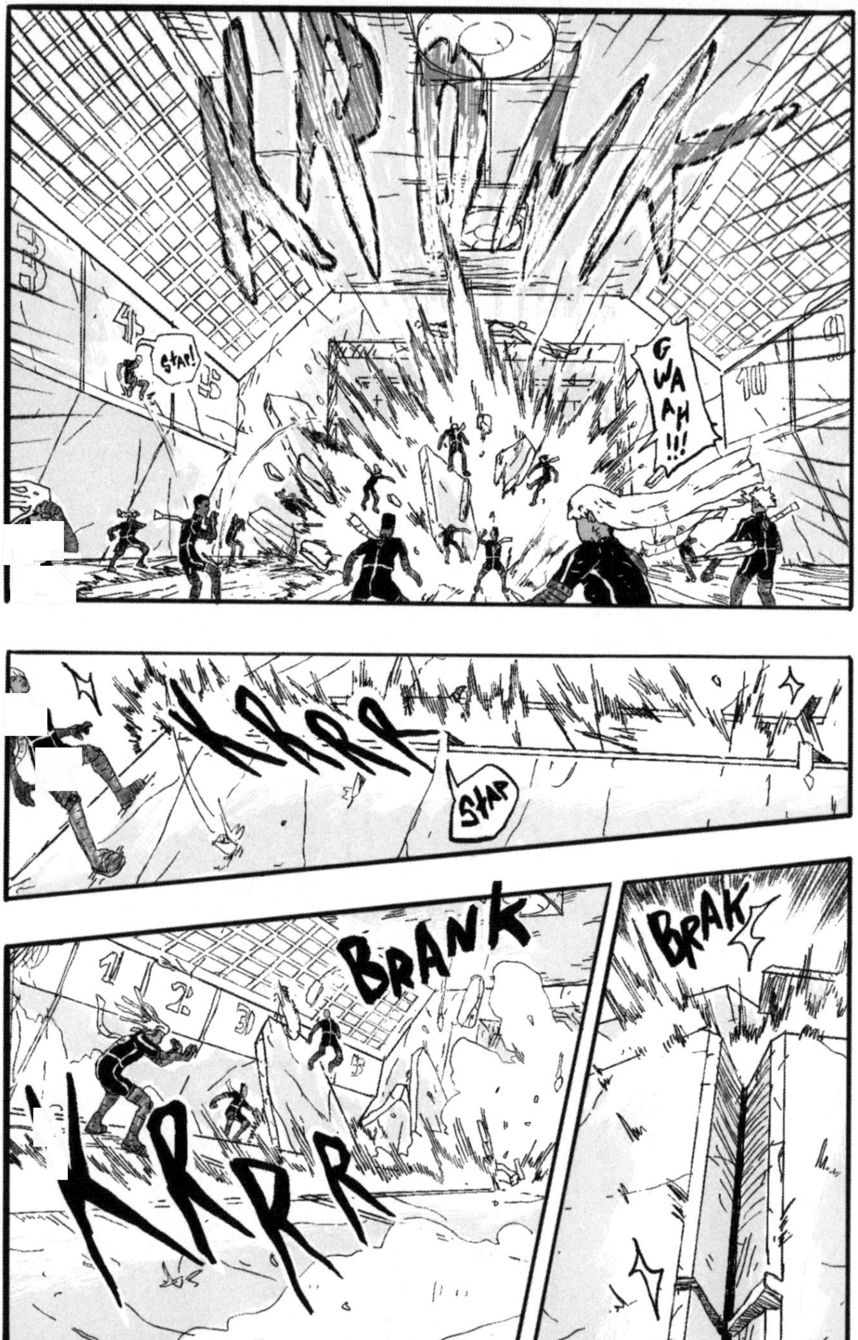
STAP!
GWAH!!!
KRRP
STAP
BRANK
KRRR
BRAK

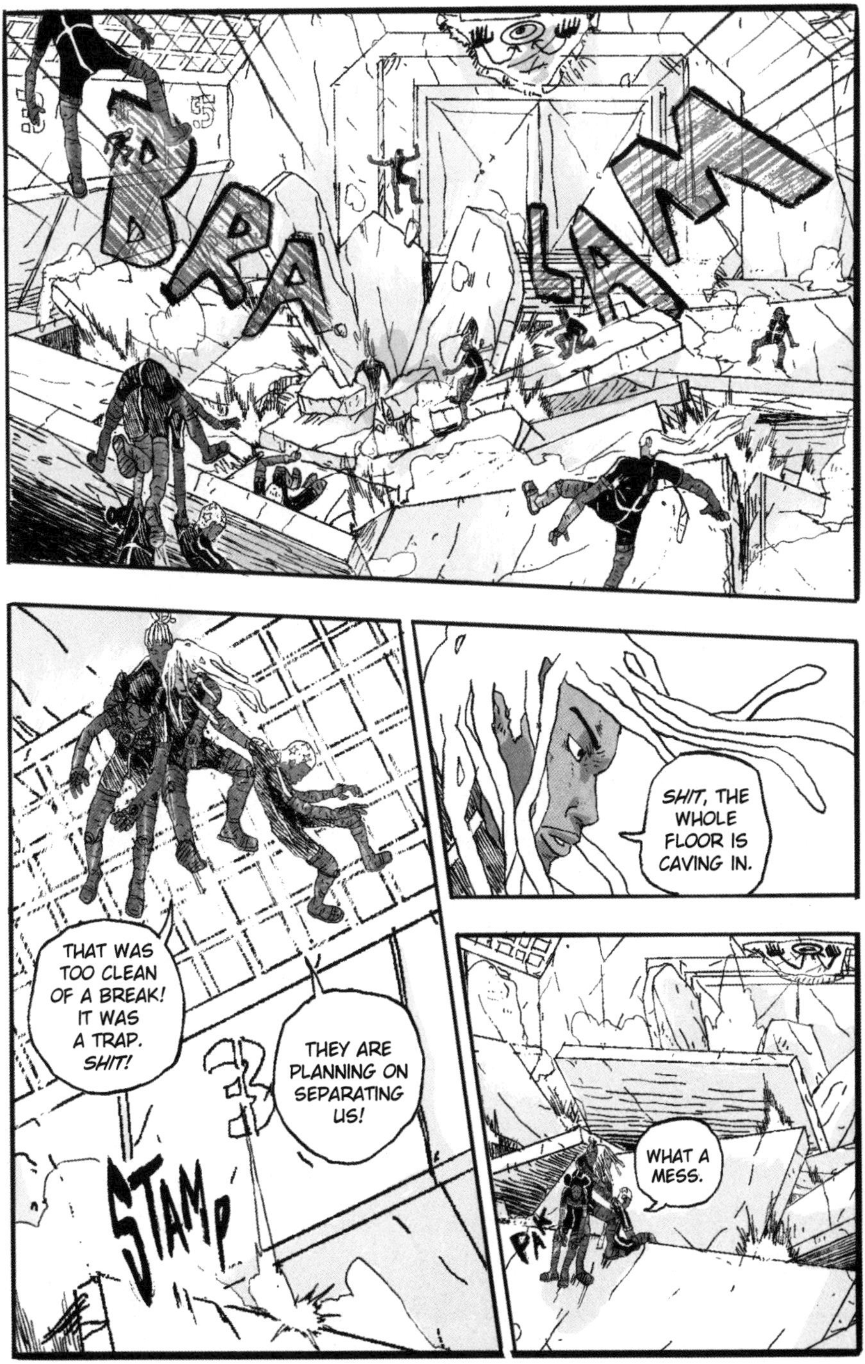
BRALAM
SHIT, THE WHOLE FLOOR IS CAVING IN.
THAT WAS TOO CLEAN OF A BREAK! IT WAS A TRAP. SHIT!
THEY ARE PLANNING ON SEPARATING US!
STAMP
WHAT A MESS.

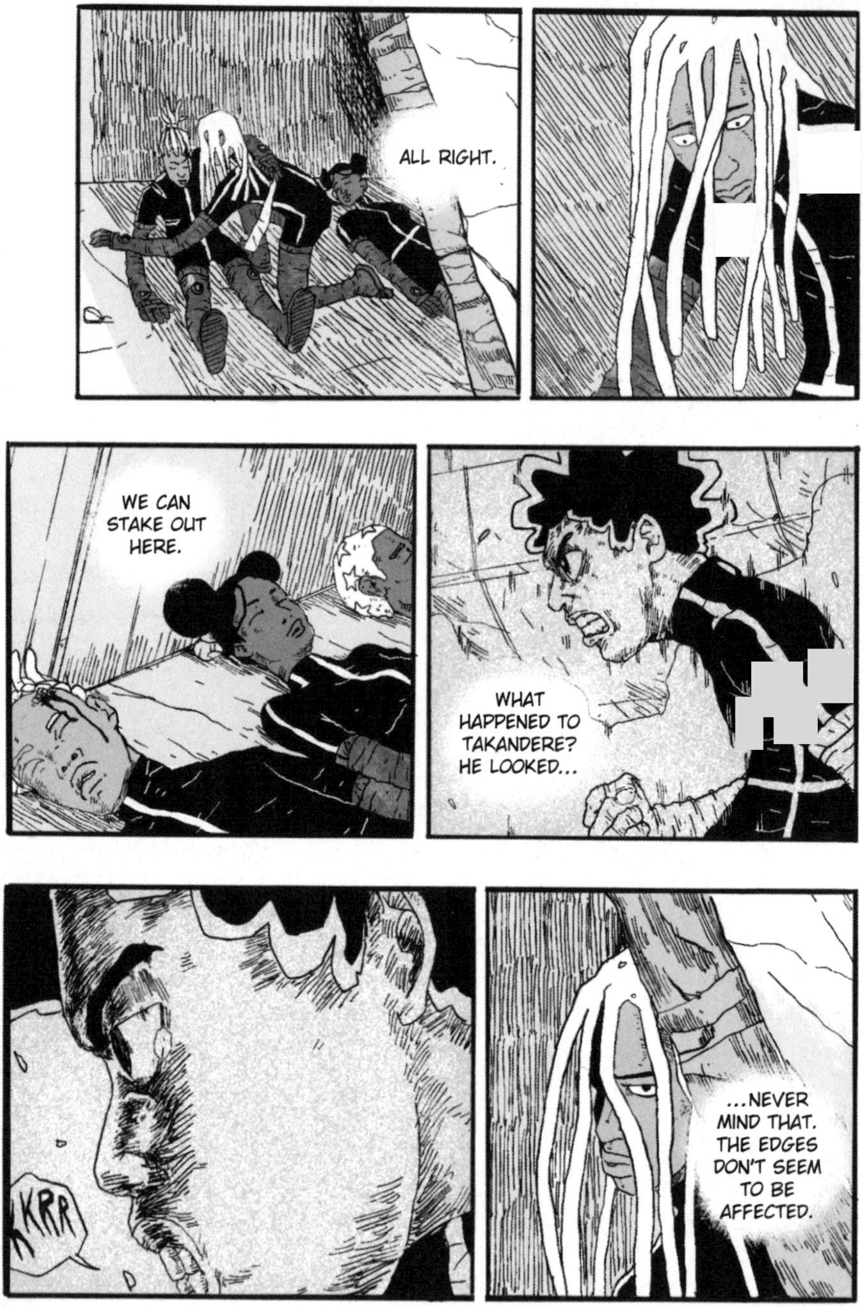
ALL RIGHT.
WE CAN STAKE OUT HERE.
WHAT HAPPENED TO TAKANDERE? HE LOOKED...
KRR
...NEVER MIND THAT. THE EDGES DON'T SEEM TO BE AFFECTED.

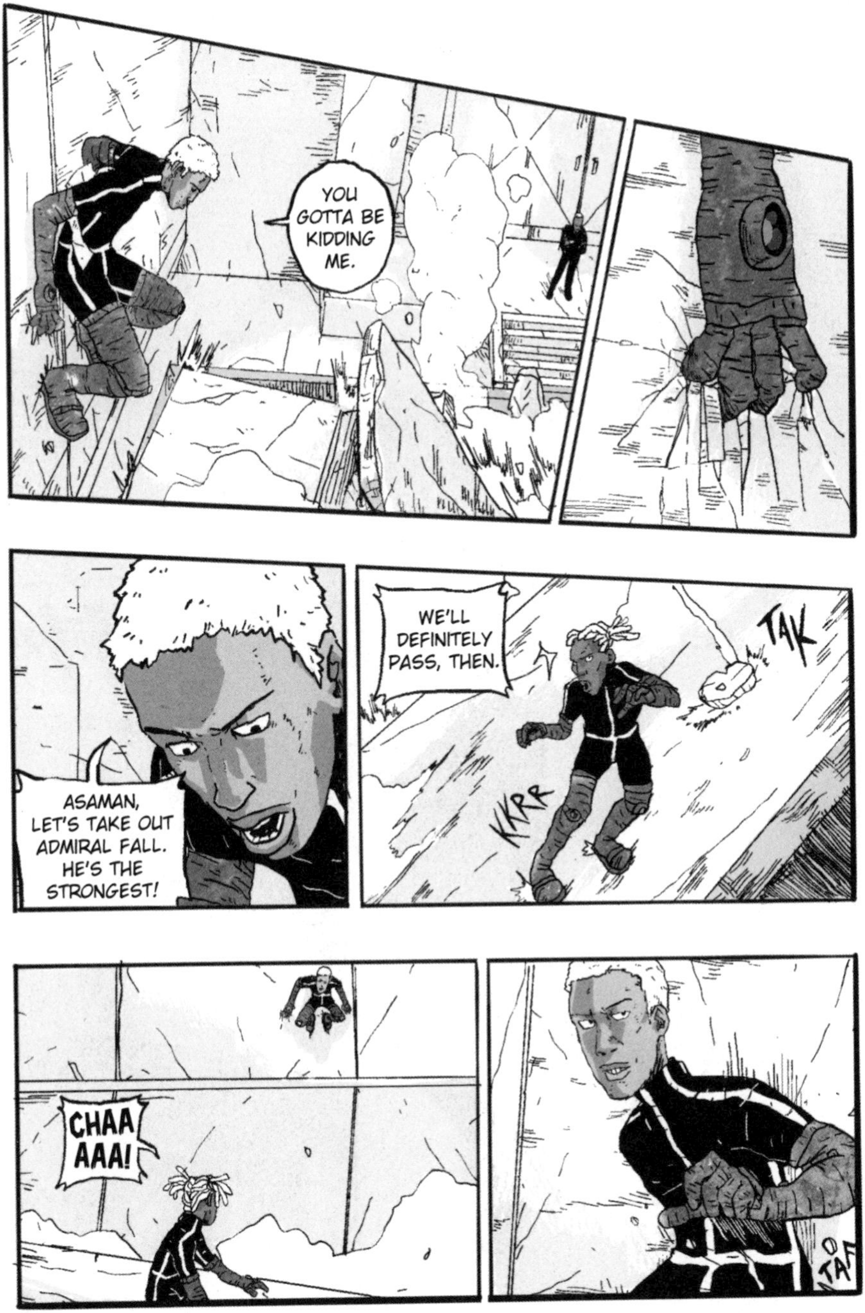
YOU GOTTA BE KIDDING ME.
ASAMAN, LET'S TAKE OUT ADMIRAL FALL. HE'S THE STRONGEST!
WE'LL DEFINITELY PASS, THEN.
TAK
KKRR
CHAA AAA!
TAP

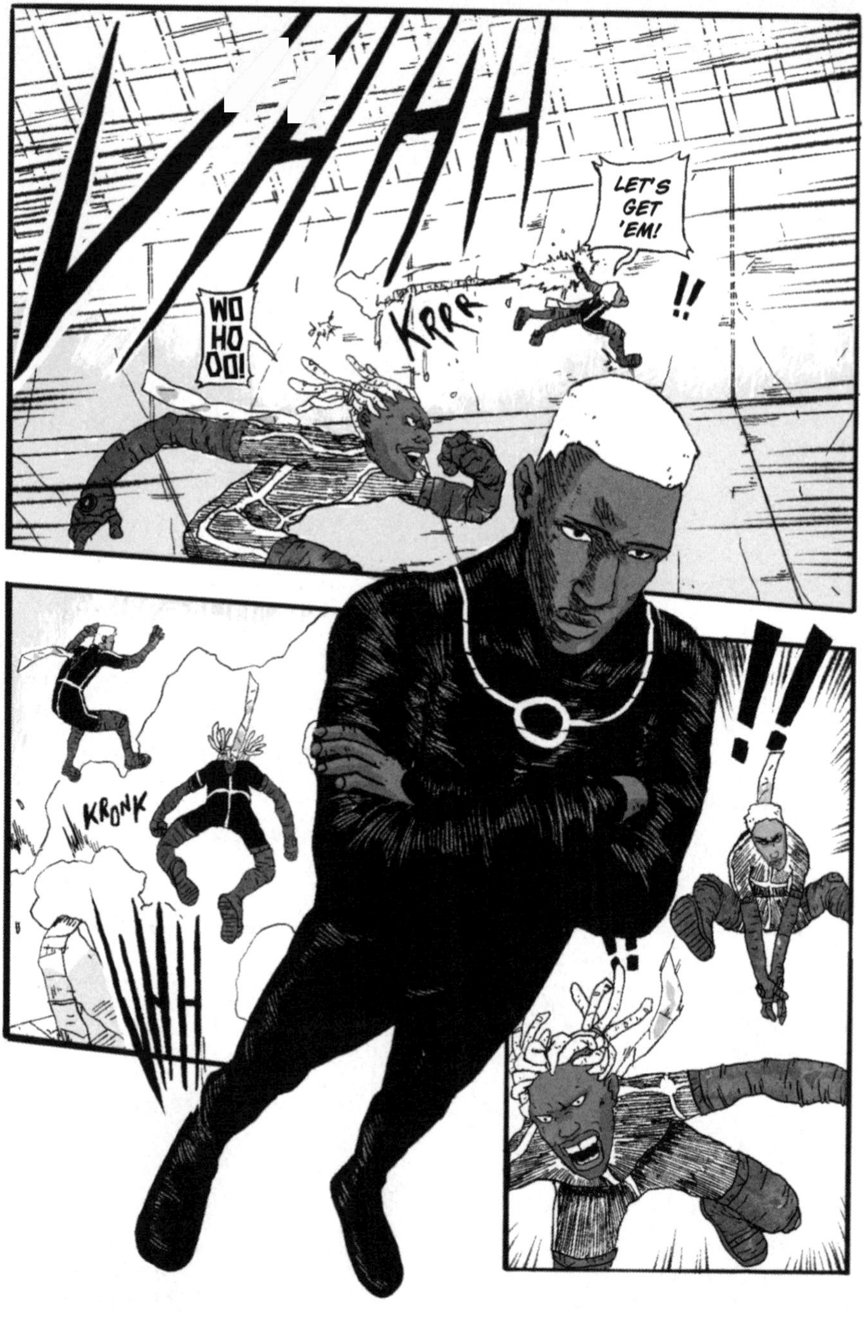
WO
HO
OO!
KRRA
LET'S
GET
'EM!
!!
KRONK
!!
!!

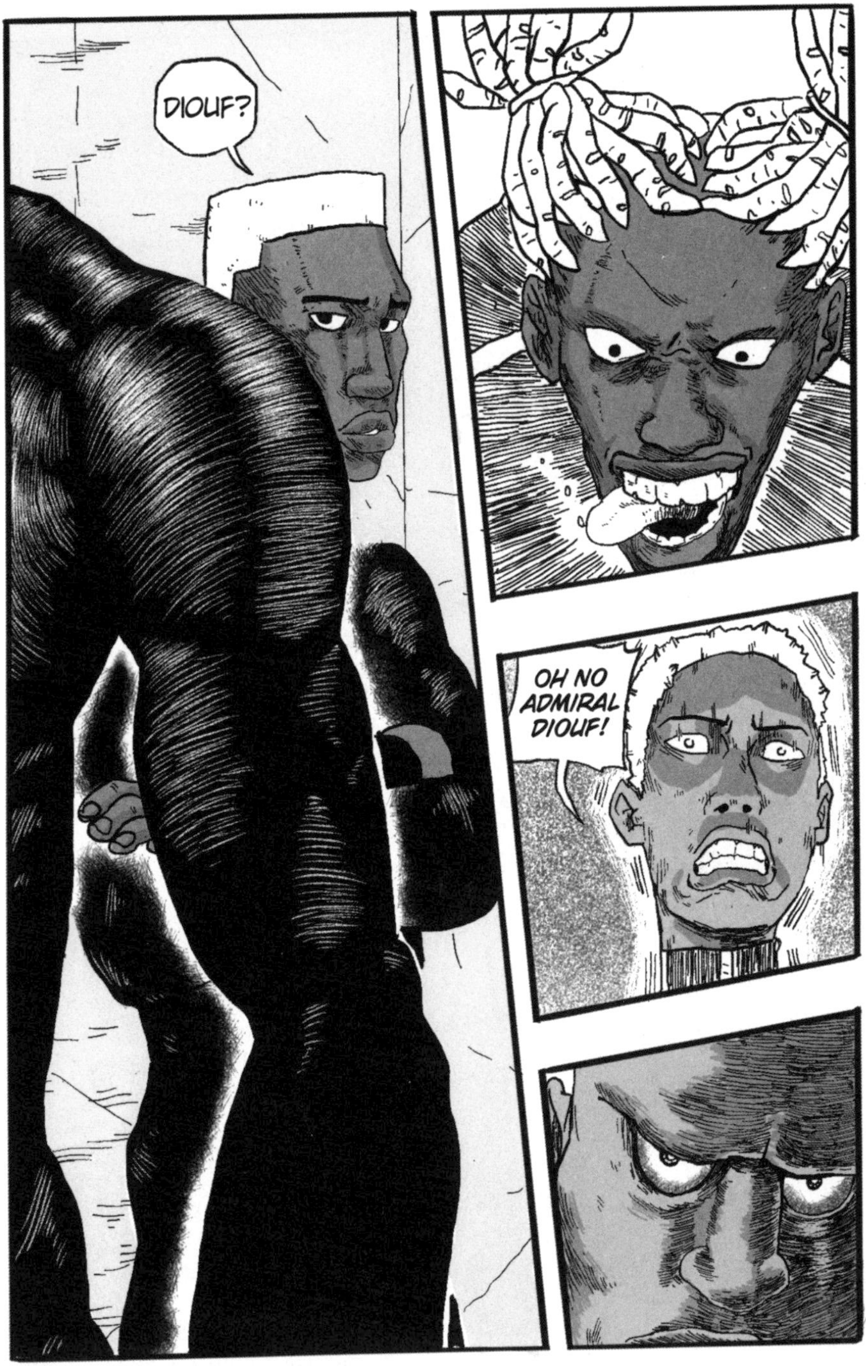
DIOUF?
OH NO ADMIRAL DIOUF!

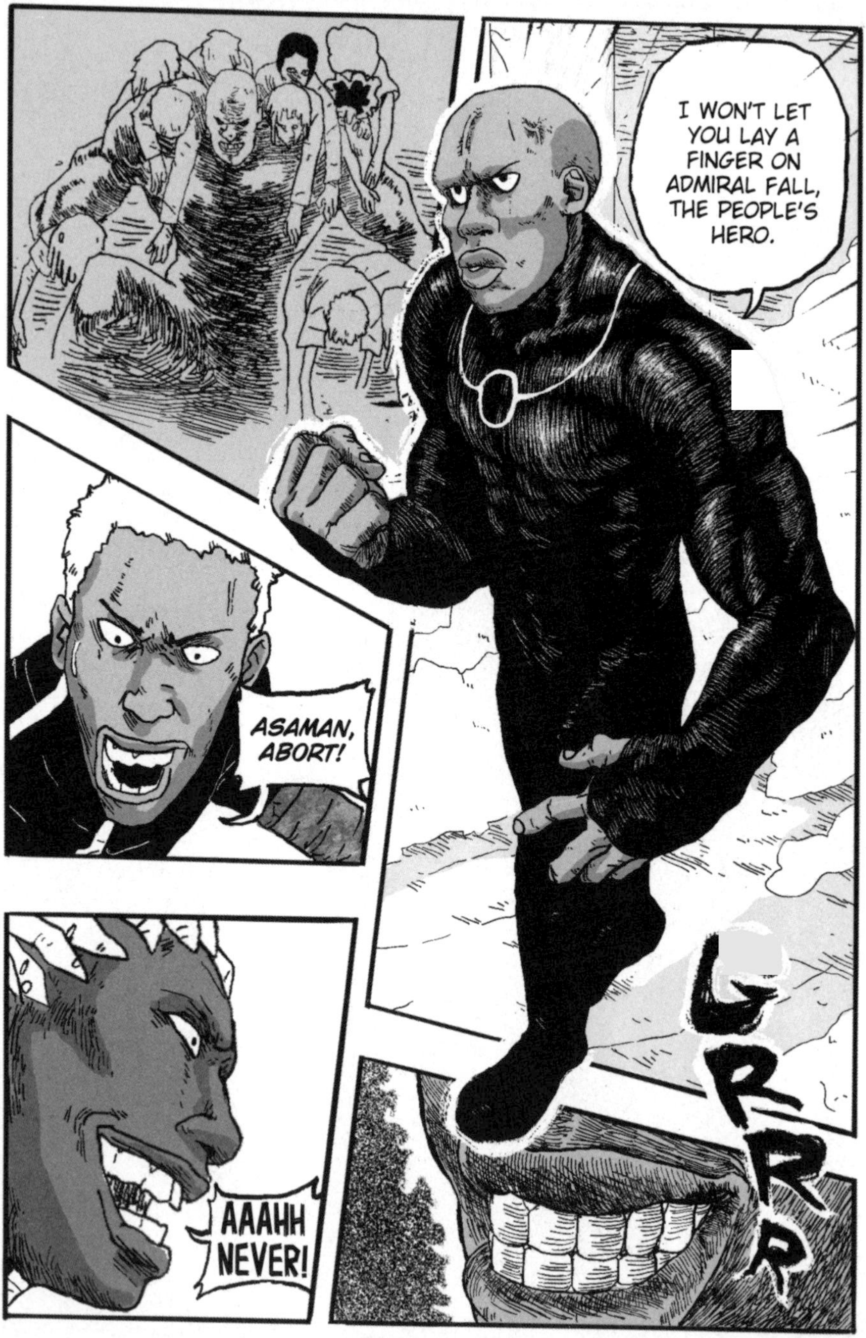
I WON'T LET YOU LAY A FINGER ON ADMIRAL FALL, THE PEOPLE'S HERO.
ASAMAN, ABORT!
AAAHH NEVER!
GRRR

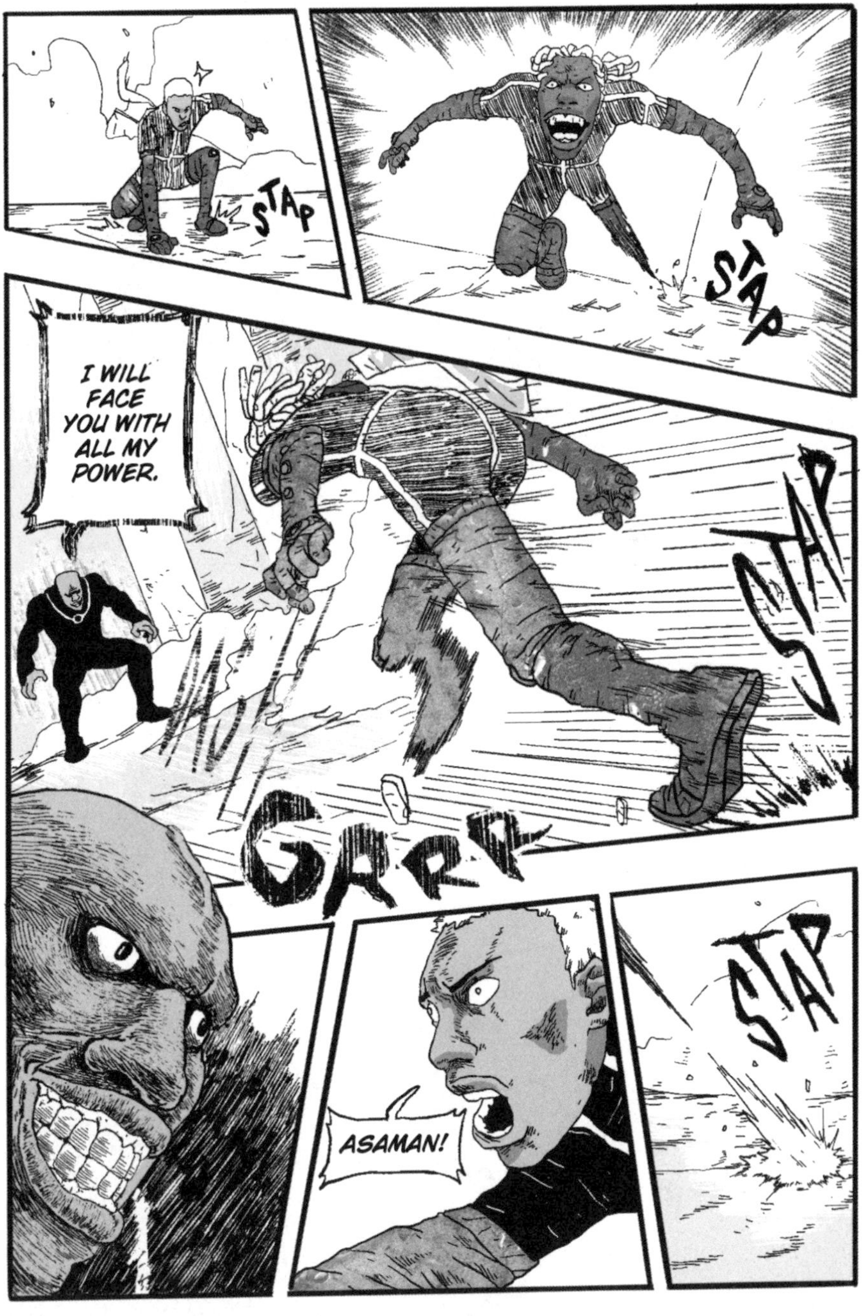
STAP
STAP
I WILL FACE YOU WITH ALL MY POWER.
STAP
GARR
ASAMAN!
STAP

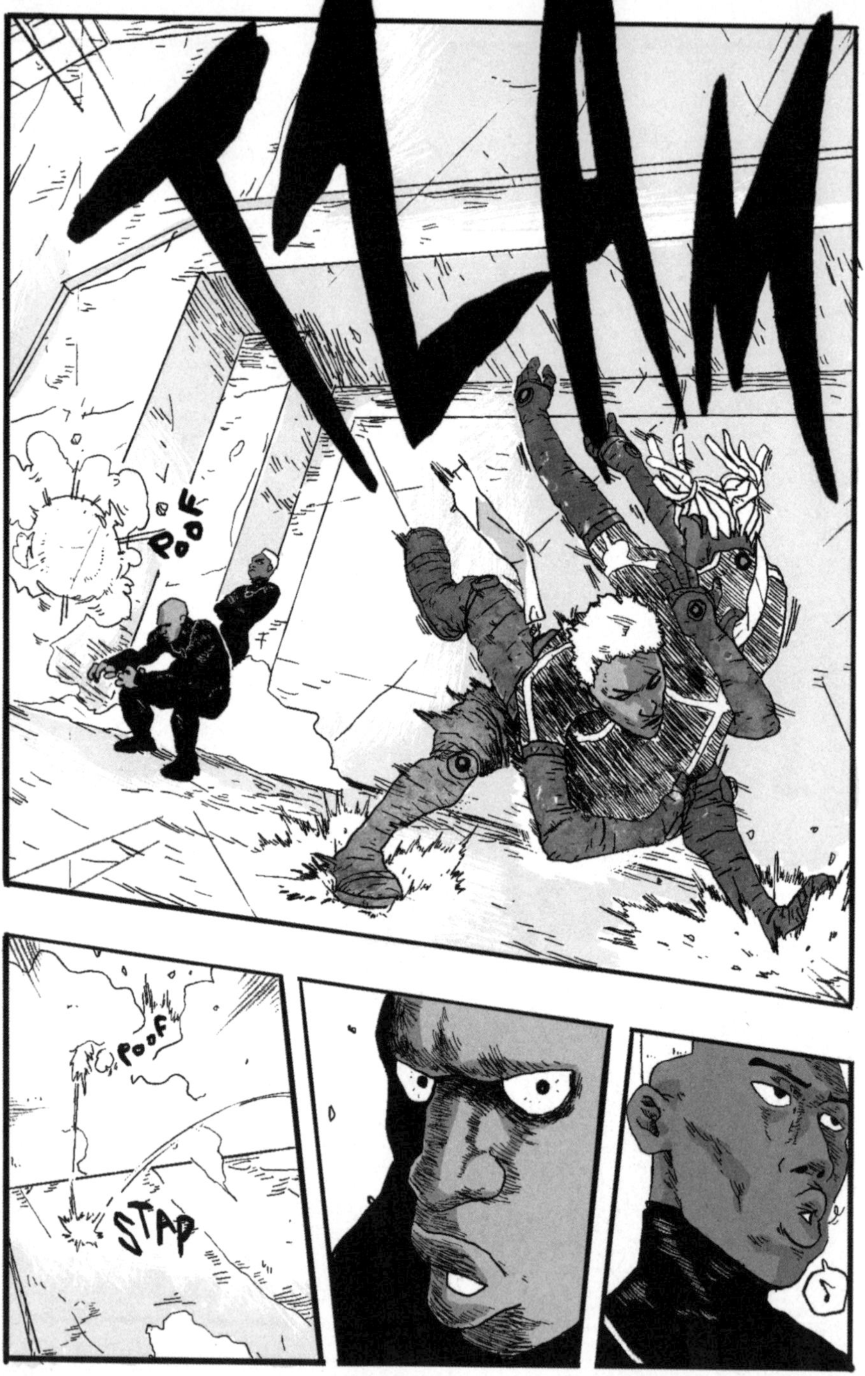

TZAM
POOF
POOF
STAP
♪

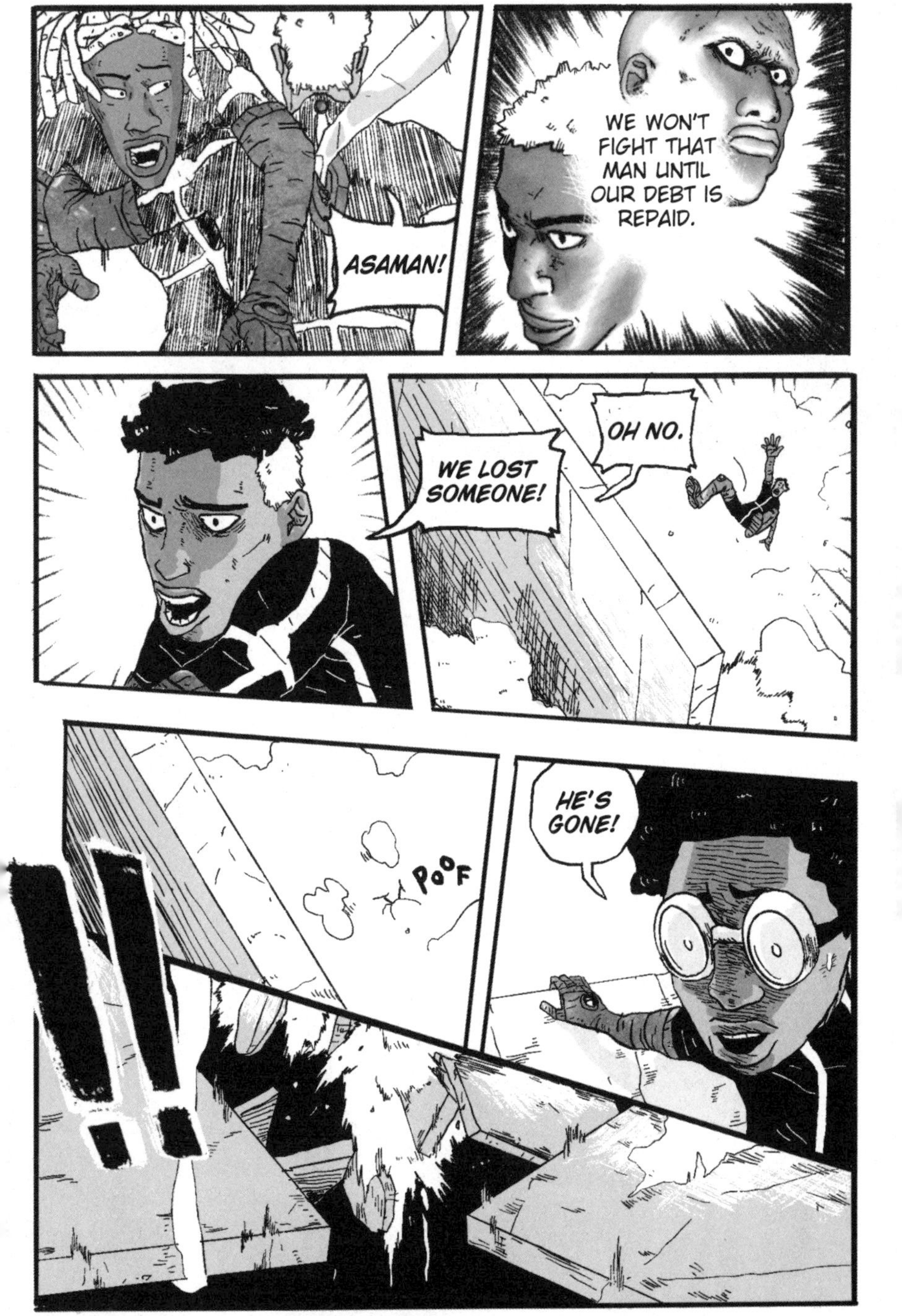
ASAMAN!
WE WON'T FIGHT THAT MAN UNTIL OUR DEBT IS REPAID.
WE LOST SOMEONE!
OH NO.
POOF
HE'S GONE!

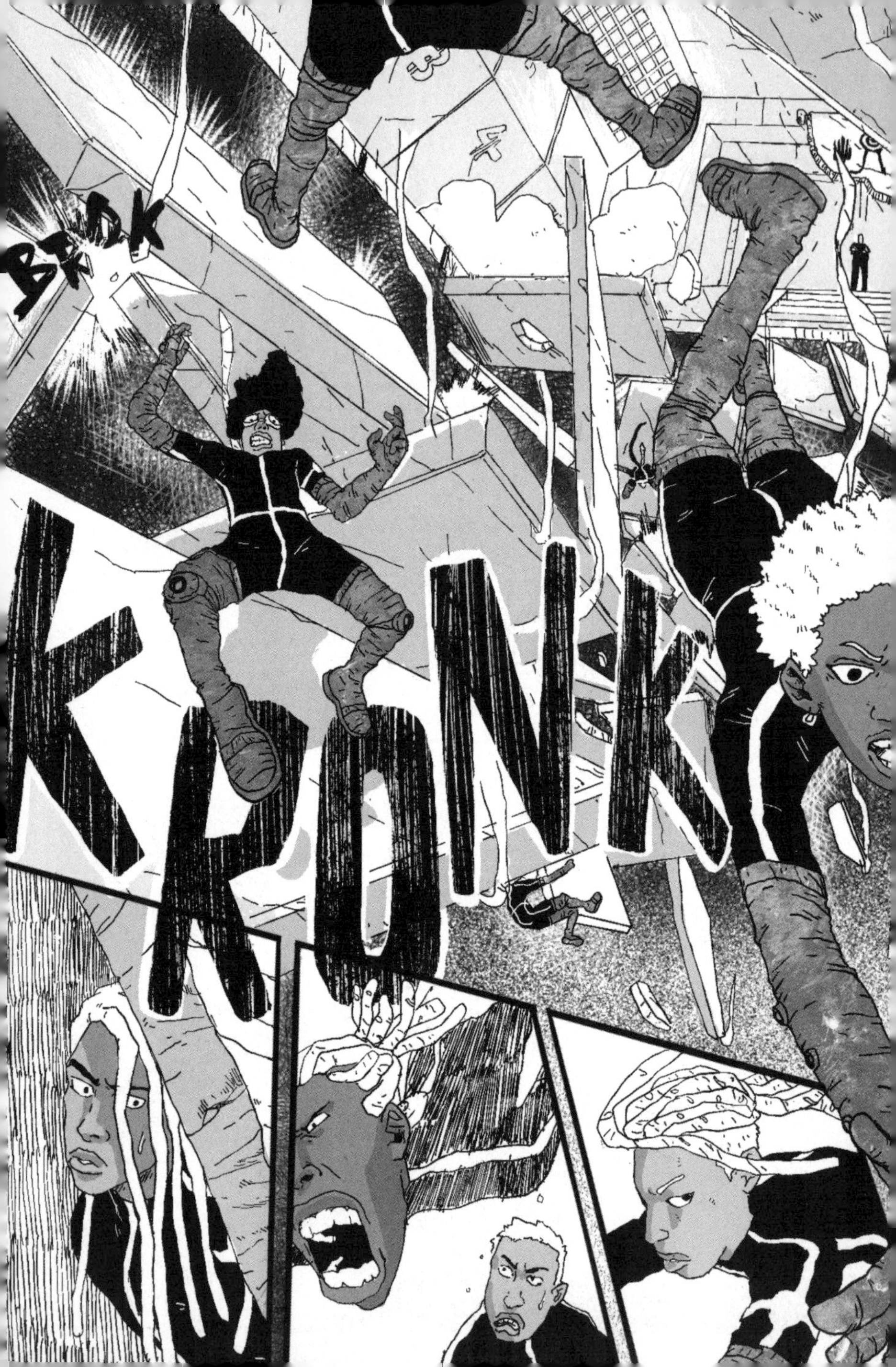
BRDK
KRONK

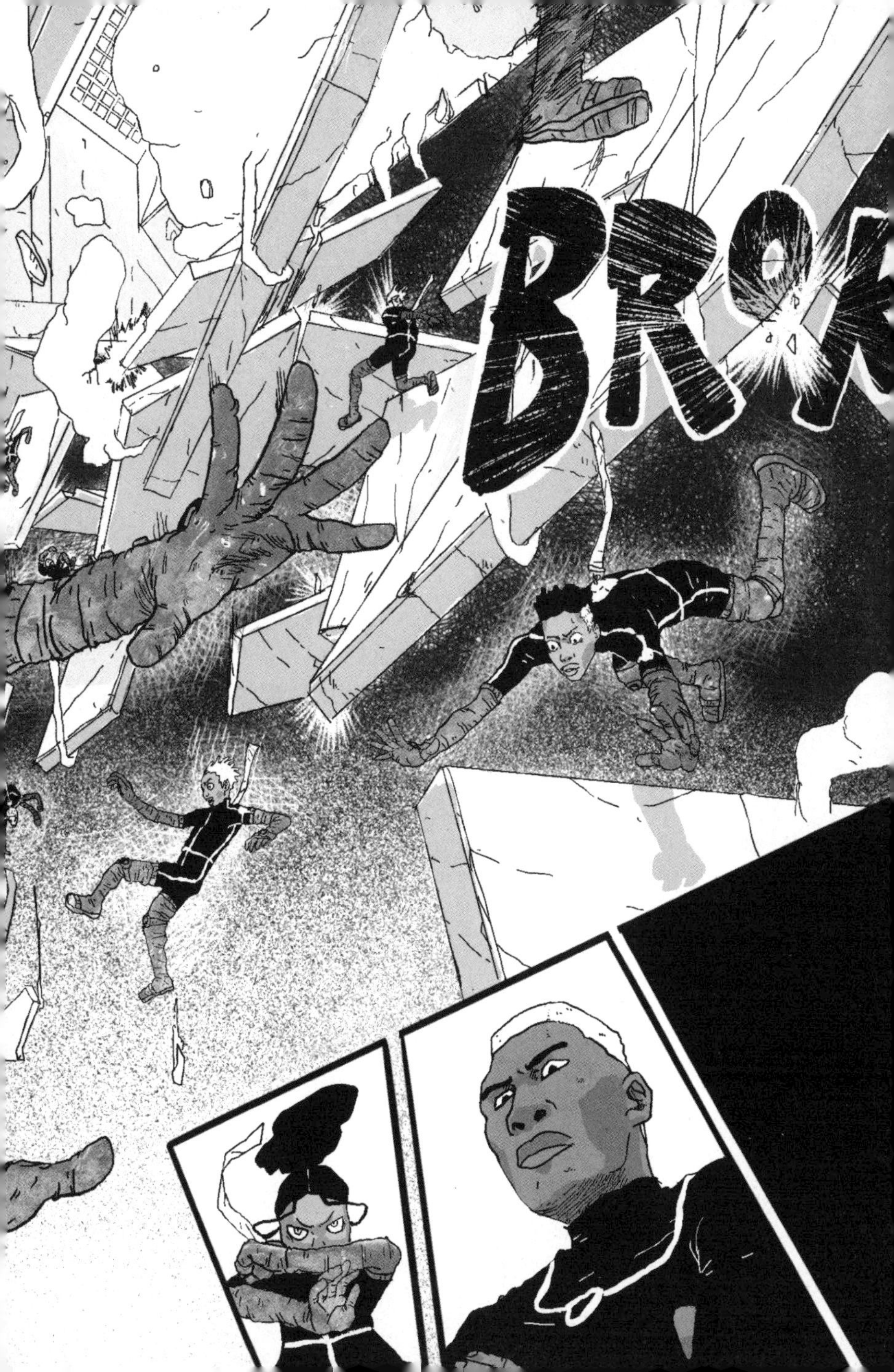
BROK

OBLIVION ROUGE

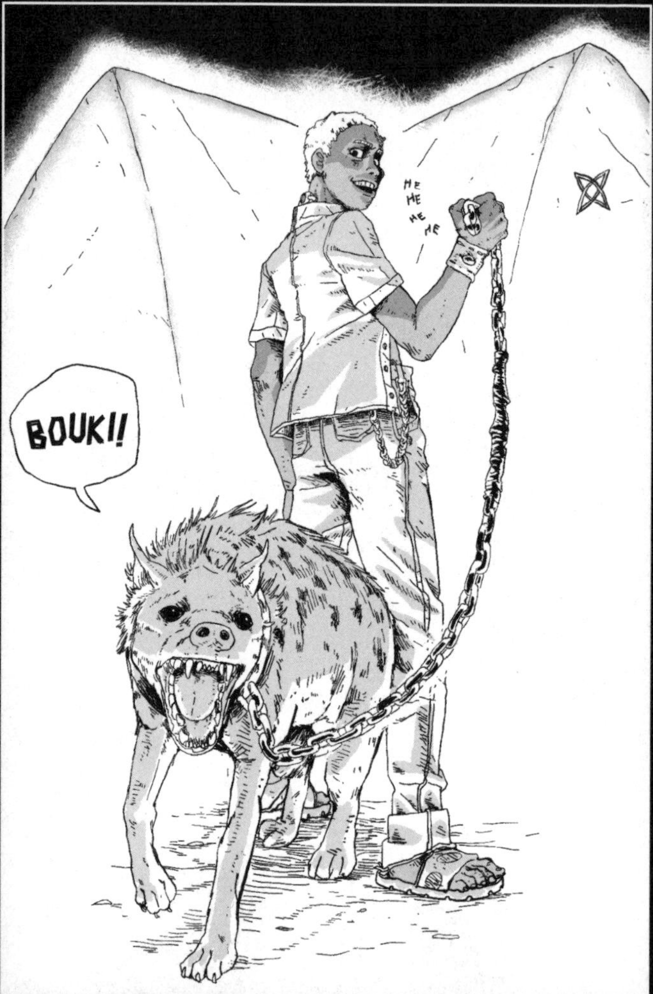
HE HE HE HE
BOUK!!

CHAPTER 4

Neverland Battleground - 0%

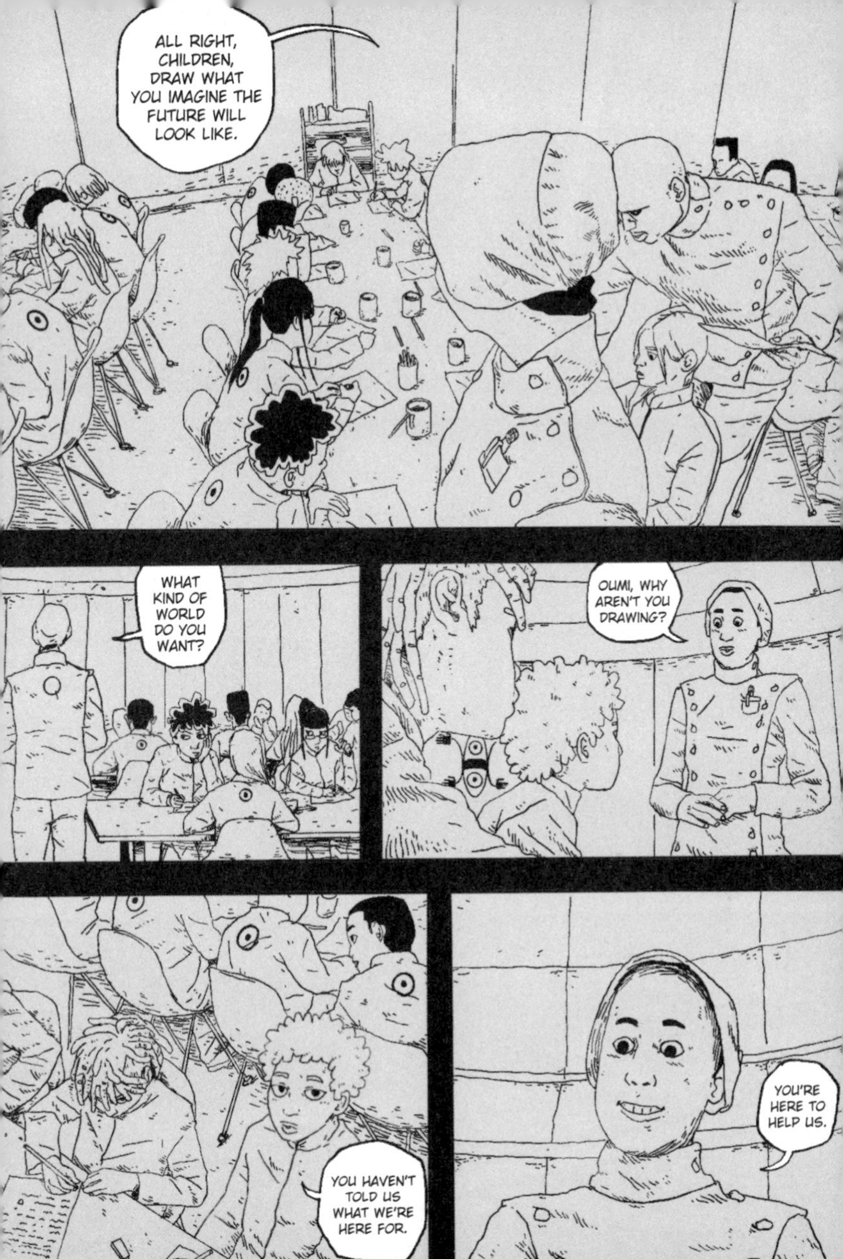
ALL RIGHT, CHILDREN, DRAW WHAT YOU IMAGINE THE FUTURE WILL LOOK LIKE.
WHAT KIND OF WORLD DO YOU WANT?
OUMI, WHY AREN'T YOU DRAWING?
YOU HAVEN'T TOLD US WHAT WE'RE HERE FOR.
YOU'RE HERE TO HELP US.

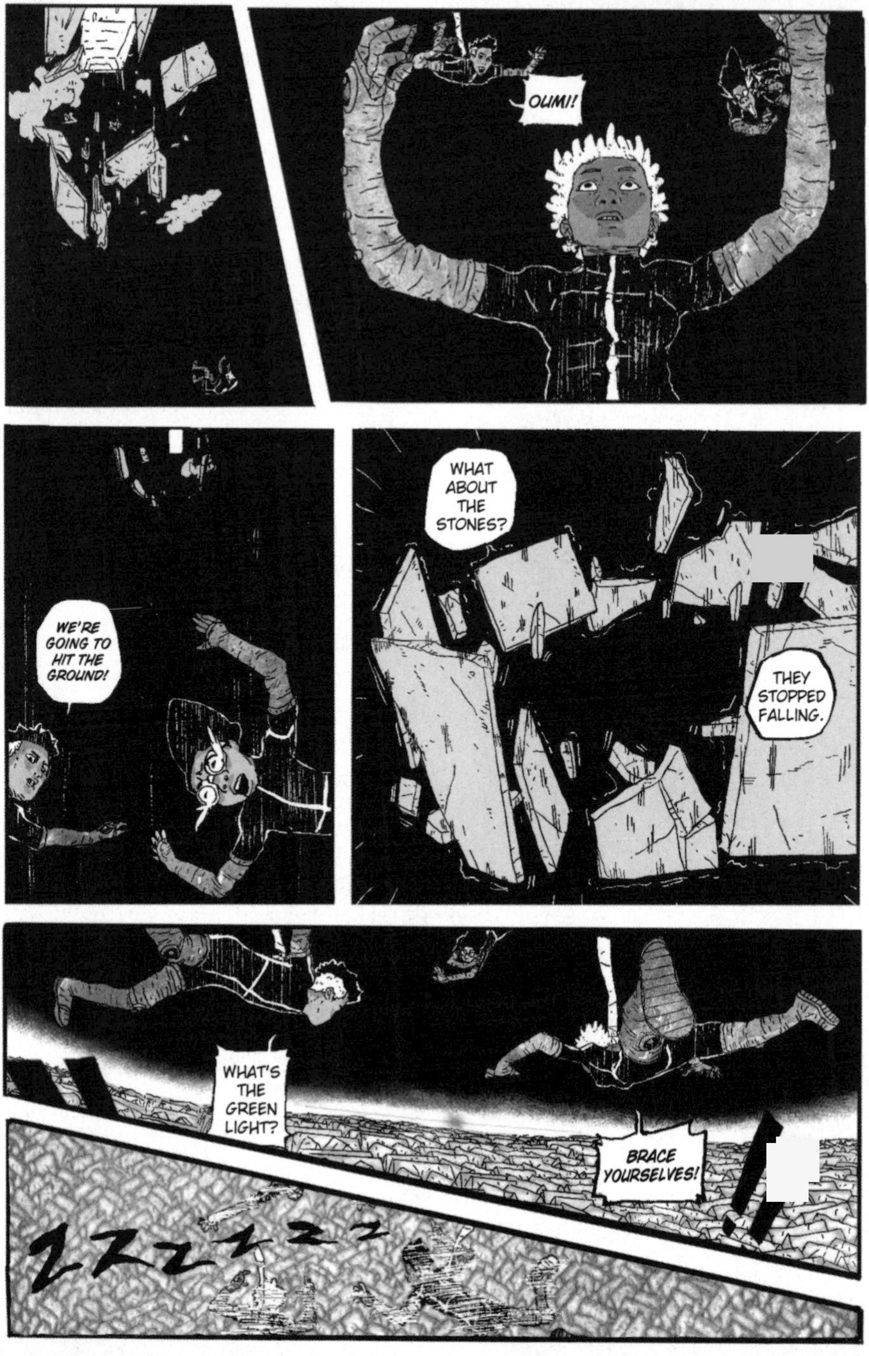
OUMI!
WE'RE GOING TO HIT THE GROUND!
WHAT ABOUT THE STONES?
THEY STOPPED FALLING.
WHAT'S THE GREEN LIGHT?
BRACE YOURSELVES!
ZZZZZZZ

ZUSH
WE TELEPORTED!
plop
PAK
!

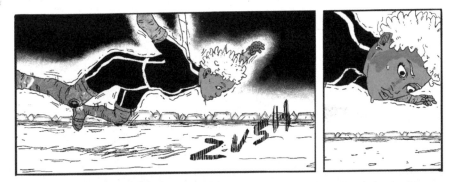

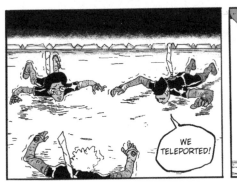

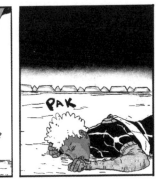

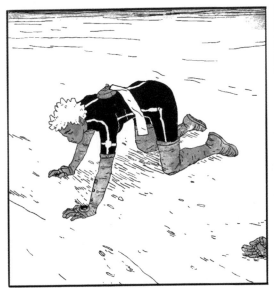

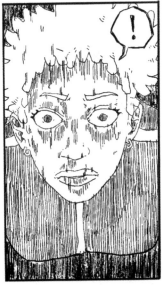

ASTOU!
WE HAVE TO GO NOW. THIS IS A BLOODBATH.
THEY'RE TAKING OUT THE WEAK.

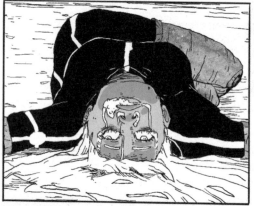

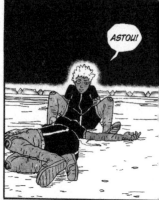

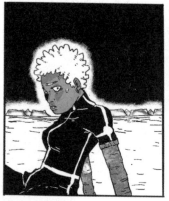

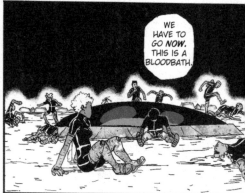

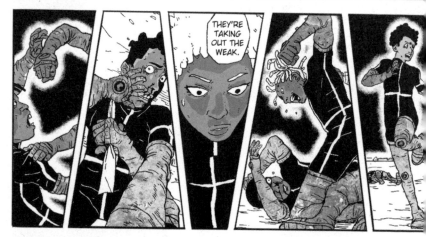

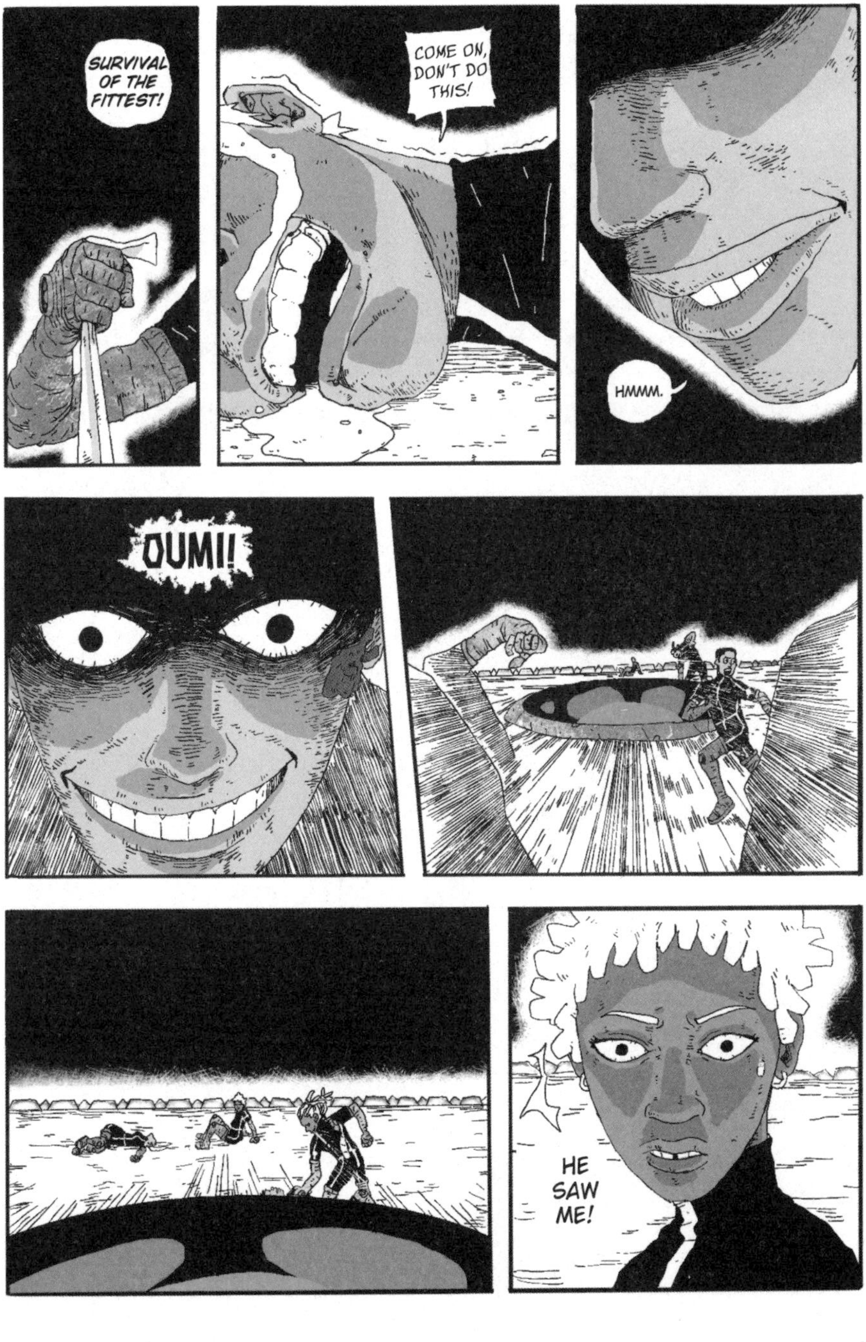
SURVIVAL OF THE FITTEST!
COME ON, DON'T DO THIS!
HMMM.
OUMI!
HE SAW ME!

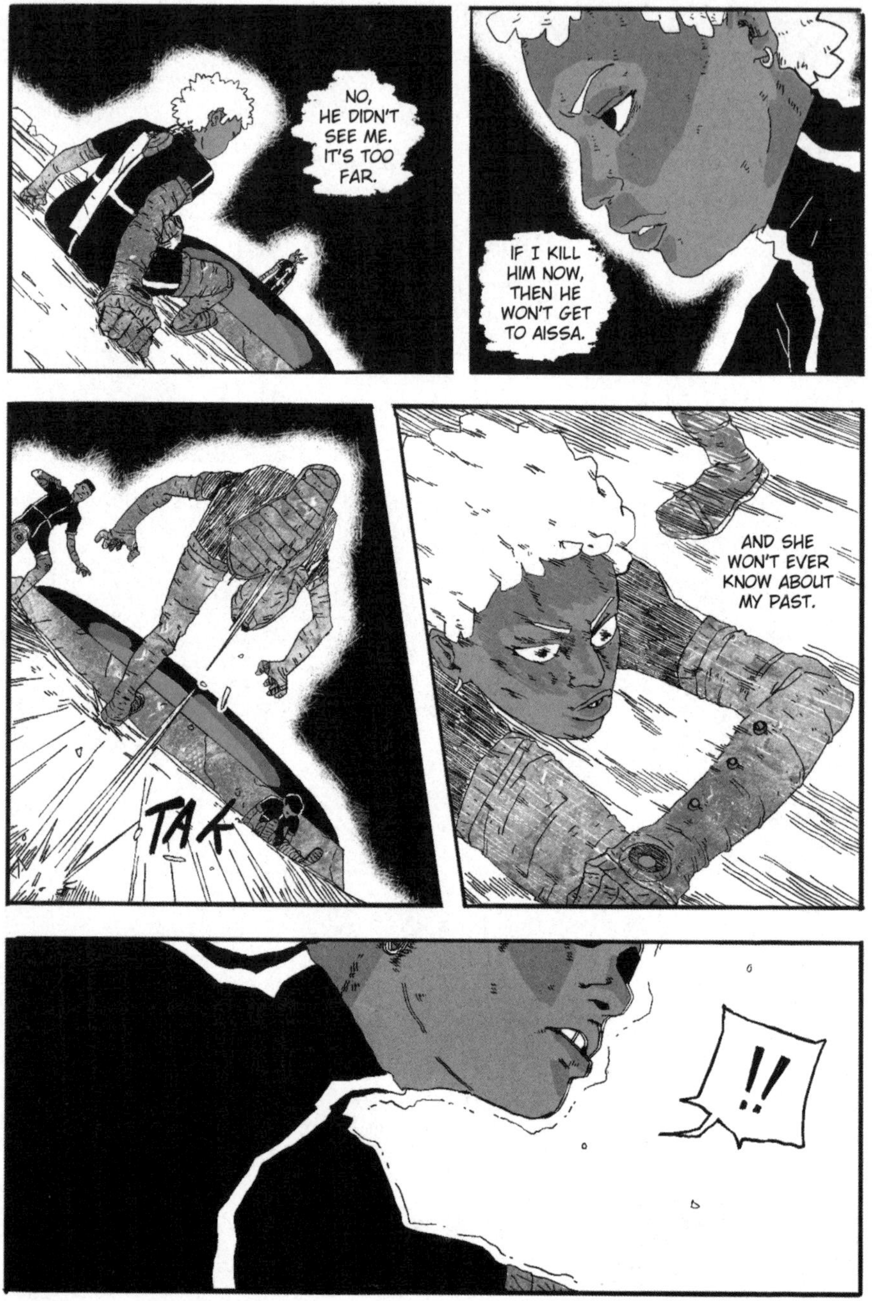
NO, HE DIDN'T SEE ME. IT'S TOO FAR.
IF I KILL HIM NOW, THEN HE WON'T GET TO AISSA.
TAK
AND SHE WON'T EVER KNOW ABOUT MY PAST.
!!

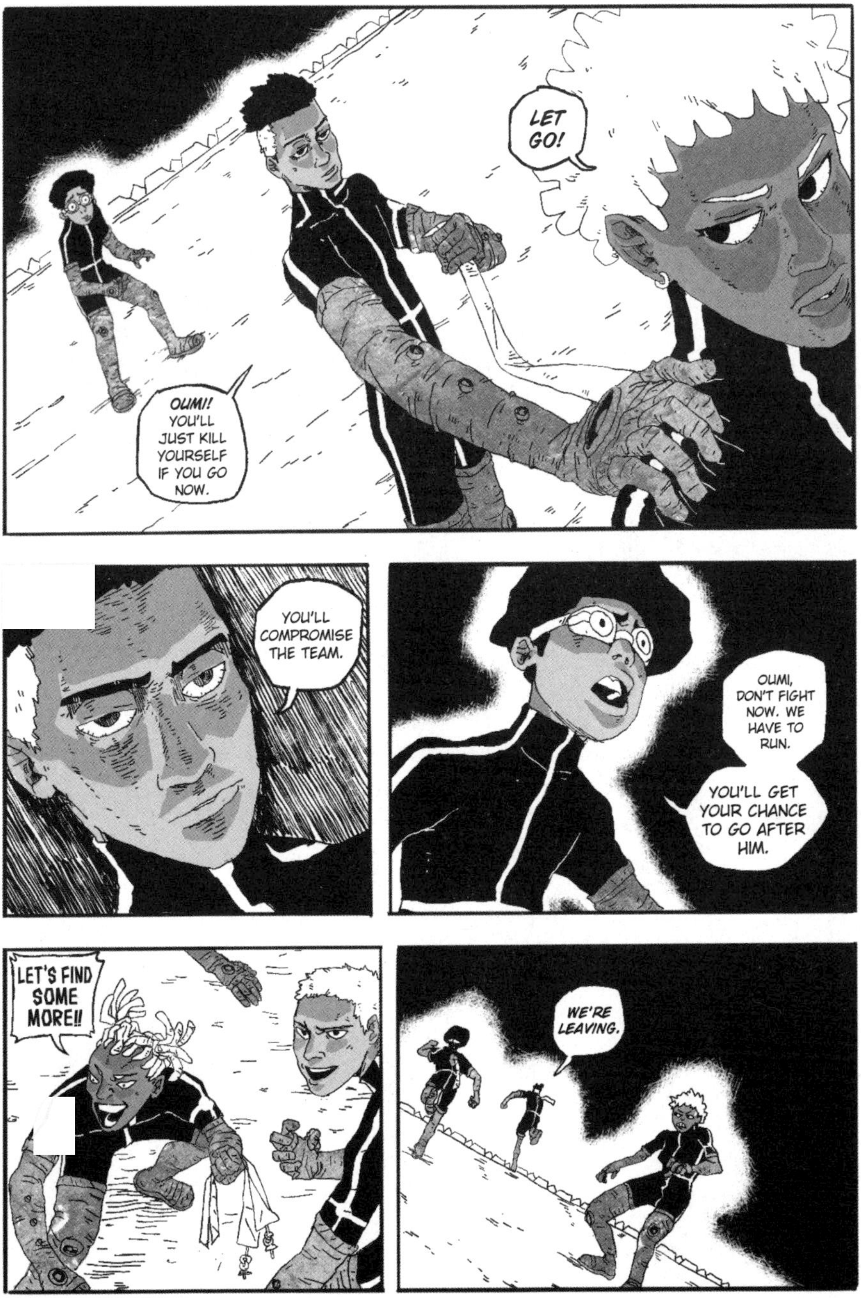
LET GO!
OUMI! YOU'LL JUST KILL YOURSELF IF YOU GO NOW.
YOU'LL COMPROMISE THE TEAM.
OUMI, DON'T FIGHT NOW. WE HAVE TO RUN.
YOU'LL GET YOUR CHANCE TO GO AFTER HIM.
LET'S FIND SOME MORE!!
WE'RE LEAVING.

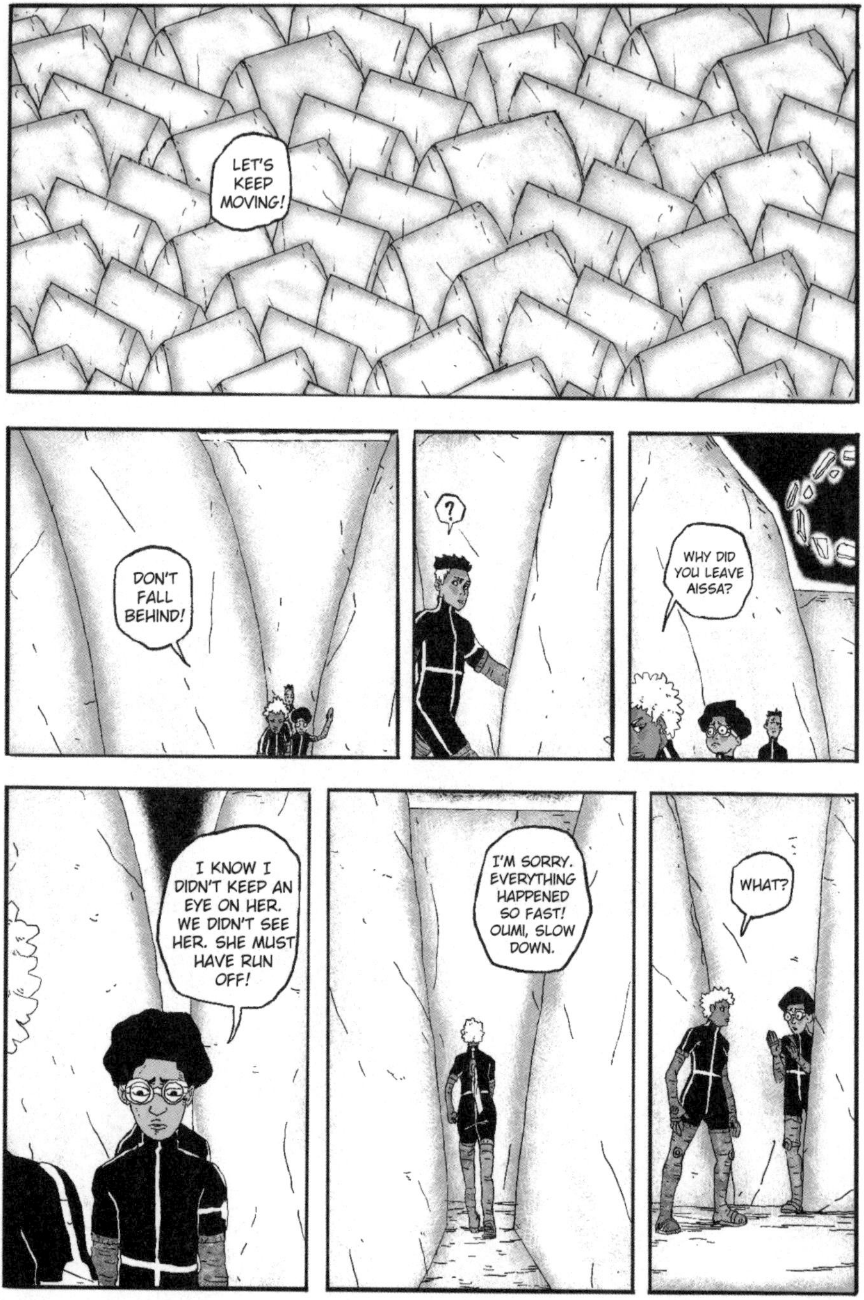

LET'S KEEP MOVING!
DON'T FALL BEHIND!
?
WHY DID YOU LEAVE AISSA?
I KNOW I DIDN'T KEEP AN EYE ON HER. WE DIDN'T SEE HER. SHE MUST HAVE RUN OFF!
I'M SORRY. EVERYTHING HAPPENED SO FAST! OUMI, SLOW DOWN.
WHAT?

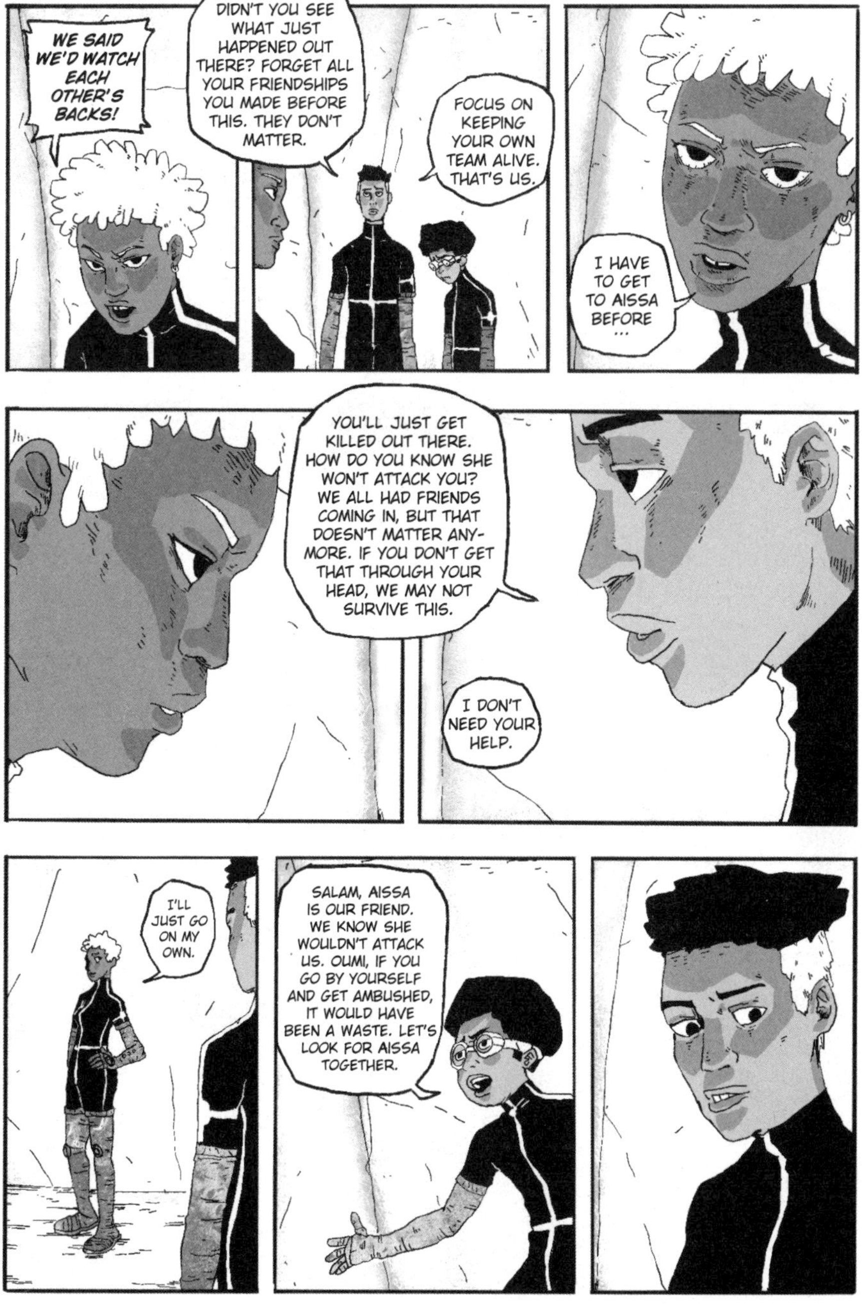
WE SAID WE'D WATCH EACH OTHER'S BACKS!
DIDN'T YOU SEE WHAT JUST HAPPENED OUT THERE? FORGET ALL YOUR FRIENDSHIPS YOU MADE BEFORE THIS. THEY DON'T MATTER.
FOCUS ON KEEPING YOUR OWN TEAM ALIVE. THAT'S US.
I HAVE TO GET TO AISSA BEFORE ...
YOU'LL JUST GET KILLED OUT THERE. HOW DO YOU KNOW SHE WON'T ATTACK YOU? WE ALL HAD FRIENDS COMING IN, BUT THAT DOESN'T MATTER ANY-MORE. IF YOU DON'T GET THAT THROUGH YOUR HEAD, WE MAY NOT SURVIVE THIS.
I DON'T NEED YOUR HELP.
I'LL JUST GO ON MY OWN.
SALAM, AISSA IS OUR FRIEND. WE KNOW SHE WOULDN'T ATTACK US. OUMI, IF YOU GO BY YOURSELF AND GET AMBUSHED, IT WOULD HAVE BEEN A WASTE. LET'S LOOK FOR AISSA TOGETHER.

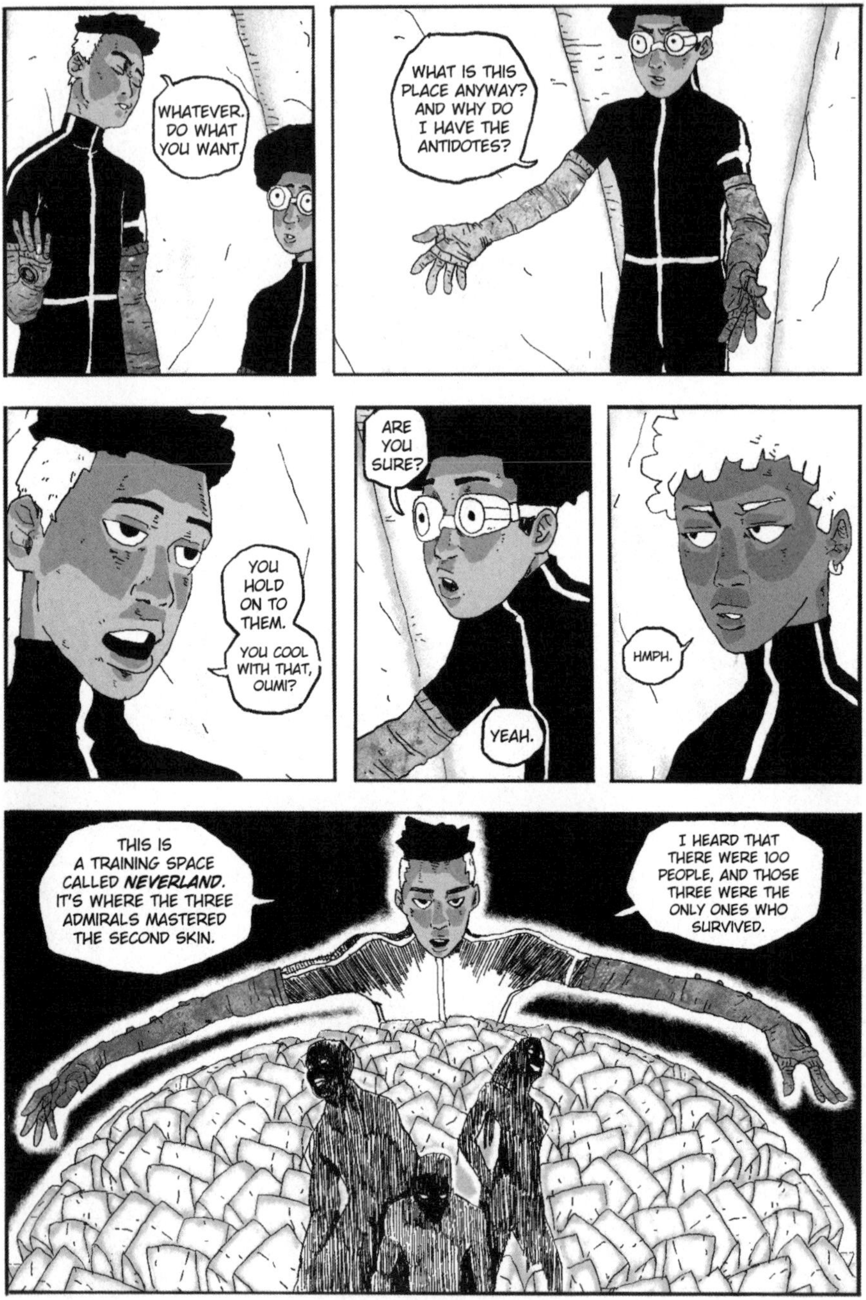
WHATEVER. DO WHAT YOU WANT.
WHAT IS THIS PLACE ANYWAY? AND WHY DO I HAVE THE ANTIDOTES?
YOU HOLD ON TO THEM.
YOU COOL WITH THAT, OUMI?
ARE YOU SURE?
YEAH.
HMPH.
THIS IS A TRAINING SPACE CALLED ***NEVERLAND***. IT'S WHERE THE THREE ADMIRALS MASTERED THE SECOND SKIN.
I HEARD THAT THERE WERE 100 PEOPLE, AND THOSE THREE WERE THE ONLY ONES WHO SURVIVED.

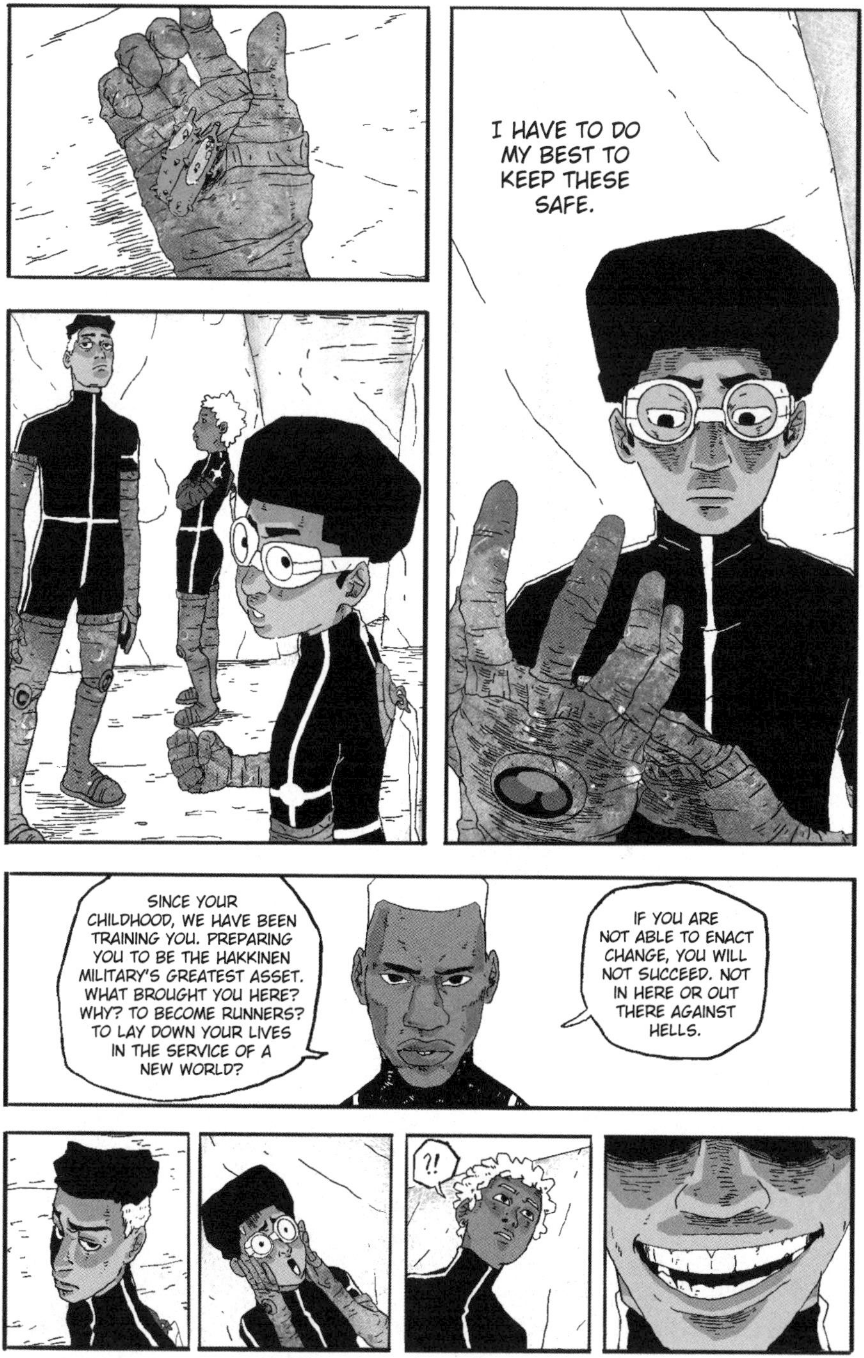
I HAVE TO DO MY BEST TO KEEP THESE SAFE.
SINCE YOUR CHILDHOOD, WE HAVE BEEN TRAINING YOU. PREPARING YOU TO BE THE HAKKINEN MILITARY'S GREATEST ASSET. WHAT BROUGHT YOU HERE? WHY? TO BECOME RUNNERS? TO LAY DOWN YOUR LIVES IN THE SERVICE OF A NEW WORLD?
IF YOU ARE NOT ABLE TO ENACT CHANGE, YOU WILL NOT SUCCEED. NOT IN HERE OR OUT THERE AGAINST HELLS.
?!

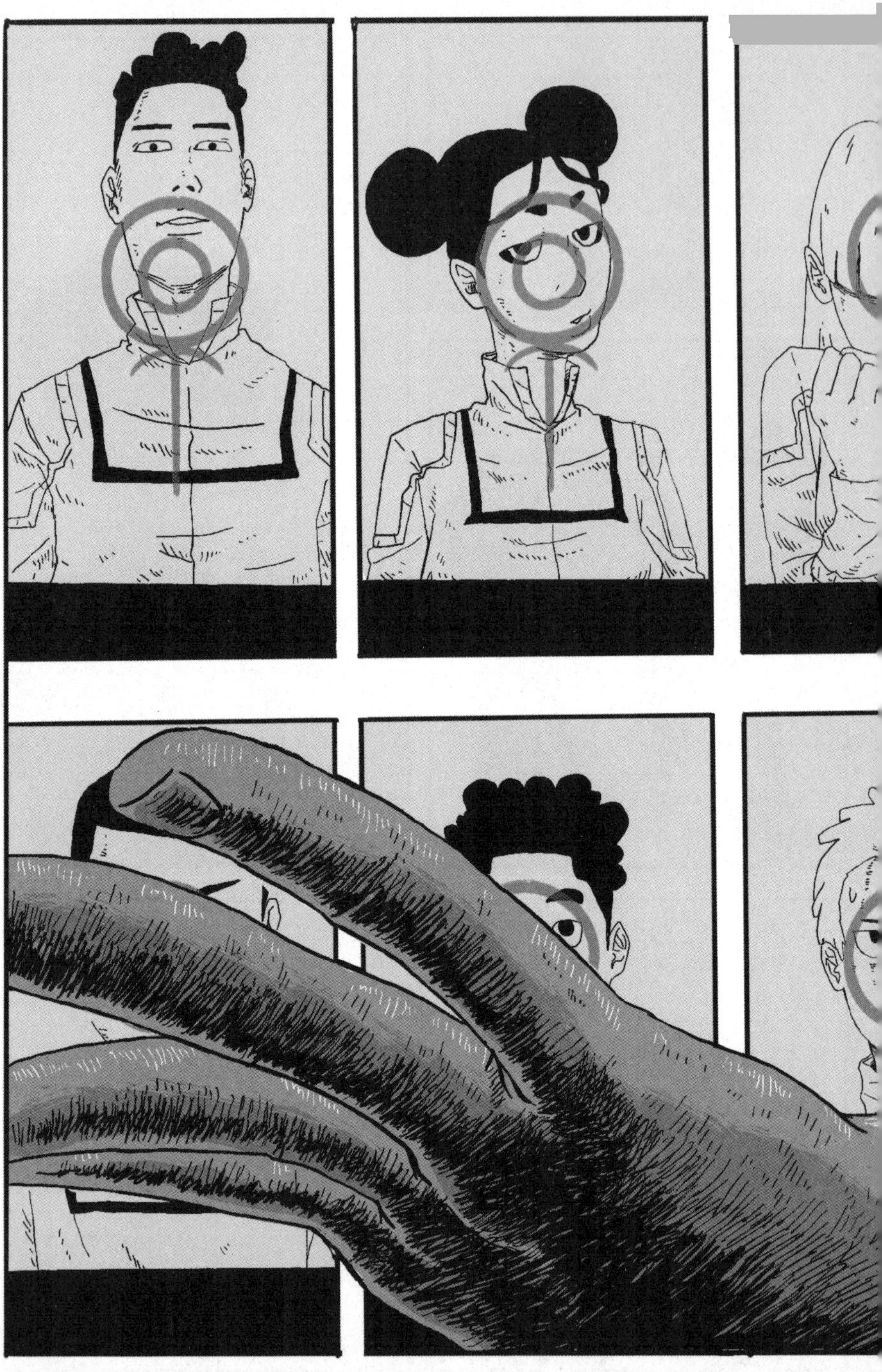

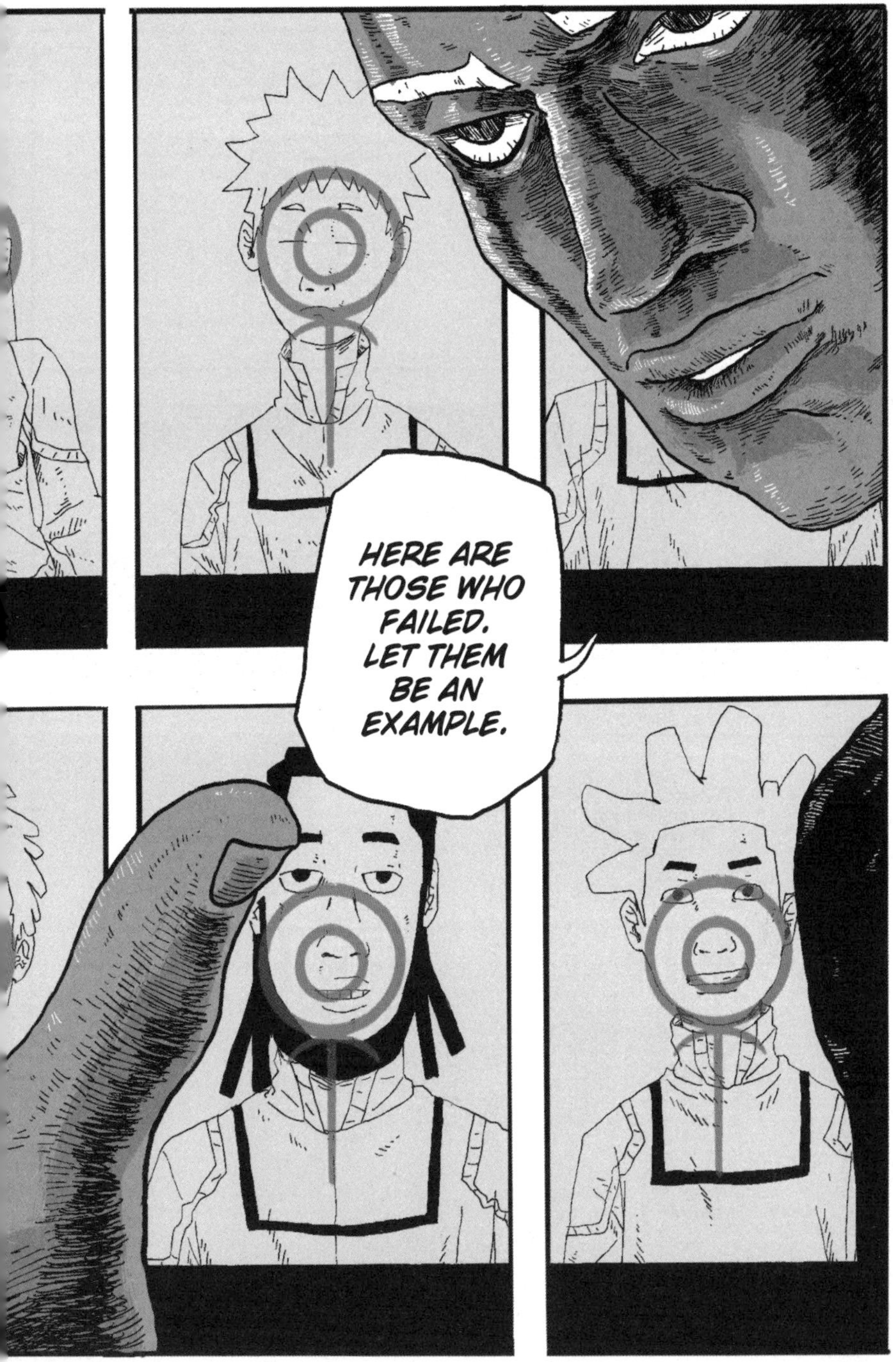
HERE ARE THOSE WHO FAILED. LET THEM BE AN EXAMPLE.

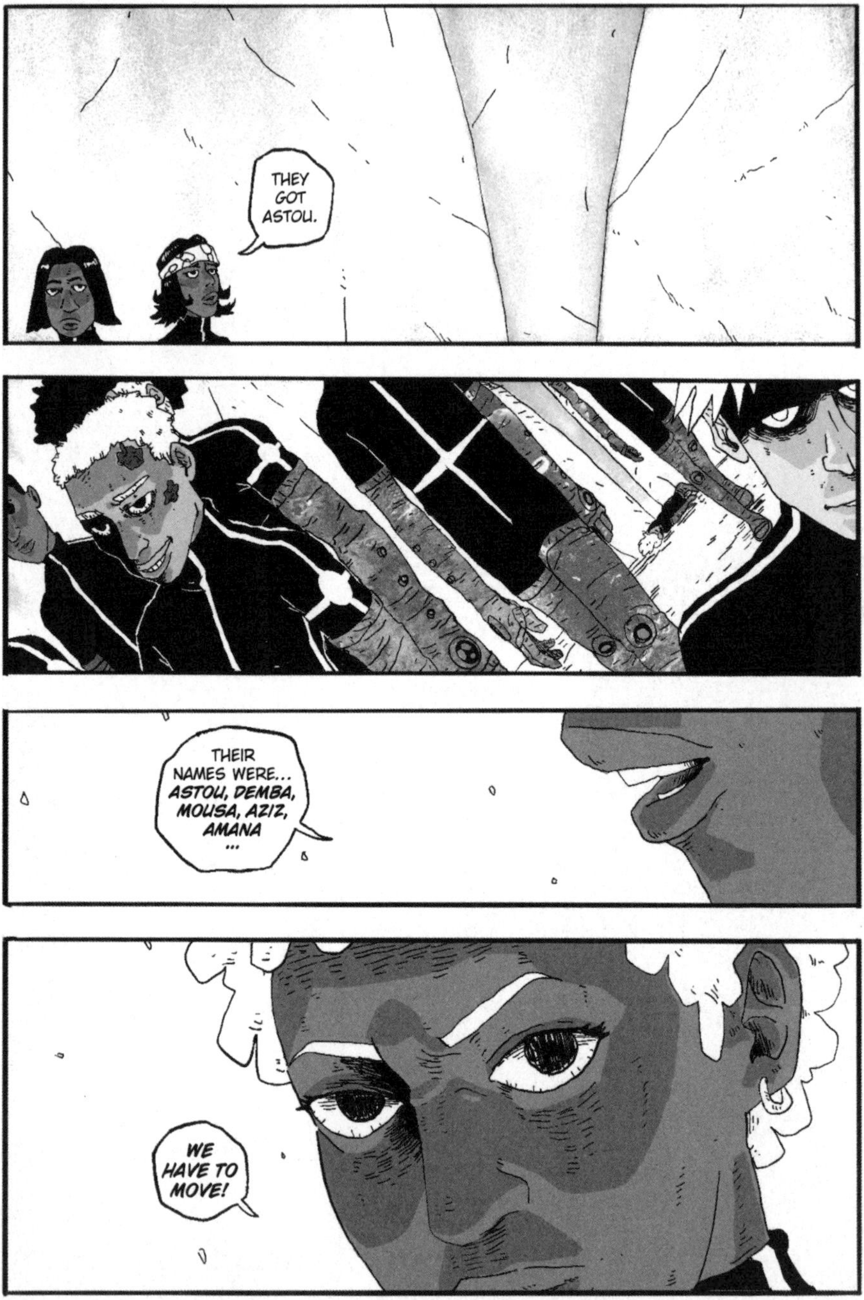
THEY GOT ASTOU.
THEIR NAMES WERE... ASTOU, DEMBA, MOUSA, AZIZ, AMANA ...
WE HAVE TO MOVE!

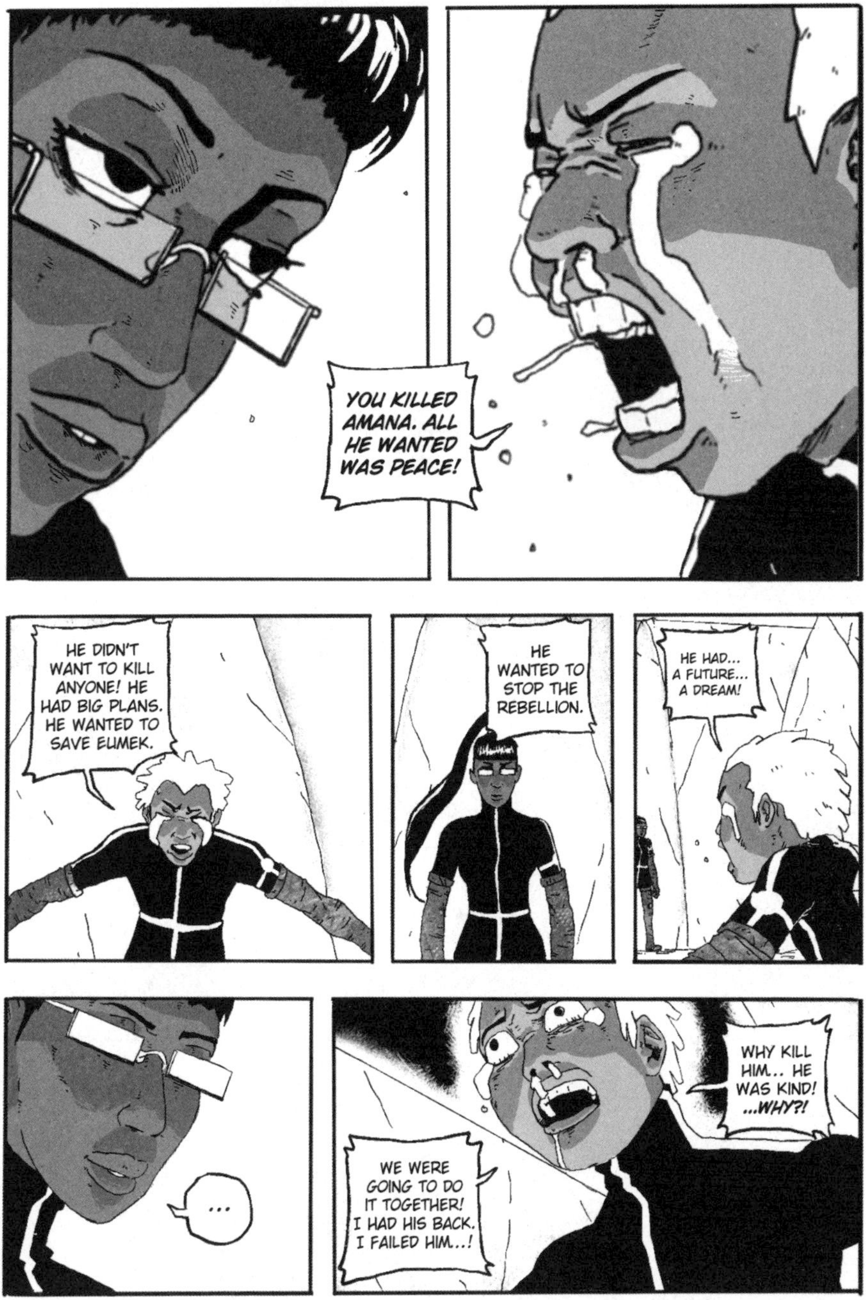
YOU KILLED AMANA. ALL HE WANTED WAS PEACE!
HE DIDN'T WANT TO KILL ANYONE! HE HAD BIG PLANS. HE WANTED TO SAVE EUMEK.
HE WANTED TO STOP THE REBELLION.
HE HAD... A FUTURE... A DREAM!
...
WE WERE GOING TO DO IT TOGETHER! I HAD HIS BACK. I FAILED HIM...!
WHY KILL HIM... HE WAS KIND! ...WHY?!

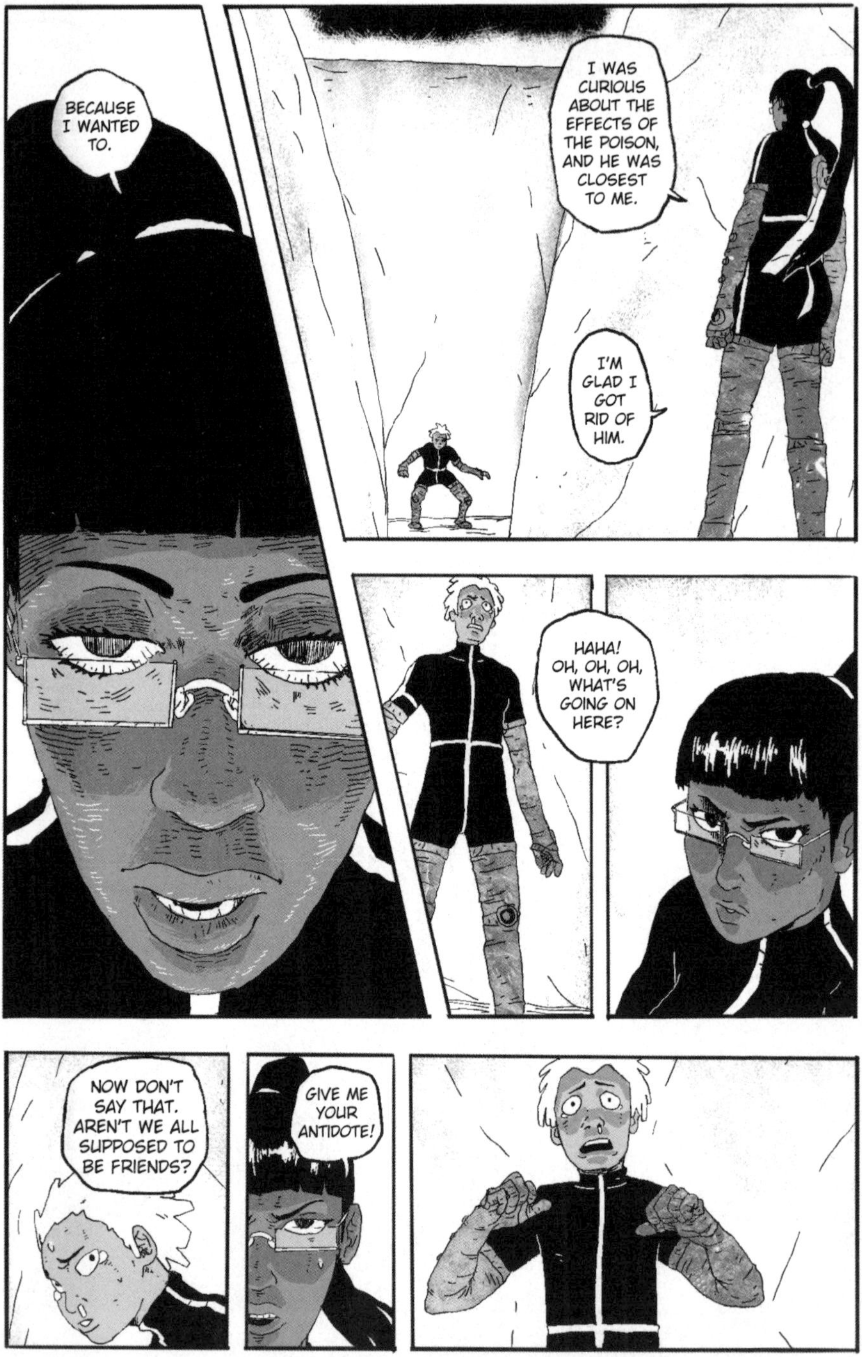
BECAUSE I WANTED TO.
I WAS CURIOUS ABOUT THE EFFECTS OF THE POISON, AND HE WAS CLOSEST TO ME.
I'M GLAD I GOT RID OF HIM.
HAHA! OH, OH, OH, WHAT'S GOING ON HERE?
NOW DON'T SAY THAT. AREN'T WE ALL SUPPOSED TO BE FRIENDS?
GIVE ME YOUR ANTIDOTE!

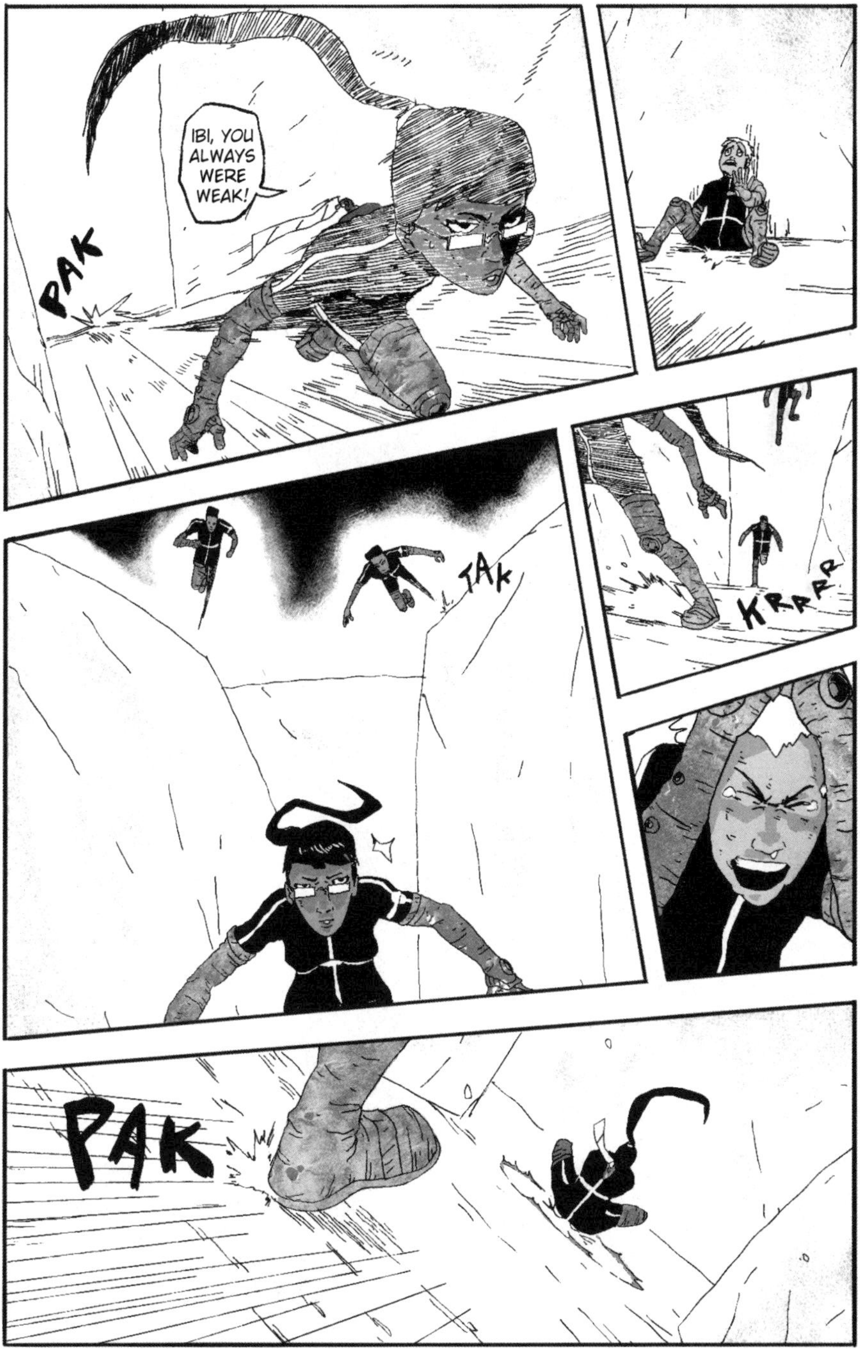
IBI, YOU ALWAYS WERE WEAK!
PAK
TAK
KRRRR
PAK

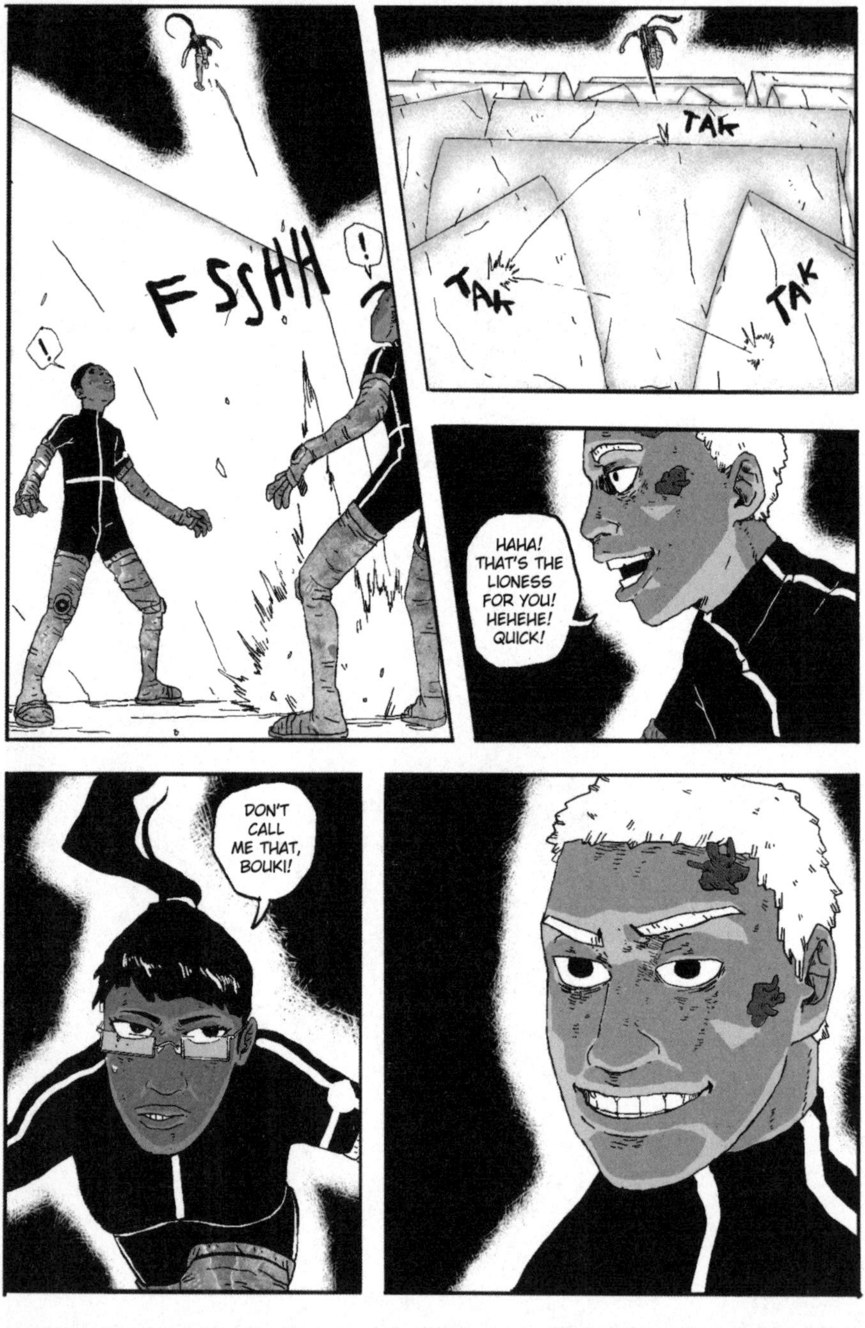

FSSHH
!
!
TAK
TAK
TAK
HAHA! THAT'S THE LIONESS FOR YOU! HEHEHE! QUICK!
DON'T CALL ME THAT, BOUKI!

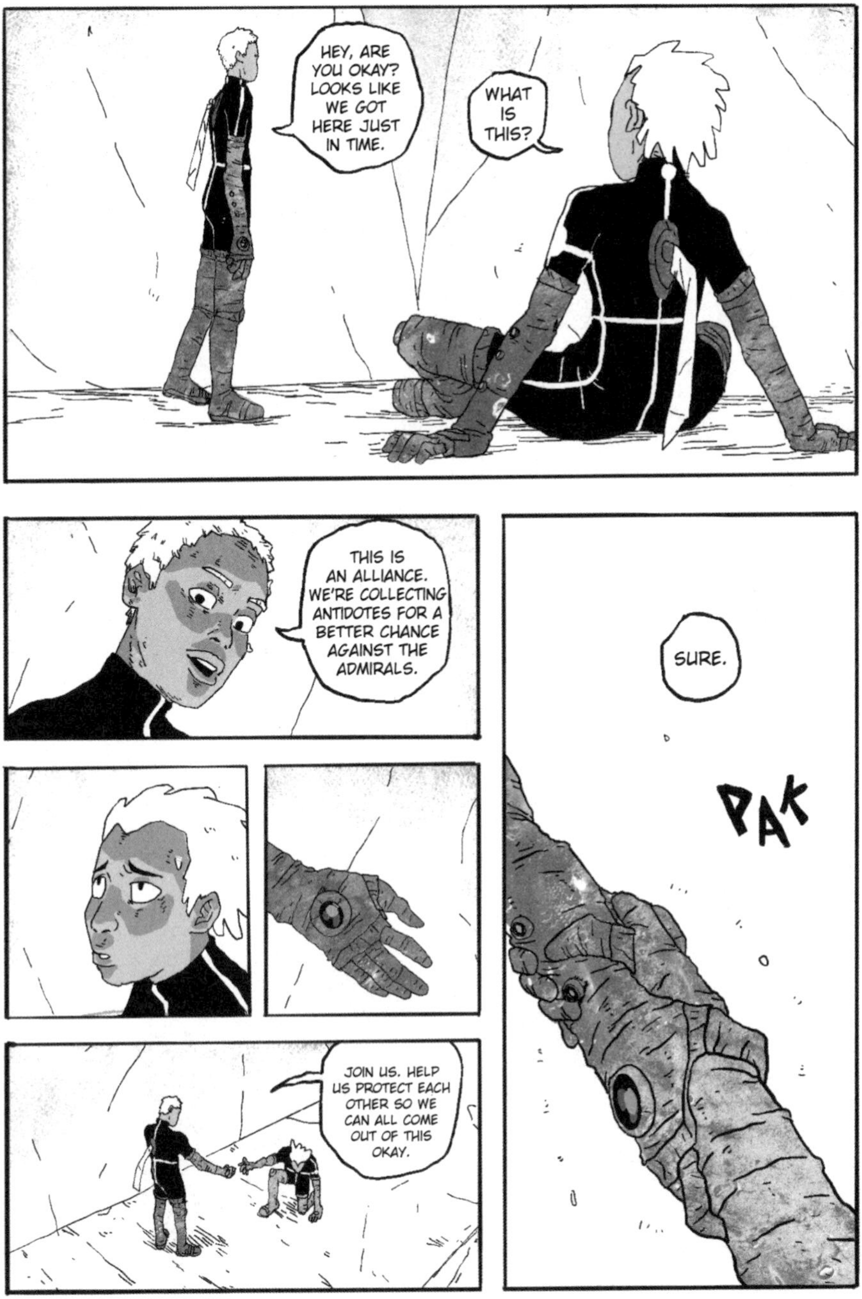
HEY, ARE YOU OKAY? LOOKS LIKE WE GOT HERE JUST IN TIME.
WHAT IS THIS?
THIS IS AN ALLIANCE. WE'RE COLLECTING ANTIDOTES FOR A BETTER CHANCE AGAINST THE ADMIRALS.
JOIN US. HELP US PROTECT EACH OTHER SO WE CAN ALL COME OUT OF THIS OKAY.
SURE.
PAK

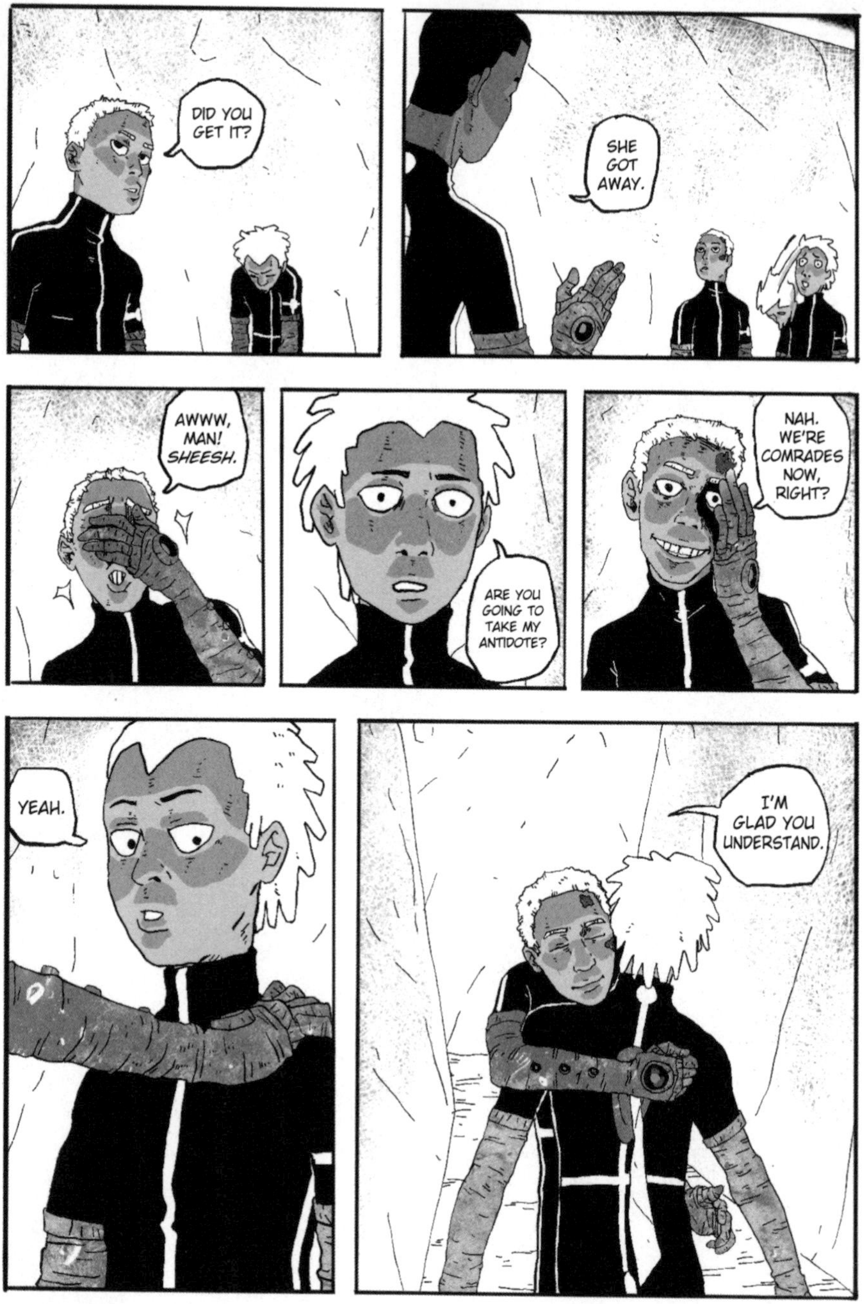
DID YOU GET IT?
SHE GOT AWAY.
AWWW, MAN! SHEESH.
ARE YOU GOING TO TAKE MY ANTIDOTE?
NAH. WE'RE COMRADES NOW, RIGHT?
YEAH.
I'M GLAD YOU UNDERSTAND.

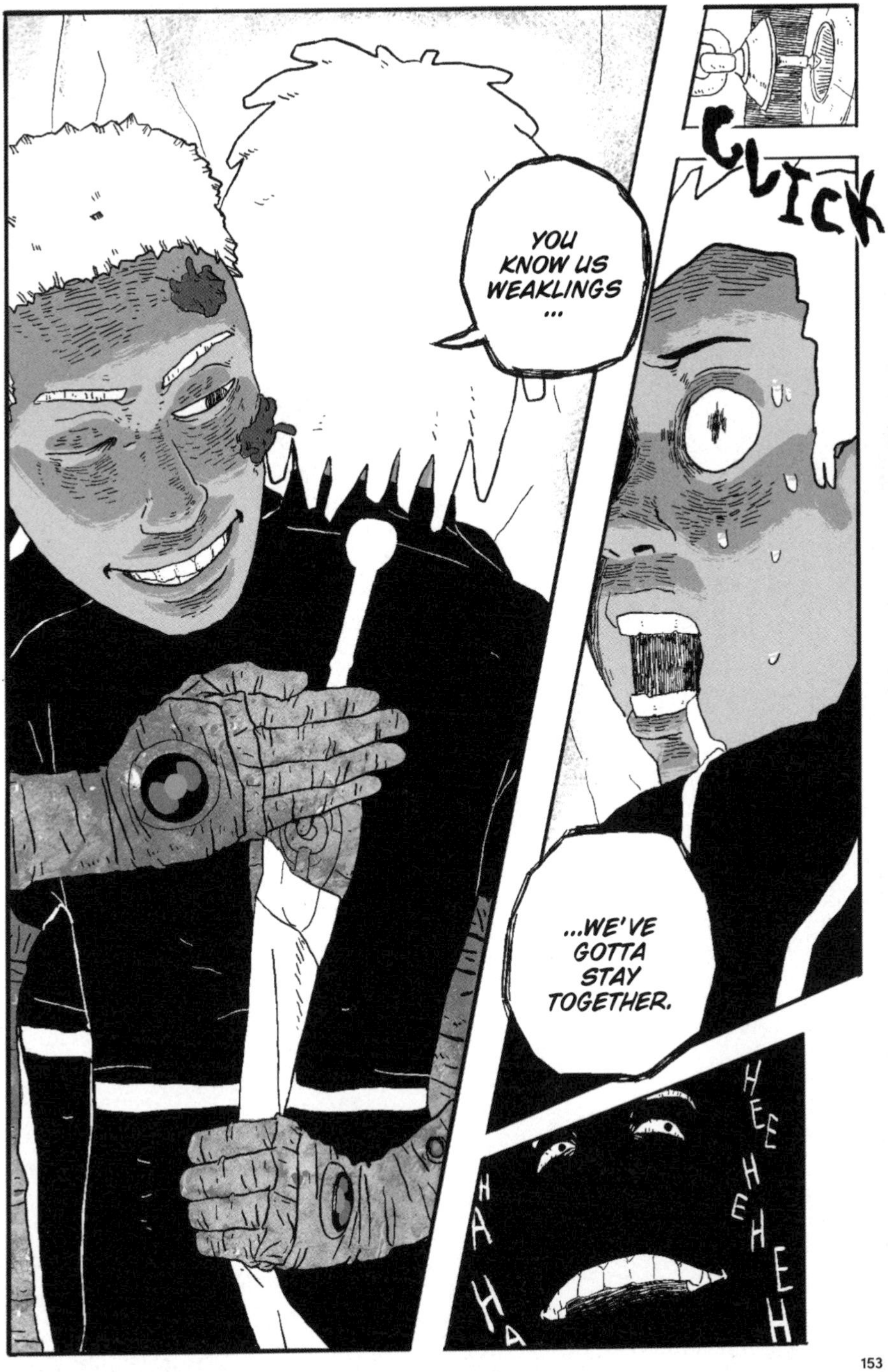
YOU KNOW US WEAKLINGS ...
CLICK
...WE'VE GOTTA STAY TOGETHER.
HEE HEH HEH HEH
HA HA HA

OBLIVION ROUGE

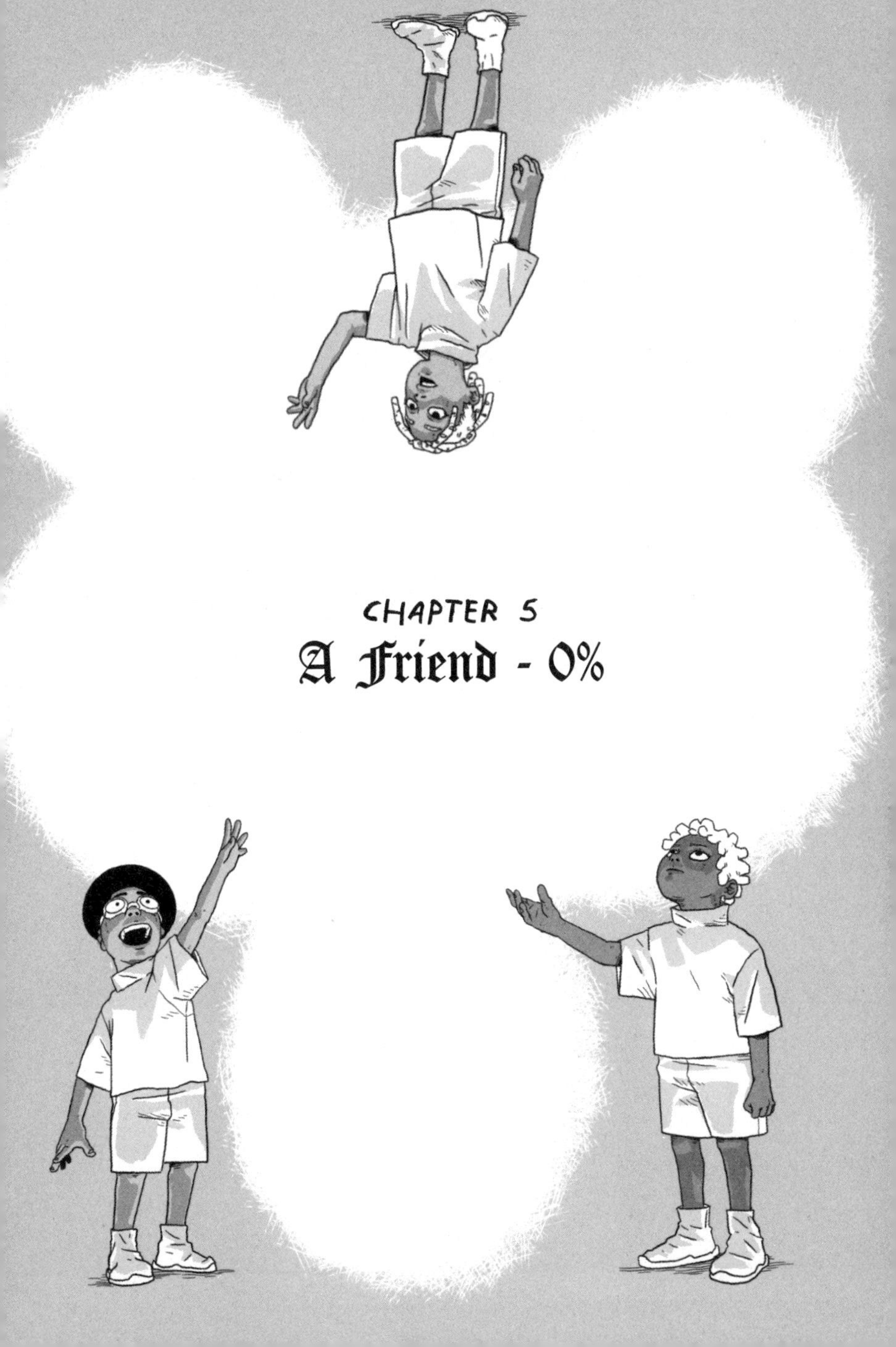

CHAPTER 5

A Friend - 0%

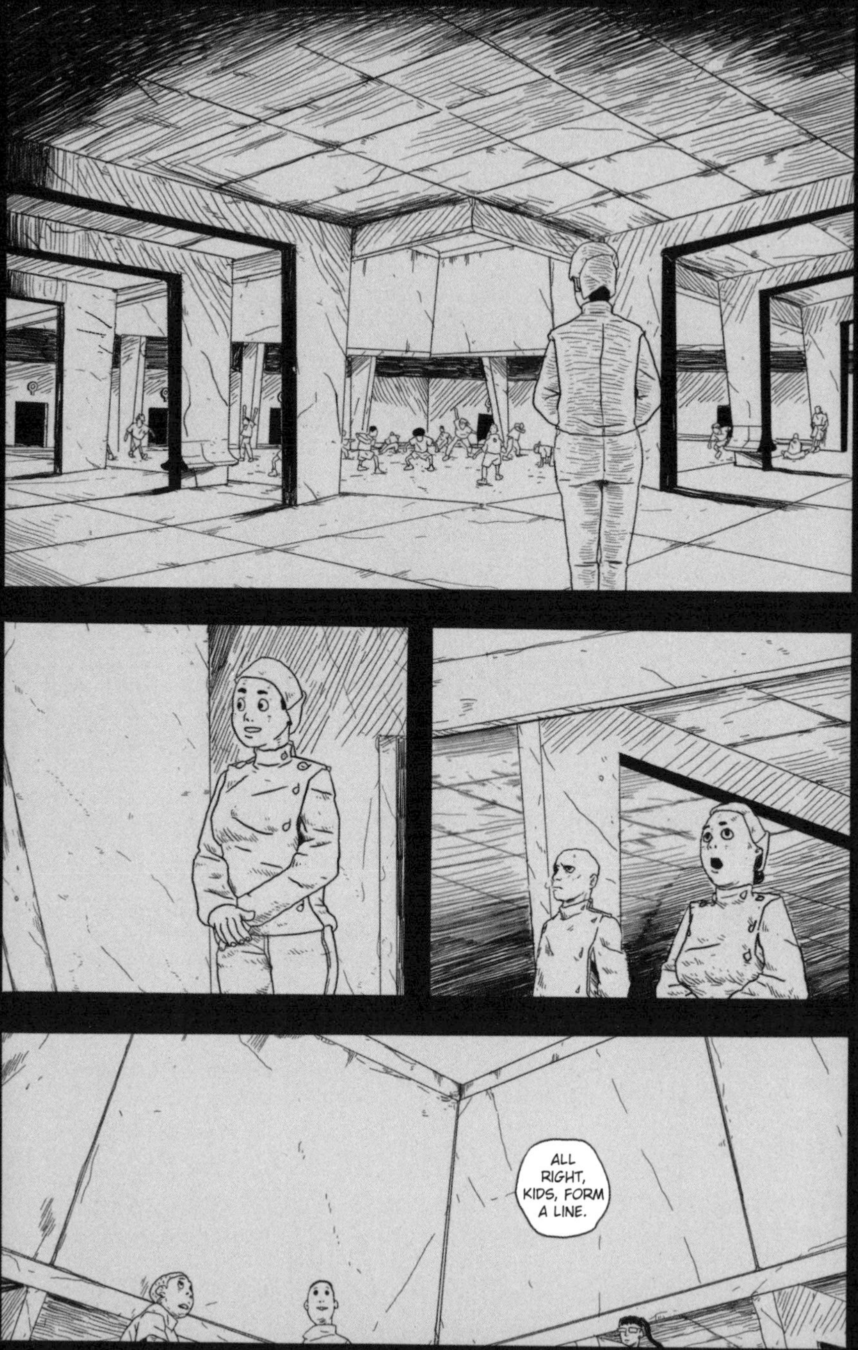
ALL RIGHT, KIDS, FORM A LINE.

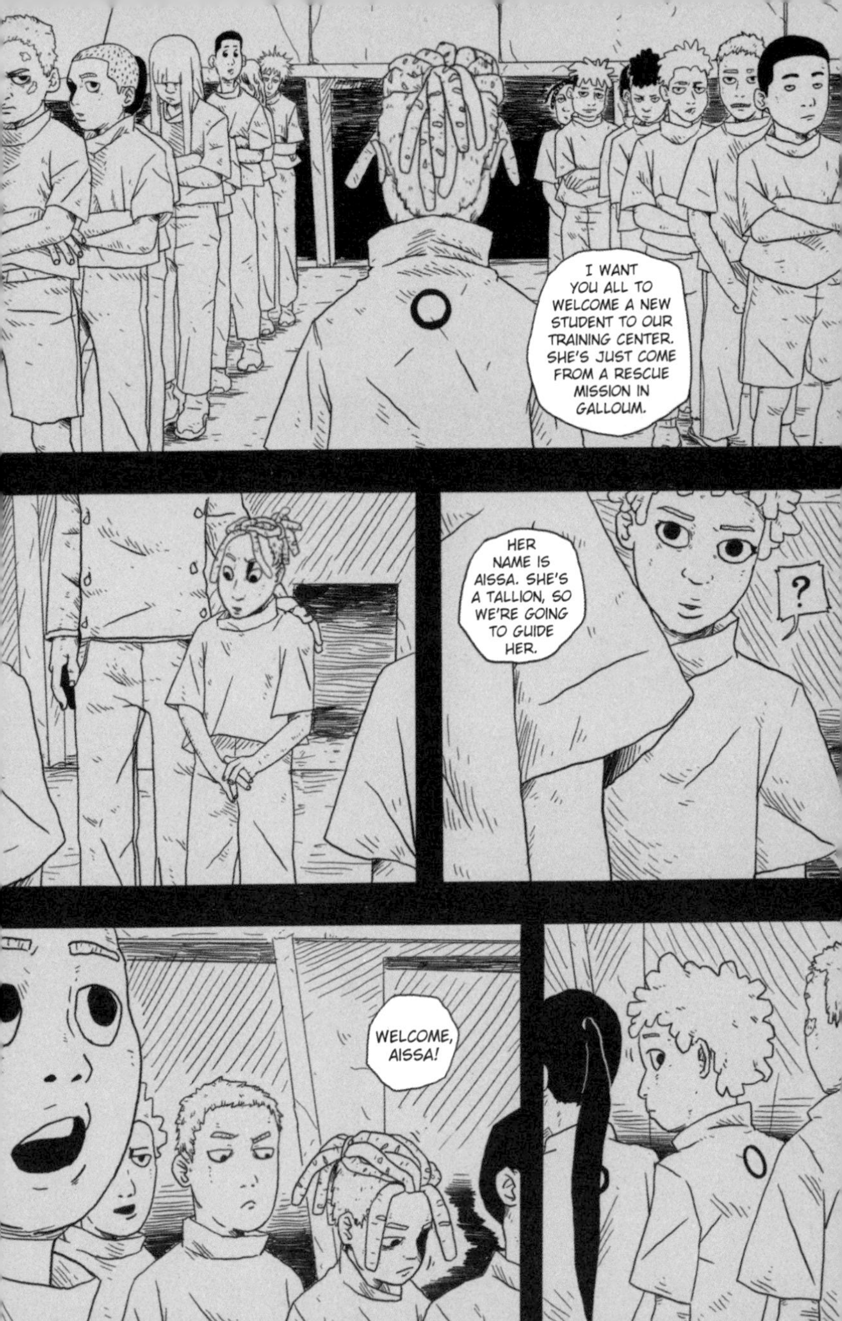
I WANT YOU ALL TO WELCOME A NEW STUDENT TO OUR TRAINING CENTER. SHE'S JUST COME FROM A RESCUE MISSION IN GALLOUM.
HER NAME IS AISSA. SHE'S A TALLION, SO WE'RE GOING TO GUIDE HER.
?
WELCOME, AISSA!

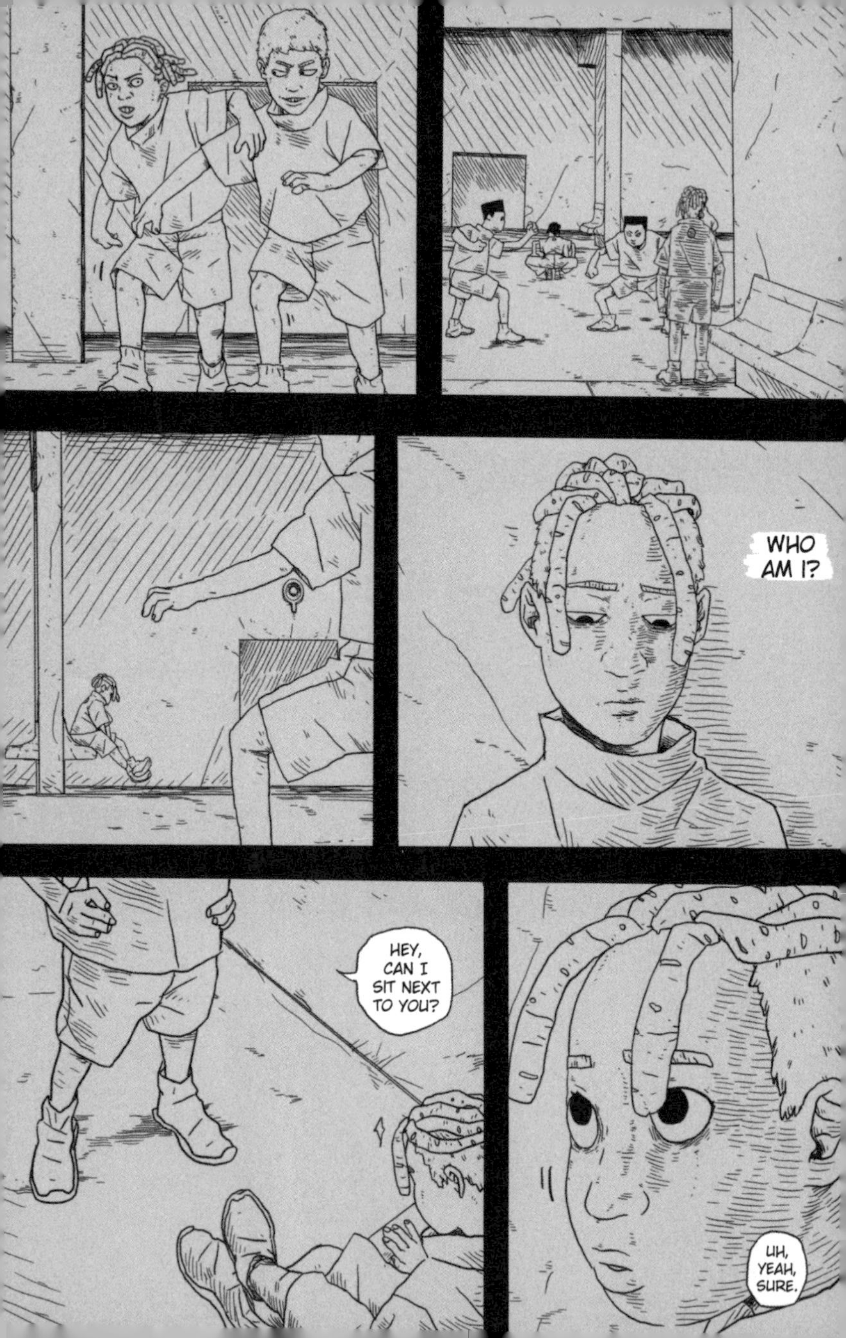
WHO AM I?
HEY, CAN I SIT NEXT TO YOU?
UH, YEAH, SURE.

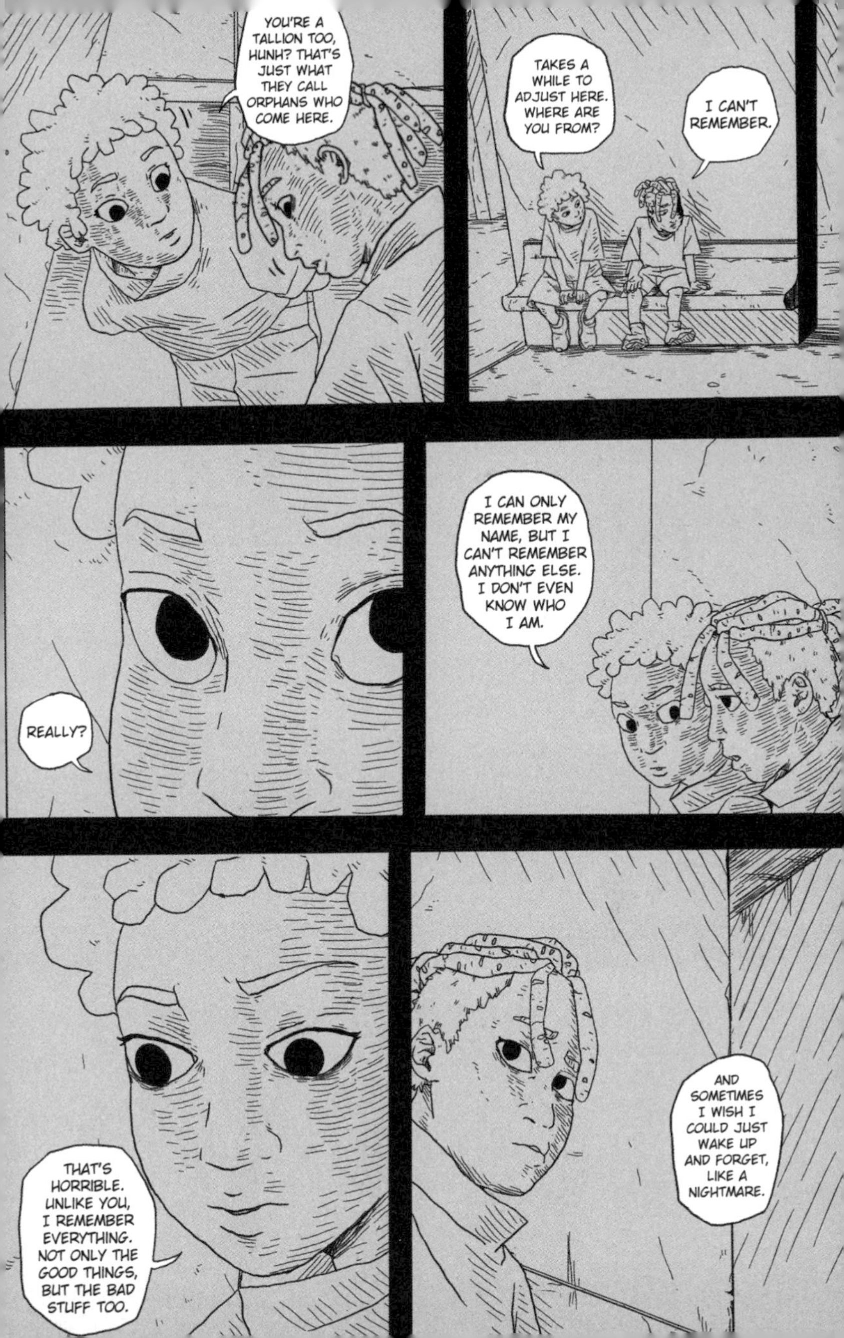
YOU'RE A TALLION TOO, HUNH? THAT'S JUST WHAT THEY CALL ORPHANS WHO COME HERE.
TAKES A WHILE TO ADJUST HERE. WHERE ARE YOU FROM?
I CAN'T REMEMBER.
REALLY?
I CAN ONLY REMEMBER MY NAME, BUT I CAN'T REMEMBER ANYTHING ELSE. I DON'T EVEN KNOW WHO I AM.
THAT'S HORRIBLE. UNLIKE YOU, I REMEMBER EVERYTHING. NOT ONLY THE GOOD THINGS, BUT THE BAD STUFF TOO.
AND SOMETIMES I WISH I COULD JUST WAKE UP AND FORGET, LIKE A NIGHTMARE.

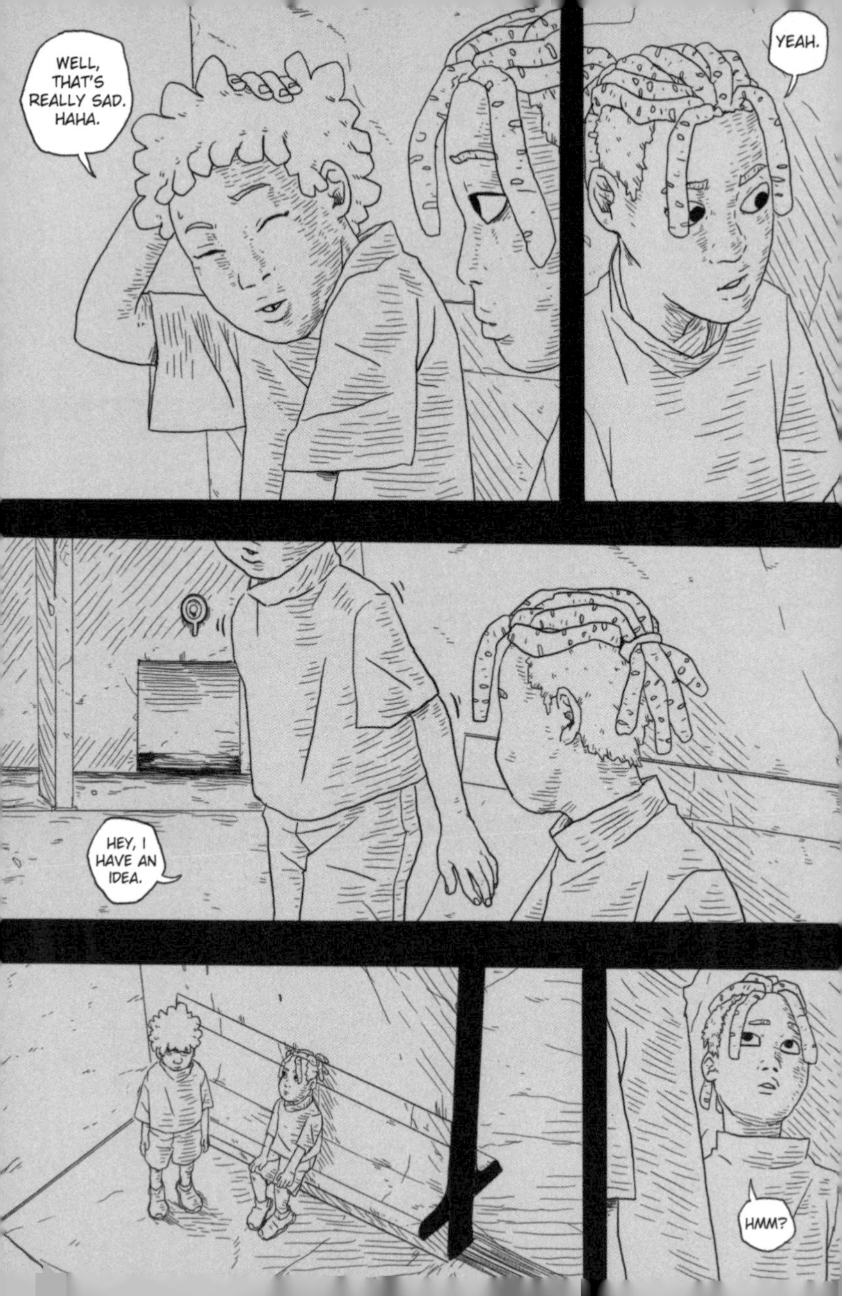
WELL, THAT'S REALLY SAD. HAHA.
YEAH.
HEY, I HAVE AN IDEA.
HMM?

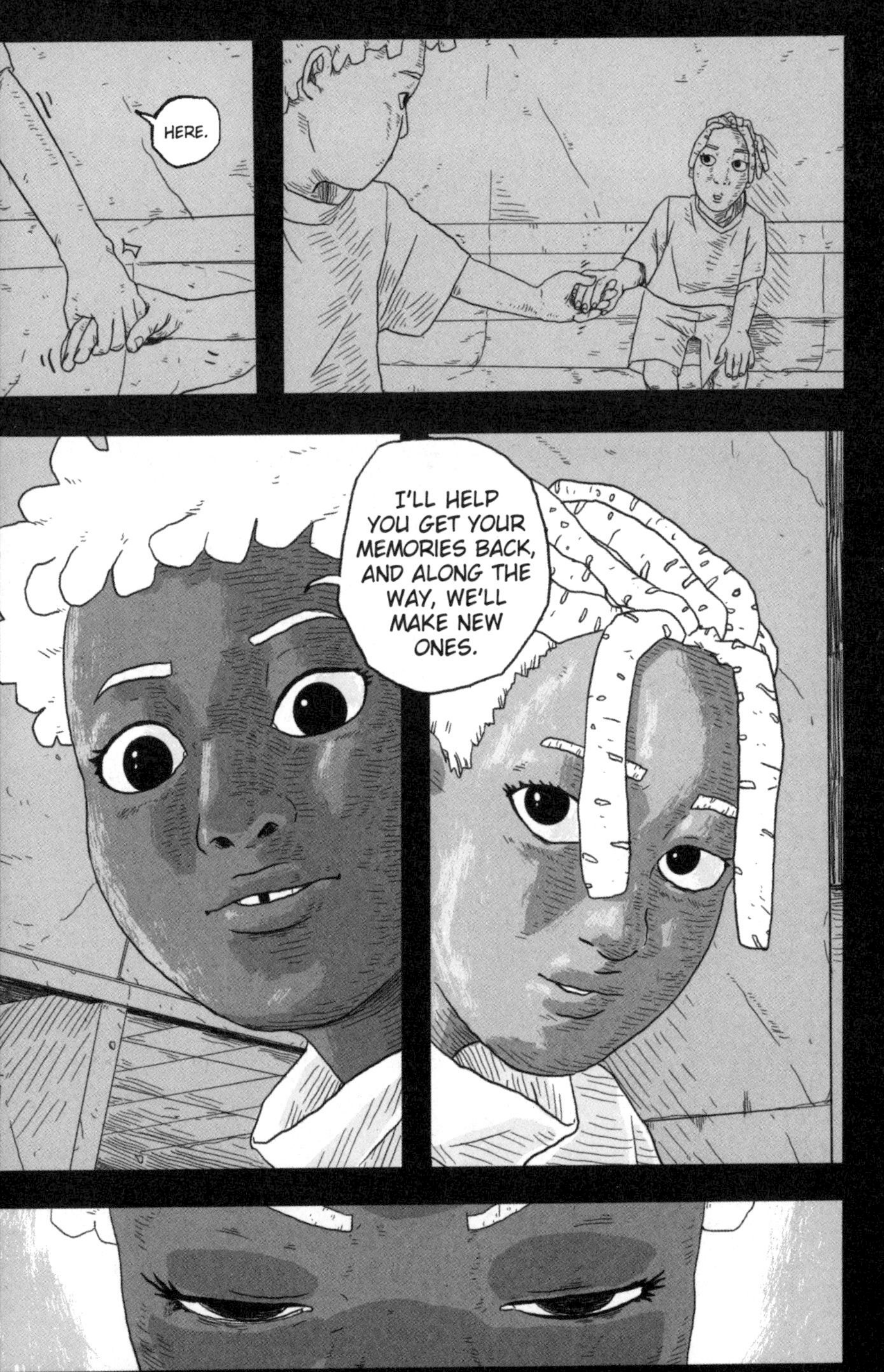
HERE.
I'LL HELP YOU GET YOUR MEMORIES BACK, AND ALONG THE WAY, WE'LL MAKE NEW ONES.

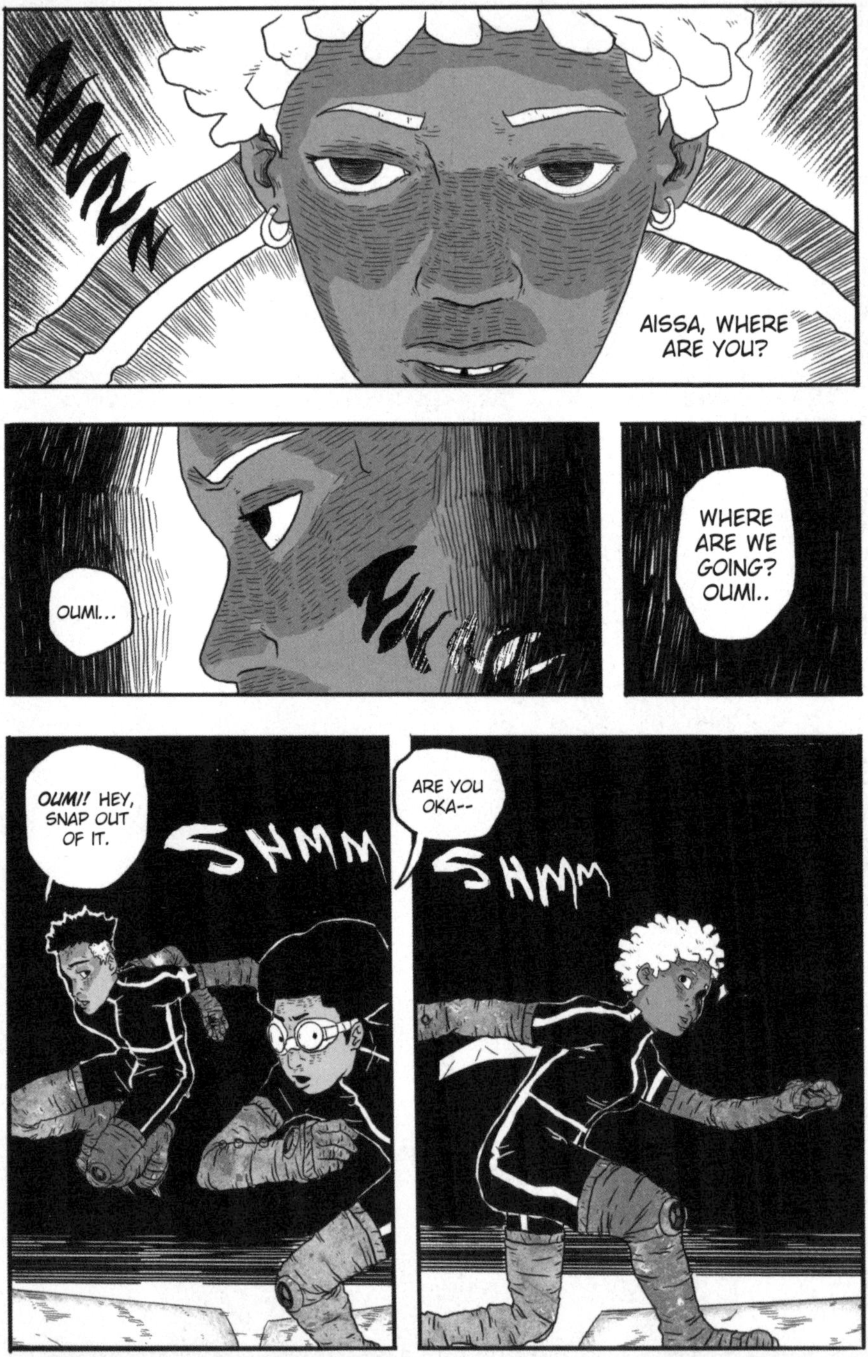
AISSA, WHERE ARE YOU?
OUMI...
WHERE ARE WE GOING? OUMI..
OUMI! HEY, SNAP OUT OF IT.
SHMM
ARE YOU OKA--
SHMM

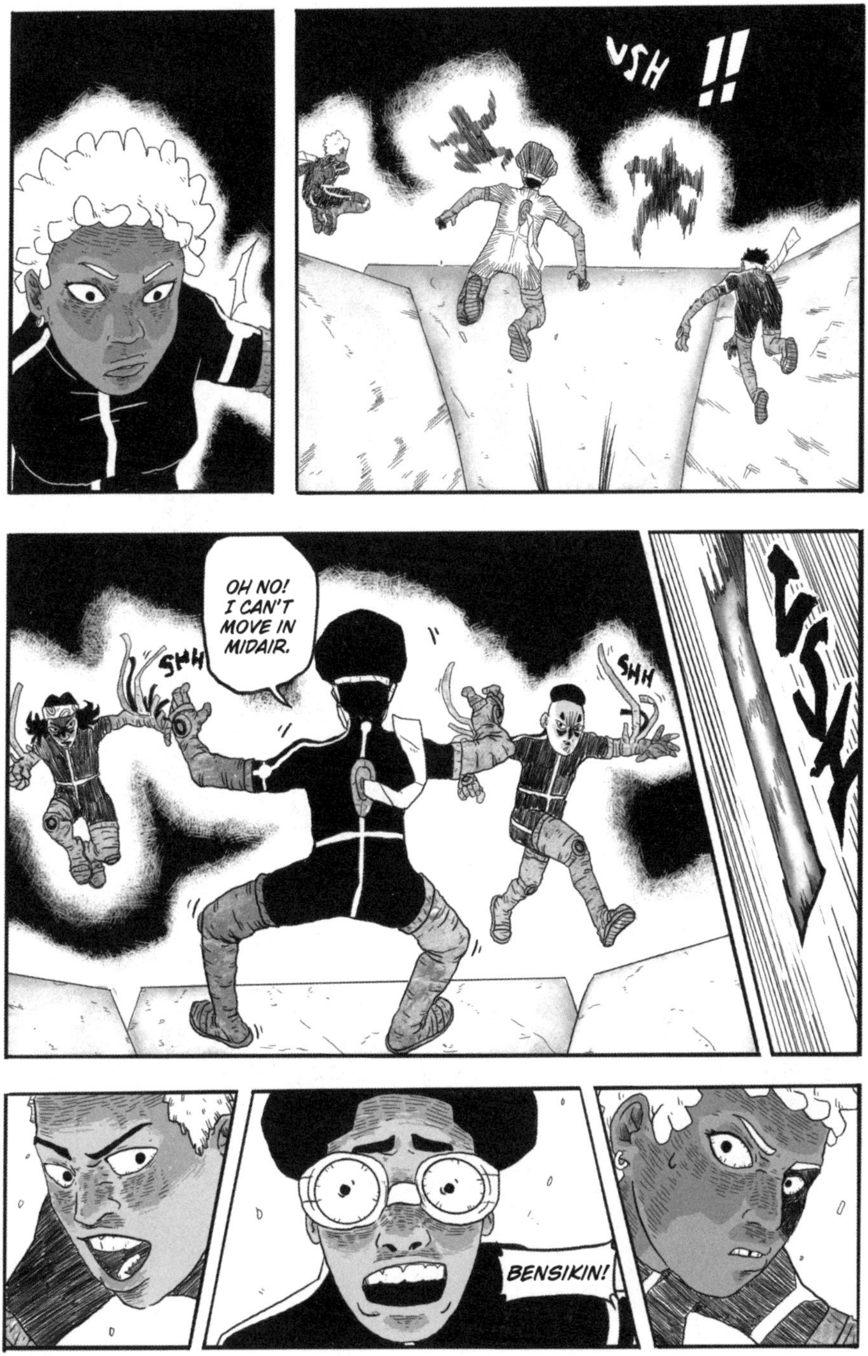
VSH!!
SHH
OH NO! I CAN'T MOVE IN MIDAIR.
SHH
VSH
BENSIKIN!

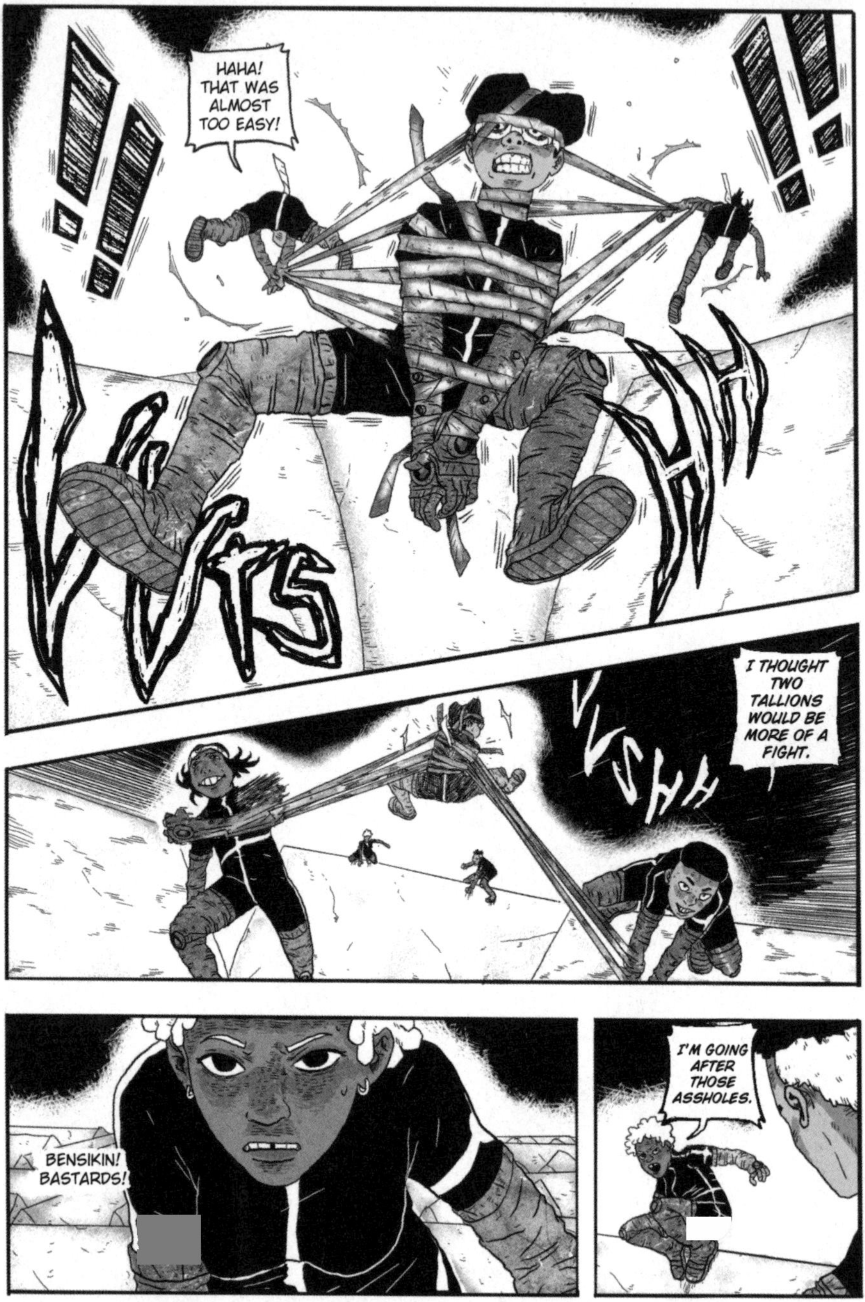
HAHA! THAT WAS ALMOST TOO EASY!
I THOUGHT TWO TALLIONS WOULD BE MORE OF A FIGHT.
BENSIKIN! BASTARDS!
I'M GOING AFTER THOSE ASSHOLES.

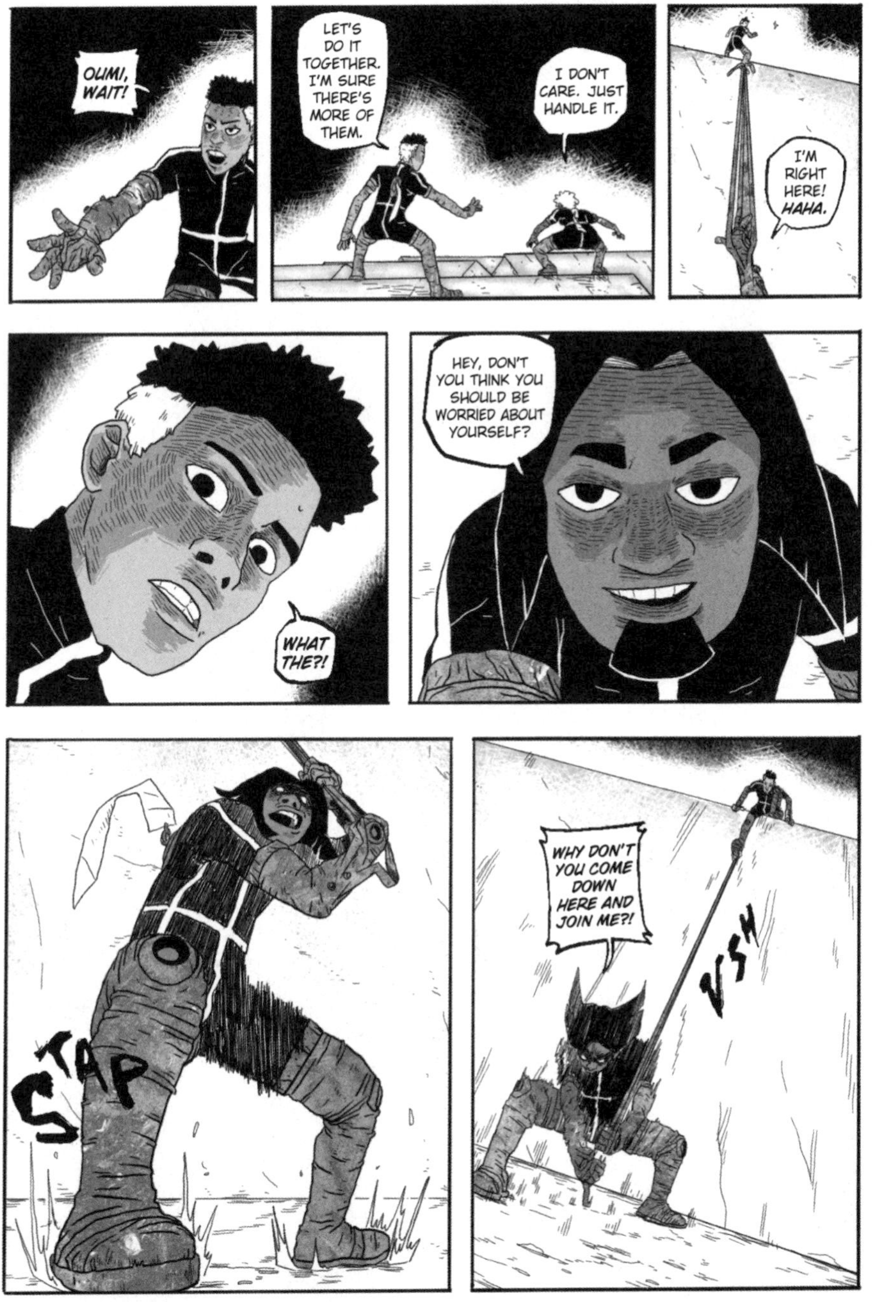
OUMI, WAIT!
LET'S DO IT TOGETHER. I'M SURE THERE'S MORE OF THEM.
I DON'T CARE. JUST HANDLE IT.
I'M RIGHT HERE! HAHA.
WHAT THE?!
HEY, DON'T YOU THINK YOU SHOULD BE WORRIED ABOUT YOURSELF?
STAP
WHY DON'T YOU COME DOWN HERE AND JOIN ME?!
VSH

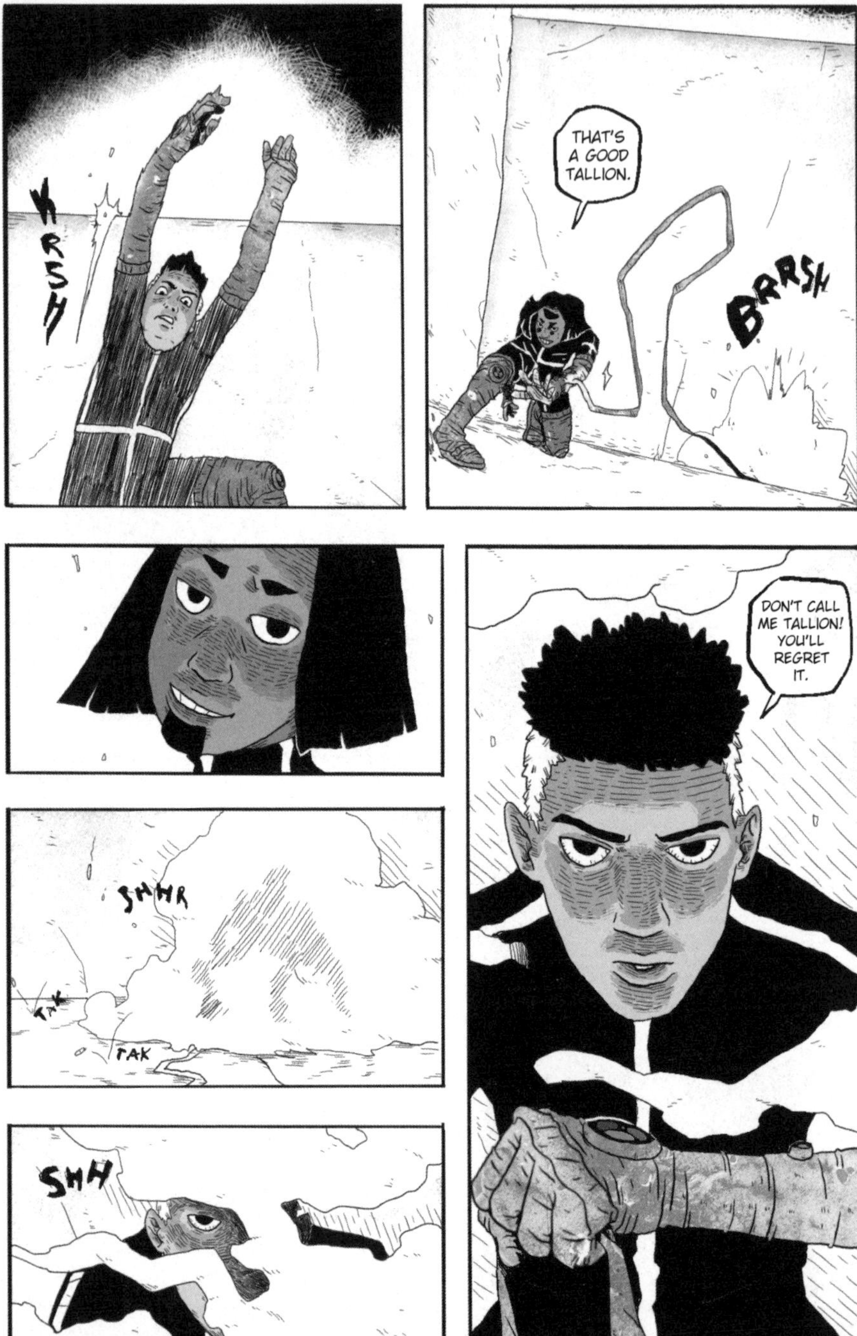
KRSH
THAT'S A GOOD TALLION.
BRRSH
SHHR
TAK
TAK
DON'T CALL ME TALLION! YOU'LL REGRET IT.
SHH

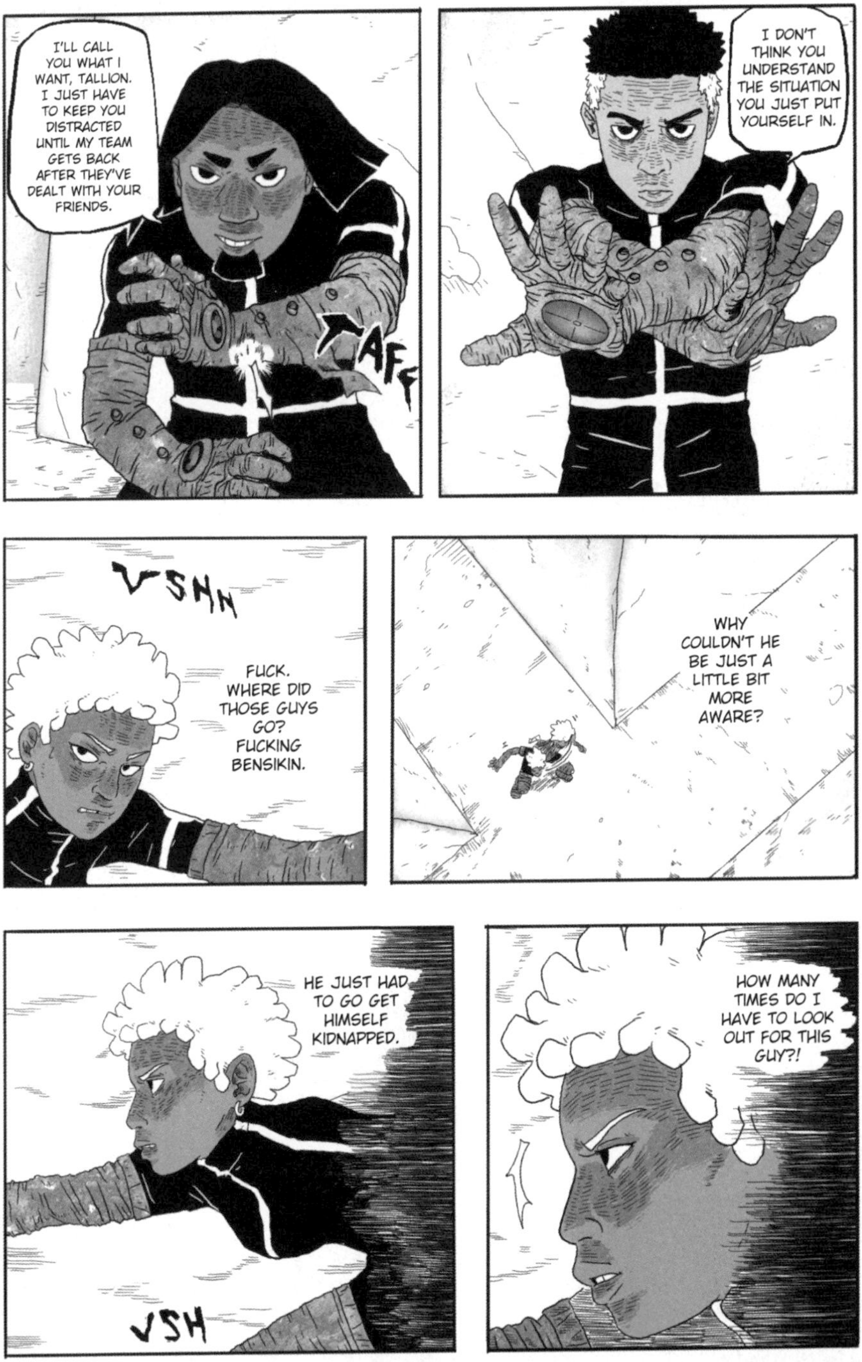
I'LL CALL YOU WHAT I WANT, TALLION. I JUST HAVE TO KEEP YOU DISTRACTED UNTIL MY TEAM GETS BACK AFTER THEY'VE DEALT WITH YOUR FRIENDS.
TAFF
I DON'T THINK YOU UNDERSTAND THE SITUATION YOU JUST PUT YOURSELF IN.
VSHN
FUCK. WHERE DID THOSE GUYS GO? FUCKING BENSIKIN.
WHY COULDN'T HE BE JUST A LITTLE BIT MORE AWARE?
HE JUST HAD TO GO GET HIMSELF KIDNAPPED.
VSH
HOW MANY TIMES DO I HAVE TO LOOK OUT FOR THIS GUY?!

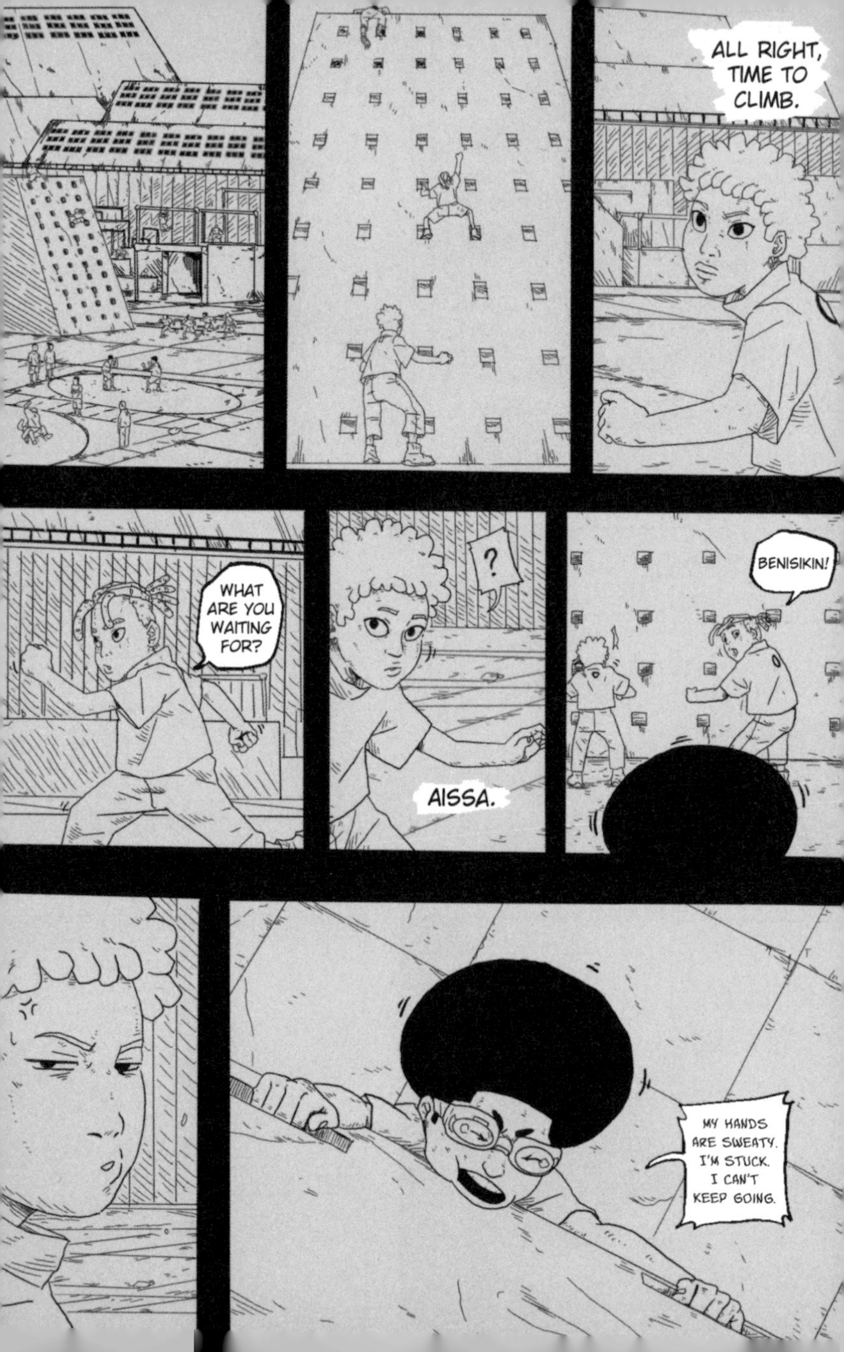
ALL RIGHT, TIME TO CLIMB.
WHAT ARE YOU WAITING FOR?
?
AISSA.
BENISIKIN!
MY HANDS ARE SWEATY. I'M STUCK. I CAN'T KEEP GOING.

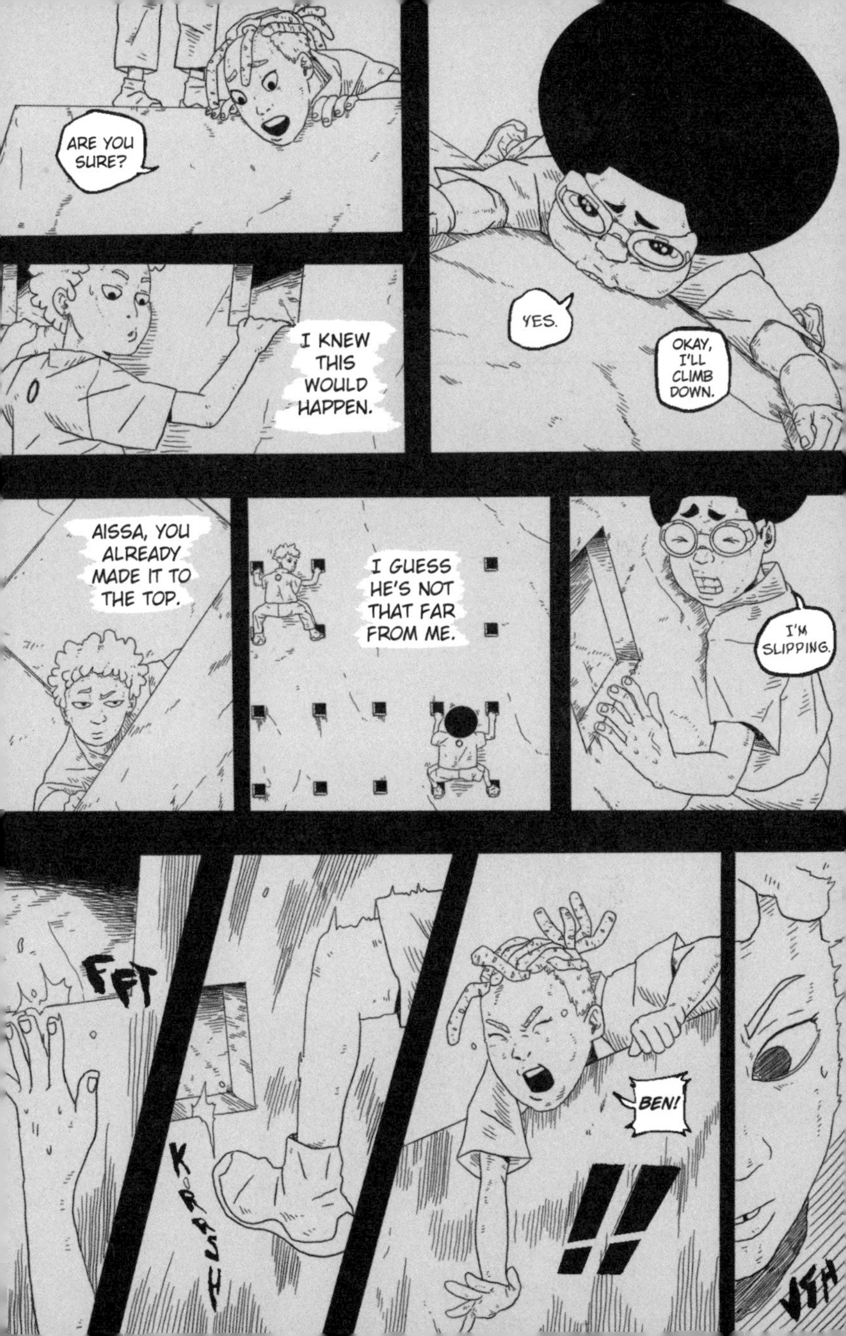
ARE YOU SURE?
YES.
OKAY, I'LL CLIMB DOWN.
I KNEW THIS WOULD HAPPEN.
AISSA, YOU ALREADY MADE IT TO THE TOP.
I GUESS HE'S NOT THAT FAR FROM ME.
I'M SLIPPING.
FFT
KRRUSH
BEN!
!!
VFH

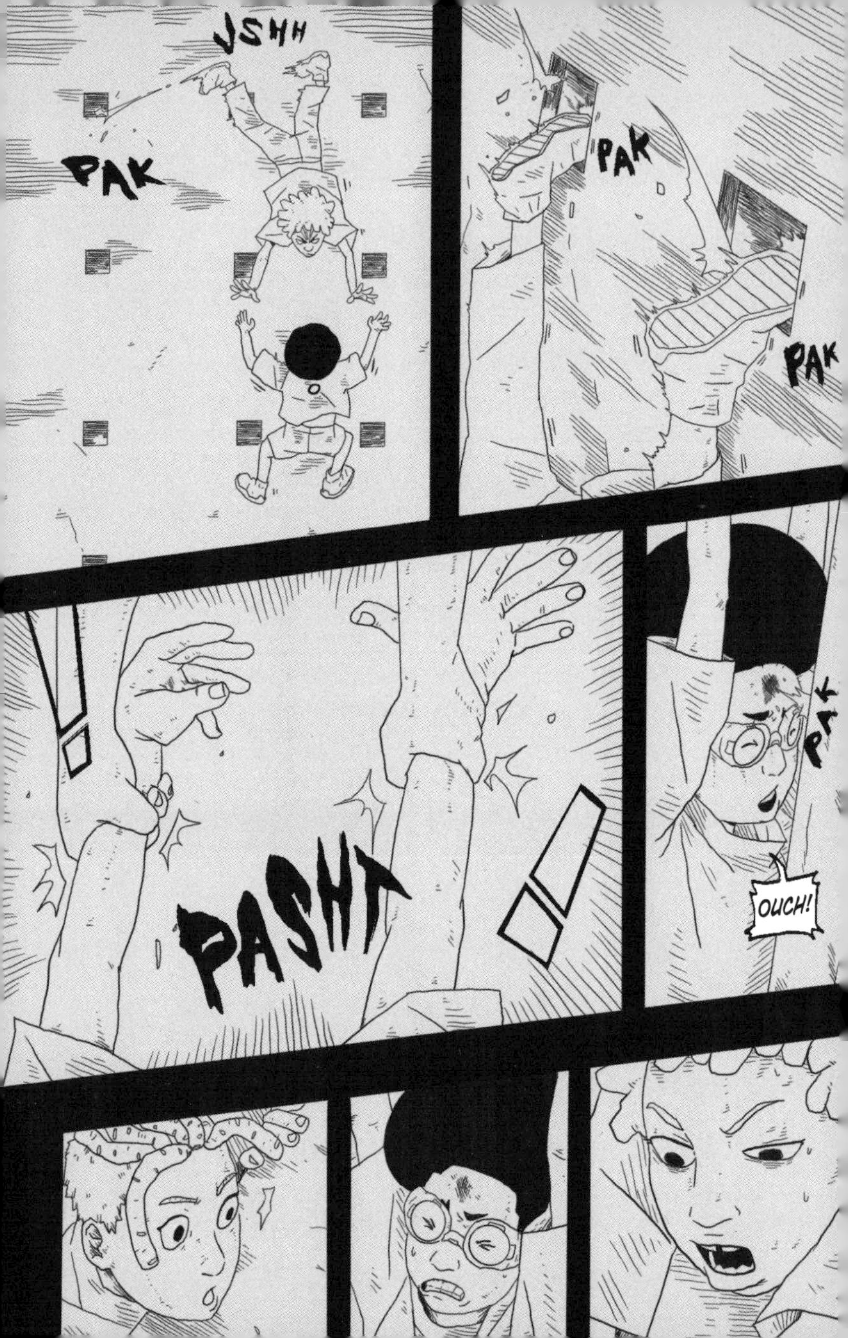
JSHH
PAK
PAK
PAK
PASHT
PAK
OUCH!

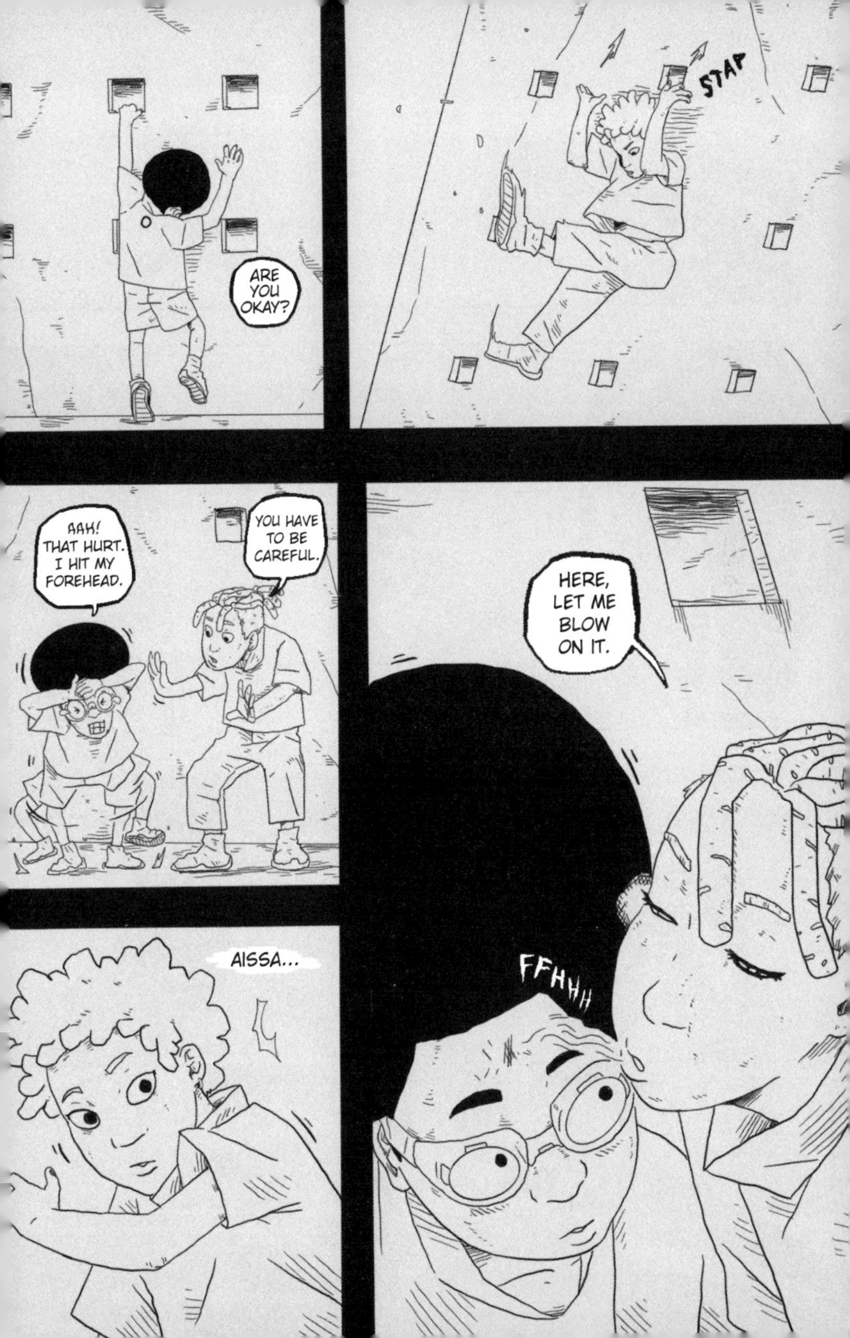
ARE YOU OKAY?
STAP
AAH! THAT HURT. I HIT MY FOREHEAD.
YOU HAVE TO BE CAREFUL.
AISSA...
HERE, LET ME BLOW ON IT.
FFHHH

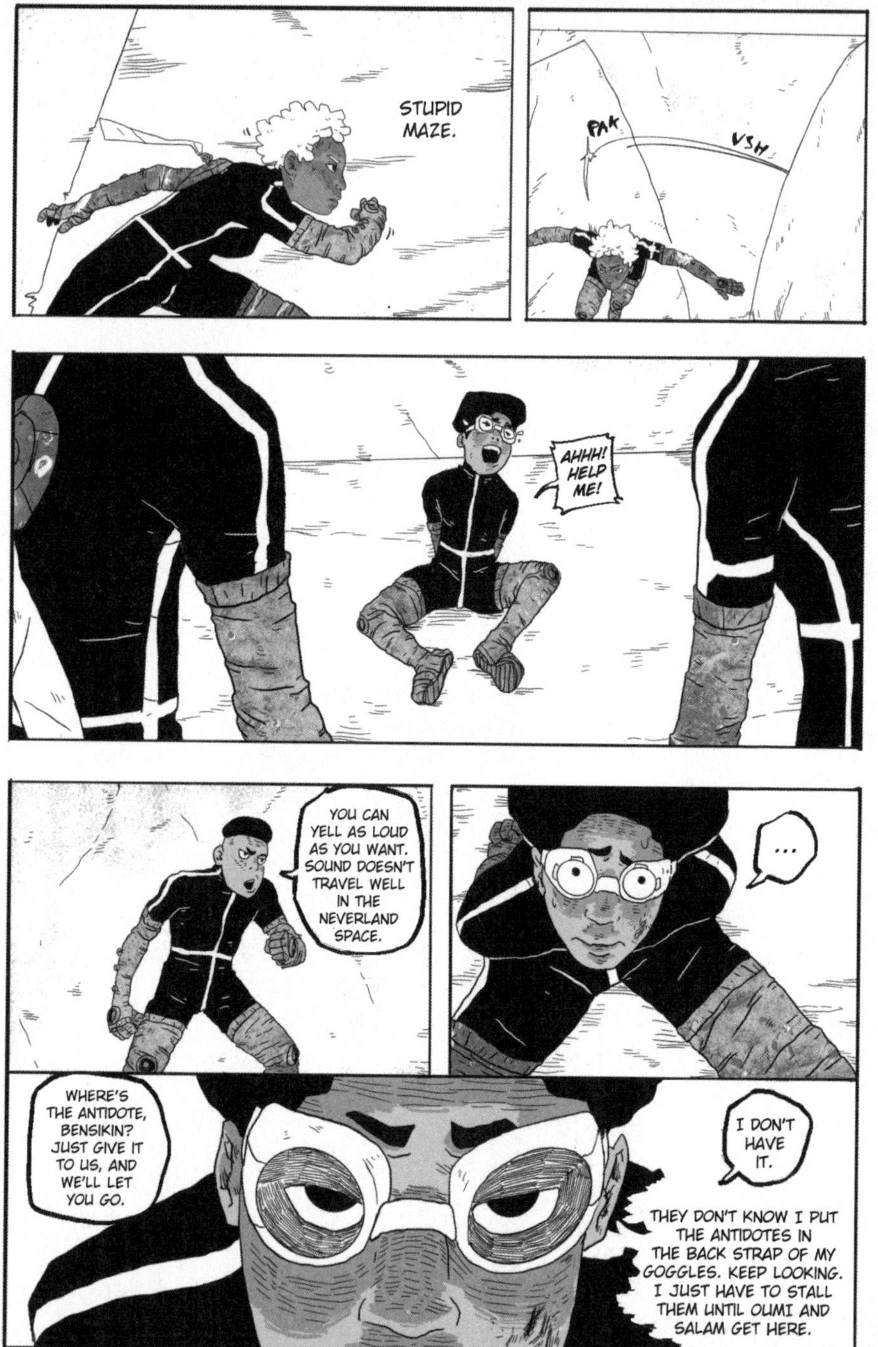
STUPID MAZE.
PAK
VSH
AHHH! HELP ME!
YOU CAN YELL AS LOUD AS YOU WANT. SOUND DOESN'T TRAVEL WELL IN THE NEVERLAND SPACE.
...
WHERE'S THE ANTIDOTE, BENSIKIN? JUST GIVE IT TO US, AND WE'LL LET YOU GO.
I DON'T HAVE IT.
THEY DON'T KNOW I PUT THE ANTIDOTES IN THE BACK STRAP OF MY GOGGLES. KEEP LOOKING. I JUST HAVE TO STALL THEM UNTIL OUMI AND SALAM GET HERE.

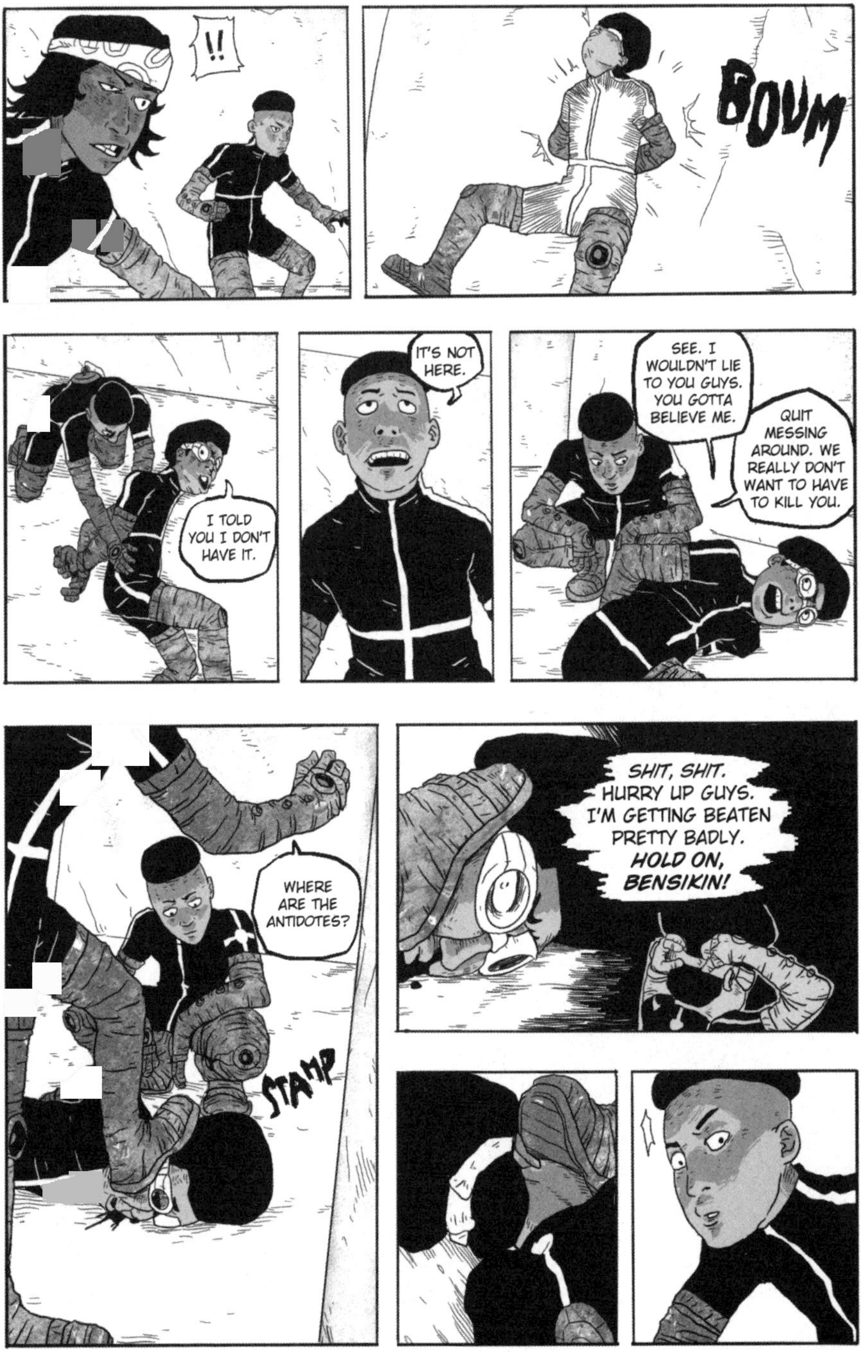
!!
BOUM
I TOLD YOU I DON'T HAVE IT.
IT'S NOT HERE.
SEE. I WOULDN'T LIE TO YOU GUYS. YOU GOTTA BELIEVE ME.
QUIT MESSING AROUND. WE REALLY DON'T WANT TO HAVE TO KILL YOU.
WHERE ARE THE ANTIDOTES?
STAMP
SHIT, SHIT. HURRY UP GUYS. I'M GETTING BEATEN PRETTY BADLY. HOLD ON, BENSIKIN!

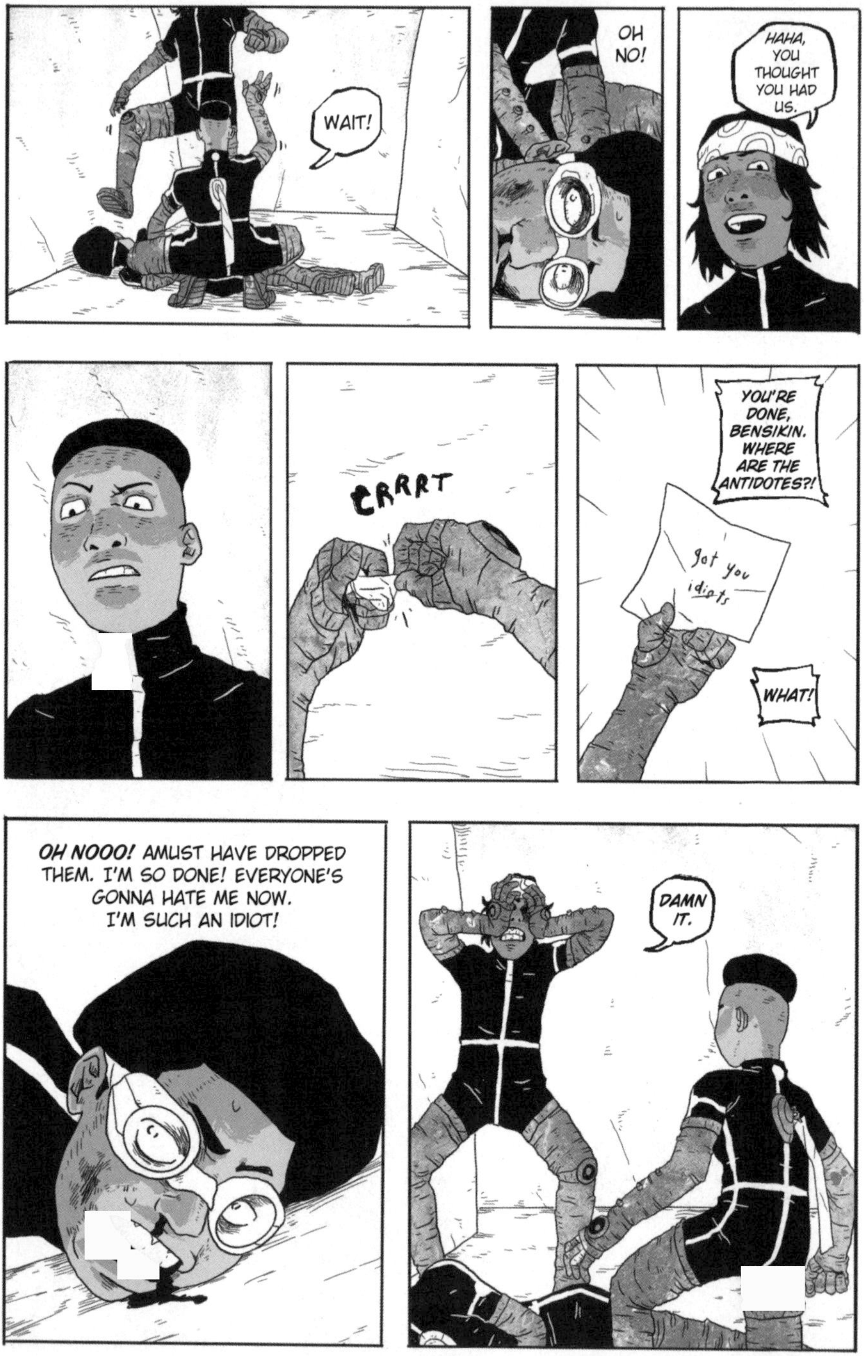
WAIT!
OH NO!
HAHA, YOU THOUGHT YOU HAD US.
CRRRT
YOU'RE DONE, BENSIKIN. WHERE ARE THE ANTIDOTES?!
got you idiots
WHAT!
OH NOOO! AMUST HAVE DROPPED THEM. I'M SO DONE! EVERYONE'S GONNA HATE ME NOW. I'M SUCH AN IDIOT!
DAMN IT.

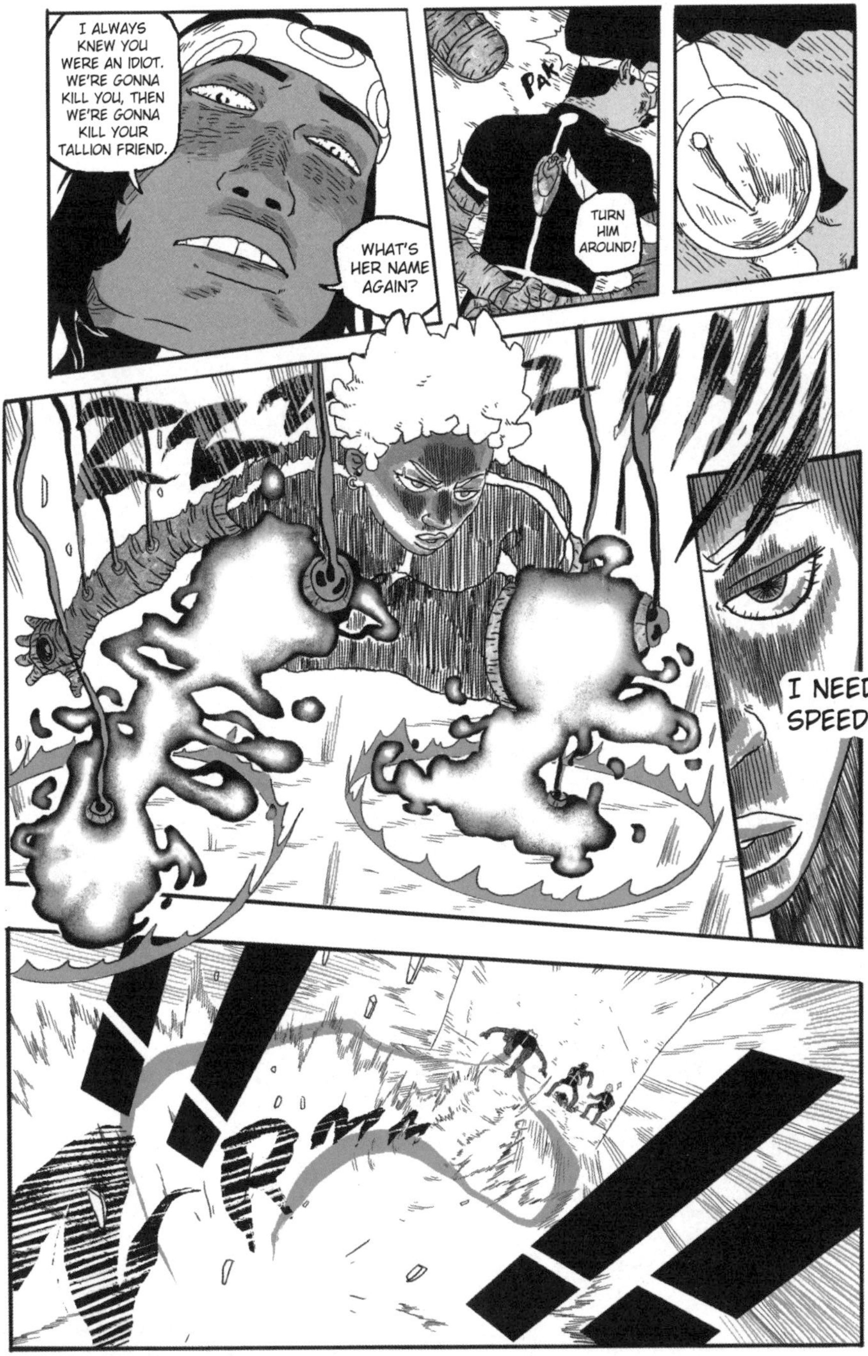
I ALWAYS KNEW YOU WERE AN IDIOT. WE'RE GONNA KILL YOU, THEN WE'RE GONNA KILL YOUR TALLION FRIEND.
WHAT'S HER NAME AGAIN?
PAK
TURN HIM AROUND!
I NEED SPEED!

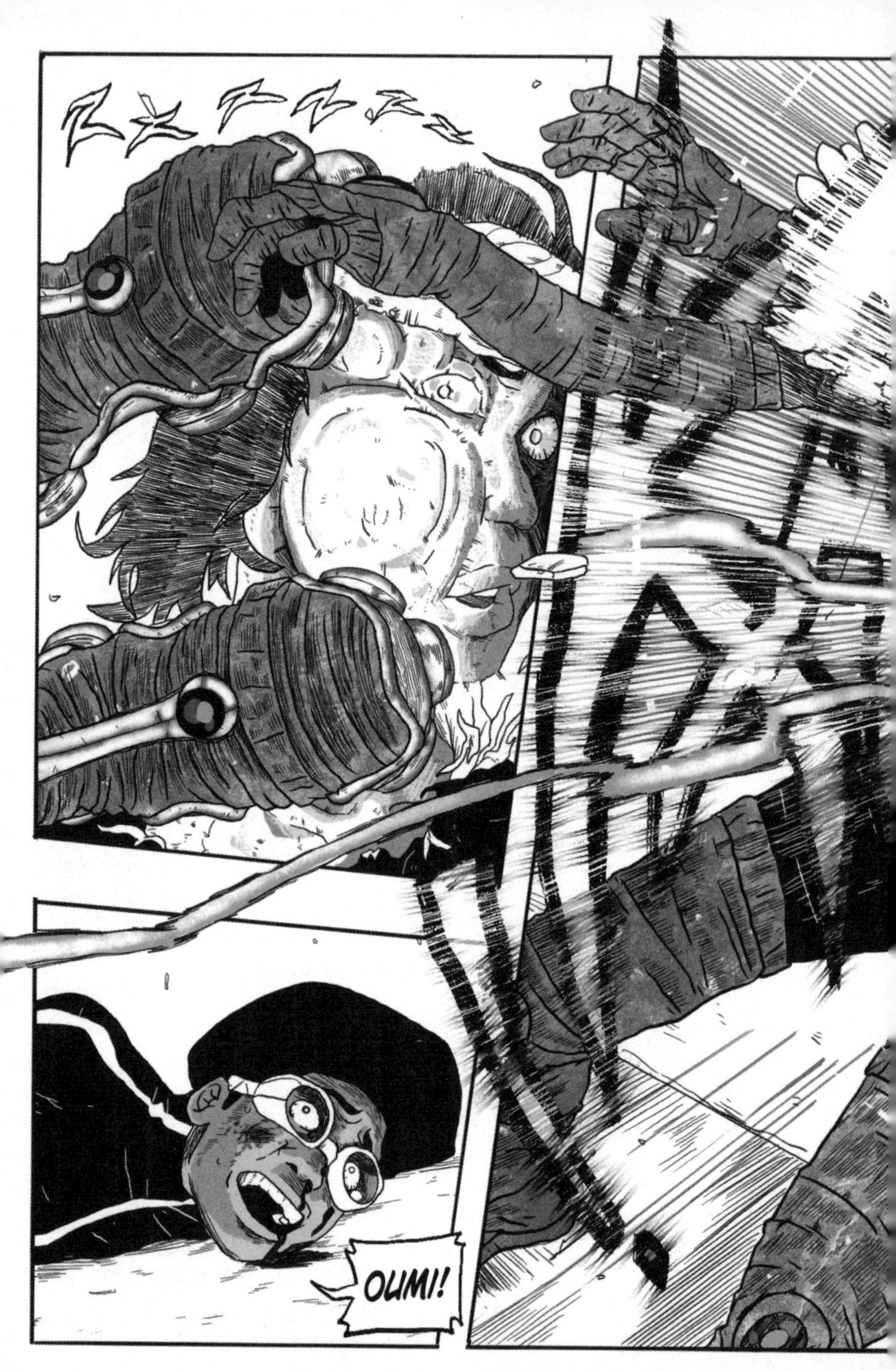
OUMI!

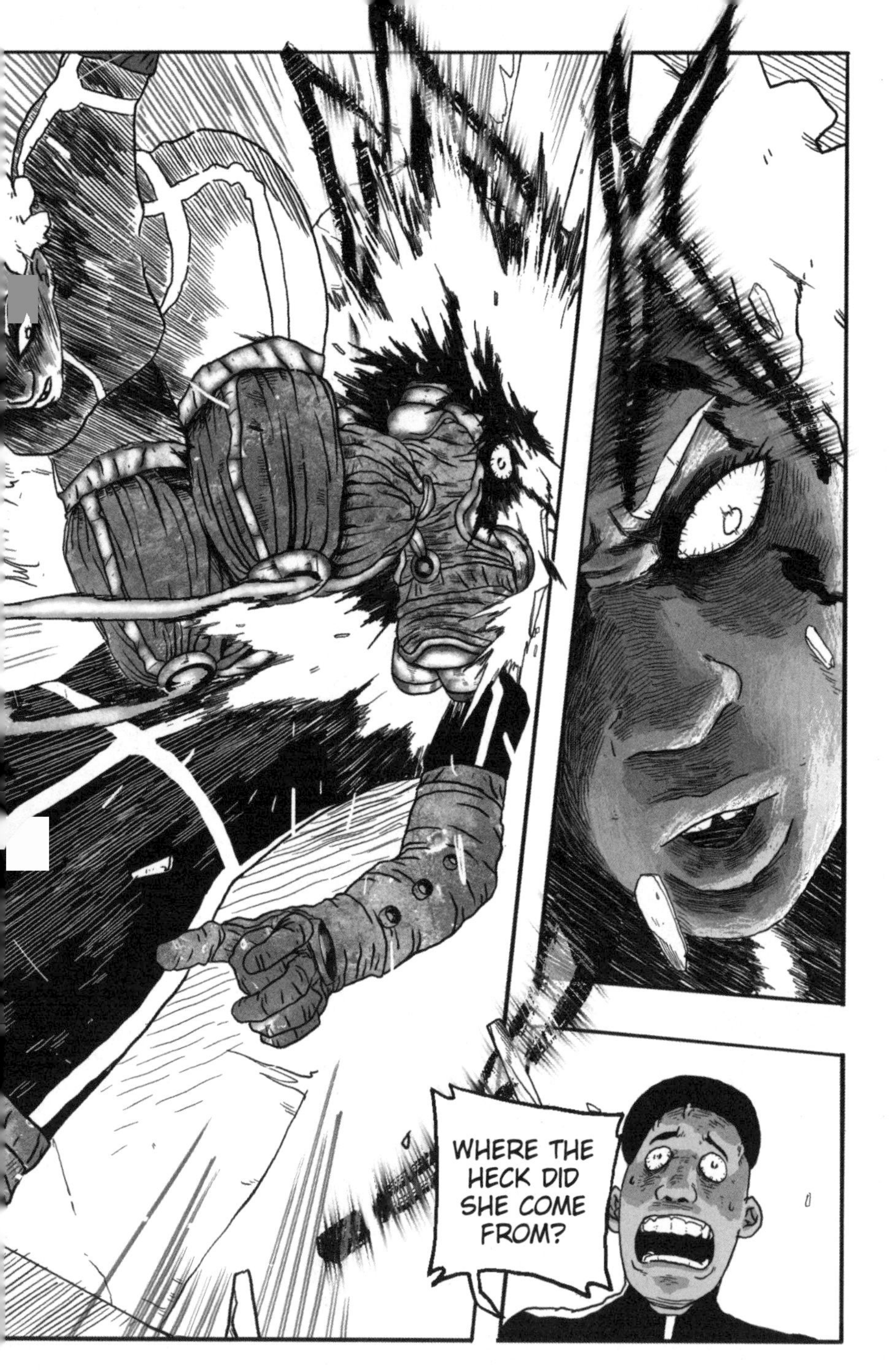
WHERE THE HECK DID SHE COME FROM?

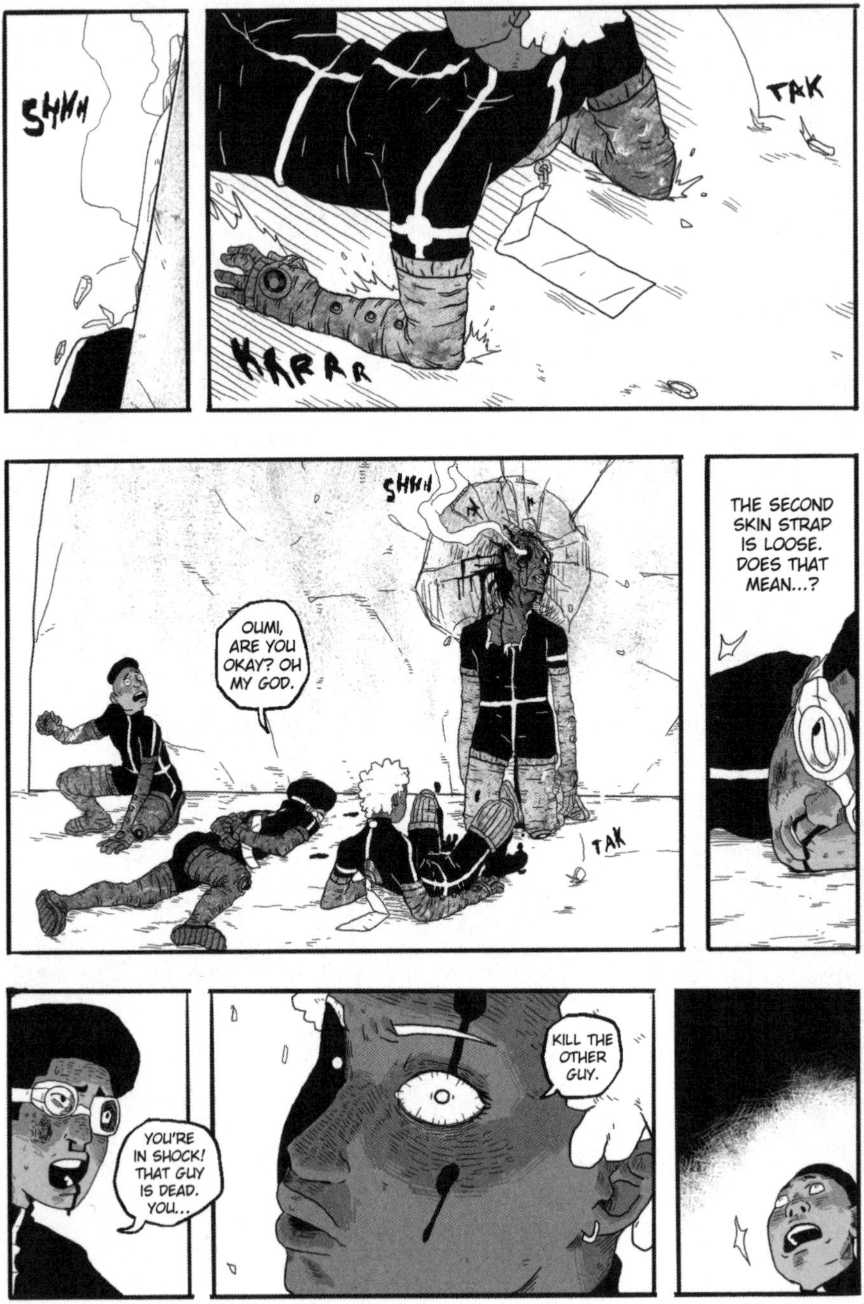
SHHH
TAK
KRRRR
SHHH
OUMI, ARE YOU OKAY? OH MY GOD.
TAK
THE SECOND SKIN STRAP IS LOOSE. DOES THAT MEAN...?
YOU'RE IN SHOCK! THAT GUY IS DEAD. YOU...
KILL THE OTHER GUY.

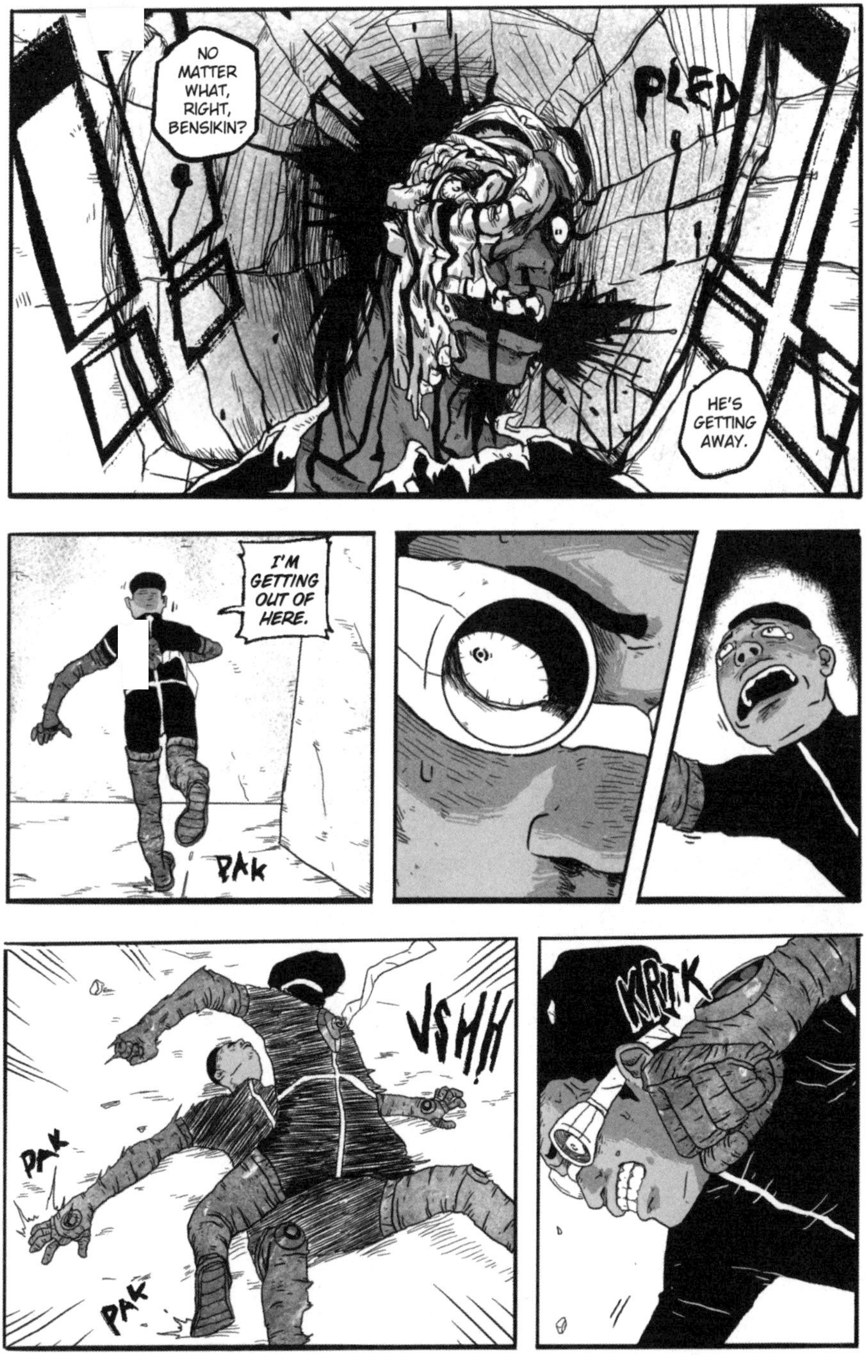
NO MATTER WHAT, RIGHT, BENSIKIN?
PLED
HE'S GETTING AWAY.
I'M GETTING OUT OF HERE.
PAK
PAK
PAK
VSHH
KRIK

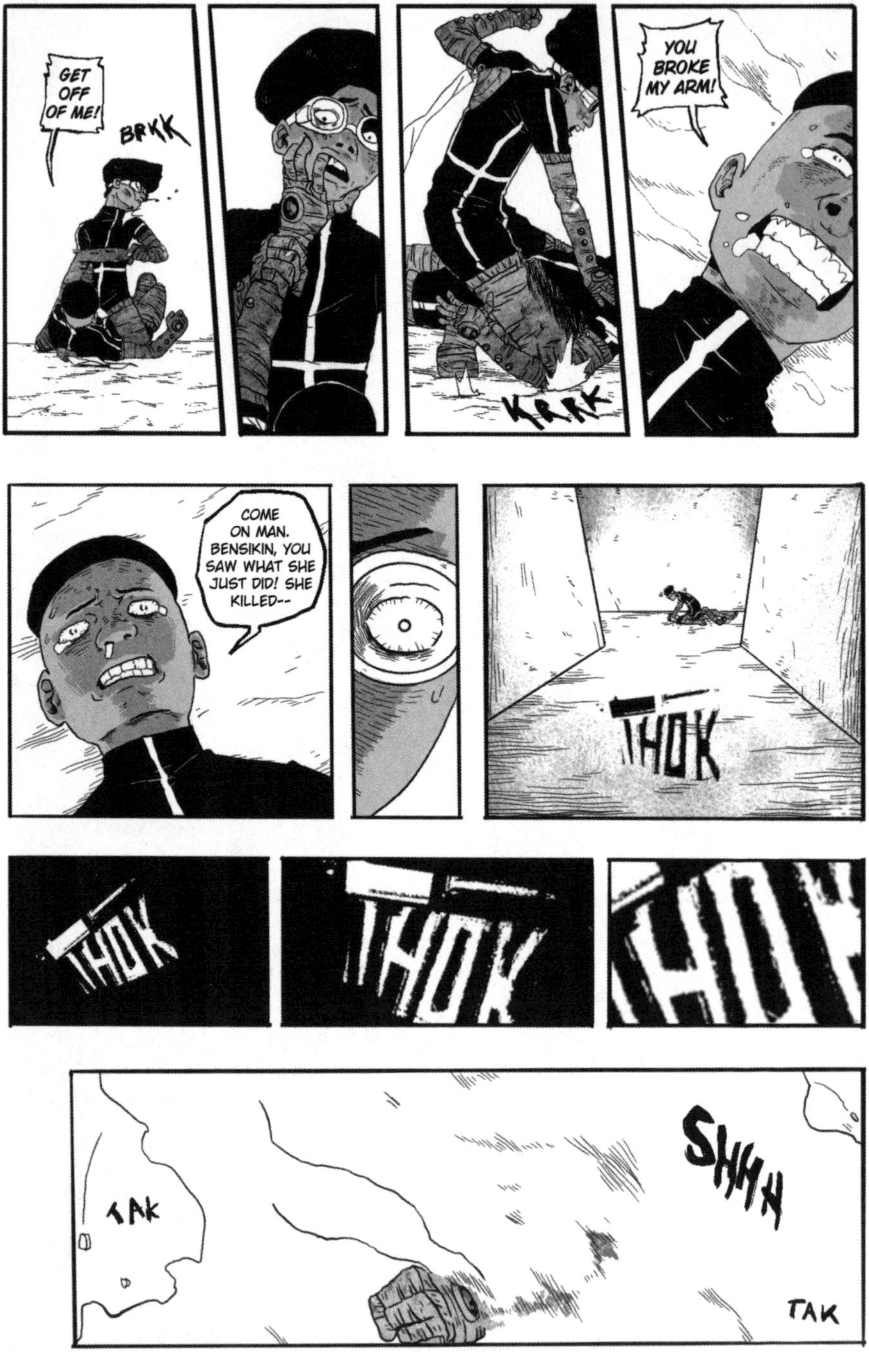
GET OFF OF ME!
BRKK
KRRK
YOU BROKE MY ARM!
COME ON MAN. BENSIKIN, YOU SAW WHAT SHE JUST DID! SHE KILLED--
THOK
THOK
THOK
TAK
SHHH
TAK

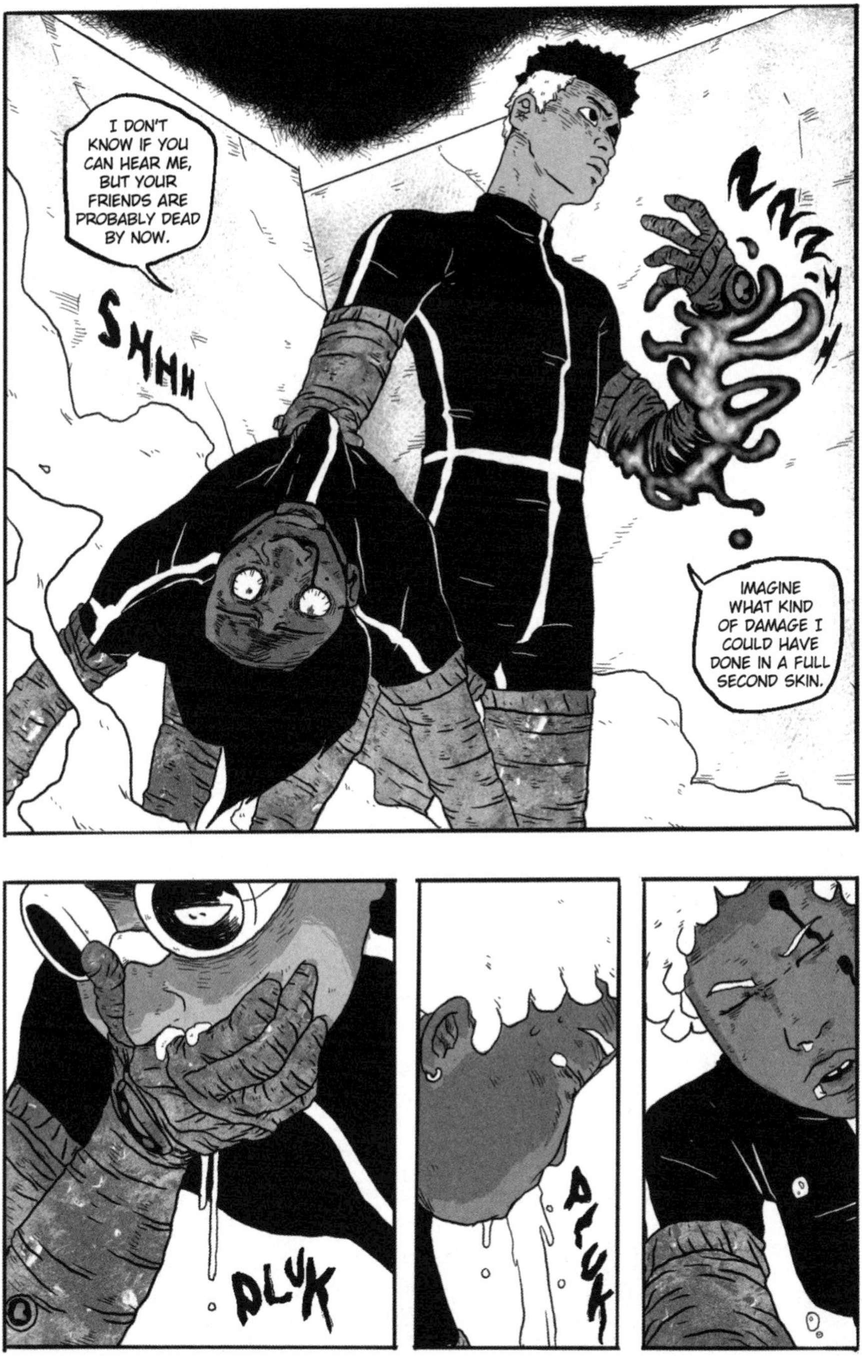
I DON'T KNOW IF YOU CAN HEAR ME, BUT YOUR FRIENDS ARE PROBABLY DEAD BY NOW.
SHHH
NNN...
IMAGINE WHAT KIND OF DAMAGE I COULD HAVE DONE IN A FULL SECOND SKIN.
PLUK
PLUK

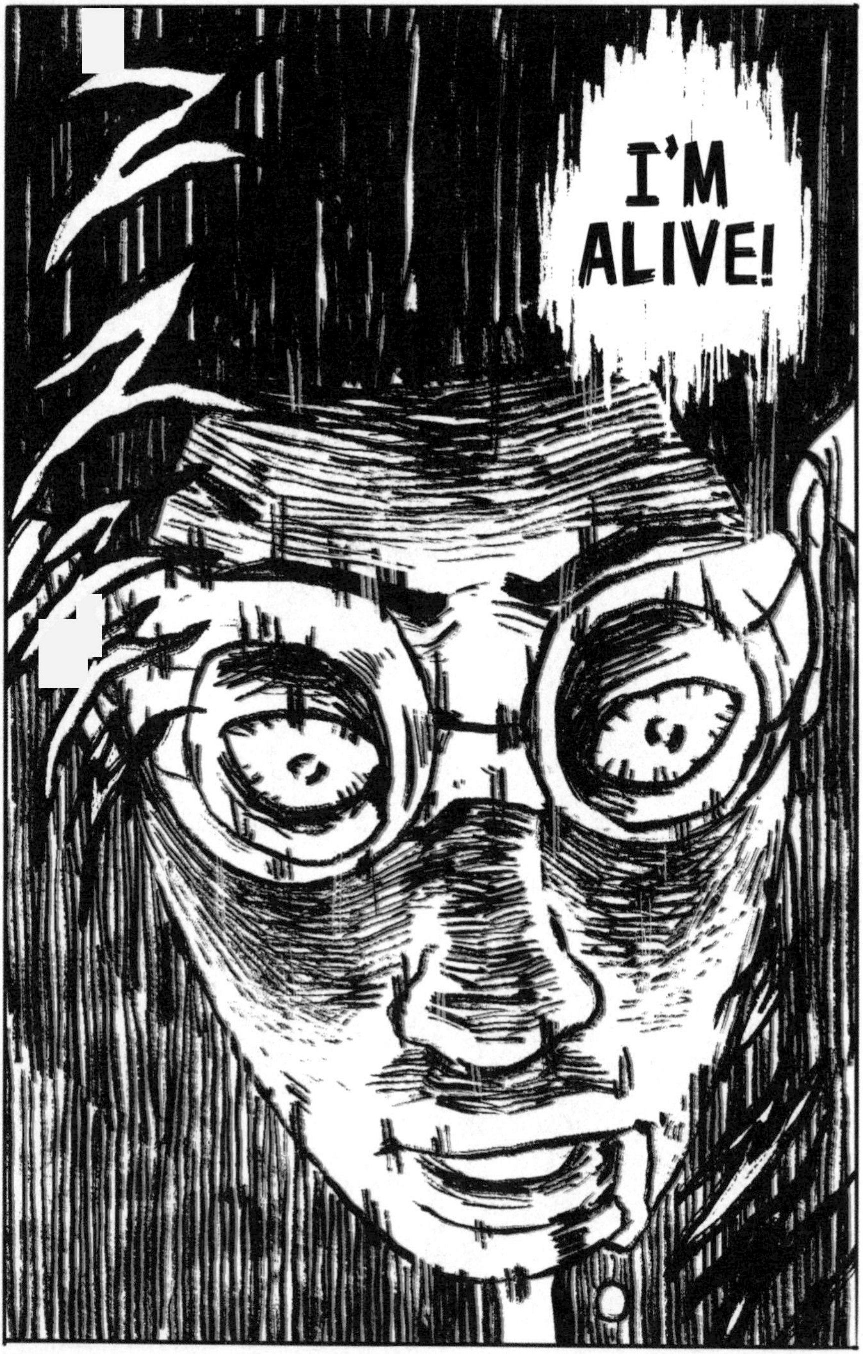
I'M ALIVE!

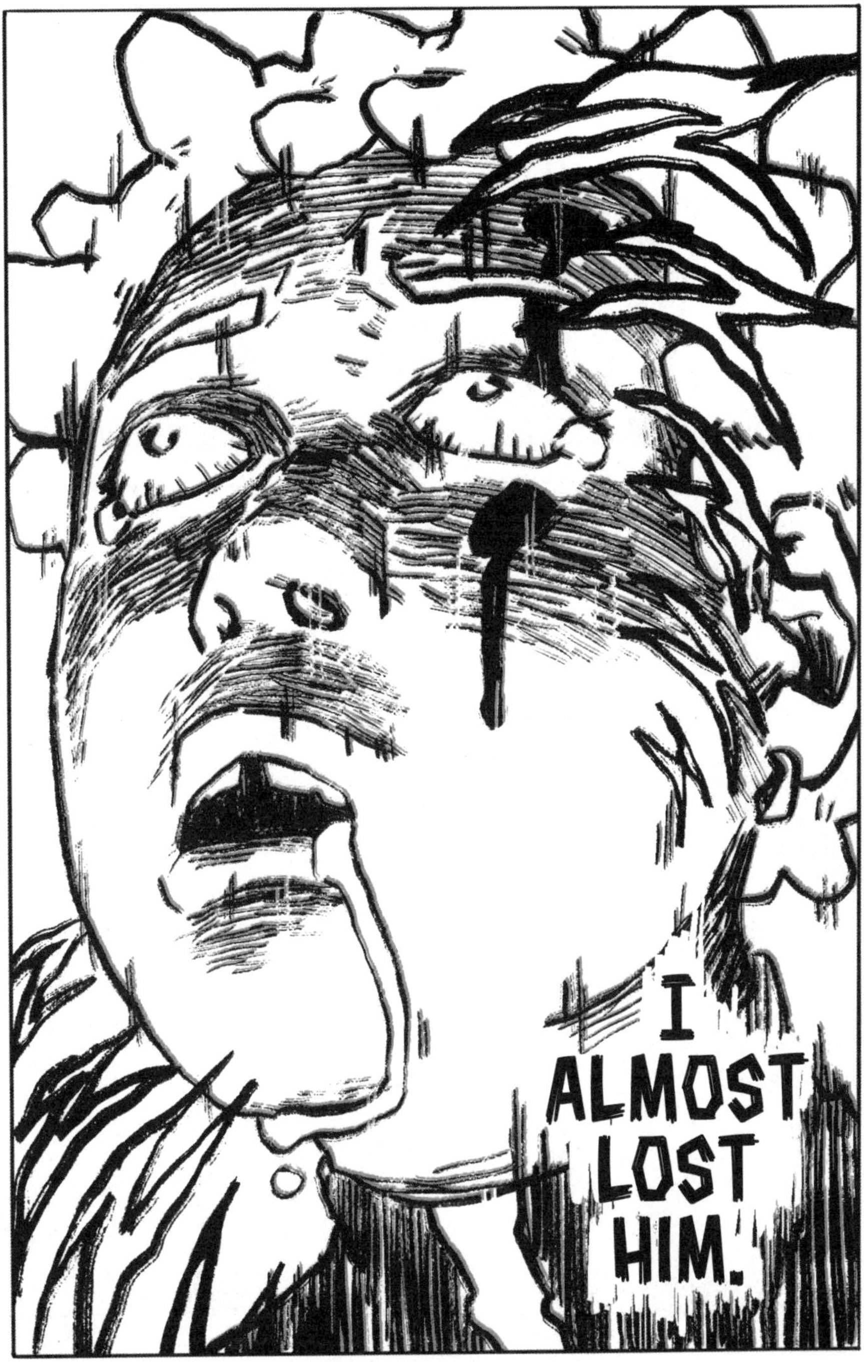
I ALMOST LOST HIM.

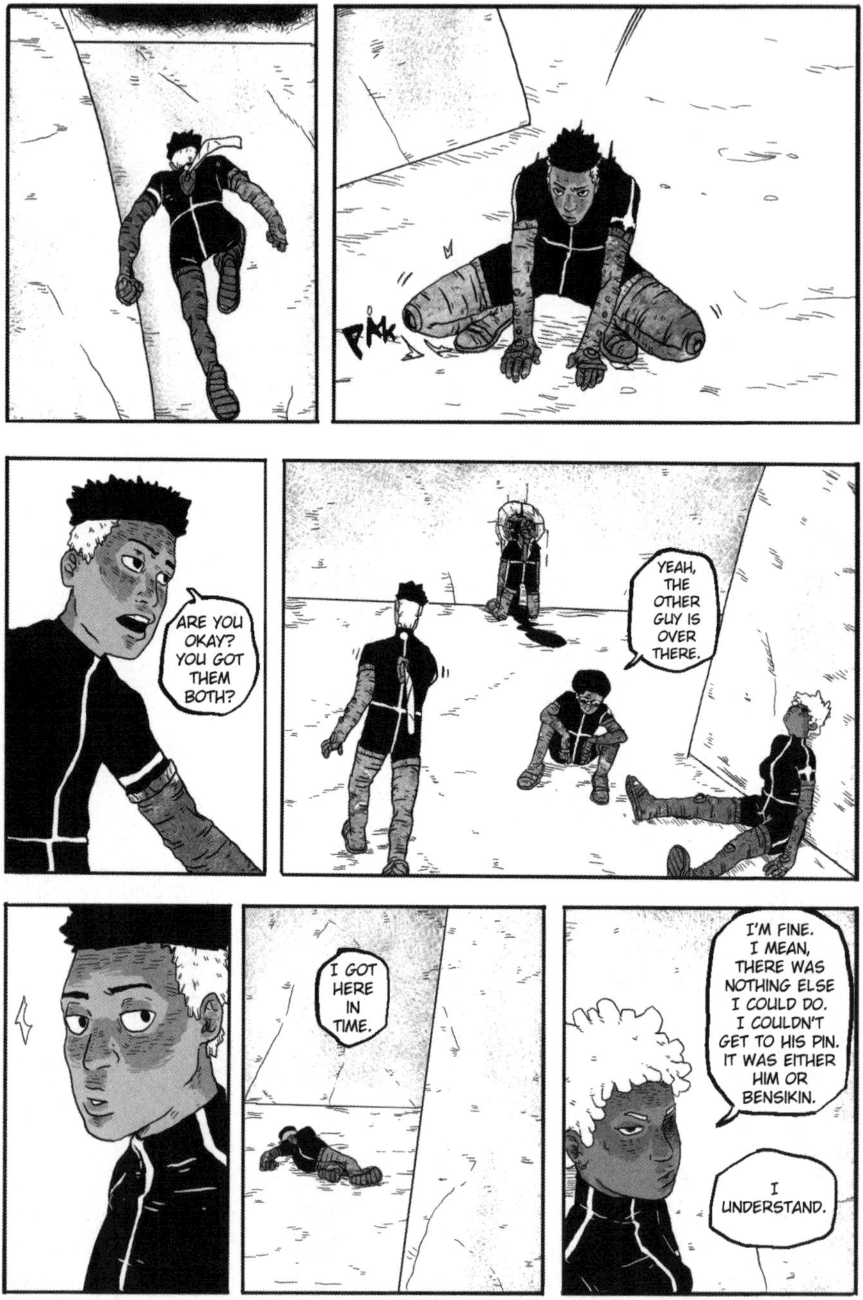
PIKK
ARE YOU OKAY? YOU GOT THEM BOTH?
YEAH, THE OTHER GUY IS OVER THERE.
I GOT HERE IN TIME.
I'M FINE. I MEAN, THERE WAS NOTHING ELSE I COULD DO. I COULDN'T GET TO HIS PIN. IT WAS EITHER HIM OR BENSIKIN.
I UNDERSTAND.

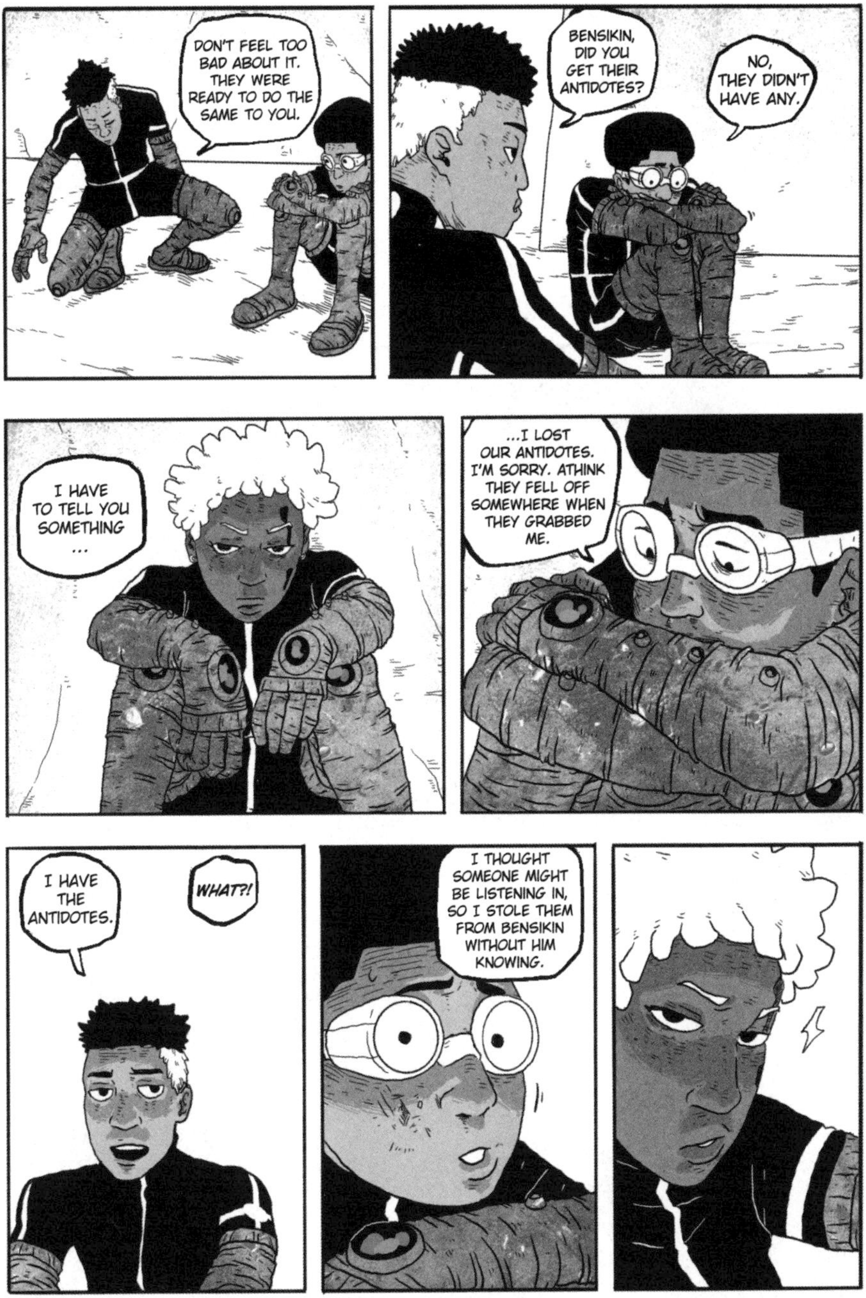
DON'T FEEL TOO BAD ABOUT IT. THEY WERE READY TO DO THE SAME TO YOU.
BENSIKIN, DID YOU GET THEIR ANTIDOTES?
NO, THEY DIDN'T HAVE ANY.
I HAVE TO TELL YOU SOMETHING ...
...I LOST OUR ANTIDOTES. I'M SORRY. ATHINK THEY FELL OFF SOMEWHERE WHEN THEY GRABBED ME.
I HAVE THE ANTIDOTES.
WHAT?!
I THOUGHT SOMEONE MIGHT BE LISTENING IN, SO I STOLE THEM FROM BENSIKIN WITHOUT HIM KNOWING.

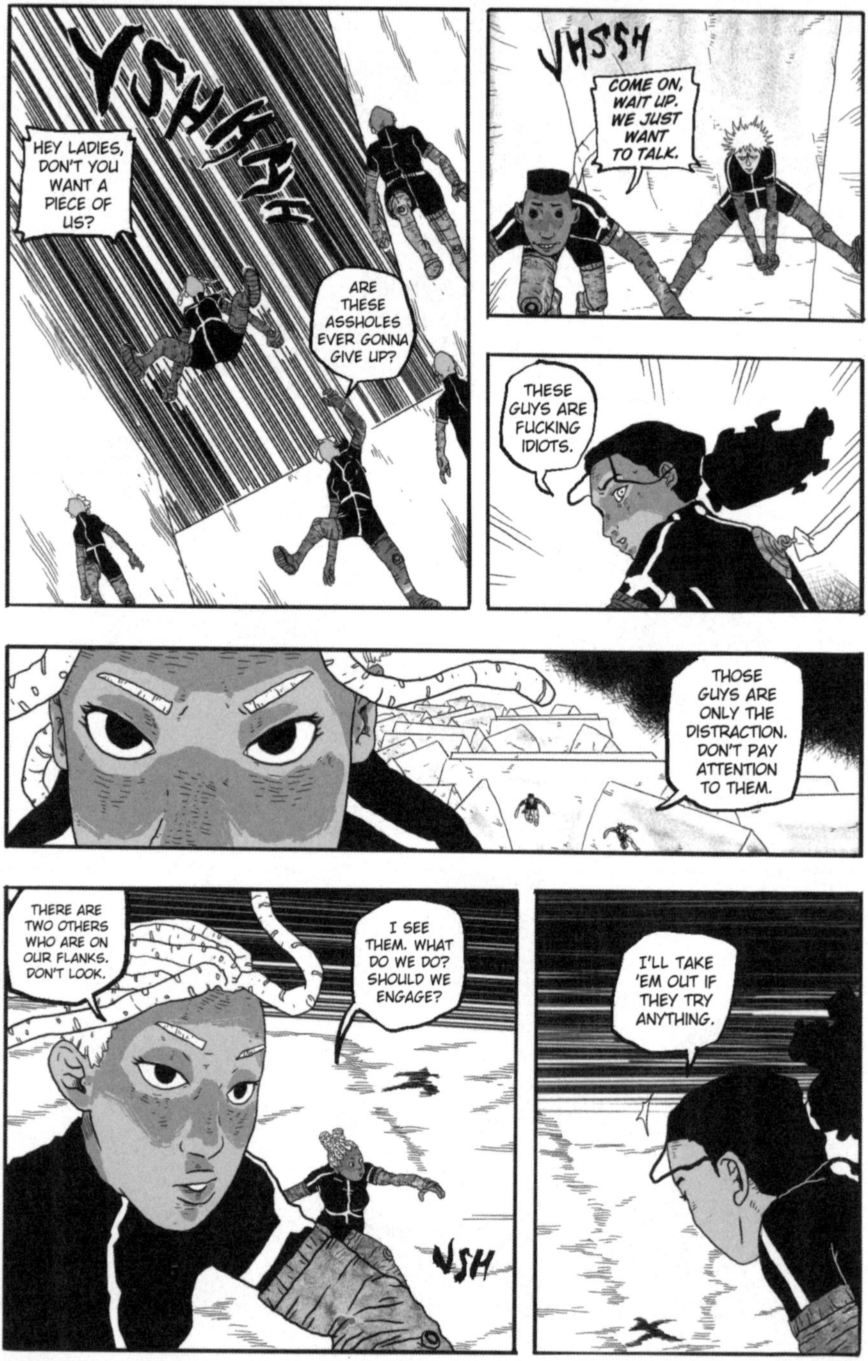
YSHHAH
HEY LADIES, DON'T YOU WANT A PIECE OF US?
ARE THESE ASSHOLES EVER GONNA GIVE UP?
VHSSH
COME ON, WAIT UP. WE JUST WANT TO TALK.
THESE GUYS ARE FUCKING IDIOTS.
THOSE GUYS ARE ONLY THE DISTRACTION. DON'T PAY ATTENTION TO THEM.
THERE ARE TWO OTHERS WHO ARE ON OUR FLANKS. DON'T LOOK.
I SEE THEM. WHAT DO WE DO? SHOULD WE ENGAGE?
VSH
I'LL TAKE 'EM OUT IF THEY TRY ANYTHING.

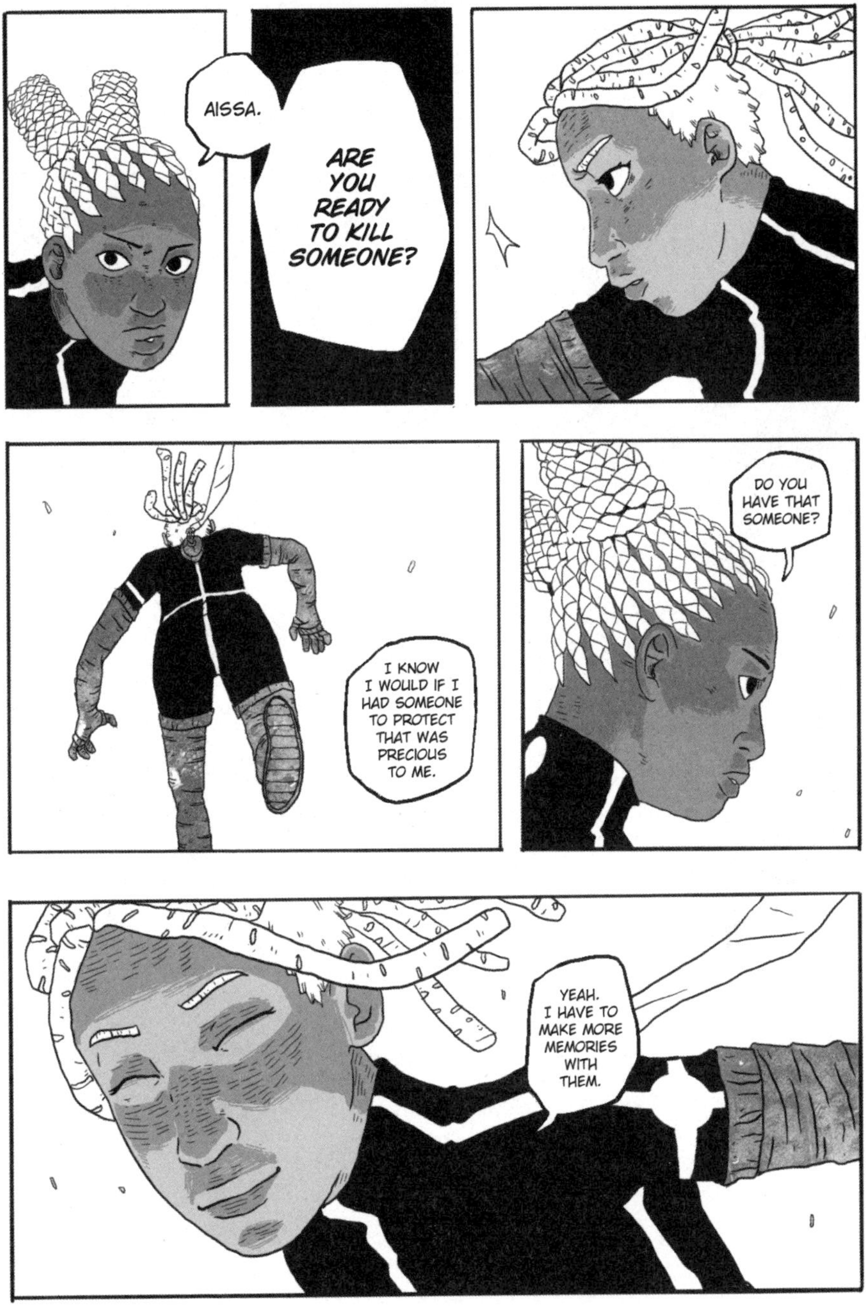
AISSA.
ARE YOU READY TO KILL SOMEONE?
I KNOW I WOULD IF I HAD SOMEONE TO PROTECT THAT WAS PRECIOUS TO ME.
DO YOU HAVE THAT SOMEONE?
YEAH. I HAVE TO MAKE MORE MEMORIES WITH THEM.

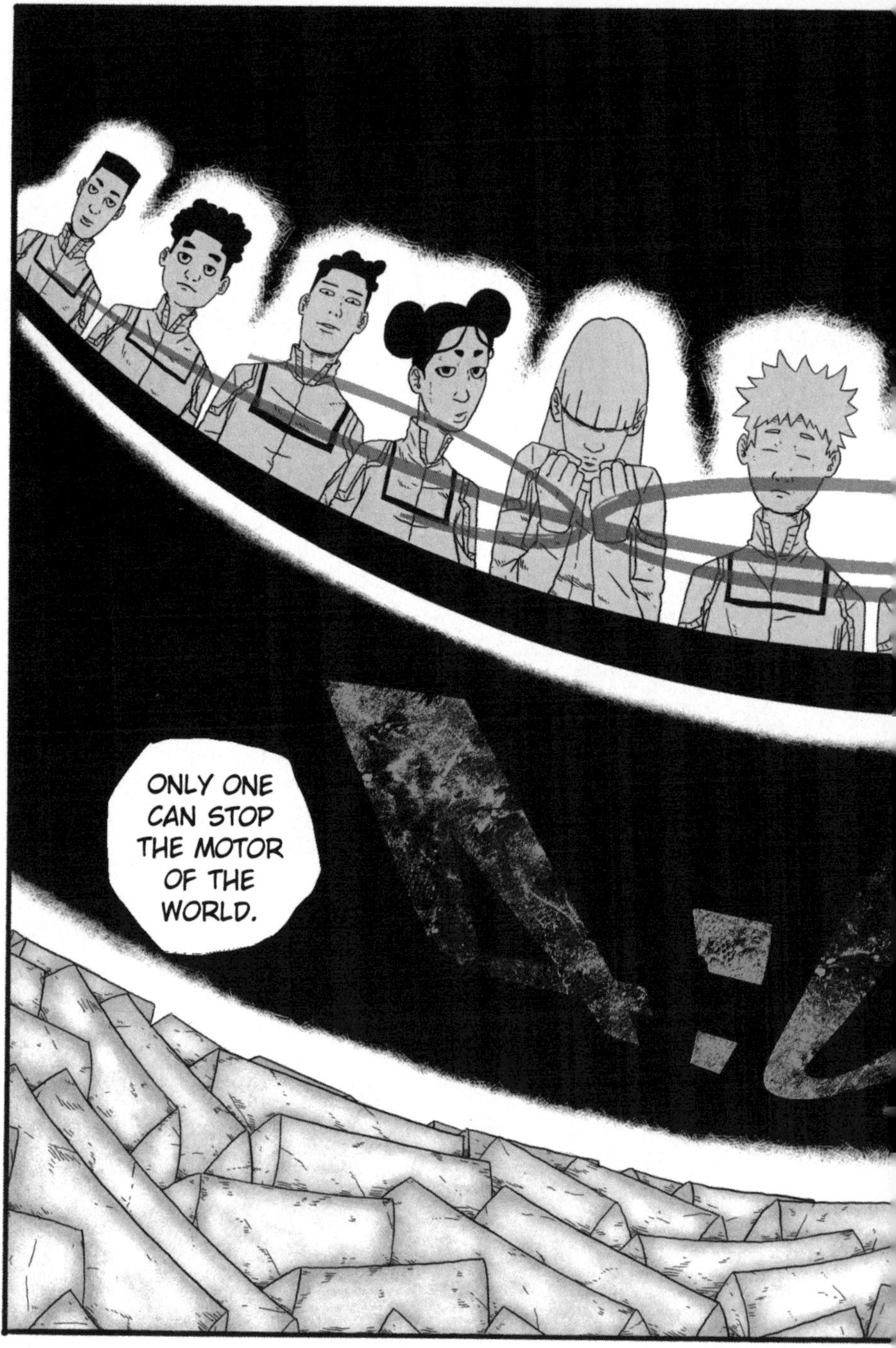
ONLY ONE CAN STOP THE MOTOR OF THE WORLD.

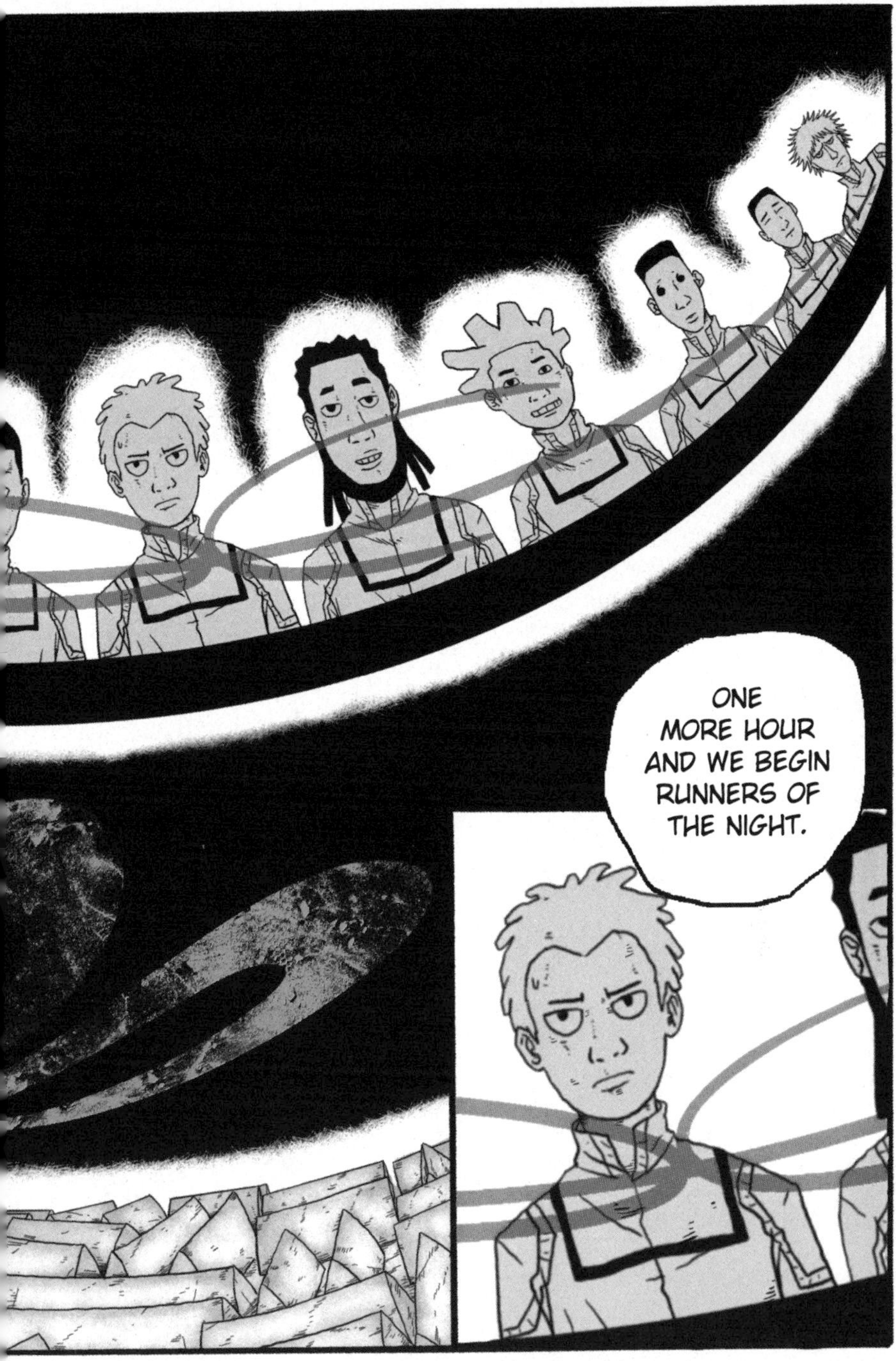
ONE MORE HOUR AND WE BEGIN RUNNERS OF THE NIGHT.

OBLIVION ROUGE

CHAPTER 6
Remember Me - 0%

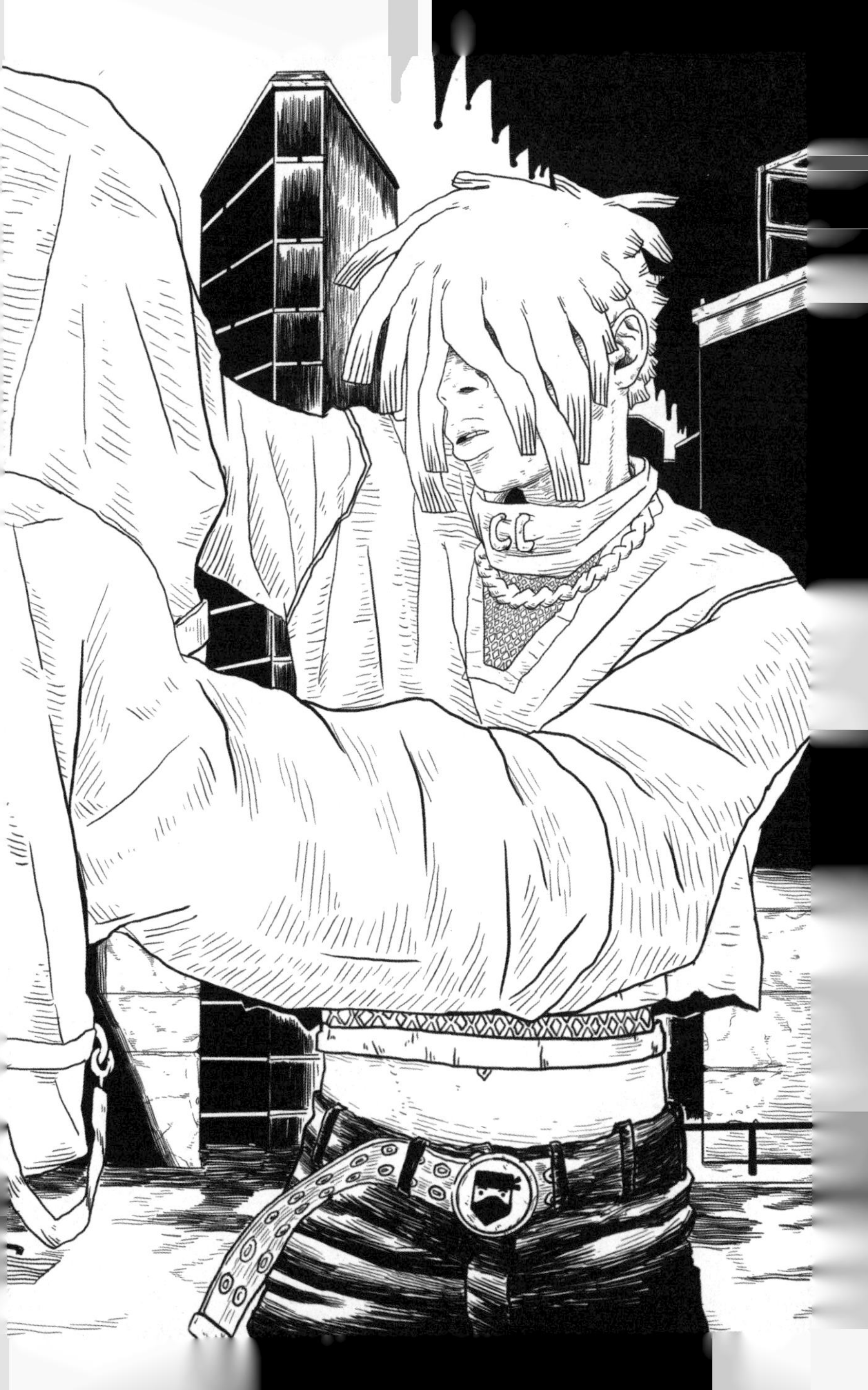

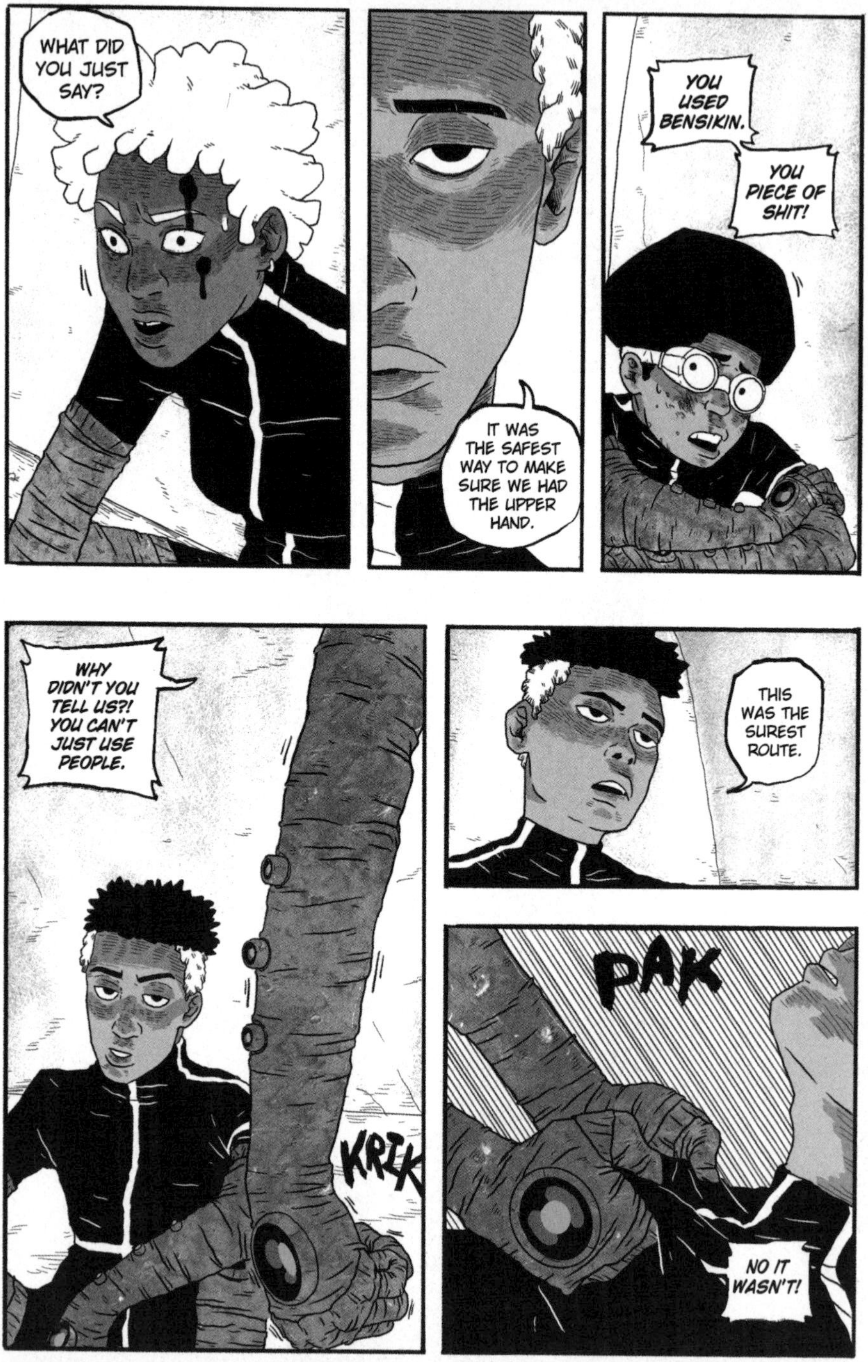
WHAT DID YOU JUST SAY?
IT WAS THE SAFEST WAY TO MAKE SURE WE HAD THE UPPER HAND.
YOU USED BENSIKIN.
YOU PIECE OF SHIT!
WHY DIDN'T YOU TELL US?! YOU CAN'T JUST USE PEOPLE.
KRIK
THIS WAS THE SUREST ROUTE.
PAK
NO IT WASN'T!

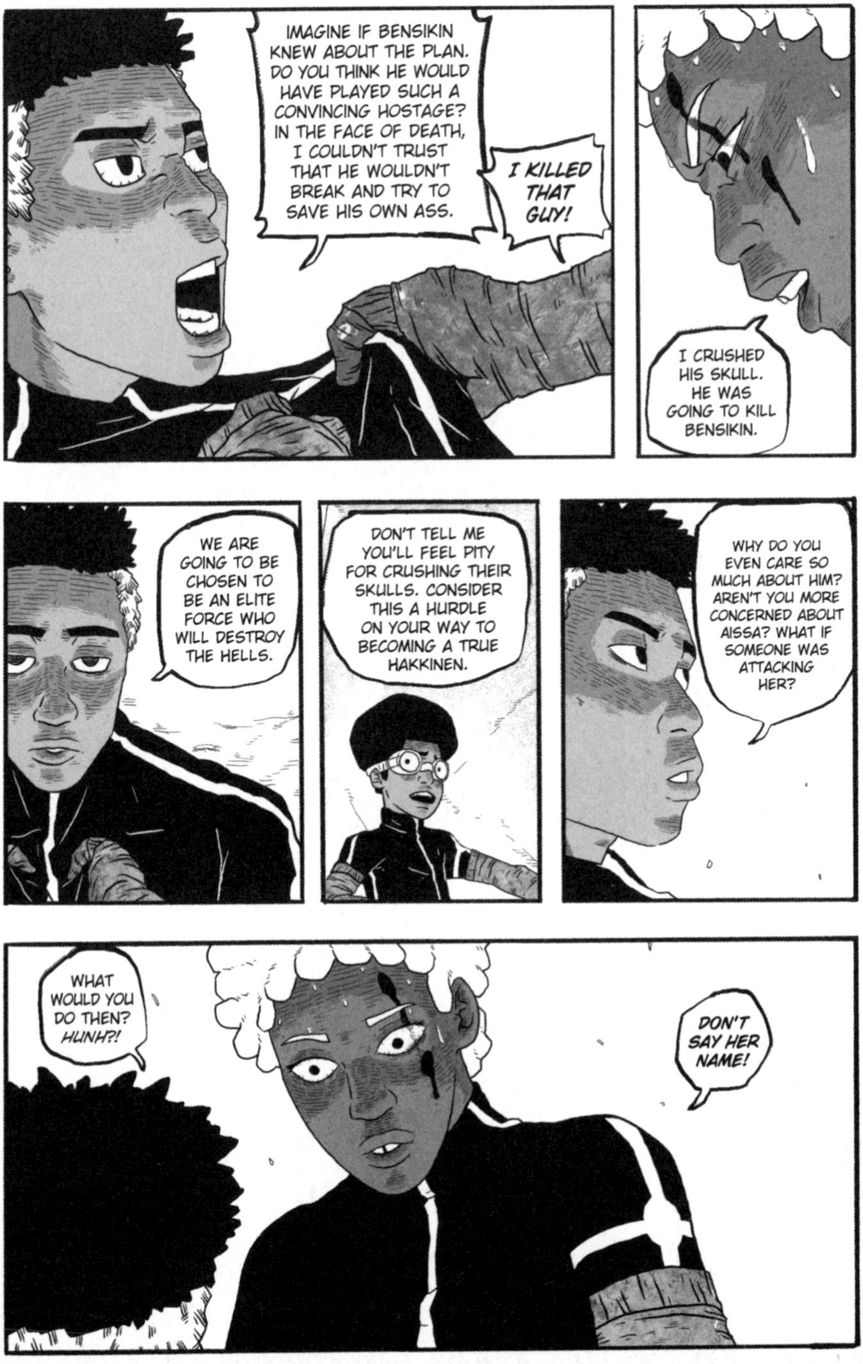

IMAGINE IF BENSIKIN KNEW ABOUT THE PLAN. DO YOU THINK HE WOULD HAVE PLAYED SUCH A CONVINCING HOSTAGE? IN THE FACE OF DEATH, I COULDN'T TRUST THAT HE WOULDN'T BREAK AND TRY TO SAVE HIS OWN ASS.
I KILLED THAT GUY!
I CRUSHED HIS SKULL. HE WAS GOING TO KILL BENSIKIN.
WE ARE GOING TO BE CHOSEN TO BE AN ELITE FORCE WHO WILL DESTROY THE HELLS.
DON'T TELL ME YOU'LL FEEL PITY FOR CRUSHING THEIR SKULLS. CONSIDER THIS A HURDLE ON YOUR WAY TO BECOMING A TRUE HAKKINEN.
WHY DO YOU EVEN CARE SO MUCH ABOUT HIM? AREN'T YOU MORE CONCERNED ABOUT AISSA? WHAT IF SOMEONE WAS ATTACKING HER?
WHAT WOULD YOU DO THEN? *HUNH?!*
DON'T SAY HER NAME!

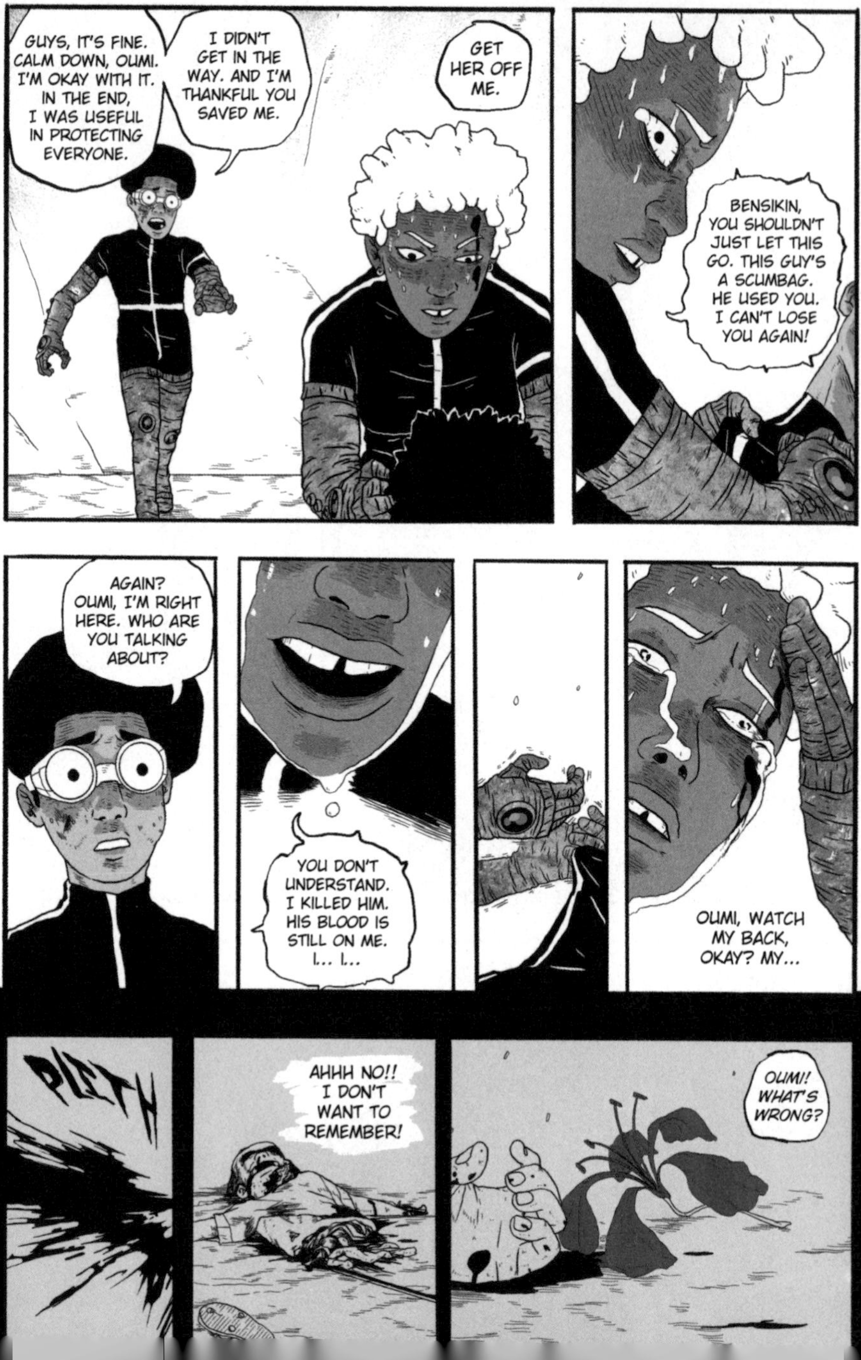
GUYS, IT'S FINE. CALM DOWN, OUMI. I'M OKAY WITH IT. IN THE END, I WAS USEFUL IN PROTECTING EVERYONE.
I DIDN'T GET IN THE WAY. AND I'M THANKFUL YOU SAVED ME.
GET HER OFF ME.
BENSIKIN, YOU SHOULDN'T JUST LET THIS GO. THIS GUY'S A SCUMBAG. HE USED YOU. I CAN'T LOSE YOU AGAIN!
AGAIN? OUMI, I'M RIGHT HERE. WHO ARE YOU TALKING ABOUT?
YOU DON'T UNDERSTAND. I KILLED HIM. HIS BLOOD IS STILL ON ME. I... I...
OUMI, WATCH MY BACK, OKAY? MY...
PLETH
AHHH NO!! I DON'T WANT TO REMEMBER!
OUMI! WHAT'S WRONG?

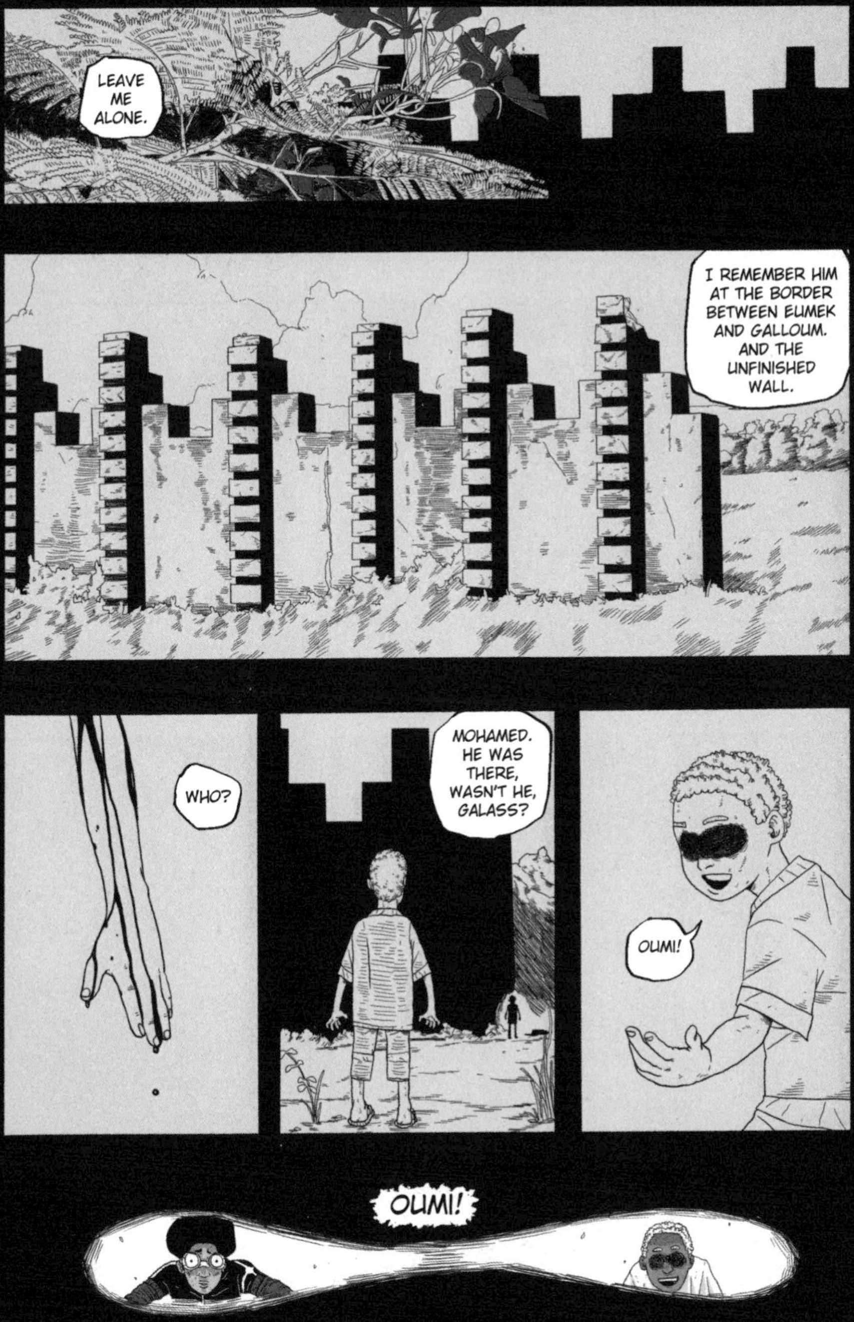
LEAVE ME ALONE.
I REMEMBER HIM AT THE BORDER BETWEEN EUMEK AND GALLOUM. AND THE UNFINISHED WALL.
WHO?
MOHAMED. HE WAS THERE, WASN'T HE, GALASS?
OUMI!
OUMI!

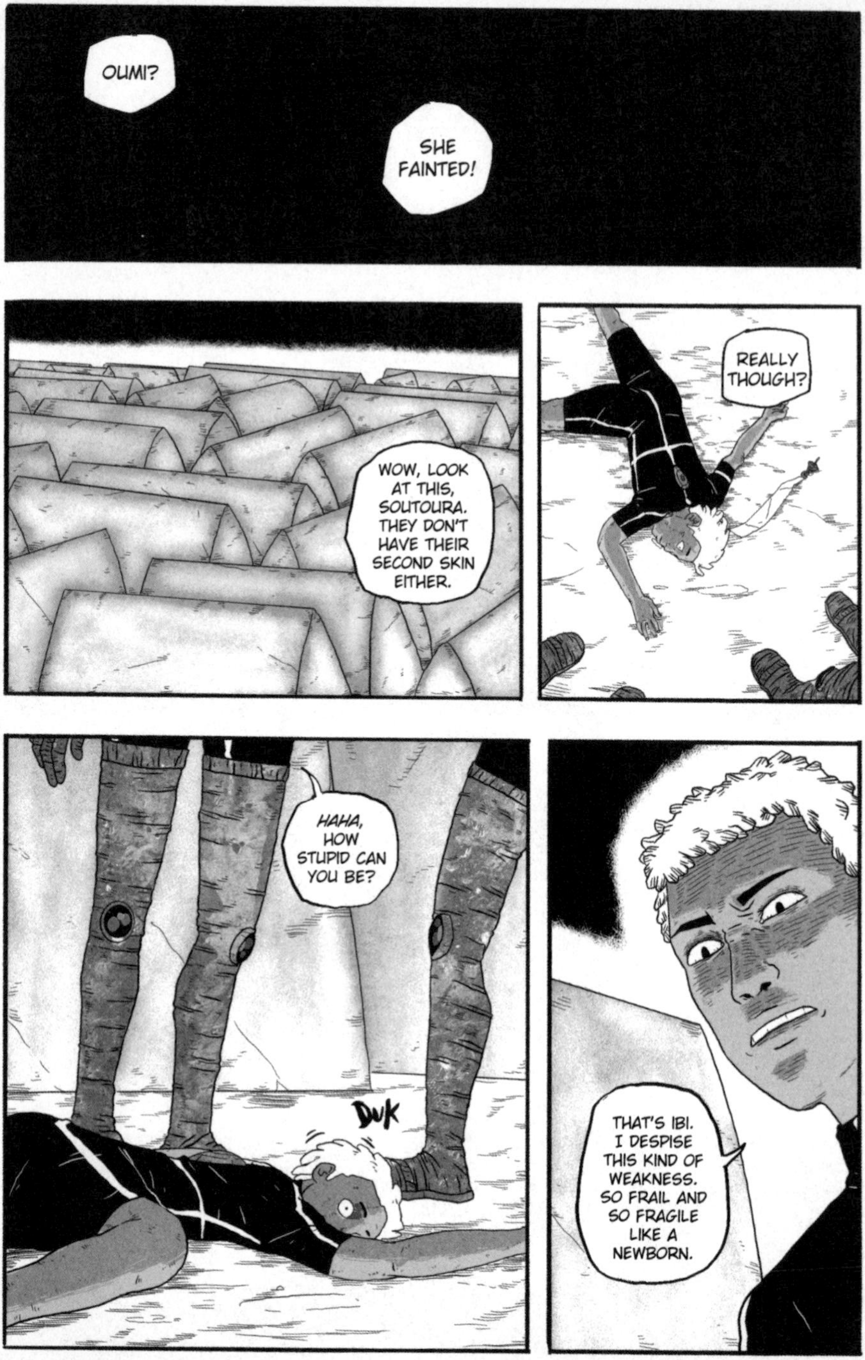
OUMI?
SHE FAINTED!
WOW, LOOK AT THIS, SOUTOURA. THEY DON'T HAVE THEIR SECOND SKIN EITHER.
REALLY THOUGH?
HAHA, HOW STUPID CAN YOU BE?
DUK
THAT'S IBI. I DESPISE THIS KIND OF WEAKNESS. SO FRAIL AND SO FRAGILE LIKE A NEWBORN.

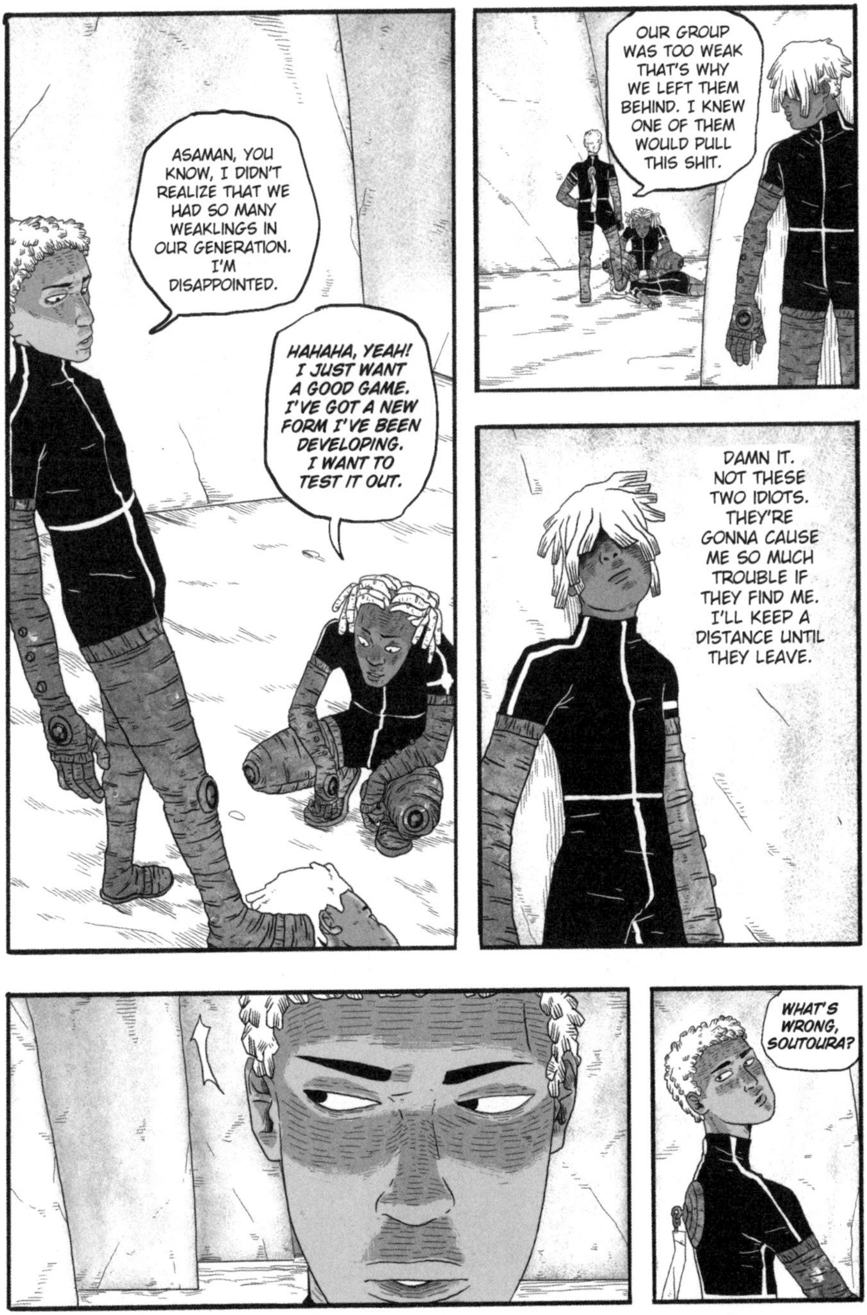
ASAMAN, YOU KNOW, I DIDN'T REALIZE THAT WE HAD SO MANY WEAKLINGS IN OUR GENERATION. I'M DISAPPOINTED.
HAHAHA, YEAH! I JUST WANT A GOOD GAME. I'VE GOT A NEW FORM I'VE BEEN DEVELOPING. I WANT TO TEST IT OUT.
OUR GROUP WAS TOO WEAK THAT'S WHY WE LEFT THEM BEHIND. I KNEW ONE OF THEM WOULD PULL THIS SHIT.
DAMN IT. NOT THESE TWO IDIOTS. THEY'RE GONNA CAUSE ME SO MUCH TROUBLE IF THEY FIND ME. I'LL KEEP A DISTANCE UNTIL THEY LEAVE.
WHAT'S WRONG, SOUTOURA?

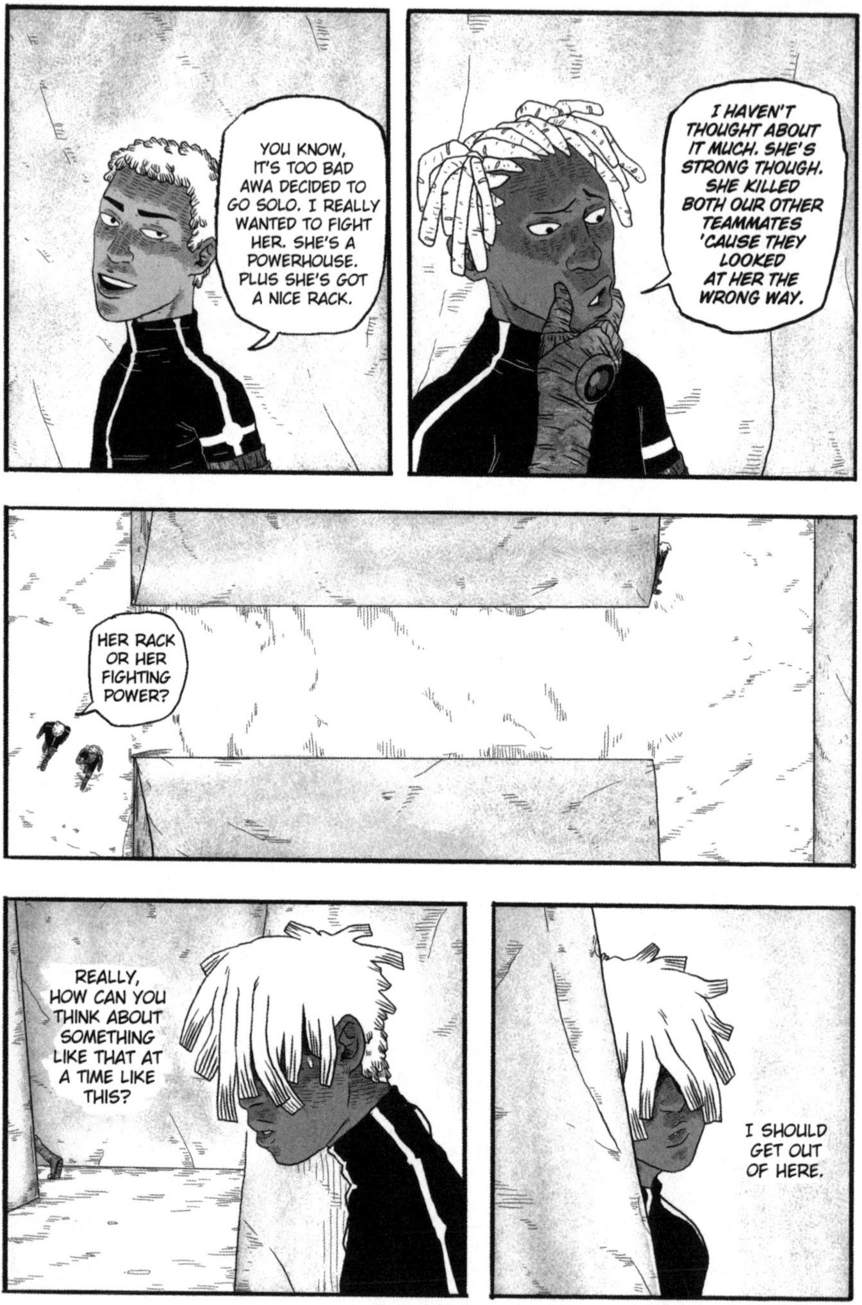
YOU KNOW, IT'S TOO BAD AWA DECIDED TO GO SOLO. I REALLY WANTED TO FIGHT HER. SHE'S A POWERHOUSE. PLUS SHE'S GOT A NICE RACK.
I HAVEN'T THOUGHT ABOUT IT MUCH. SHE'S STRONG THOUGH. SHE KILLED BOTH OUR OTHER TEAMMATES 'CAUSE THEY LOOKED AT HER THE WRONG WAY.
HER RACK OR HER FIGHTING POWER?
REALLY, HOW CAN YOU THINK ABOUT SOMETHING LIKE THAT AT A TIME LIKE THIS?
I SHOULD GET OUT OF HERE.

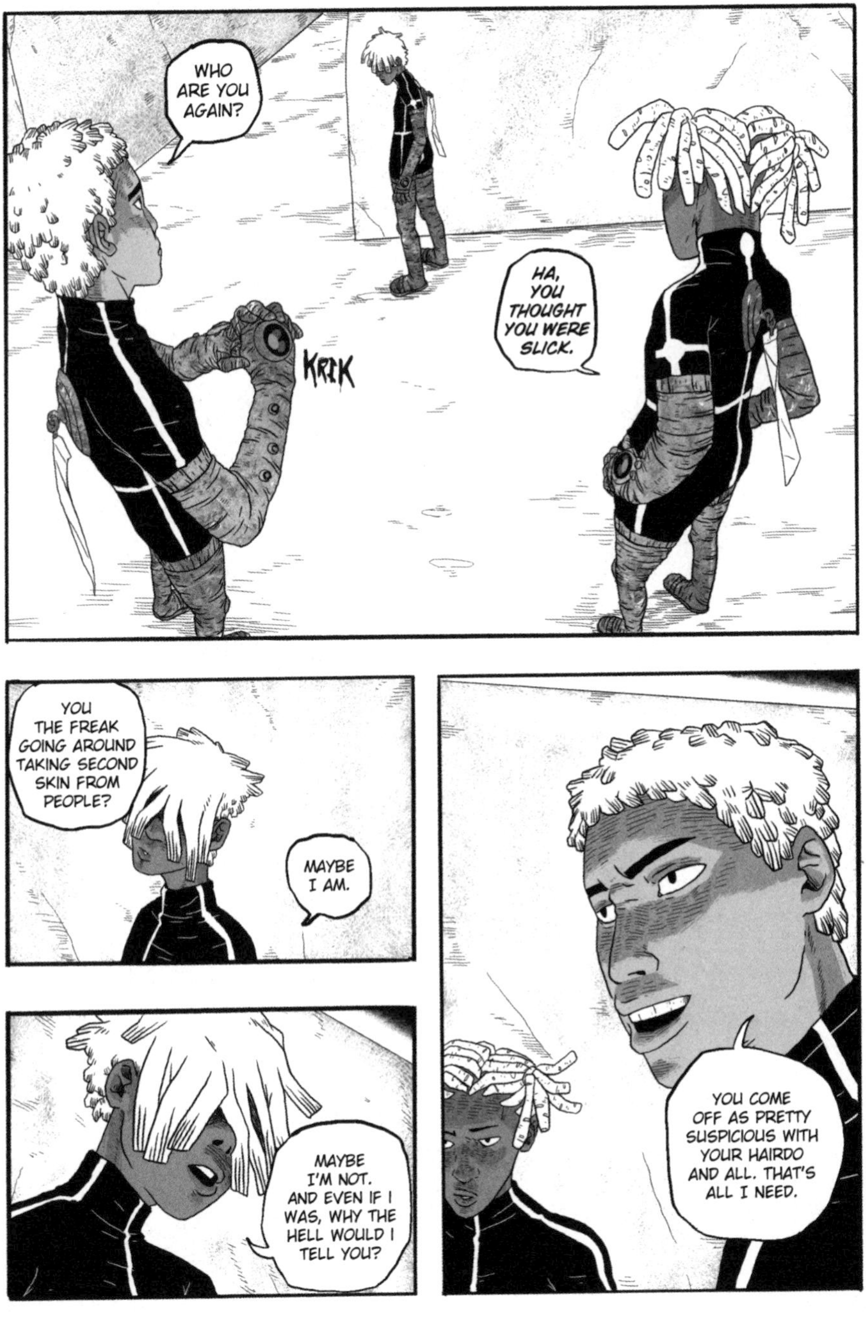
WHO ARE YOU AGAIN?
KRIK
HA, YOU THOUGHT YOU WERE SLICK.
YOU THE FREAK GOING AROUND TAKING SECOND SKIN FROM PEOPLE?
MAYBE I AM.
MAYBE I'M NOT. AND EVEN IF I WAS, WHY THE HELL WOULD I TELL YOU?
YOU COME OFF AS PRETTY SUSPICIOUS WITH YOUR HAIRDO AND ALL. THAT'S ALL I NEED.

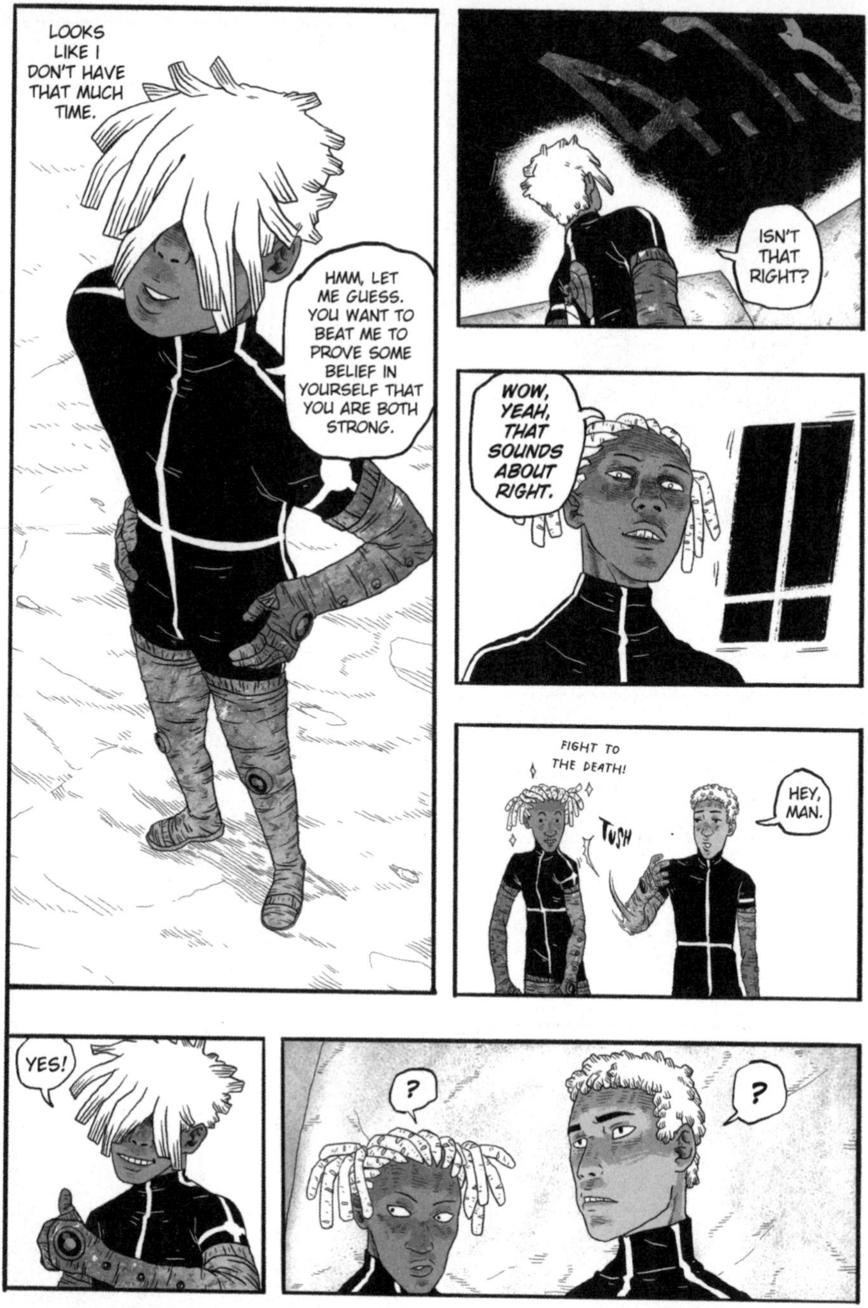
LOOKS LIKE I DON'T HAVE THAT MUCH TIME.
HMM, LET ME GUESS. YOU WANT TO BEAT ME TO PROVE SOME BELIEF IN YOURSELF THAT YOU ARE BOTH STRONG.
ISN'T THAT RIGHT?
WOW, YEAH, THAT SOUNDS ABOUT RIGHT.
FIGHT TO THE DEATH!
TUSH
HEY, MAN.
YES!
?
?

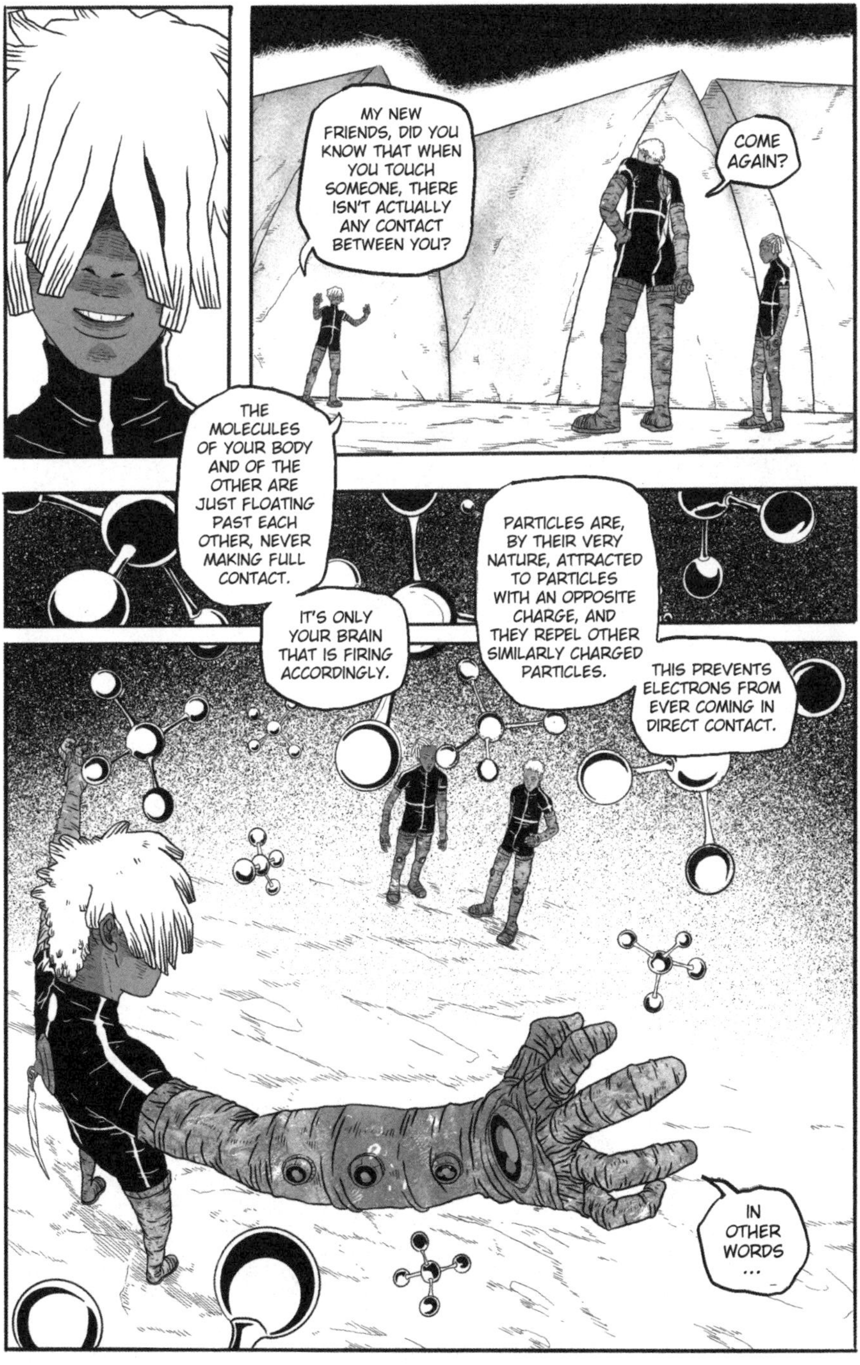
MY NEW FRIENDS, DID YOU KNOW THAT WHEN YOU TOUCH SOMEONE, THERE ISN'T ACTUALLY ANY CONTACT BETWEEN YOU?
COME AGAIN?
THE MOLECULES OF YOUR BODY AND OF THE OTHER ARE JUST FLOATING PAST EACH OTHER, NEVER MAKING FULL CONTACT.
IT'S ONLY YOUR BRAIN THAT IS FIRING ACCORDINGLY.
PARTICLES ARE, BY THEIR VERY NATURE, ATTRACTED TO PARTICLES WITH AN OPPOSITE CHARGE, AND THEY REPEL OTHER SIMILARLY CHARGED PARTICLES.
THIS PREVENTS ELECTRONS FROM EVER COMING IN DIRECT CONTACT.
IN OTHER WORDS ...

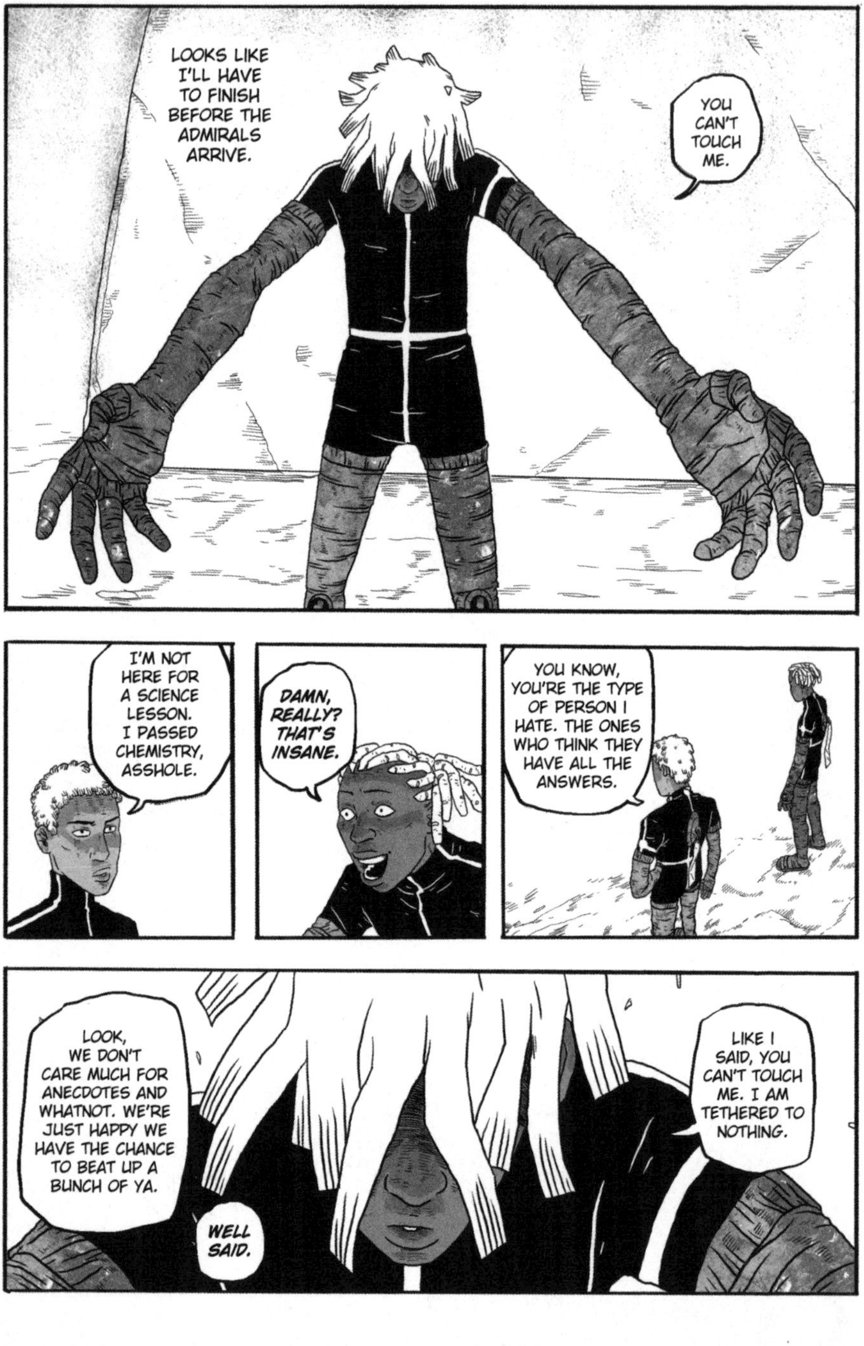
LOOKS LIKE I'LL HAVE TO FINISH BEFORE THE ADMIRALS ARRIVE.
YOU CAN'T TOUCH ME.
I'M NOT HERE FOR A SCIENCE LESSON. I PASSED CHEMISTRY, ASSHOLE.
DAMN, REALLY? THAT'S INSANE.
YOU KNOW, YOU'RE THE TYPE OF PERSON I HATE. THE ONES WHO THINK THEY HAVE ALL THE ANSWERS.
LOOK, WE DON'T CARE MUCH FOR ANECDOTES AND WHATNOT. WE'RE JUST HAPPY WE HAVE THE CHANCE TO BEAT UP A BUNCH OF YA.
WELL SAID.
LIKE I SAID, YOU CAN'T TOUCH ME. I AM TETHERED TO NOTHING.

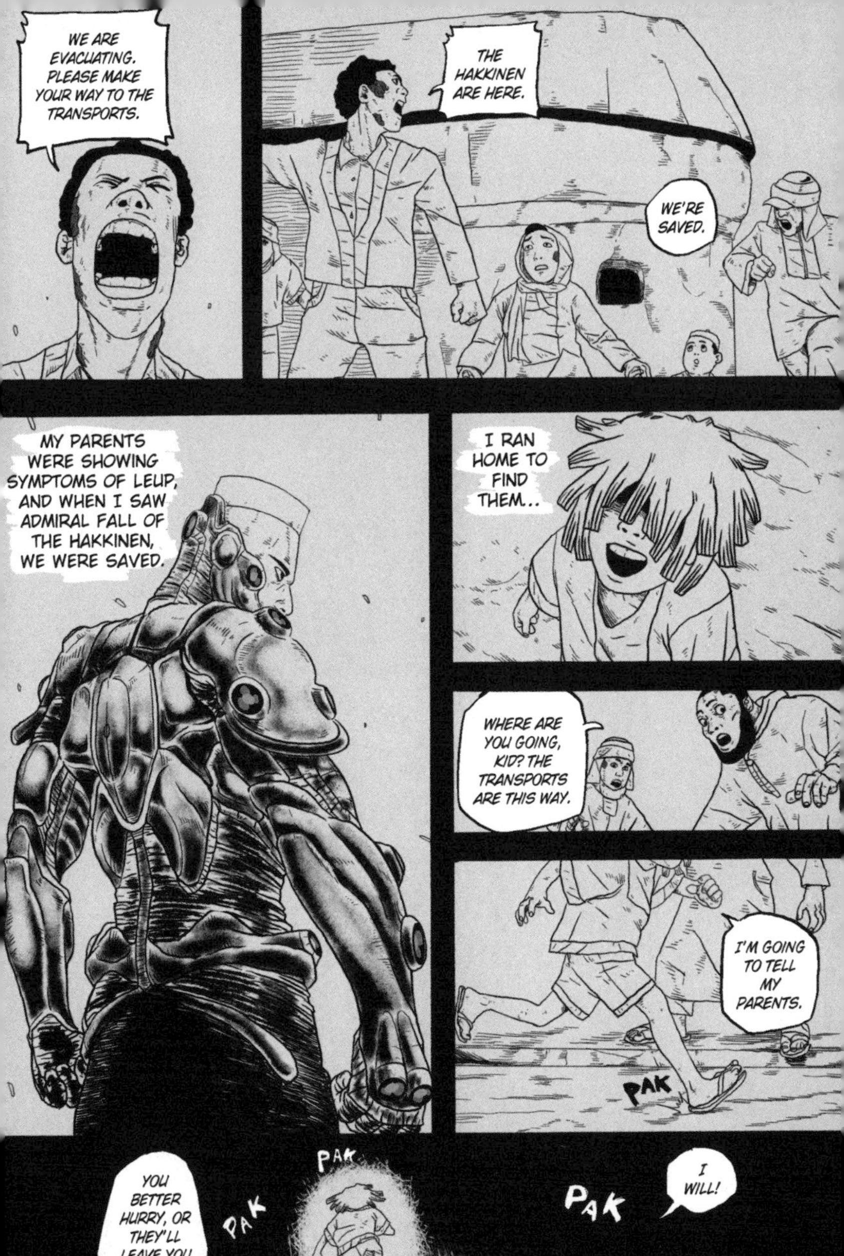
WE ARE EVACUATING. PLEASE MAKE YOUR WAY TO THE TRANSPORTS.
THE HAKKINEN ARE HERE.
WE'RE SAVED.
MY PARENTS WERE SHOWING SYMPTOMS OF LEUP, AND WHEN I SAW ADMIRAL FALL OF THE HAKKINEN, WE WERE SAVED.
I RAN HOME TO FIND THEM...
WHERE ARE YOU GOING, KID? THE TRANSPORTS ARE THIS WAY.
I'M GOING TO TELL MY PARENTS.
PAK
YOU BETTER HURRY, OR THEY'LL LEAVE YOU BEHIND.
PAK
PAK
PAK
I WILL!

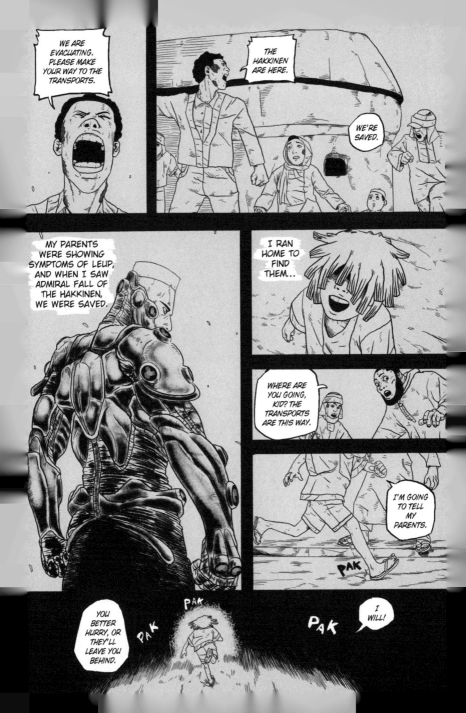

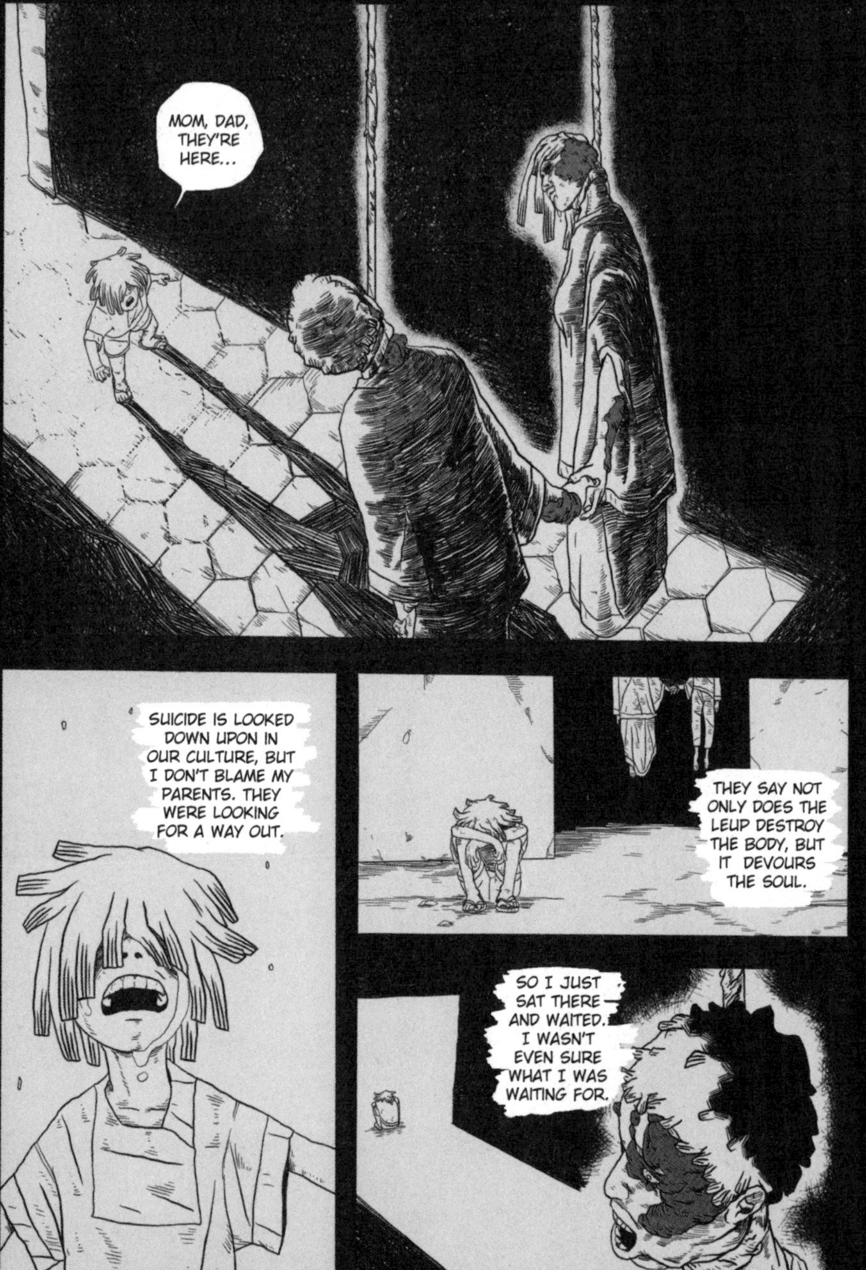
MOM, DAD, THEY'RE HERE...
SUICIDE IS LOOKED DOWN UPON IN OUR CULTURE, BUT I DON'T BLAME MY PARENTS. THEY WERE LOOKING FOR A WAY OUT.
THEY SAY NOT ONLY DOES THE LEUP DESTROY THE BODY, BUT IT DEVOURS THE SOUL.
SO I JUST SAT THERE AND WAITED. I WASN'T EVEN SURE WHAT I WAS WAITING FOR.

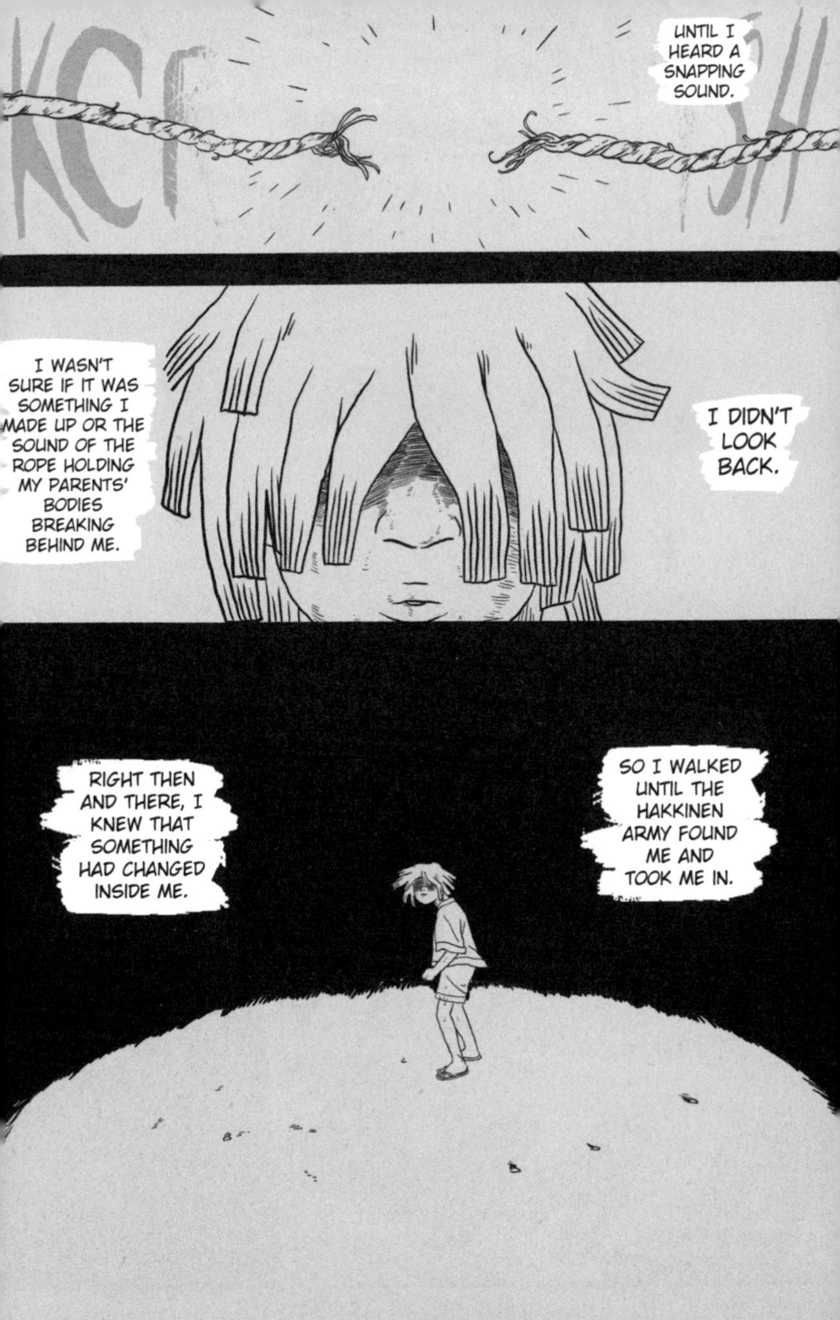
UNTIL I HEARD A SNAPPING SOUND.
I WASN'T SURE IF IT WAS SOMETHING I MADE UP OR THE SOUND OF THE ROPE HOLDING MY PARENTS' BODIES BREAKING BEHIND ME.
I DIDN'T LOOK BACK.
RIGHT THEN AND THERE, I KNEW THAT SOMETHING HAD CHANGED INSIDE ME.
SO I WALKED UNTIL THE HAKKINEN ARMY FOUND ME AND TOOK ME IN.

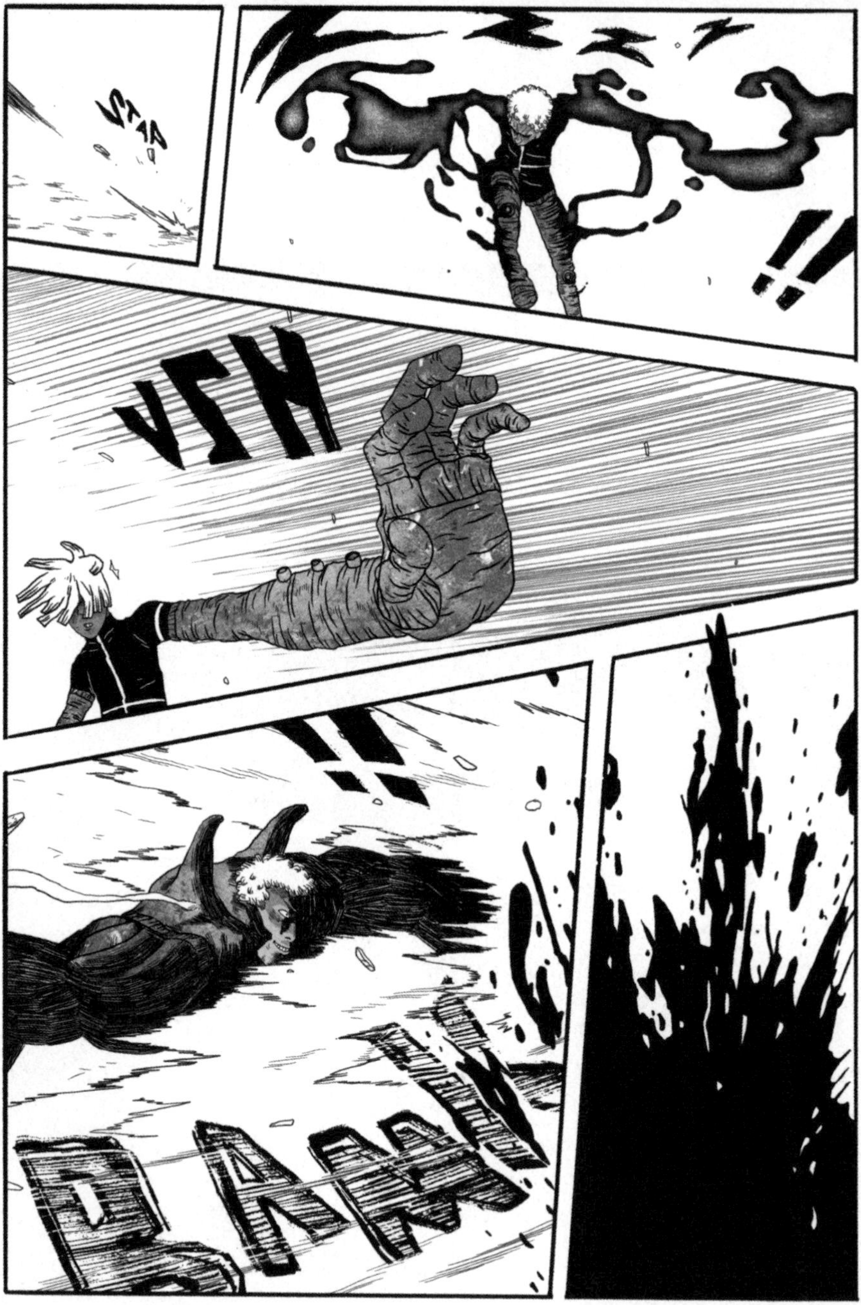
!!
!!

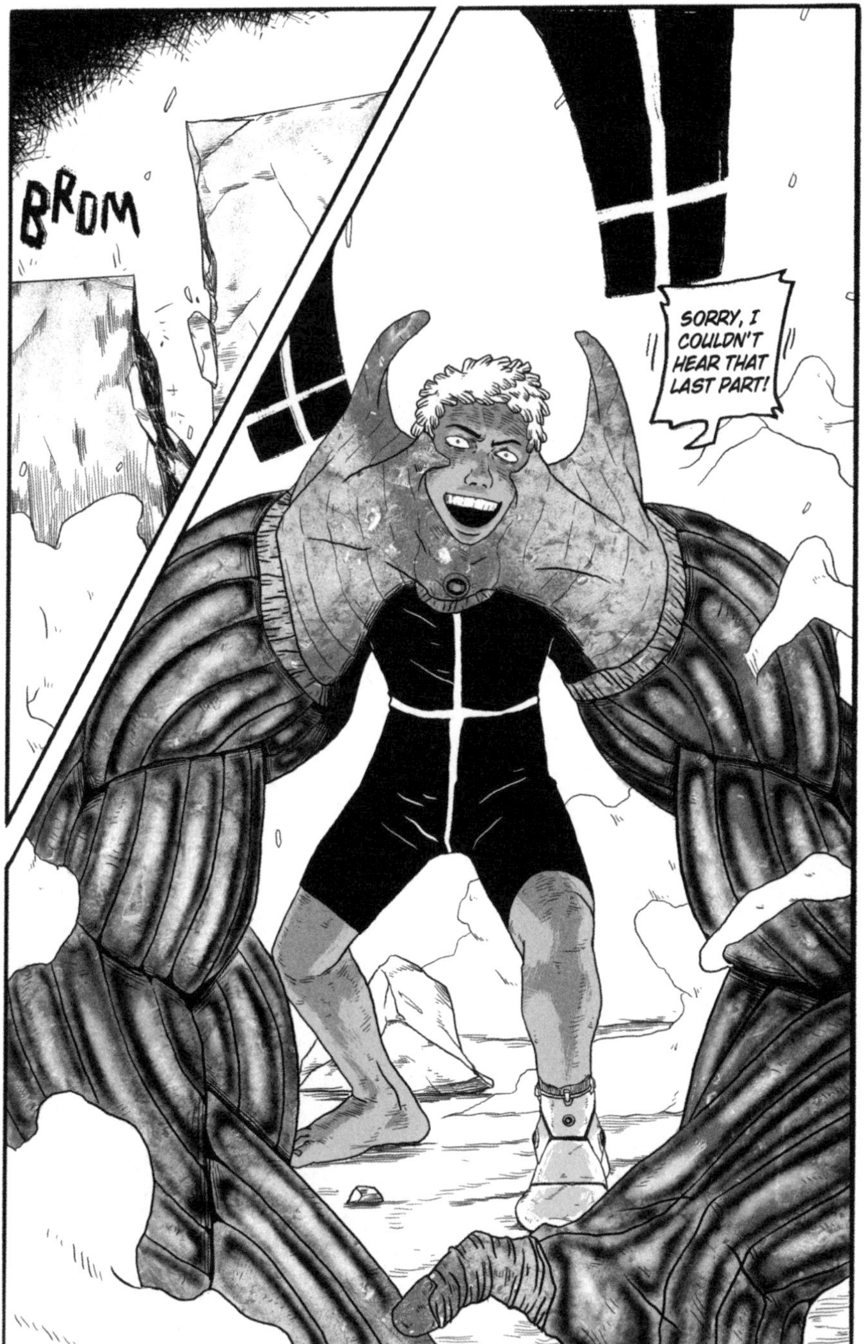
BROM
SORRY, I COULDN'T HEAR THAT LAST PART!

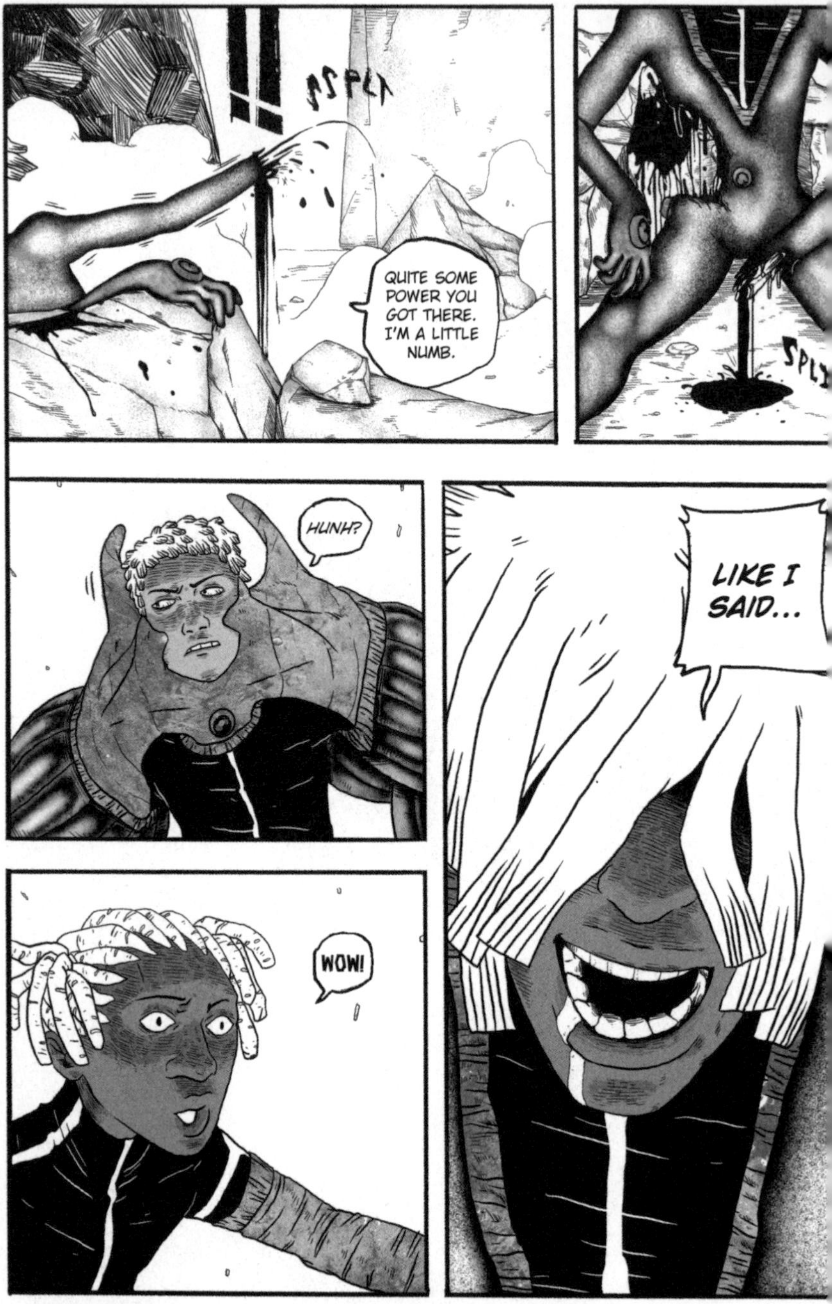
QUITE SOME POWER YOU GOT THERE. I'M A LITTLE NUMB.
HUNH?
WOW!
LIKE I SAID...

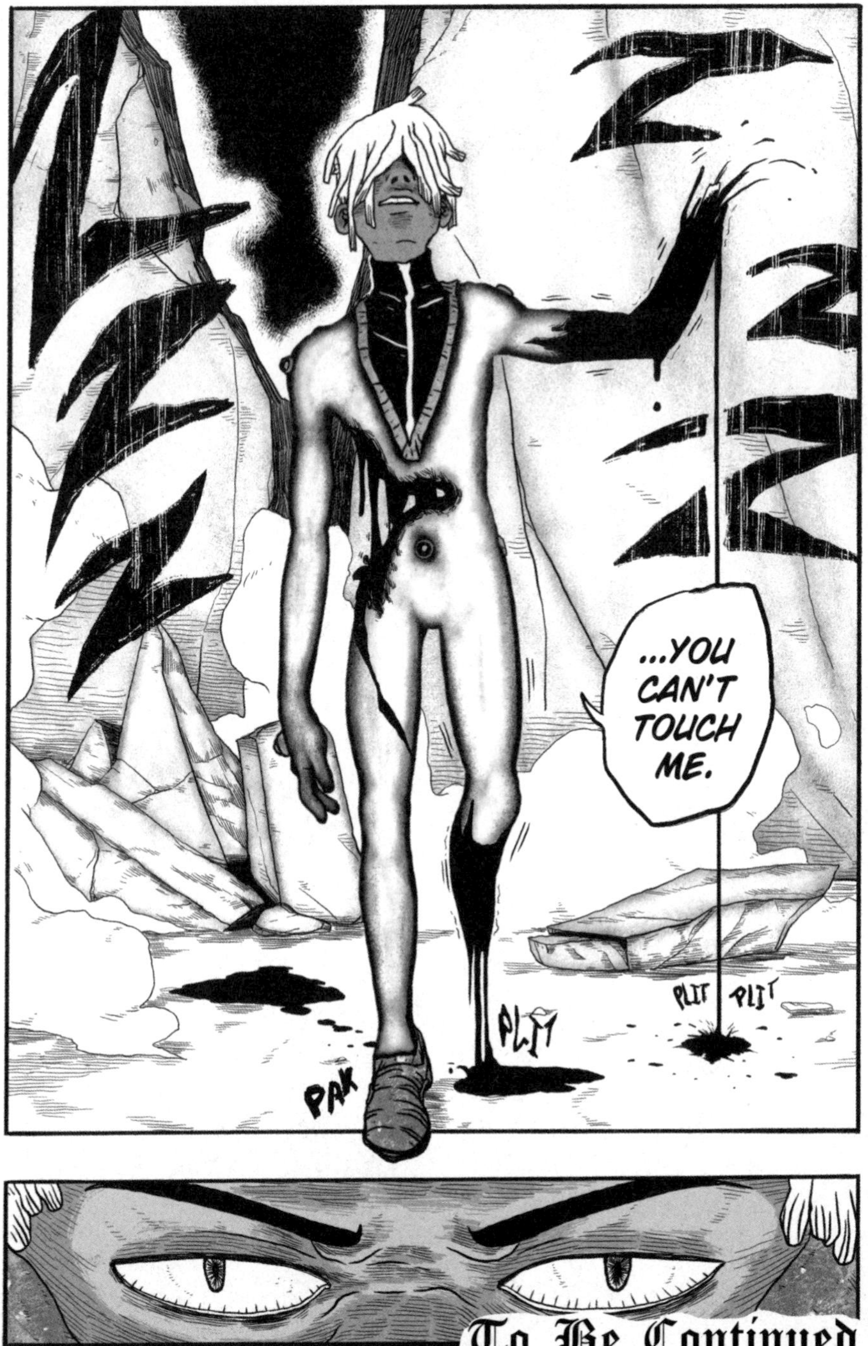
...YOU CAN'T TOUCH ME.
PLIT PLIT
PLIT
PAK
To Be Continued

OBLIVION ROUGE

END OF VOLUME 1

STORY AND ART BY Pap Souleye Fall

ABOUT THE AUTHOR

Pap Souleye Fall

Pap Souleye Fall is a Senegalese-American artist who lives and works in Dakar, Senegal. His work deals with themes such as identity, suspended disbelief, and utopian/dystopian ideas of community. *Oblivion Rouge* was born out of his thoughts on neocolonialism and has developed into a whole universe over two years. He is currently an MFA student in the Yale School of Art sculpture program.

ACKNOWLEDGMENTS

LET'S GO, SATURDAY AM!

WE'RE MAKING MOVES! THIS HAS BEEN A FANTASTIC
JOURNEY! THANK YOU TO ALL MY FAMILY AND FRIENDS WHO
HAVE LISTENED TO ME RANT FOR HOURS ABOUT THE WORLD
OF *OBLIVION ROUGE*. I'M SO HAPPY TO FINALLY GET THE
CHANCE TO SHARE THIS STORY WITH Y'ALL.

I'D LIKE TO THANK JEAN JAQUE TOUE, WHOM I MET AT
A PARTY AND TALKED WITH FOR HOURS ABOUT CREATING
COMICS. THANKS TO A LOT OF LONG HOURS WITH HIM,
I WAS ABLE TO REALLY BUILD THE *OBLIVION ROUGE*
UNIVERSE. LET'S KEEP BUILDING WORLDS TOGETHER!
I'D LIKE TO ALSO THANK MY FRIENDS, FAMILY, AND
ACQUAINTANCES WHO LET ME FILL THEIR EARS WITH
DREAMS OF WORLDS FILLED WITH FANTASY AND ADVENTURE.

-Pap Souleye Fall

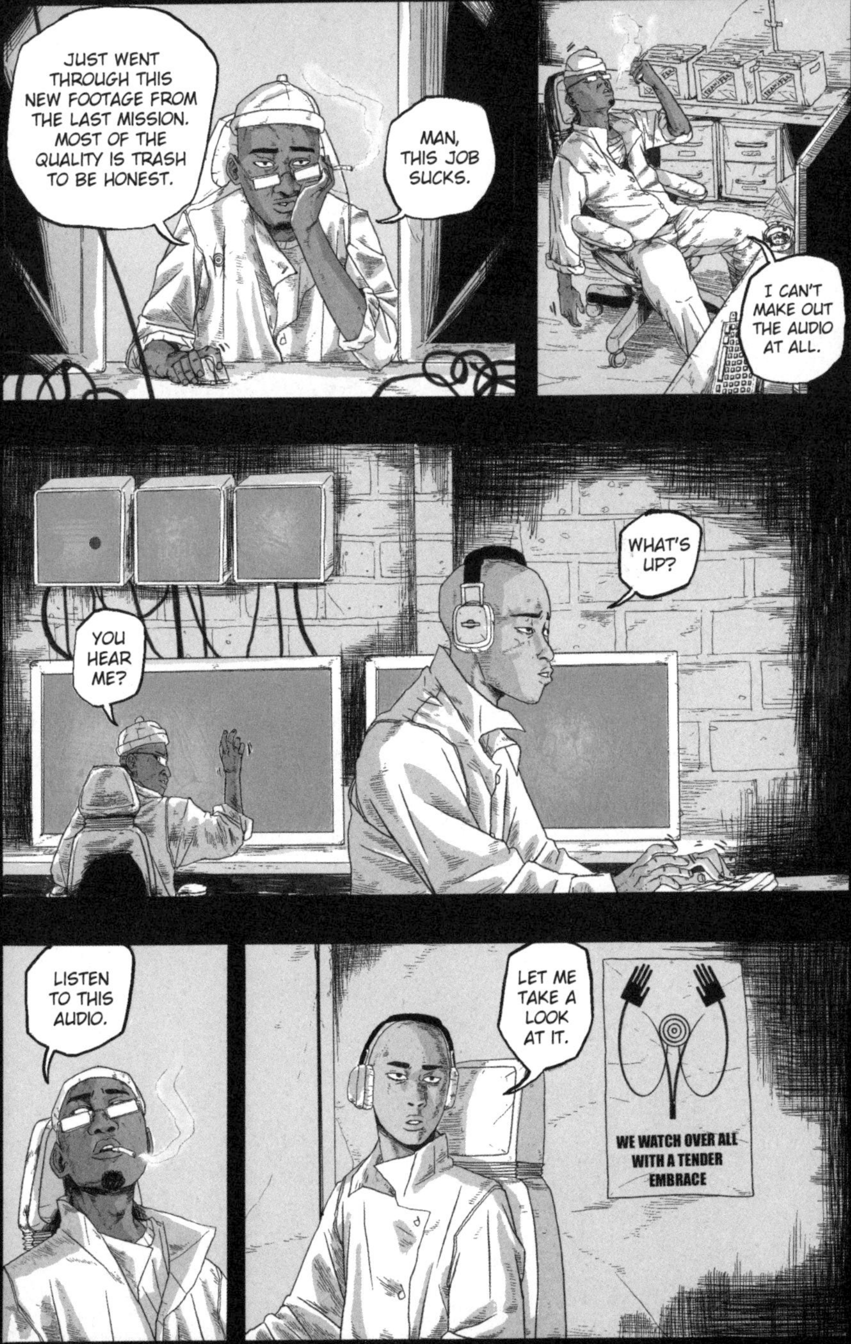
JUST WENT THROUGH THIS NEW FOOTAGE FROM THE LAST MISSION. MOST OF THE QUALITY IS TRASH TO BE HONEST.
MAN, THIS JOB SUCKS.
I CAN'T MAKE OUT THE AUDIO AT ALL.
YOU HEAR ME?
WHAT'S UP?
LISTEN TO THIS AUDIO.
LET ME TAKE A LOOK AT IT.
WE WATCH OVER ALL WITH A TENDER EMBRACE

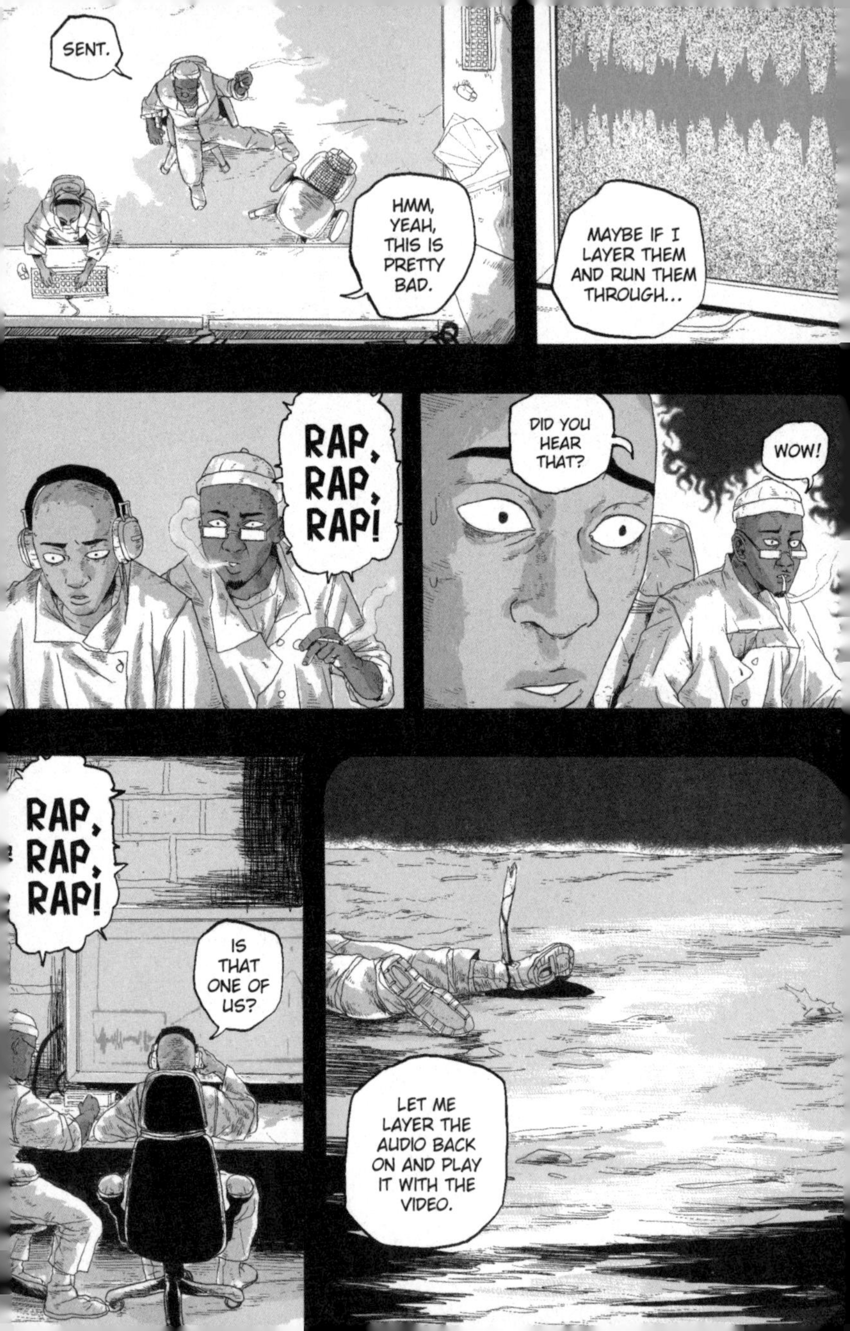
SENT.
HMM, YEAH, THIS IS PRETTY BAD.
MAYBE IF I LAYER THEM AND RUN THEM THROUGH...
RAP, RAP, RAP!
DID YOU HEAR THAT?
WOW!
RAP, RAP, RAP!
IS THAT ONE OF US?
LET ME LAYER THE AUDIO BACK ON AND PLAY IT WITH THE VIDEO.

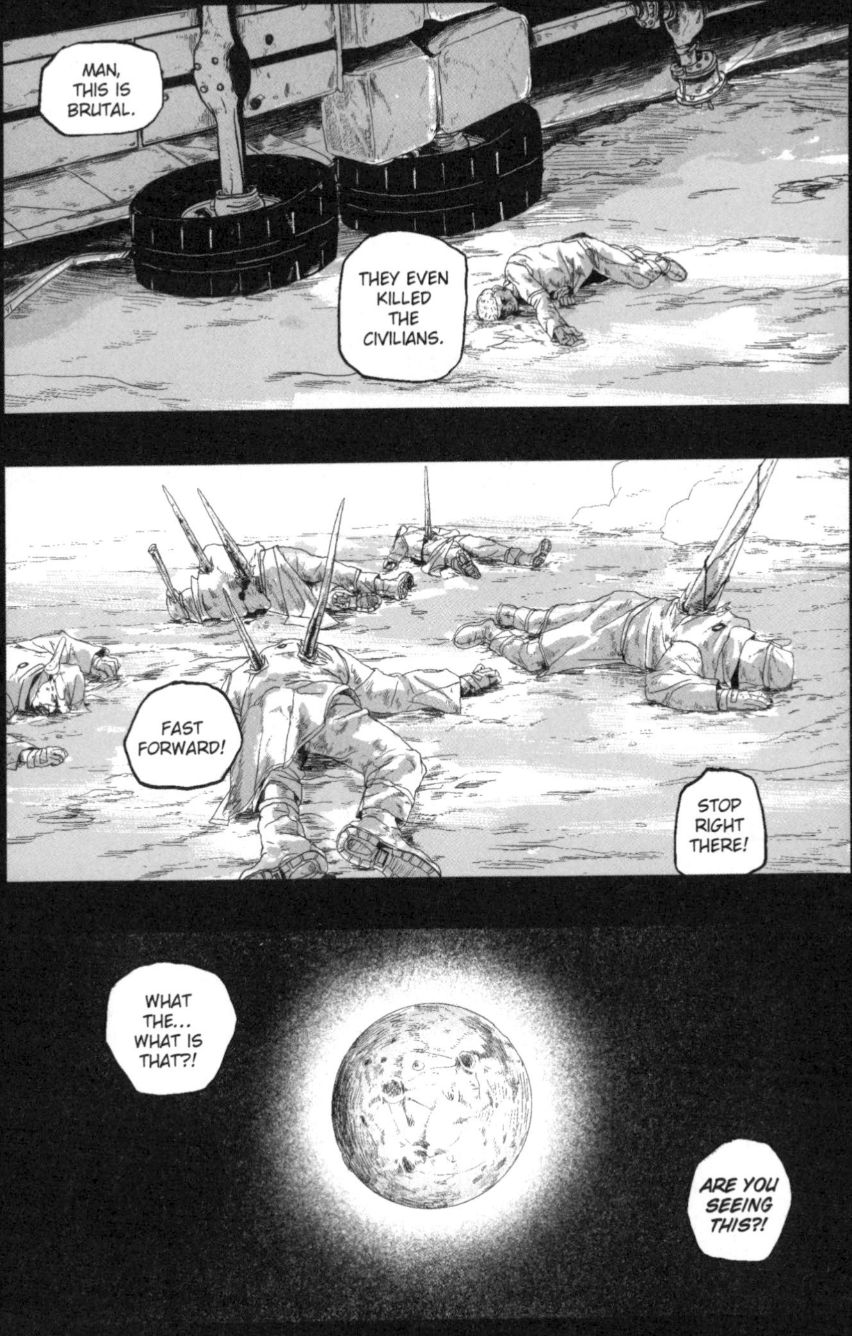
MAN, THIS IS BRUTAL.
THEY EVEN KILLED THE CIVILIANS.
FAST FORWARD!
STOP RIGHT THERE!
WHAT THE... WHAT IS THAT?!
ARE YOU SEEING THIS?!

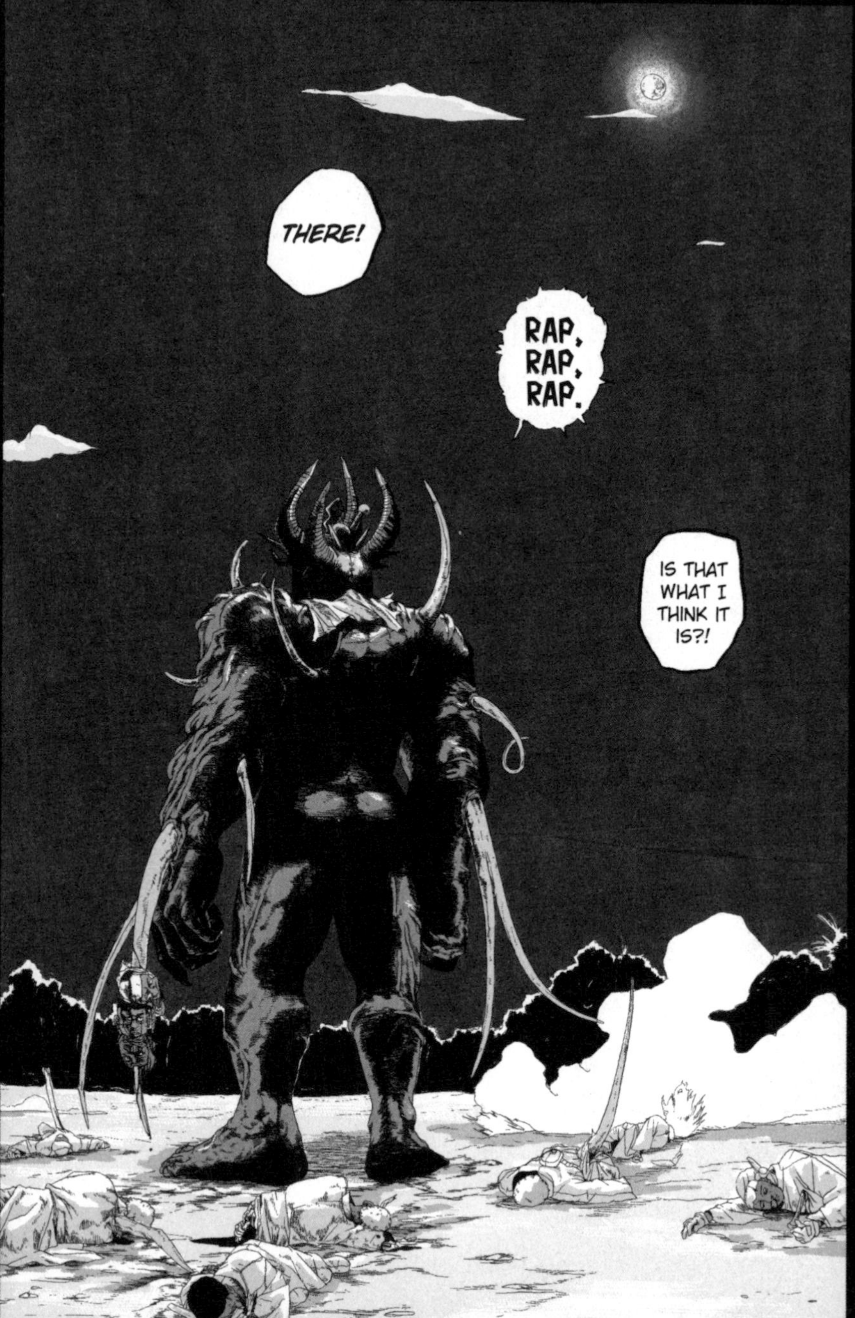
THERE!
RAP, RAP, RAP.
IS THAT WHAT I THINK IT IS?!

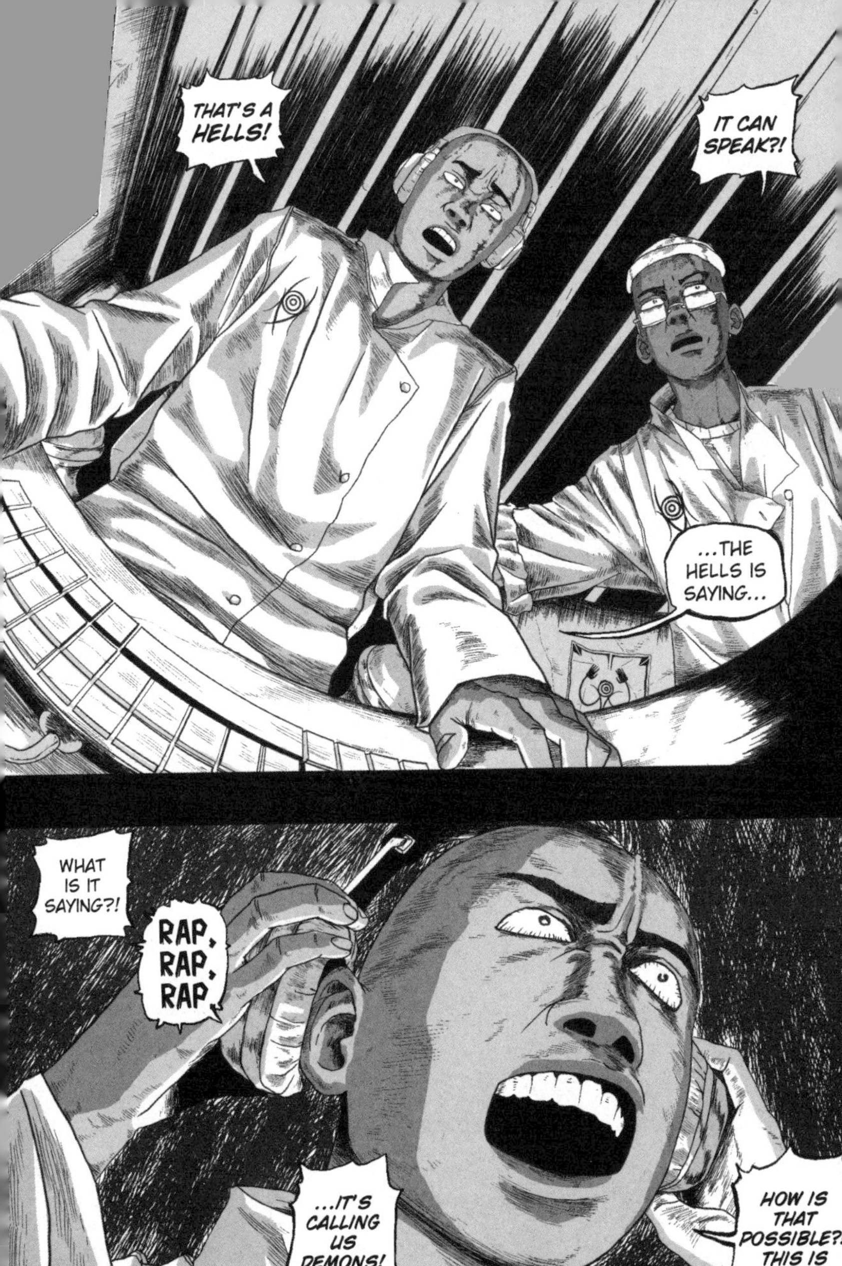
THAT'S A HELLS!
IT CAN SPEAK?!
...THE HELLS IS SAYING...
WHAT IS IT SAYING?!
RAP, RAP, RAP
...IT'S CALLING US DEMONS!
HOW IS THAT POSSIBLE?! THIS IS HUGE!

OBLIVION ROUGE

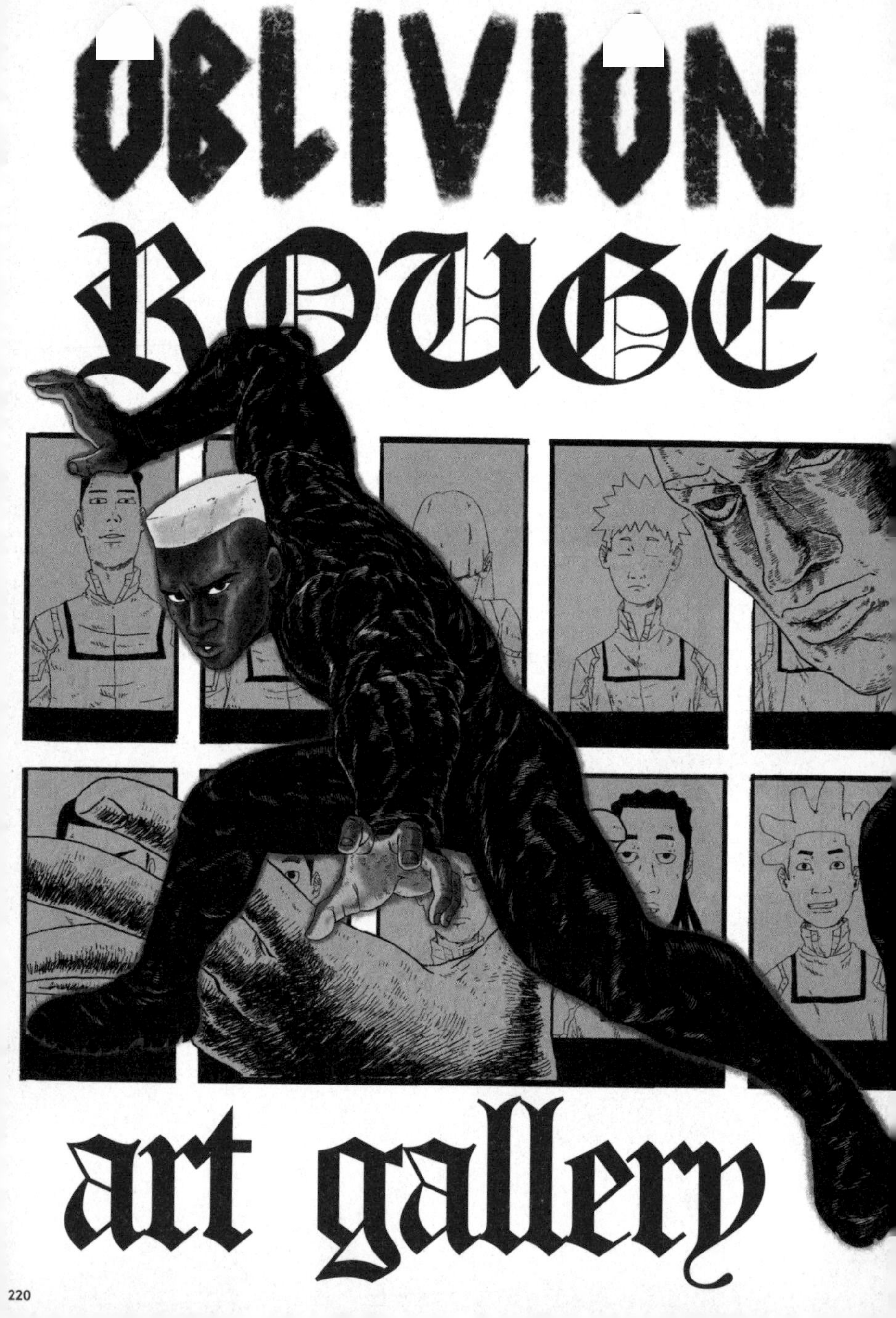

art gallery

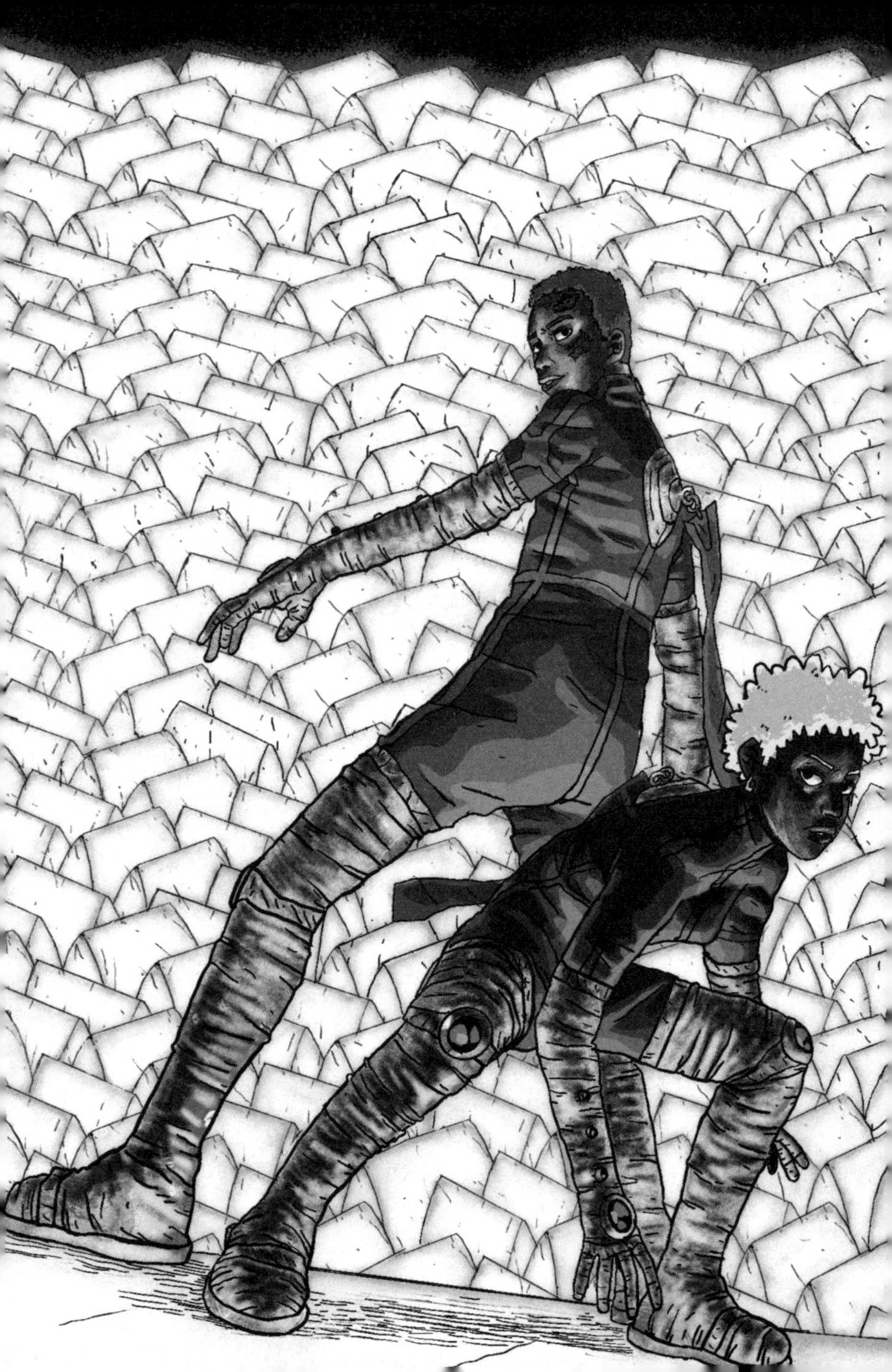

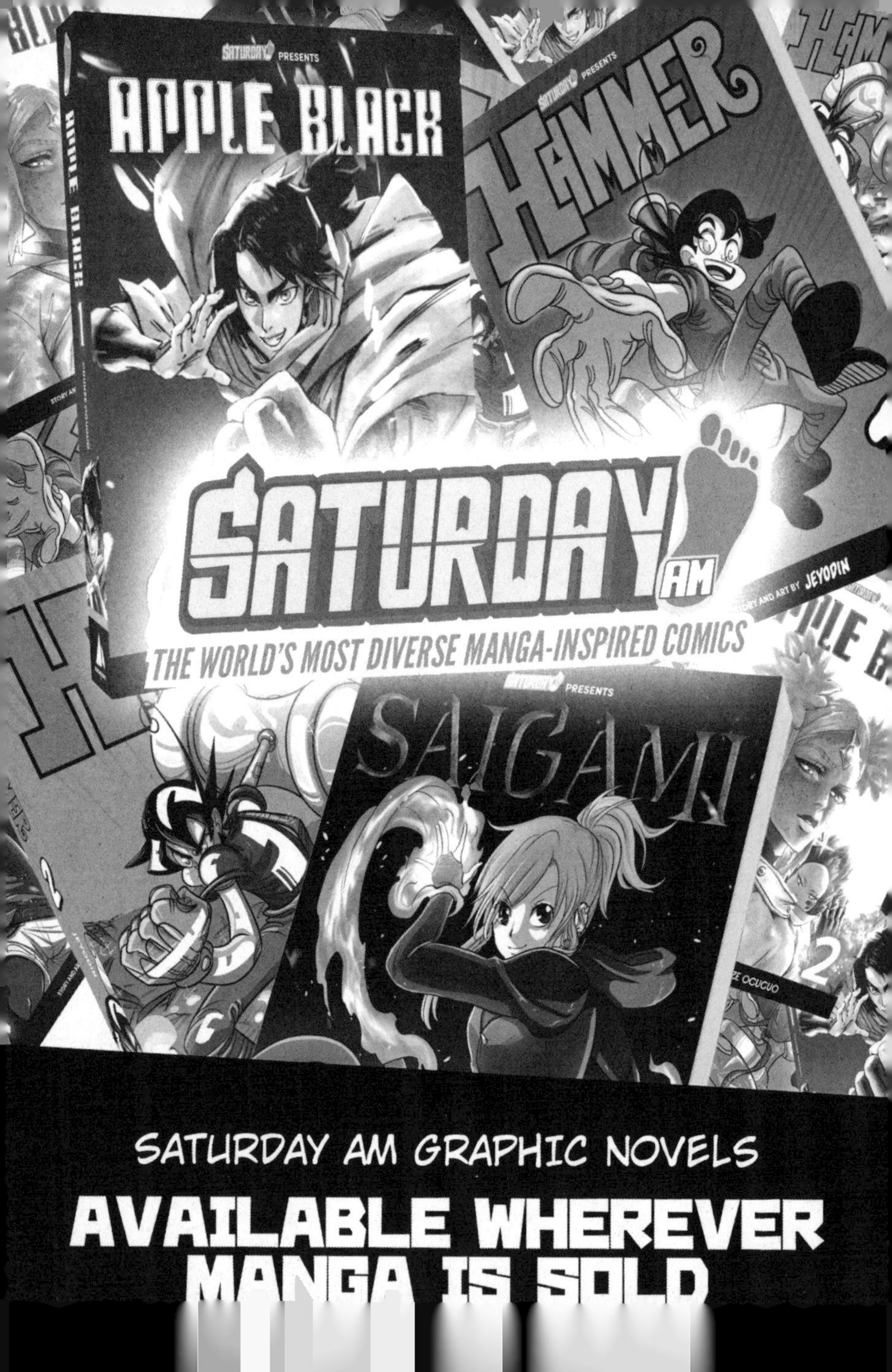

READ FREE DIVERSE MANGA

Saturday AM
Global Comics

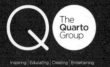

Brimming with creative inspiration, how-to projects, and useful information to enrich your everyday life, quarto.com is a favorite destination for those pursuing their interests and passions.

First published in 2022 by Rockport Publishers,
an imprint of The Quarto Group,
100 Cummings Center, Suite 265-D, Beverly, MA 01915, USA.
T (978) 282-9590 F (978) 283-2742 Quarto.com

Rockport Publishers titles are also available at discount for retail, wholesale, promotional, and bulk purchase. For details, contact the Special Sales Manager by email at specialsales@quarto.com or by mail at The Quarto Group, Attn: Special Sales Manager, 100 Cummings Center, Suite 265-D, Beverly, MA 01915, USA.

10 9 8 7 6 5 4 3 2 1

iSBN: 978-0-7603-7686-7

Library of Congress Cataloging-in-Publication Data is available.

Story and Art: Pap Souleye Fall
Design and Lettering: Mitch Proctor
Editors: Frederick L. Jones, Peter Doney, and Austin Harvey

Printed in China

RATED FOR OT OLDER TEEN AGES 16+

Oblivion Rouge, Volume 1 is rated OT for Older Teens and is recommended for ages 16 and up. It contains profanity and some violent scenes.